Film Review
1991-2

Film Review 1991-2

INCLUDING VIDEO RELEASES

F. Maurice Speed

AND

James Cameron-Wilson

VIRGIN

First published in Great Britain in 1991 by
VIRGIN BOOKS
an imprint of Virgin Publishing Ltd
338 Ladbroke Grove, London W10 5AH

British Library Cataloguing in Publication Data

Film Review
1. Cinema films – Serials
791.43′05

ISBN 1–85227–318–6 Hbk
ISBN 0–86369–374–1 Pbk

Designed by Fred Price

Phototypeset by Intype Ltd, London

Printed in Great Britain
by Scotprint Ltd, Musselburgh

Contents

Introduction

F. MAURICE SPEED surveys the cinematic year

Are we at last coming to the end of the quite ludicrous overspending and waste that has so often been the principal characteristic of the Hollywood film during the past few years? Are we finally to see the major studio bosses curbing the demands of the greedy, overpriced stars (and of course their greedier agents); the end of the ridiculous unrealistic amounts that have been paid to scriptwriters; and the crazy rewards that directors and producers have been demanding for their services?

Are we in fact going to see some sort of financial sanity coming to Hollywood film production costs? Recent statements from some of the major companies make one hopeful, even if past history has shown that while the talk of economies and rationalisation has been coming from the front office the same old profligate spending was continuing in the studios.

But this time the climate of stricter and more careful control, allied to the disastrous showing at the box office of some of the year's priciest productions (and the red figures looming large in the company ledgers) may in fact forcibly lead to belt-tightening and reorganisation in Hollywood. Certainly the talking is getting tougher. Jack Valenti, the head of the Motion Picture Association of America, recently said, at a celebration of the 25th anniversary of his taking up the post, that in view of the 'paucity of available capital', film companies will have to 'adopt a strong policy of fiscal discipline' and that 'planned budgets will be lower in the future'. After all, it isn't by any means certain that the big spenders are the big earners, so maybe things are set to change at last. Maybe . . .

Some signs and portents. Disney Chairman Jeffrey Katzenberg is on record as saying recently that, despite his own company's good financial results, for most of the major film companies 1990 was a year of steady decline. Christmas in particular brought disastrous business in the USA, at a time when the movies normally enjoy a bonanza, with several major productions released. And apparently most of Katzenberg's fellow company leaders were in full agreement with him when he said: 'Like lemmings we are all racing faster and faster into the sea, each of us trying to outrun and outspend the others in a mad rush towards the mirage of making the next blockbuster.'

But in spite of hopeful signs for the future, there is not much tangible evidence as yet of the new philosophy being adopted for films now in production or pre-production. How can anyone, for instance, justify the payment of $1.75 million that was paid for the script of *The Last Boy Scout* (working out at $12,500 per page!) or, even crazier, the $2

million that, according to *Variety*, was paid to Ronald Bass for his adaptation of T. M. Wright's book *Manhattan Ghost Story*? One single script can now, it seems, make a writer or adaptor a dollar millionaire. And the craziest script story of the year (again from *Variety*) was the $3 million paid to Joe Eszterhas, writer of *Basic Instinct*. Can you imagine the sheer insanity of loading a production with a $3 million outlay before the film has even got on the floor? It really is a Mad, Mad, Mad, Mad World out there in Hollywood.

Happily there are by contrast some saner examples around: films conceived and budgeted on more reasonable terms, which have brought their makers both financial and popular success, outshining in both respects many of the year's supposed blockbusters-to-be. Films like *Ghost*, which brought some $94 million into the Paramount coffers; and *Pretty Woman*, which made $81 million for the Disney studios from the American release alone. (*Pretty Woman* since made another $15 million from the UK release, not to mention substantial returns from other European countries . . . and all this from a film that costs only $20 million to make.) Compare these successes with such expensive flops as *Havana*, *Dick Tracy*, *Days of Thunder* and *Rocky V*. And while mentioning modest winners and megabuck losers, it is astonishing that although *Batman* has so far contributed $253 million to Warners, it still showed in mid-1991 a deficit of nearly $35 million on the books.

An interesting sidelight on the inflated costs of many recent movies was the list of the top-earning stars of 1989–90 which was published in *Variety*. At no. 1 was Sylvester Stallone (who has recently signed a new contract which will bring him between $12 and $17 million a movie!); no. 2, Arnold Schwarzenegger; no. 3, Jack Nicholson; no. 4, Eddie Murphy; no. 5, Bruce Willis (reportedly getting $10 million for *The Last Boy Scout*); no. 6, Sean Connery; no. 7, Michael J. Fox; no. 8, Tom Cruise. Any of these stars can now demand around $10 million per performance.

Of course, you may think actors like these are worth the money, but it certainly means that when a film has to bear this sort of financial stone around its neck from the beginning, only a major success can hope to cover the costs of a big-budget film.

One wonders what impact (if any) the increasing financial involvement of the Japanese in Hollywood will have? Toshiba has apparently been taking an increasing interest in the Time–Warner set-up, while Sony has already obtained the ownership of Columbia/CBS Records, and Matsushita now owns the MCA giant and is helping to finance a number of

Martin Scorsese (right) *directs Robert De Niro in a scene from* GoodFellas, *one of the most highly acclaimed films of the 'nineties.*

films. And Disney has accepted $365 million to finance 60 per cent of the cost of 25 movies over the next 18 months. Not bad for starters!

Something of a storm was caused by Katzenberg's public remarks (in spite of the Disney studio's involvement) that 'The Japanese are getting into a business that to some extent is outside their cultural context.' His statement brought acid comments from some of the Japanese investors, who claimed that they were only interested in the financial side of American showbiz and they had no intention of interfering in the artistic side of things. Maybe. But one can't help wondering if they will remain silent when they see their yen being squandered on films which have from the start no profit possibilities. (By the way, it is estimated that the Japanese invested a total of some $600 million in Hollywood films during 1990.)

I mentioned last year that America was making too many movies; far too many for all of them to get a cinema showing, with most going straight to video, a few to cable TV, and some just getting shelved. Even with US production down by about 20 per cent – the 1990 total was about 430 movies, compared with 1988's all-time high of more than 600 – it is still estimated that about 40 per cent of the year's total will never get to a cinema in the USA.

But if too many films are being made in the States, there are certainly too few in Britain. It says something for the disastrous state of the British film industry that, of the hundreds of movies from all over the world competing in this year's Cannes Film Festival, only two British productions were entered, and even then not for the major awards. Ken Loach's *Riff-Raff* was shown in the Directors' Fortnight and *Young Soul Rebels* was selected for inclusion in the International Critics' Week section. It is significant that both these films were partly financed by Channel 4 TV and were obviously aimed at a very restricted cinema release before becoming part of Channel 4's TV feature library.

Yet, while British film production has become virtually extinct, cinema attendance in this country is still rising healthily. Though we no longer have any official figures it appears certain that in spite of the long hot summer and the Gulf War the magical figure of 100 million admissions will have been reached or even exceeded.

The ten most successful films to be shown in British cinemas during the year, in financial order, were: no. 1, *Ghost*; no. 2, *Pretty Woman*; no. 3, *Look Who's Talking*; no. 4, *Honey, I Shrunk the Kids*; no. 5, *Total Recall*; no. 6,

Ghostbusters 2; no. 7, *Back to the Future 3*; no. 8, *Back to the Future 2*; no. 9, *Gremlins 2*; and no. 10, *When Harry Met Sally*.

It may also interest you to know that the top ten money-making non-American films to be shown in the US between 1960 and 1990 were: *I Am Curious Yellow* (which earned $19 million); *La Dolce Vita* ($18 million); *La Cage aux Folles* ($18 million); *Z* ($15 million); *A Man and a Woman* ($13 million); *Emmanuelle* ($13.5 million); *Cinema Paradiso* ($11.25 million); *Das Boot* ($11 million); *Story of O* ($10 million); and *8½* ($9.5 million).

It is somewhat ironical that the American moviemakers are now facing a problem that has been plaguing their British counterparts for years. With their inflated production costs the Americans can no longer, as in the past, depend on a US release to make a profit, and now have to rely on a British release and showings elsewhere in Europe to do more than break even. Confirming this, Warner executive Robert Derby recently went on record saying: 'We've come to recognise that you can't really proceed with a production any more unless you have a real potential overseas.'

Virtually unnoticed, at least by the media, was a part of British film history that vanished this year, when the oldest working film studios in the UK were razed at Elstree, the birthplace of some of the biggest and best of British movies. At some point a new but smaller studio complex is scheduled to rise from the ashes – the greater part of the site has been taken by a new supermarket/superstore – but this will be principally devoted to TV productions.

Another film landmark, this time in the USA, was also lost this year, when the 100-year-old Golden State Theater in Riverside, California, was knocked down after a fire had gutted it. It was at this cinema that D. W. Griffith premiered his *Birth of a Nation* in 1915, and here too Sarah Bernhardt, W. C. Fields and Al Jolson all performed live.

Technically there have been few great advances in the period under review – whatever happened to all those perfected, exciting forms of 3-D which we have read about fairly regularly during the past few years? But there have been some developments in cinema sound. Eastman Kodak and Optical Radiation seem to have come up with a winner in a cinema sound system which compares with the old level of reproduction much as today's CD compares with the old 33⅓ rpm records. Called 'Cinema Digital Sound', the system made its public debut in the summer of 1990 with the release of *Dick Tracy* at five Los Angeles and two New York cinemas, boasting 'a playback mode to provide 6-track optical stereo from the special 70mm Eastman Digital Sound Recording Film 2374.' Few cinemas are at present equipped to show these prints, but the developers (who have invested $5 million in the enterprise) hope that within a few years it will have become the normal sound system in all but the very smallest and oldest cinemas.

TV is steadily taking over what little film production is left in the UK, as is shown by the fact that of the 35 feature films of all kinds produced in British film studios last year, 22 had varying degrees of TV investment in them. And this ratio is likely to increase when the BBC complete their plans to set up their own productions in their own studios, where they will produce first features which, after a short cinema life, will then go into the TV library. As there is a considerable difference between films made for the small and the large screens, we are clearly witnessing a major change in the nature of filmmaking in this country.

1991 saw yet another chapter in the Goldcrest Films saga when the management team organised a buyout from the previous owner, George Walker, for nearly £25 million and immediately announced plans to make three films: *Agaguk* (but surely that won't be the final title?), *Killing Time* and *Madame Solario*. It is good to see Goldcrest (makers of *Chariots of Fire*, *Gandhi*, *The Killing Fields* and a number of other outstanding British films) battling on.

And now a couple of things to look forward to; firstly, early 1992 should see the premiere of the first ever – after 50 years of shorts – Tom and Jerry feature film, now being made. And secondly, the re-release of Orson Welles's *Citizen Kane* in the US – and soon in Britain too, surely – makes it increasingly likely we'll see his *The Other Side of the Wind*. This 1972 feature starring John Huston has never hitherto been shown, and has now been assembled from the unedited footage by a team including Frank Marshall and Peter Bogdanovich. There's one to look out for!

I'd like to conclude this year's Introduction on a personal note. Last March, I was considerably moved when, at a little ceremony at the Ritz Hotel in London, my fellow critics saw fit to present me with a special award for long service to the film industry. That award, now facing me as I write this, is something I shall always treasure.

Top Ten Box-Office Stars

STAR OF THE YEAR

Julia Roberts

Arnold Schwarzenegger

Kevin Costner

Harrison Ford

Mel Gibson

Michael J. Fox

Bruce Willis

Warren Beatty

Patrick Swayze

Gerard Depardieu

This UK list was calculated on the strength of box-office returns in the UK. Whereas *most* films' popularity more or less corresponds on both sides of the Atlantic, this is not *always* the case. While *Arachnophobia* was a catastrophe in US cinemas, it did very well in the UK, thanks to a laundered advertising campaign (the spiders were played down). Likewise, the third biggest grossing film of all time, *Home Alone*, failed to engender the same kind of enthusiasm in the UK as it did in the States.

However, without exception, the reigning star of both American and UK cinema audiences was Julia Roberts, listed in our Promising Faces section only last year. Since then every film Ms Roberts has touched has turned to box-office gold (reputedly making her the highest-paid actress in the world). *Pretty Woman* was the surprise hit of the summer, followed by *Flatliners* last winter and then the potent thriller *Sleeping with the Enemy*. Good reviews or no, Julia Roberts has won herself a die-hard audience.

On the male front, Arnold Schwarzenegger pretty much domi-

nated the box office last summer with the muscular *Total Recall* and then again at Christmas with *Kindergarten Cop*. Kevin Costner continued his reign with *Dances with Wolves*, a three-hour Western that insiders predicted would be a financial bomb. Instead, it made a fortune and walked off with seven Oscars. Can Kevin do no wrong? Placed fourth, Harrison Ford proved in his intelligent courtroom thriller *Presumed Innocent* he didn't have to have a fedora and bullwhip to bring in the crowds, while Mad Mel was very busy, clocking up three big movies, *Bird on a Wire*, *Air America* and *Hamlet*. The other stars speak for themselves, although special mention must go to Gerard Depardieu, the first Frenchman to make it on to the list.

For the record, last year's top ten were: 1 Harrison Ford; 2 Pauline Collins; 3 Robin Williams; 4 Mel Gibson; 5 Jack Nicholson; 6 Rick Moranis; 7 Michael J. Fox; 8 Bill Murray; 9 Tom Hanks; 10 Tom Cruise.

[JC-W]

Releases of the Year

In this section you will find details of all the films released in Great Britain from 1 July 1990 to the end of June 1991 – the period covered by all the reference features in the book. The precise dating of some of these releases is a little tricky in view of the lack of any rigidity in the release pattern, but the date given generally refers to the film's London release, unless otherwise stated.

In the case of films sent out on a 'floating' release the date of the film's first London showing has been added because usually this is also the first British showing.

The normal abbreviations operate as follows: Dir – for Director; Pro – for Producer; Assoc Pro – for Associate Producer; Ex Pro – for Executive Producer; Pro Ex – for Production Executive; Pro Sup – for Production Supervisor; Co-Pro – for Co-Producer; Pro Co-Ord – for Production Co-Ordinator; Ph – for Photographer; Ed – for Editor; Art – for Art Director; Pro Des – for Production Designer; M – for Music; and a few others which will be obvious.

Abbreviations for the names of film companies are also pretty obvious when used, such as Fox for 20th Century-Fox, Rank for Rank Film Distributors, and UIP for Universal International Pictures. Where known, the actual production company is given first, the releasing company last.

When it comes to nationality of the film, you will find that this is noted wherever possible – those films without any mention of country of origin can usually be taken as being American – but in these days of increasing international co-productions between two, three or even four countries it is sometimes a little difficult to sort out where the premier credit is due.

Finally, unless otherwise specified (i.e. in black-and-white), it can safely be taken that the film is made in Technicolor or some similar process.

Censorship certificates: *U* represents films suitable for persons of any age: *PG* (Parental Guidance) represents films which some parents might consider unsuitable for their children; *12* or *15* means no persons under that age will be admitted; and films certified with an *18* (approximately the old 'X' certificate) means that nobody under that age will be admitted to the cinema while that film is showing. 'No cert' means that no certificate has been issued by the *initial showing of the film* but this does not mean that one will not subsequently be issued.

Films are reviewed by F. Maurice Speed and James Cameron-Wilson, with Frederick Deeps Malone, Charles Bacon and Michael Darvell. Each review is followed by its writer's initials.

The Adventures of Ford Fairlane. Andrew Dice Clay, a popular target of the Activists Against Sexist Pigs lobby, is best known as The Diceman, a controversial, proudly offensive stand-up comic. If enough people had seen this, his starring film debut, he could've become as controversial a film star. No such luck. *Ford Fairlane* bombed at the box office and forced Twentieth Century-Fox to abandon the theatrical release of Clay's concert film *Dice*. It is easy to see why. The comedian plays a dumb, insensitive, hateful male chauvinist pig, otherwise known as the rock'n'roll detective Ford Fairlane. Asked to locate a missing groupie, Fairlane uncovers a hornet's nest of corruption in the LA music business and loses everything but his libido along the way. Even his pet koala bear is murdered. *The Adventures of Ford Fairlane* attempts to be tasteless, but doesn't even have the courage of its own convictions. What remains is an excruciating mess of overacting, duff dialogue and infantile histrionics. Avoid. [JC-W]

Also with: Wayne Newton (Julian Grendel), Priscilla Presley (Colleen Sutton), Morris Day (Don Cleveland), Lauren Holly (Jazz), Maddie Corman (Zuzu Petals), Gilbert Gottfried (Johnny Crunch), Cody Jarrett (Kyle Troy), Patrick Kelly, Brandon Call, Robert Englund, Ed O'Neill, Vince Neil, Sheila E., David Arnott, Mark Goldstein, William Shockley, Mark Zuelke, Pamela Segall, David Bowe, Lori Pfeiffer, Randy Crenshaw, Tone Loc. Dir: Renny Harlin. Pro: Joel Silver and Steve Perry. Ex Pro: Michael Levy. Screenplay: Daniel Waters, James Cappe and David Arnott; based on characters created by Rex Weiner. Ph: Oliver Wood. Ed: Michael Tronick. Pro Des: John Vallone. M: Yello; songs performed by Billy Idol, Teddy Pendergrass, Motley Crue, Dion, Sheila E., Tone Loc, Andrew Dice Clay, Bobby Darin etc. Costumes: Marilyn Vance-Straker. Sound: Tim Cooney. (Fox.) Rel: 8 February 1991. 102 mins. Cert 18.

Air America. 1969, Laos. From the heart of Laos, American ace pilot Gene Ryack watches a black-and-white TV screen on which Richard M. Nixon declares, 'There are no American combat forces in Laos.' It is this official invisibility that makes the flyers of Air America, the world's largest clandestine airline, so reckless. If they don't exist, then nothing they get up to actually happens. Mel Gibson is the veteran pilot, airlifting everything from live pigs to heroin; Robert Downey Jr is the rookie airman, straight from traffic patrol in LA. A gung-ho comedy a few shades lighter than *M*A*S*H*, *Air America* is competently directed and played, but is neither funny enough nor feels authentic enough to grip the imagination or funny bone. Still, it wears its heart on its sleeve and the stunts are spectacular. Full marks, too, to the throwaway period detail and fluid editing. [JC-W]

Also with: Robert Downey Jr (Billy Covington), Nancy Travis (Corrine Landreaux), Ken Jenkins (Major Donald Lemond), David Marshall Grant (Rob Diehl), Lane Smith (Senator Davenport), Burt Kwouk (General Lu Soong), Art La Fleur, Ned Eisenberg, Marshall Bell, David Bowe, Tim Thomerson, Harvey Jason, Sinjai Hongthai. Dir: Roger Spottiswoode. Pro: Daniel Field. Ex Pro: Mario Kassar and Andrew Vajna. Screenplay: John Eskow and Richard Rush. Ph: Roger Deakins. Ed: John Bloom and Lois Freeman-Fox. Pro Des: Allan Cameron. M: Charles Gross; songs performed by Aerosmith, B. B. King, Bonnie Raitt, The Temptations, Steely Dan, Creedence Clearwater Revival, The Four Tops, The Mamas and the Papas, The Rolling Stones, Frank Sinatra etc. Costumes: John Mollo. Sound: Simon Kaye. (Carolco-Guild.) Rel: 4 January 1991. 112 mins. Cert 15.

√ **Akira.** Lavish, $8 million Japanese animation feature by the writer-director Katsuhiro Otomo, based on his comic books, which are apparently very popular in Japan and the USA. Tokyo has been destroyed by atomic assault and although now rebuilt – well, sort of – it is under threat from a secret new source of energy which the army doesn't know how to control. And in the world of the future there are all the old troubles; students demonstrating and terrorists plotting to unseat the government. Imaginative and fascinating; the jerky human beings are the only real snag. [FDM]

Dir and (with Izo Hashimoto) Screenplay: Katsuhiro Otomo; based on his comic books. Ph: Katsuji Misawa. Art: Toshiharu Mizutani. M: Shoji Yamashiro. (Akira Committee Pro.–ICA.) Rel: floating; first shown London (ICA) 25 January 1991. 124 mins. No cert.

Almost an Angel. Paul Hogan returns as another likeable rogue, this time

playing Terry Dean, a hardened crook who thinks he's an angel after recovering from a road accident. Hogan has fun as the holy safebreaker and electronics wizard (bypassing his prison's circuits *after* he's released), and sidesteps the schmaltz with his trademark laid-back machismo. Co-star Elias Koteas is also very good, as a cripple

Mel Gibson and Robert Downey Jr show off their machismo while frittering away a fascinating subject – in Roger Spottiswoode's Air America *(Guild).*

Paul Hogan, alias Rod Stewart, as a bank robber-cum-master of disguise who becomes Almost an Angel *(Paramount).*

The diary of a stuffed shirt: Michael Palin in his fine labour of love, American Friends *(from Virgin Vision).*

dying of spinal cancer – or, as Terry Dean puts it, 'a jerk in a wheelchair'. Very sentimental, very whimsical, often amusing, always engaging. Paul Hogan not only stars, but executive produced the film from his own screenplay, while Mrs Hogan, *alias* Linda Kozlowski, plays his romantic interest for the third time. [JC-W]

Also with: Elias Koteas (Steve), Linda Kozlowski (Rose Garner), Doreen Lang (Mrs Garner), Douglas Seale (Father), Parley Baer (George Bealeman), Charlton Heston (God), Robert Sutton, Travis Venable, Ruth Warshawsky, Ben Slack, Michael Alldredge, Linda Kurimoto, Joe Dallesandro. Dir and Pro: John Cornell. Ex Pro and Screenplay: Paul Hogan. Ph: Russell Boyd. Ed: David Stiven. Pro Des: Henry Bumstead. M: Maurice Jarre. Costumes: April Ferry. Sound: Tom Brandau. (Ironbark Films/Paramount–UIP.) Rel: 26 December 1990. 95 mins. Cert PG.

American Friends. The heroine of *American Friends*, Miss Elinor Hartley (Trini Alvarado), is referred to at one point as 'frail and eager', an apt description of the film itself. Inspired by the travel journals of Michael Palin's great-grandfather, this is a gentle, eager-to-please romantic drama, co-scripted by Palin himself. The actor plays Francis Ashby, a shy, stuffy Fellow of St John's College, Oxford, whose life is turned upside down when he meets two American women on holiday in Switzerland. A leisurely, delectable piece, *American Friends* is structured like fine filigree and executed with enormous care and love. Once and for all, Palin has laid his Monty Python ghost to rest. [JC-W]

Also with: Connie Booth (Miss Caroline Hartley), Alfred Molina (Oliver Syme), Alun Armstrong (Dr Weeks), Robert Eddison (Rushden), Bryan Pringle (Haskell), David Calder, Simon Jones, Sheila Reid, Edward Rawle-Hicks, Jonathan Firth, Ian Dunn, John Nettleton, Charles McKeown,

Roger Lloyd Pack, Jimmy Jewel, Wensley Pithey, Arthur Howard. Dir: Tristram Powell. Pro: Patrick Cassavetti and Steve Abbott. Screenplay: Palin and Powell. Ph: Philip Bonham-Carter. Ed: George Akers. Pro Des: Andrew McAlpine. M: Georges Delerue. Costumes: Bob Ringwood. Sound: John Ireland. (Prominent Features–Virgin Vision.) Rel: 22 March 1991. 95 mins. Cert PG.

La Amiga – The Girlfriend. See The Girlfriend – La Amiga.

An Angel at My Table. Haunting and beautifully composed New Zealand biopic about Jane Frame, one of that country's outstanding authors. Based on the writer's own trilogy, which in turn served for a three-part TV mini-series. Once seen, not easily forgotten. [FDM]

An enormous cast includes: Kerry Fox (Janet Frame), Karen Fergusson (Janet as a teenager), Alexis Keogh (Janet as a girl),

Melina Bernecker (Myrtle Frame), Glynis Angell (Isabel Frame), Samantha Townsley (Isabel as a teenager), Catherine Murray-Cowper (Isabel as a child), Sarah Smuts-Kennedy (June Frame), Susan McGregor (teenager June), Sarah Llewellyn (June as a child), Andrew Binns (Bruddie Frame), Christopher Lawrence (teenager Bruddie), Mark Morrison (Bruddie as a child), Iris Churn (Mum), K. J. Wilson (Dad), Carla Hedgeman (young Poppy), Caroline Somerville (teenager Poppy), Colin McColl, Martyn Sanderson, Jessica Wilcox, Mark Clare, Michael Harry, William Brandt, Peter Dennett, David McKenzie, Eleanor Wragge, Jessie Mune, etc. Dir: Jane Campion. Pro: Bridge Ikin. Co-Pro: John Maynard. Pro Co-Ord: Sam Thompson. Screenplay: Laura Jones; based on the trilogy by Janet Frame: *To the Island, An Angel at My Table* and *The Envoy from Mirror City*. Ph: Stuart Dryburgh. Pro Des: Grant Major. Art: Jackie Gilmore. M: Don McGlashan. (Hibiscus Films in assoc with New Zealand Film Commission/Television New Zealand/ Australian Broadcasting Corp. and Channel 4–Artificial Eye.) Rel: floating; first shown London (Lumiere) 28 September 1990. 158 mins. Cert 15.

Anita: Dances of Vice – Anita: Tanze des Lasters. Fascinating West German film set in the decadent 'twenties in Berlin, the period of the notorious Weimar Republic. It's the story of Anita, a nude cabaret dancer and lesbian, told by a mixture of black-and-white film and conventional sound (the present) and garishly coloured silent sequences (the past). A brilliant performance by Loti Huber as the old Anita, who relates her life as she recalls – and imagines – it while dying in hospital. [FDM]

Also with: Ina Blum (the young Anita), Mikael Honesseu (her partner Droste), Tillmann Lehnert, Marion Kutscke, Bernd Henckels, Nadja Reichardt, Andreas Hof, Gertrud Goroncy, Jörg Dauscher, Hanne-lene Limpach, Eva Kutz, Helge Musial, Michael Morris, Reiner Kranich, Beate Zeidler, Friedrich Steinhauer, Dieter Dorst, Ovel, Dorit Quast, Alix Buchen, Sabine von Recke, Maria Hasenhäcker. Dir: Rosa von Praunheim. Ex Pro: Renée Gundelach. Pro Co-Ord: Nani Mahlo. Screenplay: Praunheim, with Hannelene Limpach, Marianne Enzensberger and Lotti Huber. Ph: Elfi Mikesch. Ed: Praunheim and Michael Schafer. Art: Inge Stiborski, Michael Fechner, Christa Kleemann, Volker Marz and Wolfgang Peetz. M: Konrad Elfers; Rainer Rubbert, Alan Marks, Ed Lieber and Dieter Siebert. (Rosa von Praunheim/Road Movies in assoc with ZDF–ICA Projects.) Rel:

floating; first shown London (ICA) 13 July 1990. 85 mins. No cert.

Another 48HRS. San Francisco, eight years later. Nick Nolte and Eddie Murphy return as tough cop Jack Cates and fast-talking, foul-mouthed convict Reggie Hammond – in the sequel that reportedly cost Paramount more than $100 million to set up, produce and market worldwide. A local drug-dealing crimelord, The Iceman, has put out a contract on Reggie – and Jack needs to know why. Walter Hill directs the familiar clutter like a macho commercial for tequila, and then revs up the bodycount to (presumably) keep our attention. What starts out as a stylish B-movie thriller soon collapses under a welter of clichés, stereotypical villains and foul language. The dialogue should be ashamed of itself. [JC-W]

Also with: Brion James (Ben Kehoe), Kevin Tighe (Blake Wilson), Ed O'Ross (Frank Cruise), David Anthony Marshall (Willie Hickok), Andrew Divoff (Cherry Ganz), Bernie Casey (Kirkland Smith), Brent Jen-

Yet Another 48HRS: *Nick Nolte and Eddie Murphy squabble over honour as the bodycount rises in this opulent, lazy and very, very boring sequel from UIP.*

nings (Tyrone Burroughs), Ted Markland (Malcolm Price), Tisha Campbell (Amy Kirkland), Felice Orlandi, Edward Walsh, Page Leong, Cathy Haase, Nancy Everhard. Dir: Walter Hill. Pro: Lawrence Gordon and Robert D. Wachs. Ex Pro: Mark Lipsky and Ralph S. Singelton. Assoc Pro: Raymond L. Murphy Jr and Kenneth H. Frith Jr. Screenplay: John Fasano, Jeb Stuart and Larry Gross; from a story by Fred Braughton. Ph: Matthew F. Leonetti. Ed: Freeman Davies, Carmel Davies and Donn Aron. Pro Des: Joseph C. Nemec III. M: James Horner. Costumes: Dan Moore. Sound: Willie D. Burton. (Paramount–UIP.) Rel: 21 September 1990. 95 mins. Cert 18.

Arachnophobia. Corny, over-slick and predictable comic-thriller in the *Jaws* mould, with director Steven Spielberg producing and producer Frank Marshall directing. Arachnophobic GP Ross Jennings (Jeff Daniels) and his pretty wife and two kids move to the country to escape the stresses of city life. But no sooner has he secured his first patient (a healthy 68-year-old), than she mysteriously ups and dies on him. Local custom preventing the act of a routine autopsy prevents the good doctor from establishing the cause of her death or that of other seemingly hale and hearty citizens. The plot is

designed to fit like a wall-to-wall carpet and soon the creepy-crawlies take over, gnashing their chelicerae and wielding their pedipalps. But remember, without our octopod friends the world would be overrun by hordes of nasty crop-eating and disease-spreading insects. So there. [JC-W]

Also with: Julian Sands (Dr James Atherton), Harley Jane Kozak (Molly Jennings), John Goodman (Delbert McClintock), Stuart Pankin (Sheriff Parsons), Henry Jones (Dr Sam Metcalf), Peter Jason (Henry Beechwood), Mary Carver (Margaret Hollins), Brian McNamara, Mark L. Taylor, James Handy, Roy Brocksmith, Kathy Kinney, Garette Patrick Ratcliff, Marlene Katz. Dir: Frank Marshall. Pro: Kathleen Kennedy and Richard Vane. Ex Pro: Steven Spielberg and Frank Marshall. Screenplay: Don Jakoby and Wesley Strick; from a story by Jakoby and Al Williams. Ph: Mikael Salomon. Ed: Michael Kahn. Pro Des: James Bissell. M: Trevor Jones; numbers performed by Frank Sinatra, Pat Metheny, Tony Bennett, Jimmy Buffett etc. Sound: Ronald Judkins. (Hollywood Pictures/Amblin Entertainment–Warner.) Rel: 4 January 1991. 110 mins. Cert PG.

Avalon. Every now and then a filmmaker feels compelled to write and direct an epic chronicling his childhood

and roots. Few have pulled it off as well as Barry Levinson, who shapes his childhood in Baltimore with a masterful hand. Armin Mueller-Stahl stars as Sam Krichinsky, an Eastern European immigrant who arrives in America in 1914. In Baltimore he sets up home, scraping together enough money to pay for his brothers and family to move across the ocean. Levinson's alter ego is little Michael (Elijah Wood), Krichinsky's grandson, who soaks up his family's history through big soulful eyes. From the annual ritual of Thanksgiving to less regular deaths and pregnancies, Levinson weaves a dense, magical tale of humanity that is touching and funny and gives a dignified perspective on the world we live in. *Avalon* doesn't strike a single false note. [JC-W]

Also with: Elizabeth Perkins (Ann Kaye), Joan Plowright (Eva Krichinsky), Aidan Quinn (Jules Kaye), Eve Gordon (Dottie Kirk), Lou Jacobi (Gabriel Krichinsky), Kevin Pollak (Izzy Kirk), Ronald Guttman (Simka), Tom Wood (Michael Kaye, as an adult), Leo Fuchs, Israel Rubinek, Grant

The director as a young man: Elijah Wood portrays Michael, the alter ego of Barry Levinson, in Levinson's autobiographical masterpiece Avalon – seen here with Armin Mueller-Stahl.

Gelt, Frania Rubinek, Neil Kirk, Miles A. Perman, Herb Levinson, Paul Quinn, Michael Krauss, Ava Eileen Quinn, Irv Stein. Dir and Screenplay: Barry Levinson. Pro: Levinson and Mark Johnson. Ph: Allen Daviau. Ed: Stu Linder. Pro Des: Norman Reynolds. M: Randy Newman. Costumes: Gloria Gresham. Sound: Richard Beggs. (Tri-Star Columbia.) Rel: 1 March 1991. 128 mins. Cert U.

Awakenings. The Bronx, 1969. True story about Dr Malcolm Sayer (Robin Williams), a timid neurologist, amateur botanist and expert on earthworms, who accidentally lands a job at the New York Bainbridge Hospital. His brief is to look after a ward of catatonics, but through painstaking care and experimentation he discovers that his vegetable-like patients are in fact curable. One patient in particular, Leonard Lowe (Robert De Niro), responds to human contact and the drug L-dopa and evolves into a normal human state after thirty years of 'sleep'. The Rip Van Winkle story updated, *Awakenings* is a well-crafted, 'feel good' drama that is only marginally too sentimental for its own good, and although it falls apart in its final third, it dispenses enough positive food for thought to make it a memorable, worthwhile experience. Again, Robin Williams is superb. [JC-W]

Also with: John Heard (Dr Kaufman), Julie Kavner (Eleanor Costello), Penelope Ann Miller (Paula), Max Von Sydow (Dr Peter Ingham), Ruth Nelson (Mrs Lowe), Alice Drummond (Lucy), Judith Malina, Barton Heyman, George Martin, Anne Meara, Richard Libertini, Laura Esterman, Dexter Gordon. Dir: Penny Marshall. Pro: Walter F. Parkes and Lawrence Lasker. Ex Pro: Marshall, Arne Schmidt and Elliot Abbott. Screenplay: Steven Zillian; based on the book by Oliver Sacks. Ph: Miroslav Ondricek. Ed: Jerry Greenberg and Battle Davies. Pro Des: Anton Furst. M: Randy Newman. Costumes: Cynthia Flynt. Sound: Les Lazarowitz. (Columbia Tri-Star.) Rel: 15 March 1991. 121 mins. Cert 12.

A.W.O.L. – Absent Without Leave (US: *Lionheart*). Corny, predictable and totally unbelievable kickboxing action-thriller. Jean-Claude Van Damme, star of *Bloodsport, Cyborg* and *Kickboxer*, plays Lyon, a soldier of the Foreign Legion who discovers that his brother has been seriously burned by drug dealers in Los Angeles. Fighting

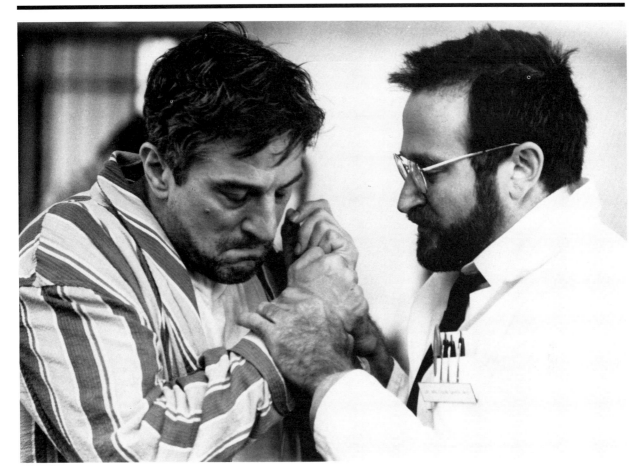

his way out of the desert, Lyon works his passage to New York where he partakes in illegal streetfighting to pay for his fare to LA. The fights, choreographed by Van Damme (and set in underground car parks, half-emptied swimming pools and squash courts), are strong meat, but somewhat unconvincing, while the acting leaves an enormous amount to be desired. Manipulative and formulaic stuff. Previously known as *Wrong Bet*. [JC-W]

Also with: Deborah Rennard (Cynthia), Harrison Page (Joshua), Lisa Pelikan (Helene), Ashley Johnson (Nicole), Brian Thompson (Russell). Dir: Sheldon Lettich. Pro: Ash R. Shah and Eric Karson. Ex Pro: Sunil R. Shah, Anders P. Jensen and Sundip R. Shah. Screenplay: Sheldon Lettich and Jean-Claude Van Damme. Ph: Robert New. Ed: Mark Conte. Pro Des: Gregory Pickerell. M: John Scott. (Imperial Entertainment–Guild.) Rel: 21 September 1990. 110 mins. Cert 18.

Ay, Carmela! Carmela, her husband and a homeless mute entertain the Republican troops during the Spanish Civil War. When they inadvertently stray into Nationalist territory they are taken prisoner. However, when the commanding lieutenant discovers that they are entertainers, he releases them, gives them decent food and drink and arranges for a theatrical 'spectacle'. It is up to Carmela & Co. to adapt their patriotic songs and poems to the Fascist cause. An atmospheric attempt to cap-

Robert De Niro and Robin Williams battle for the acting honours in Penny Marshall's thoughtful, funny, bittersweet Awakenings *(from Columbia Tri-Star).*

Andres Pajares and Carmen Maura mock the Fascist cause in Carlos Saura's comic-tragic look at the Spanish Civil War in Ay Carmela! *(from Palace).*

Babar, king of the elephants, makes his film debut in Winston's Babar: The Movie: *here he meets his subjects.*

ture the ambiguity and desolation of civil war, *Ay, Carmela!* at times succeeds in touching the emotions, but at others proves merely to be farcical and gauche. An Italian-Spanish co-production. [JC-W]

Cast includes: Carmen Maura (Carmela), Andres Pajares (Paulino, her husband), Gabino Diego (Gustavete), Maurizio Di Razza (Lt Ripamonte), Miguel A. Rellan, Edward Zentara, Mario De Candia. Dir: Carlos Saura. Ex Pro: Andres Vicente Gomez. Screenplay: Saura and Rafael Azcona; based on a book by Sanchis Sinisterra. Ph: Jose Luis Alcaine. Ed: Pablo G. Del Amo. Art: Rafael Palmero. M: Alejandro Masso. Sound: Guilles Ortion. (Iberoamericana Films (Madrid)/Ellepi (Rome)/Television Espanola–Palace.) Rel: 3 May 1991. 104 mins. Cert 12.

Babar: The Movie. French-Canadian animated feature. On the annual Celesteville Victory Day Parade, the King of Elephantland tells his children about a youthful adventure, when he rescued the inhabitants of his sweetheart's village from attack by the villainous rhinoceros. Aimed at the kiddies, it should certainly please them – *and* the young at heart – with its simple moral tale and charming atmosphere. [FDM]

The voices of Gordon Pinsent (the king), Gavin Magrath (the king as a boy), Elizabeth Hanna (as the queen), Sarah Polley (the queen as a girl), Chris Wiggins, Stephen Ouimette, John Stocer, Charles Kerr. Dir:

Alan Bunce. Pro: Peter Lambert and Michael Clive. Ex Pro: Patrick Loubert, Michael Hirsh and Clive A. Smith. Screenplay: Peter Sauder, J. D. Smith, John de Klein, Raymond Jafelice and Alan Bunce; based on characters created by Jean and Laurent de Brunhoff. Pro Des: Ted Bastien.

Art: Clive Powsey and Carol Bradbury. M: Milan Kymkicka. (Melvana-Ellipse Pro. in assoc with Clifford Ross Co.–Habbey Home Entertainment–Winstone Films.) Rel: floating; first shown London (Cannon, Panton St, Tottenham Ct Rd and Chelsea) 27 July 1990. 70 mins. Cert U.

Back to the Future – Part III. You're not going to believe this: Marty McFly discovers that good ol' Doc Brown was killed back in 1885, so the time travelling duo go back to save him. The distortion of logic is too much even for this sequel to take. I mean, why bring Doc back from 1885 if he is already alive and well and bouncing between 1955 and 2015? Beats me. As it turns out, director Robert Zemeckis is a Western fan and so the cowboy genre is re-born (yet again), with very little

Back to the Western: Michael J. Fox as Clint Eastwood in Back to the Future Part III *(UIP), a wasted opportunity to explore the real West. And, below: Thomas F. Wilson as your archetypal villain, Buford 'Mad Dog' Tannen.*

attention to futurism and heavy homage to Clint Eastwood. Mary Steenburgen guest stars as Doc's love interest, reuniting her with actor Christopher Lloyd from her very first film, *Goin' South* – a Western! [JC-W]

Cast includes: Michael J. Fox (Marty McFly/Clint Eastwood/Seamus McFly), Christopher Lloyd (Dr Emmett Brown), Mary Steenburgen (Clara Clayton), Thomas F. Wilson (Buford 'Mad Dog' Tannen/Biff Tannen), Lea Thompson (Maggie McFly/Lorraine McFly), Elisabeth Shue (Jennifer), Matt Clark, Richard Dysart, Pat Buttram, Harry Carey Jr, Dub Taylor, James Tolkan, Marc McClure, Wendie Jo Sperber, Jeffrey Weissman, Christopher Wynne, Sean Gregory Sullivan, Mike Watson, Hugh Gillin, Bill McKinney, Donovan Scott, Flea, Marvin J. McIntyre, Dean Cundey (as the photographer). Dir: Robert Zemeckis. Pro:

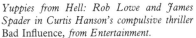

Vanessa Redgrave stretches her range – even for her – in Simon Callow's fiercely atmospheric The Ballad of the Sad Café, *from Carson McCullers's novella (from HoBo).*

Bob Gale and Neil Canton. Ex Pro: Steven Spielberg, Frank Marshall and Kathleen Kennedy. Screenplay: Bob Gale; from a story by Zemeckis and Gale. Ph: Dean Cundey. Ed: Arthur Schmidt and Harry Keramidas. Pro Des: Rick Carter. M: Alan Silvestri; 'Doubleback' written and perfor-

Yuppies from Hell: Rob Lowe and James Spader in Curtis Hanson's compulsive thriller Bad Influence, *from Entertainment.*

med by ZZ Top. Costumes: Joanna Johnston. Sound: William B. Kaplan. (Universal–UIP.) Rel: 11 July 1990.

Bad Influence. On paper this thriller looked too good to be true. Rob Lowe, fresh from his sex video scandal, plays the smooth bad guy we first saw in *Masquerade*. James Spader (star of *sex, lies and videotape*) co-stars as the engaged LA drip videotaped *in flagrante delicto* with a one-night stand. Soon, Mr Lowe is controlling Spader's every move, skilfully spinning a spider's web around the loser who wants to improve his life. Lowe is convincing as the devil in Armani suits, and director Hanson (*The Bedroom Window*) artfully nudges his story of ego and paranoia to its satisfactory conclusion. [JC-W]

Cast includes: Rob Lowe (Alex), James Spader (Michael Boll), Lisa Zane (Claire), Christian Clemenson (Pismo Boll), Kathleen Whilhoite (Leslie), Tony Maggio (Patterson), Marcia Cross (Ruth Fielding). Dir: Curtis Hanson. Pro: Steve Tisch. Ex Pro: Morrie Eisenman and Richard Becker. Screenplay: David Koepp. Ph: Robert Elswit. Ed: Bonnie Koehler. Pro Des: Ron Foreman. M: Trevor Jones. Sound: Dane A. Davis. (Epic/PRO–Entertainment.) Rel: 5 October 1990. 100 mins. Cert 18.

The Ballad of the Sad Café. Powerful directorial debut from the actor Simon Callow, who combines a keen cinematic

Rip Torn as the 'free thinker' and controversial poet Walt Whitman in John Kent Harrison's superb first feature, Beautiful Dreamers *(Blue Dolphin).*

eye with an actor's sensibility. Vanessa Redgrave is bravely cast as Miss Amelia, the androgynous owner of a sleepy Southern café, a woman treated with fearful respect – at a distance – by the locals. She exhibits an untapped tenderness when a hunchbacked cousin arrives out of the blue, but the latter's fascination with the myth surrounding Miss Amelia's banished husband – shortly to be released from prison – produces yet another change in the café owner's personality. An extraordinary,

strange film, dominated by Vanessa Redgrave's towering performance and a vivid sense of atmosphere and other-worldliness. Based on the novel by Carson McCullers, a literary exercise in melding myth with fairy tale. [JC-W]

Also with: Keith Carradine (replacing Sam Shepard as Marvin Macy), Cork Hubbert (Cousin Lymon), Rod Steiger (Revd Willin), Austin Pendleton, Beth Dixon, Lanny Flaherty, Mert Hatfield, Earl Hindman, Anne Pitoniak, Keith Wommack, Kevin Wommack, Don Stroud. Dir: Simon Callow. Pro: Ismail Merchant. Ex Pro: Paul Bradley. Screenplay: Michael Hirst. Ph: Walter Lassally. Ed: Andrew Marcus. Pro Des: Bruno Santini. M: Richard Robbins. Costumes: Marianna Elliott. Sound: John Foster. (Film Four International–HoBo.) Rel: 26 April 1991. 100 mins. Cert 15.

Beautiful Dreamers. 1880–2, London, Ontario. Sensitive, moving account of the friendship between the great American poet Walt Whitman (1819–92) and Dr Maurice Bucke, superintendent of an asylum for the insane. Pictured at first as a timid, retiring man, Dr Bucke loses his cool at a conference in Philadelphia, and rails against the inhumanity of science, attracting the attention of Whitman. Bucke is made furious by the practice of removing the ovaries as a treatment for nymphomania. But Whitman (whose book of poems, *Leaves of Grass*, has already been banned in Boston) is more interested in Bucke's treatment of the insane. Whitman himself has a 'mentally incompetent' brother and asks Bucke to examine him. From here, the poet's influence on Bucke changes the doctor's life, transforming in turn his stuffy wife and ultimately the attitude of the local community towards his asylum and its occupants. A gentle, articulate film, superbly realised. [JC-W]

Cast includes: Colm Feore (Dr Maurice Bucke), Rip Torn (Walt Whitman), Wendel Meldrum (Jessie Bucke), Colin Fox (Revd Haines), David Gardner (Dr Lett), Tom McCamus (Leonard Thomas), Barbara Gordon (Agatha Haines), Marsha Moreau (Birdie Bucke), Sheila McCarthy, Albert Schultz, Angelo Rizacos, Gordon Masten, Gerry Quigley, Roland Hewgill. Dir and Screenplay: John Kent Harrison. Pro: Michael Maclear and Martin Walters. Co-Pro: Sally Bochner. Ex Pro: Stephen J. Roth. Ph: François Protat. Ed: Ron Wisman. Pro Des: Seamus Flannery. M: Lawrence Shragge. Costumes: Ruth Secord. (Cinexus/Famous Players/C/FP Distributors Inc/Telefilm Canada/Ontario Film Development Corp./National Film Board of Canada–Blue Dolphin.) Rel: 18 January 1991. 108 mins. Cert 15.

Berlin Jerusalem. Two women, one a German Expressionist poet, the other a Russian revolutionary, both Zionist idealists, finally realise that their dream is just a dream. A cool, cerebral film, this French–Israeli co-production is by no means easy to take in, though the camerawork is remarkable. Minority viewing, but nonetheless exciting and fascinating. [FDM]

Cast: Lisa Kreuzer (Elsa), Rivka Neuman (Mania), Markus Stockhausen, Benjamin Levy, Vernon Dobtcheff. Dir and, with Gudie Lawaetz, Screenplay: Amos Gitai.

Ph: Henri Alekan. Ed: Luke Barnier. Sound: Antoine Bonfanti. Art: Marc Petit-jean and Emmanuel Amrami. M: Markus Stockhausen. (AGAV Films/Channel 4/La Sept Nova Films/RA12/Orthel Films/NOS/ Transfax/La Maison de Culture du Havre/ Hubert Bals Fund/CNC–ICA.) Rel: floating; first shown London (ICA) 8 March 1991. 89 mins. No cert.

Betsy's Wedding. Celluloid weddings are seldom the stuff of poetry, and Betsy's is no exception. Betsy Hopper, a Jewish-Italian design student, and Jake Lovell, a wealthy New York WASP, want a quiet, inexpensive cere-mony. But Betsy's father Eddie (Alan Alda) intends to give his first daughter a 'fantastic' wedding. 'That doesn't mean big and expensive, does it?' begs Betsy. 'No, that means cheap and ugly. What do you think?' While everybody tries to have their say, Eddie plummets into debt after making a shady deal with the (now ubiquitous) Mob. But this is Alan Alda territory, so you know there's got to be a sentimental, warm-hearted happy ending. Although Alda (who also writes and directs) comes up with the blandest of comedies, he is a great entertainer and invariably supplies a wealth of interesting characters and a decent quota of laughs. [JC-W]

Also with: Joey Bishop (Eddie's father), Madeline Kahn (Lola Hopper), Catherine O'Hara (Gloria Henner), Joe Pesci (Oscar Henner), Ally Sheedy (Connie Hopper), Burt Young (Uncle Georgie), Molly Ring-wald (Betsy Hopper), Anthony LaPaglia (Stevie Dee), Julie Bovasso (Grandma Hopper), Nicolas Coster (Henry Lovell), Bibi Besch (Nancy Lovell), Dylan Walsh (Jake Lovell), Camille Saviola, Allan Rich, Sully Boyar, Larry Block, Helen Hanft. Dir and Screenplay: Alan Alda. Pro: Martin Bregman and Louis A. Stroller. Ph: Kelvin Pike. Ed: Michael Polakow. Pro Des: John Jay Moore. M: Bruce Broughton; songs per-formed by The Dixie Cups, Frankie Avalon etc. Costumes: Mary Malon. Sound: John Pritchett and Frank Haber. (Touchstone/ Silver Screen Partners–Warner.) Rel: 26 October 1990. 94 mins. Cert 15.

The Big Man. Powerful drama about an unemployed Scottish miner who trains for a bare-knuckle contest to bring his family the readies. As the date of the fight approaches, the 'big man' sees the corruption that is part and parcel of the main event but is never-theless seduced by the fresh money in his pocket. David Leland (*Wish You*

The big day has arrived: Alan Alda and Molly Ringwald at Betsy's Wedding *(Warner).*

Were Here, Checking Out) directs the film as if he were staging a Wagnerian opera, while Ennio Morricone's epic score drowns the action in orchestral hysteria. However, the brutality and realism of the scenario and the fresh-ness of the locales (Glasgow, Coalburn) add up to some impressive cinema, not far off a Scottish *Raging Bull*. Based on

Liam Neeson is The Big Man, *a local hero who 'organises his life with the precision of a road accident' – from Palace.*

The superb Martin Short as the Hollywood agent as artificial as Sweet 'n' Low in HoBo's periodically hilarious The Big Picture.

William McIlvanney's cult angry novel. [JC-W]

Cast includes: Liam Neeson (Danny Scoular), Joanne Whalley-Kilmer (Beth Scoular), Ian Bannen (Matt Mason), Billy Connolly (Frankie), Hugh Grant (Gordon), Maurice Roeves (Cam Colvin), George Rossi, Tom Watson, Julie Graham, Pat Roach, Kenny Ireland, Ken Drury, Jack Shepherd. Dir: David Leland. Pro: Stephen Woolley. Ex Pro: Nik Powell. Screenplay: Don McPher-

Rosanna Arquette as the sham medium with unusual gifts in Mike Hodges' intriguing Black Rainbow, *from Palace.*

son; based on the novel by William McIlvanney. Ph: Ian Wilson. Ed: George Akers. Pro Des: Caroline Amies. M: Ennio Morricone. Costumes: Mary-Jane Reyner. Sound: Colin Nicholson. (Miramax/BSB/British Screen–Palace.) Rel: 31 August 1990. 116 mins. Cert 18.

The Big Picture. Nick Chapman (Kevin Bacon) is a promising film student who believes in black-and-white, simple camera moves and heterosexual love stories. When he walks off with the coveted first prize at his LA film school he finds himself the toast of Hollywood. His answering machine is jammed with calls, beautiful actresses beg his company and Martin Short becomes his agent. Soon, the pressures of a house in Beverly Hills and a ground-level sports car force Chapman to junk his dream film in favour of *Beach Nuts*. What co-scripters Christopher Guest and Michael McKean did for the rock industry with *This Is Spinal Tap*, they do here for the movies. A lot of the parody is *too* broad (even for Hollywood), but the subtler stuff is hilarious. And at the heart of this sporadically successful spoof is a rather sweet film about 'the bigger picture' – life. [JC-W]

Also with: Emily Longstreth (Susan Rawlings), J. T. Walsh (Allen Habel), Jennifer Jason Leigh (Lydia Johnson), Michael McKean (Emmet Sumner), Kim Miyori (Jenny Sumner), Tery Hatcher (Gretchen), Martin Short (Neil Sussman), Dan Schneider, Jason Gould, Tracy Brooks Swope, Don Franklin, Gary Kroeger, Fran Drescher, Eddie Albert, June Lockhart, Stephen Collins, Roddy McDowall, Elliott Gould, Caitlin Clarke, Nancy Valen, John Cleese. Dir: Christopher Guest. Pro: Michael Varhol. Ex Pro: William E. McEuen and Richard Gilbert Abramson. Screenplay: Varhol, Guest and Michael McKean; from a story by Varhol and Guest. Ph: Jeff Jur. Ed: Martin Nicholson. Pro Des: Joseph T. Garrity. M: David Nichtern. Costumes: Karen Patch. Sound: John Huck. (Aspen Film Society–HoBo.) Rel: 30 November 1990. 100 mins. Cert 15.

The Big Steal. Lightweight but amusing and once or twice really hilarious Australian comedy about the feud between a dodgy car dealer and the youngster to whom he sells a dud. The

third film from the husband and wife team of David Parker (writer and photographer) and Nadia Tass (director). [FDM]

Cast: Ben Mendelsohn (Danny), Claudia Karvan (Joanna), Steve Bisley (Gordon Farkas), Angelo D'Angelo (Vangoli Petrakis), Tim Robertson (Mr Johnson), Maggie King, Sheryl Munks, Lise Rodgers, Frankie J. Holden. Pro: Tass and Parker. Dir: Tass. Ph: Parker. Screenplay: Parker. Ed: Peter Carrodus. Pro Des: Paddy Reardon. M: Chris Gough. (Cascade Films–HoBo.) Rel: floating; first shown London (Cannon, Haymarket, Tottenham Ct Rd and Chelsea) 29 March 1991. 100 mins. Cert 15.

√**Bird on a Wire.** Mindless chase caper with Mel Gibson as a double-crossed federal witness on the run with ex-girlfriend Goldie Hawn. Formerly involved with a South American drug cartel (remember *Tequila Sunrise*?), Rick Jarmin (Gibson) has been fingered by a corrupt FBI man in contact with Goldie's current beau. Mel and Goldie scream and giggle and smooch as the cartoon violence erupts around them, transporting us to a variety of colourful locations (luxury hotel, Chinatown, animal hospital, woods, fourth-rate hotel, zoo etc.). John Badham is a fine action director (*Blue Thunder, Stakeout*), but loses control of his story as it careers aimlessly from one showdown to the next. The good news is that the plentiful animal cast escapes with nary a scratch. Filmed in British Columbia. [JC-W]

Also with: Goldie Hawn (Marianne Graves), David Carradine (Eugene Sorenson), Bill Duke (Albert Diggs), Stephen Tobolowsky (Joe Weyburn), Joan Severance (Rachel Varney), Harry Caesar (Marvin), Jeff Corey, Alex Bruhanski, John Pyper-Ferguson, Clyde Kusatsu, Jackson Davies, Florence Paterson, Tim Healy. Dir: John Badham. Pro: Rob Cohen. Ex Pro: Ted Field and Robert W. Cort. Screenplay: David Seltzer, Louis Venosta and Eric Lerner; from a story by Venosta and Lerner. Ph: Robert Primes. Ed: Frank Morriss and Dallas Puett. Pro Des: Philip Harrison. M: Hans Zimmer; numbers performed by The Neville Brothers, The Allman Brothers, Bob Dylan etc. Costumes: Wayne Finkelman and Eduardo Castro. Sound: Rick Patton. Animal Coordinator: Monty Cox. Rel: 19 October 1990. 111 mins. Cert 12.

Black Rainbow. Martha Travis is in the business of theatrical 'entertainment', reassuring the bereaved that

Quick as a snake, blind as a bat: Rutger Hauer wields his stuff in Phillip Noyce's Blind Fury *(Columbia Tri-Star).*

their loved ones are in a restful state of nirvana. She is a popular medium, doling out safe platitudes, preying on the gullible and turning their innocent reactions into solid information 'from the grave'. And Martha Travis is a sham. Or so she thinks. When she correctly foresees the violent deaths of her audience's nearest and dearest, her popularity is challenged, her gift confirmed. But Martha's identification of an assassin puts her life in danger. *Black Rainbow* is a serious examination of the art and artifice of the psychic sideshow, and is to be commended for its down-to-earth approach. However, as a thriller it undermines its good intentions, neither succeeding as a genre piece nor as an authentic examination of its subject. A brave attempt, but ultimately an unsatisfactory and unconvincing foray into the metaphysical. Filmed in North Carolina. [JC-W]

Cast includes: Rosanna Arquette (Martha Travis), Jason Robards (Walter Travis),

Tom Hulce (Gary Wallace), Mark Joy (Lloyd Harley a.k.a. Davidson), Ron Rosenthal (Chief Detective Irving Weinberg), John Bennes (Ted Silas), Linda Pierce, Ed L. Gray. Dir and Screenplay: Mike Hodges. Pro: John Quested and Geoffrey Helman. Ex Pro: George A. Walker. Ph: Gerry Fisher. Ed: Malcolm Cooke. Pro Des: Voytek Roman. M: John Scott. Costumes: Clifford Capone. (Goldcrest–Palace.) Rel: 27 July 1990. 95 mins. Cert 15.

Blind Fury. Vietnam, 1969; Miami/Reno, the present. Multi-genre vehicle for Rutger Hauer as a blind samurai sword-wielding Vietnam vet acting as babysitter for a spoiled brat. The kid's father, a chemist, is persuaded by gangsters to manufacture a dangerous new drug, with his son to be held as collateral should his morals intervene. But the Mob hadn't reckoned on Hauer's arbitration. Plenty of action, some nice comic touches and the odd witticism speed this action-comedy-adventure-martial arts B-movie along its merry way but, quite frankly, it's a waste of director Phillip Noyce's exceptional talents. Based on a popular Japanese potboiler in the 'Zatoichi' series. [JC-W]

Cast includes: Rutger Hauer (Nick Parker), Terry O'Quinn (Frank Devereaux), Brandon Call (Billy Devereaux), Noble Willingham (MacReady), Lisa Blount (Annie Winchester), Nick Cassavetes (Lyle Pike), Rick Overton (Tector Pike), Meg Foster (Lynn Devereaux), Randall 'Tex' Cobb, Charles Cooper, Sho Kosugi, Sharon Shackelford, Robert Manning. Dir: Phillip Noyce. Pro: Daniel Grodnik and Tim Matheson. Ex Pro: Robert W. Cort and David Madden. Screenplay: Charles Robert Carner; based upon a screenplay by Ryozo Kasahara. Ph: Don Burgess. Ed: David Simmons. Pro Des: Peter Murton. M: J. Peter Robinson. Costumes: Katherine Dover. Sound: Eric Lindemann. (Columbia Tri-Star.) Rel: 13 July 1990. 85 mins. Cert 15.

Blood Oath. December, 1945; Ambon, Indonesia. Earnest, exceedingly dull courtroom drama, with Bryan Brown as the indignant captain prosecuting Japanese officers for war crimes against their Australian prisoners. While Bryan is trying to untangle the mystery of a mass grave and four missing airmen, American politics are already stepping in to stifle justice. Look for a startling series of close-ups of Jason Donovan as a foot soldier – with one line of dialogue. [JC-W]

Cast includes: Bryan Brown (Captain Robert Cooper), George Takei (Vice-Admiral Baron Takahashi), Terry O'Quinn (Major Tom Beckett), John Bach (Major Frank Roberts), Toshi Shioya (Lt Hideo Tanaka), John Clarke, Deborah Unger, John Polson, Russell Crewe, Nicholas Eadie, Tetsu Watanabe, Sokyu Fujita, Ray Barrett, David Argue. Dir: Stephen Wallace. Pro: Charles Waterstreet, Denis Whitburn and Brian A. Williams. Ex Pro: Graham Burke, Greg Coote and John Tarnoff. Co-Pro: Annie Bleakley. Screenplay: Whitburn and Williams. Ph: Russell Boyd. Ed: Nicholas Beauman. Pro Des: Bernard Hides. M: David McHugh. Costumes: Roger Kirk. Sound: Ben Osmo. (Sovereign/Village Roadshow/ Siege Productions–Rank.) Rel: 15 March 1991. 108 mins. Cert. 15.

Blood Red. Another slice of bloody American history, *Blood Red* focuses on the Sicilian winegrowers working the land in Northern California. When their national pride prevents them from selling their homes to an exploitative developer (Dennis Hopper), a bloody

Suspended cops Joe Pantoliano and Brian Dennehy pursue a vigorous unofficial investigation in Rank's Blood Heat.

feud ensues. Eric Roberts struts and simmers as the heroic rebel defending his people's rights, while Julia Roberts debuts (*Blood Red* was made in 1986) as his little sister (which she is). The historical facts themselves are engrossing, but somehow this earnest interpretation plays like a cut-price epic. One can't help but wonder how Francis Ford Coppola would have brought the thing to life. [JC-W]

Cast includes: Eric Roberts (Marco Collogero), Giancarlo Giannini (Sebastian Collogero), Dennis Hopper (William Bradford Berrigan), Burt Young (Andrews), Carlin Glynn (Miss Jeffreys), Lara Harris (Angelica), Joseph Running Fox, Al Ruscio, Michael Madsen, Elias Koteas, Marc Lawrence, Frank Campanella, the late Aldo Ray, Gary Swanson, Susan Anspach, Kevin Cooney, Julia Roberts, Alexandra Masterson, Horton Foote Jr, Charles Diekrop. Dir: Peter Masterson. Pro: Judd Bernard and Patricia Casey. Ex Pro: John Daly and Derek Gibson. Screenplay: Ron Cutler. Ph: Toyomichi Kurita. Ed: Randy Thornton. Pro Des: Bruno Rubeo. M: Carmine Coppola. Costumes: Ruth Myers. Sound: Barney Cabral. (Hemdale.) Rel: 26 December 1990. 91 mins. Cert 15.

Blue Heat (US: *The Last of the Finest*). Good old honest cop Frank Daly (Brian

Dennehy) and his two pals are suspended when a stake-out goes wrong. In disgust they hand back their badges so they can carry on their own investigation of a drugs ring, only to end up finding a fortune in laundered money. [FDM]

Also with: Joe Pantoliano (Wayne Gross), Jeff Fahey (Ricky Rodriguez), Bill Paxton (Howard 'Hojo' Jones), Michael C. Gwynne (Anthony Reece), Henry Stolow, Guy Boyd, Henry Darrow, J. Kenneth Campbell, Deborah-Lee Furness, Lisa Jane Persky, Patricia Clipper, Michelle Little, Susannah Kelly, Sheila Kelly, Micah Rowe, Joey Wright, George Paul, John Finnegan, Ron Canada, Michael Strasser, Xander Berkeley, Pam Gidley, Burke Byrnes. Dir: John Mackenzie. Pro: John A. Davis. Ex Pro: Jere Cunningham. Screenplay: Cunningham, Thomas Lee Wright and George Armitage. Ph: Juan Ruiz-Anchia. Ed: Graham Walker. Pro: Laurence G. Paull. M: Jack Nitzsche and Michael Hoenig. (Orion– Rank.) Rel: floating; first shown London (Odeon Mezzanine) 21 September 1990. 106 mins. Cert 15.

Blue Steel. Relentless, violent thriller from Kathryn Bigelow (*Near Dark*) with Jamie Lee Curtis in a stand-out performance as the rookie cop lusted after by serial killer Ron Silver. Silver is superb as the charmer, a commodities trader by day and David Berkowitz-style killer by night, who fastens on to Curtis after she is suspended for killing an armed robber on her first night out. It is a relief that, within the limits of this genre, Ms Curtis is such a flesh-and-blood character, making the film's suspense that much more unbearable. It's a wonder the film was not more successful. [CB]

Cast includes: Jamie Lee Curtis (Megan Turner), Ron Silver (Eugene Hunt), Clancy Brown (Nick Mann), Elizabeth Pena (Tracy), Louise Fletcher (Mrs Turner), Philip Bosco (Mr Turner), Tom Sizemore (armed robber). Dir: Kathryn Bigelow. Pro: Edward R. Pressman and Oliver Stone. Ex Pro: Lawrence Kasanoff. Co-Pro: Michael Rausch. Screenplay: Bigelow and Eric Red. Ph: Amir Mokri. Ed: Lee Percy. Pro Des: Toby Corbett. M: Brad Feidel. Costumes: Richard Schissler. Sound: Tom Frandau. (Lightning Pictures/ Vestron.) Rel: 23 November 1990. 106 mins. Cert 18.

The Bonfire of the Vanities. Recovering from the harrowing subject matter of his last film, *Casualties of War*, direc-

tor Brian De Palma was determined to make a comedy – so he has turned the Great American Novel of the Eighties into a rip-roaring farce. The most eagerly awaited US film event of the 1990 Christmas season, *Bonfire* was a gift to be cherished by the top talent of Hollywood. Talks fell through with such major directors as Adrian Lyne and Norman Jewison, and when De Palma came on board he chose Tom Hanks over William Hurt for the central role of Sherman McCoy. Michelle Pfeiffer turned down the female lead, and Bruce Willis was signed to play the muck-raking English hack Peter Fallow. Hollywood couldn't believe its ears, and the US critics rightly savaged this over-directed, over-acted $45 million comedy which turns racism and justice into a circus act. Hanks and Willis are wildly miscast – particularly Hanks as the ruthless financial raider with a dangerous mistress. (Can you see Hanks as a man who brags, 'I am a Master of the Universe. I deserve more!'?) The script, by Michael Cristofer (*Falling in Love, The Witches of Eastwick*), is actually the best thing about this expensive fiasco. [JC-W]

Also with: Melanie Griffith (Maria Ruskin), Morgan Freeman (Judge White), F. Murray Abraham (uncredited, as Abe Weiss), Kim Cattrall (Judy McCoy), Saul Rubinek (Jed Kramer), John Hancock (Revd Bacon), Donald Moffat (Mr McCoy), Mary Alice (Annie Lamb), Kevin Dunn, Clifton James, Louis Giambalvo, Barton Heyman, Norman Parker, Alan King, Beth Broderick, Richard Libertini, Andre Gregory, Robert Stephens, Rita Wilson, Helen Stenborg, Vito D'Ambrosio, Paul Bates. Dir and Pro: Brian De Palma. Ex Pro: Peter Guber and Jon Peters. Co-Pro: Fred Caruso. Screenplay: Michael Cristofer; based on the novel by Tom Wolfe. Ph: Vilmos Zsigmond. Ed: David Ray and Bill Pankow. Pro Des: Richard Sylbert. M: Dave Grusin. Costumes: Ann Roth. Sound: Maurice Schell. (Warner.) Rel: 12 April 1991. 126 mins. Cert 15.

The Boost. Drugs are bad for you, and in case you didn't know it, *The Boost* shoves the message up your nose in a rollercoaster ride of grief and ecstasy. Thank God, then, for James Woods and Sean Young as the couple on the road to decline, who are at least never less than entertaining. Woods plays a real-estate hustler who, with his wife in tow, moves to Southern California to make a killing through 'tax shelter loop'

Tom Hanks as a geeky Gordon Gekko with his libidinous mistress Melanie Griffith, in Brian De Palma's disastrous film version of Tom Wolfe's The Bonfire of the Vanities *(from Warner).*

deals. Unemployed one moment, and buying an aeroplane the next, Woods moves into the heady social world of wild parties and cocaine – where he is pressurised to try a little coke. At first he demurs, but after a heavy financial setback all he needs is just a 'boost' to put him back on his feet. Darryl (*Nuts*) Ponicsan's script shines with good dialogue, but the pacing of highs and lows is a little on the predictable side. [JC-W]

Cast includes: James Woods (Lenny Brown), Sean Young (Linda), John Kapelos (Joel), Steven Hill (Max), Kelle Kerr (Rochelle), John Rothman (Ned), Amanda Blake, Grace Zabriskie, Marc Poppel, Fred McCarren, David Preston, June Chandler, Edith Fields, Scott McGinnis, Virginia Morris. Dir: Harold Becker. Pro: Daniel H. Blatt. Ex Pro: John Daly and Derek Gibson.

James Woods and Sean Young fight to keep their marriage alive under the pressure of the white stuff – in Harold Becker's The Boost *(from Hemdale).*

Screenplay: Darryl Ponicsan; based on the book *Ludes* by Benjamin Stein. Ph: Howard Atherton. Ed: Maury Winetrobe. Pro Des: Waldemar Kalinowski. M: Stanley Myers. Costumes: Susan Becker and Lisa Lovas. Sound: Walter Hoylman (Hemdale.) Rel: 27 July 1990. 95 mins. Cert 18.

The Brave Little Toaster. If you assume this 1987 animated feature is a Disney, you won't be far wrong. It was originally scheduled for Disney, but producer Tom Withite took it with him when he left, handing it over to a group of veterans who'd formerly worked at the Disney Studios. Draughtsmanship and fluidity of movement are top class, but unfortunately the script isn't: nevertheless, this story of five inanimate objects – a toaster, hoover, radio, etc. – which come to life is very good fun, and is certainly reminiscent of Disney at his best. [FDM]

With the voices of: Jon Lovitz (Radio), Tim Stack (Lampy), Timothy E. Day (Blanket), Thurl Ravencroft (Kirby), Deanna Oliver (Toaster), Phil Hartman, Jonathon Benair, Joe Ranft. Dir: Jerry Rees. Pro: Donald Kushner and Thomas L. Wilhite. Screenplay: Jerry Rees and Joe Ranft; based on the novel by Thomas M. Disch. Art: Brian McEntee. M: Davis Newman; with songs by Van Dyke Parks. (Hypericon-Kushner-

Michael Caine and Roger Moore getting carried away in Michael Winner's disappointing Bullseye! *(Castle Premier).*

Locke Pro.–Castle Premier.) Rel: floating; first shown London (Warner) 3 August 1990. 87 mins. Cert U.

Breaking In. Low-key, insipid comedy about a couple of safecrackers working in Portland, Oregon. Ernie Mullins (a grey-haired Burt Reynolds), father-figure to callow rookie Mike (Casey Siemaszko), is registered as a modern sculptor to explain his strange collection of tools (blow torch, crowbar etc.), and lives in the direct flight path of Portland airport (to muffle the sounds of gelignite explosions). Besides providing some useful tips to would-be burglars, *Breaking In* is a very slim affair – only sporadically offering examples of director Bill Forsyth's knack for squeezing humour out of the mundane. But who can forget the scene with the Dobermans? [JC-W]

Also with: Sheila Kelley (Carrie), Lorraine Toussaint (Delphine), the late Albert Salmi (Johnny Scat), Harrey Carey (Shoes), Maury Chaykin (Tucci), Steve Tobolowsky (district attorney), Richard Key Jones, Tom Laswell, Walter Shane, Eddie Driscoll, Alan Fudge, Charles Bernard. Dir: Bill Forsyth. Pro: Harry Gittes. Ex Pro: Andrew Meyer and Sarah Ryan Black. Screenplay: John Sayles. Ph: Michael Coulter. Ed: Michael Ellis. Pro Des: Adrienne Atkinson and John Willett. M: Michael Gibbs. Costumes: Louise Frogley. (Act III/Goldwyn–Castle Premiere.) Rel: 31 August 1990. 94 mins. Cert 15.

Buddy's Song. Likeable if somewhat broad musical drama about a working-class family of three struggling to stay friends. Roger Daltrey is Terry, the vulgar wide boy, whose loyalty to Des, his 'best mate', invariably lands him in trouble. Sharon Duce is Carol, Terry's wife, who's trying to better herself with computers; and newcomer Chesney Hawkes is their teenage son, Buddy (after Buddy Holly). Buddy, the film's centre of gravity, is sympathetically played by Hawkes (whose father played with The Tremeloes), who, turning his back on his father's passion for Fifties music, starts up his own 'modern' band, The Hurt. Peppered with some nice, unusual moments, the film is at its best when it's not trying to be too serious. [JC-W]

Also with: Michael Elphick (Des), Paul McKenzie (Julius), Colin Peel (Glenn), James Aubrey (Adrian), Lee Ross, Nick Moran, Barbara New, Liza Walker, Emma Amos, Julia Sawalha, Omar Salimi, Ed Devereaux, Douglas Hodge. Dir: Claude Whatham. Pro: Roy Baird, Bill Curbishley and Roger Daltrey. Screenplay: Nigel Hinton. Ph: John Hooper, with Colin Corby. Ed: John Grover. Pro Des: Grant Hicks. M: Various; numbers sung by Chesney Hawkes. Costumes: Sheelagh Killeen. Sound: Alistair Crocker. (Castle Premier.) Rel: 1 March 1991. 106 mins. Cert 12.

Bullseye! Michael Caine and Roger Moore star in this wildly complicated plot about the exploitation of a cheap way to mass-produce energy. The inventors, Dr Daniel Hicklar (Caine) and Sir John Bavistock (Moore), intend to auction their secret to the highest bidder, but are impeded by the machinations of two lookalike con men, Sidney Lipton (Caine) and Gerald Bradley-Smith (Moore). Once again director Michael Winner has managed to reduce his leading actors to the level of desperate amateurs, with Caine and Moore pulling funny faces and swapping pathetic one-liners. And they said the *Carry On* films were dead. However, the British locations are striking. [JC-W]

Also with: Sally Kirkland (Willie), Deborah Barrymore (Flo Fleming), Lee Patterson, Mark Burns, Derren Nesbitt, Deborah Leng, Christopher Adamson, Steffanie Pitt, John Woodnutt, Billy J. Mitchell, Mildred Shay, Francis Drake, Nicholas Courtney, Gordon Honeycombe, Pamela Armstrong, Patsy Kensit, Alexandra Pigg, Jenny Sea-

grove, John Cleese. Dir, Pro and Ed: Michael Winner. Ex Pro: Menahem Golan and Ami Artzi. Screenplay: Leslie Bricusse, Laurence Marks and Maurice Gran; from a story by Bricusse, Winner and Nick Mead. Ph: Alan Jones. Pro Des: John Blezard. M: John Du Prez. Costumes: John Bloomfield. Sound: Tony Lenny and Lionel Selwyn. (21st Century–Castle Premier.) Rel: 2 November 1990. 102 mins. Cert 15.

Bye Bye Blues. India and Canada, 1939–45. In spite of war clouds gathering over Europe, Daisy and Teddy Cooper lead a life of young married bliss in colonial India. There, Teddy (Michael Ontkean) is stationed as a doctor working for the British army. When he is called up to work in Singapore, Daisy (Rebecca Jenkins) is not only pregnant, but has a young son to look after. The only option is to return to her native Canada, where Daisy can bring up her children in an atmosphere of family harmony. But this proves far from possible. In order to buy her son running shoes she sings at a local dance – against her grandfather's wishes. This instils both a rebellious streak in Daisy and a yearning for professional acceptance. *Bye Bye Blues*, winner of three Canadian Genies, is a love letter dedicated to the writer-director's mother, who was also the inspiration. A sincere, beautifully told story – but not without its plodding intervals. [JC-W]

Also with: Luke Reilly (Max Gramley), Stuart Margolin (Slim Godfrey), Wayne Robson (Pete), Robyn Stevan (Frances Cooper), Kate Reid (Mary Wright), Leon Pownall, Sheila Moore, Leslie Yeo, Francis Damberger, Susan Wooldridge. Dir and Screenplay: Anne Wheeler. Pro: Wheeler and Arvi Liimatainen. Ex Pro: Tony Allard. Ph: Vic Sarin. Ed: Christopher Tate. Pro Des: John Blackie. M: George Blondheim. Costumes: Maureen Hiscox. Sound: Garrell Clark. (Allarcom/True Blue Films–Artificial Eye.) Rel: 21 September 1990. 116 mins. Cert PG.

Cadillac Man. The thought of Robin Williams as a fast-talking car salesman sounds too good to be true – which is, unfortunately, the case. This dramatic/melodramatic comedy, a Feydeau farce crossed with a siege thriller, is pitched too shrilly either to be involving or funny. Williams is Joey O'Brien, a slick Cadillac-pusher who can land more women than he can shift vehicles. When the jealous husband of a sec-

retary at Turgeon Auto's showroom breaks in with an automatic rifle and takes hostages, O'Brien reveals his true colours as a sweet, selfless hero. Nothing adds up. Director Roger Donaldson (*Marie, No Way Out*) should stick to dramatic cinema. [JC-W]

Also with: Tim Robbins (Larry), Pamela Reed (Tina), Fran Drescher (Joy Munchack), Zack Norman (Harry Munchack), Annabella Sciorra (Donna), Lori Petty (Lila), Paul Guilfoyle (Little Jack Turgeon), Eddie Jones (Benny), Bill Nelson, Mimi Cecchini, Tristine Skyler, Judith Hoag,

Rebecca Jenkins in the role that won her the Canadian Genie for best actress – in Anne Wheeler's Bye Bye Blues *(Artificial Eye).*

Lauren Tom, Anthony Powers, Paul Herman, Paul J. Q. Lee, Jim Bulleit, Richard Panebianco, Boris Leskin, Elzbieta Czyzewska, Bill Nunn, Elaine Stritch. Dir: Roger Donaldson. Pro: Donaldson and Charles Roven. Screenplay: Ken Friedman. Ph: David Gribble. Ed: Richard Francis-Bruce. Pro Des: Gene Rudolf. M: J. Peter Robinson; 'Tattler' performed by Ry Cooder. Costumes: Deborah La Gorce

Just desert: Sandrine Bonnaire faces indescribable boredom in Artificial Eye's La Captive du Desert.

Eccentric gentlemen of the Mafia: Vincent Price and Dennis Hopper plot the death of Jodie Foster in the weird and wonderful Catchfire *(Vestron).*

terrorist crew, rescues the kidnapped President of the United States, and prevents the villains from setting off their atom bomb. Get the picture? [FDM]

Cast: Matt Salinger (Captain), Ronny Cox (Tom Kimbell), Ned Beatty (Sam Kolowetz), Darren McGavin (Gen. Fleming), Michael Nouri, Melinda Dillon, Francesca Neri, Bill Mumy, Kim Gillingham, Scott Paulin (the Red Skull), Carlo Cassola (Dr Vaselli), Massimilio Massimi, Wayde Preston. Dir: Albert Pyun. Pro: Menahem Golan. Line Pro: Tom Karnowski. Assoc Pro: Stephen Tolkin. Ex Pro: Stan Lee and Joseph Calamari. Screenplay: Stephen Tolkin. Ph: Philip Alan Waters. Ed: David Reale. Ed: Jon Poll. Pro Des: Douglas Leonard. Art: Nedad Pecur, Marc Dabe and A. Rosalind Crew. M: Barry Goldberg. (21st Century in assoc with Marvel Entertainment Group and Jadran Films–Castle Pictures.) Rel: floating; regional release only from 14 December 1990. 97 mins. Cert PG.

La Captive du Desert – Captive of the Desert. Chad, 1975. True story about a young French teacher who is abducted by rebel soldiers. Watered and fed by the nomadic Toubou people, Françoise Claustre (Sandrine Bonnaire) is a prisoner of the desert and at the mercy of heat, mosquitoes, thirst and her own exhaustion. Filmmaker Raymond Derpardon provides no plot or explanations, just a relentlessly austere look at the desert, captured by a remorselessly motionless camera. You'd have more fun watching water evaporate. [JC-W]

Also with: Dobi Kore, Dobi Wachinke, Atchi Wahi-Li, Fadi Taha. Dir, Screenplay (?) and Ph: Raymond Depardon. Pro: Pascale Dauman and Jean-Luc Ormières. Ex Pro: Baudoin Capet. Ed: Roger Ikhlef, Camille Cotte and Pascale Charolais. M: Jean-Jacques Lemetre. Costumes: Françoise Clavel. Sound: Claudine Nougaret and Sophie Chiabaut. (EFDO–Artificial Eye.) Rel: 21 June 1991. 100 mins. Cert PG.

Kramer. Sound: Michael R. Tromer. (Orion–Rank.) Rel: 5 October 1990. 98 mins. Cert 15.

✓**Captain America**. Comic-strip hero CA gets involved in highly incredible heroics in an even more incredible, involved (and silly) adventure story. The Captain confronts the Red Skull's

Catchfire. Dennis Hopper's romantic *film noir* thriller is so full of ingenious surprises and plot twists that it would be unfair to reveal too much. But to whet the appetite: neon artist Anne Benton (Jodie Foster) is driving home at night when her car veers off the road with a blow-out. Running down an escarpment to escape the jeers of a carload of revellers, she stumbles on to a Mob killing. She escapes with her life, but not before being identified. The

Burrowing in the emotional closet: Julie Bataille, Nathalie Baye and Candice Lefranc in Diane Kurys's superb C'Est la Vie *(from Electric Pictures).*

Mob want her dead, the police want her evidence. She wants out. Enter enigmatic hit man Milo (Dennis Hopper), a character of few words who hunts by instinct. But Anne Benton is more than just a pretty face. Realising that police custody is an invitation to her own cremation, she opts to vanish from the world she knows. Meanwhile, Milo studies her past life and enters her personality, anticipating her thoughts before she's thought them. But you can get to know a person *too* well . . . A fast-paced, witty, handsome film that succeeds on a multitude of levels. Hopper is great as the faceless killer who gradually emerges as a man of taste and vulnerability, and Jodie Foster is in top form as his sexy, feisty prey. Music, photography, locations are all outstanding, too. (Previously known as *Backtrack*.) [JC-W]

Also with: Dean Stockwell (John Luponi), Joe Pesci (Leo Carelli), Vincent Price (Mr Avoca), John Turturro (Pinella), Fred Ward (Pauling), G. Anthony Sirico (Greek), Helena Kalianiotes (Grace Carelli), Charlie Sheen (Bob), Julie Adams, Sy Richardson, Frank Gio, Bob Dylan, Grand L. Bush, Anthony Pena. Dir: Dennis Hopper (uncredited). Pro: Dick Clark and Dan Paulson. Ex Pro: Steven Reuther and Mitchell Cannold. Screenplay: Rachel Kronstadt-Mann, Ann Louise Bardach and (uncredited) Stephen Cotler, Lanny Cotler, Alex Cox, Tod Davies and Dennis Hopper. Ph: Ed Lachman. Ed: David Rawlins. Pro Des: Ron Foreman. M: Curt Sobel. Costumes: Nancy Cone. (Vestron.) Rel: 25 January 1991. 119 mins. Cert 15.

C'Est la Vie. 1958, France. What looks like it's going to be an idyllic summer holiday on the beach is transformed into a period of mixed emotions for Frédérique, 13, and her little sister, Sophie, 6. At the very last moment their mother, Lena (Nathalie Baye), stays behind in Lyon, while the children journey on to the coastal resort of La Baule-les pins with their bossy governess. There they miss Lena but get on with the joys of childhood mischief, swimming and witnessing the high jinks of their uncle, Léon (Jean-Pierre Bacri). As Frédérique begins to fall in love with her cousin, Daniel, she gradually becomes aware of the friction in her own parents' marriage. *C'Est la Vie* is just that – a big slice of life, complete with all its traumas, joys and discoveries. It is also a very rich, multi-layered film, superbly acted by an ensemble cast and beautifully lit by Giuseppe Lanci. This is the fourth chapter in Diane Kurys's autobiographical omnibus (following on from *Peppermint Soda, Cocktail Molotov* and *Coup de Foudre*): here the director is interpreted by Julie Bataille as Frédérique. [JC-W]

Also with: Richard Berry (Michel), Zabou (Bella), Vincent Lindon (Jean-Claude), Valeria Bruni-Tedeschi (Odette), Didier Benureau (Ruffier), Candice Lefranc (Sophie), Alexis Derlon (Daniel), Emmanuelle Boidron (Suzanne), Maxime Boidron (Rene), Benjamin Sacks (Titi). Dir: Diane Kurys. Pro: Alexandre Arcady. Ex Pro: Robert Benmussa. Screenplay: Kurys and Alain Le Henry. Ph: Giuseppe Lanci. Ed: Raymonde Guyot. M: Philippe Sarde. (Alexandre Films/SGGC/Films A2/CNC–Electric.) Rel: 1 March 1991. 100 mins. Cert 12.

Family law: Mary Elizabeth Mastrantonio and Gene Hackman battle public and private grievances in Michael Apted's superior Class Action, *from Fox.*

Child's Play 2. Spectacularly stupid sequel to the hit horror film about Chucky, the walking, talking, living doll possessed by the spirit of a mass murderer. Although decapitated and burnt beyond recognition at the end of the first film, Chucky is reconstructed with a steel head by the Play Pals toy conglomerate (to dispel nasty rumours that Chucky was ever dangerous). Too foolish . . . No sooner has Chucky enjoyed his finishing touches than he electrocutes his maker and promptly goes in search of young Andy Barclay (Alex Vincent) whose soul he intends to possess. Oddly, nobody but Andy believes Chucky is for real until seconds before they die, robbing us of the satisfaction of Andy being proved right. Besides opting for the more obvious clichés, *Child's Play 2* falls down by taking itself at face value, ignoring its comic potential and distorting its own warped logic. Even something this daft

should fight for an iota of plausibility. Sadly, Chucky doesn't have an original joint in his body (compare with *Magic, Halloween III* and *The Terminator*). [JC-W]

Also with: Jenny Agutter (Joanne Simpson), Gerrit Graham (Phil Simpson), Christine Elise (Kyle), Brad Dourif (voice of Chucky), Grace Zabriskie (Grace Poole), Peter Haskell, Beth Grant, Greg Germann, Stuart Mabray. Dir: John Lafia. Pro: David Kirschner. Co-Pro: Laura Moskowitz. Ex Pro: Robert Latham Brown. Screenplay: Don Mancini; based on his characters. Ph: Stefan Czapsky. Ed: Edward Warschilka. Pro Des: Ivo Cristante. M: Graeme Revell. Costumes: Pamela Skaist. Sound: John M. Stacy. Chucky designed and engineered by: Kevin Yagher. (Universal–UIP.) Rel: 11 January 1991. 85 mins. Cert 15.

Circus Boys – Nijusseiki Shonen Dokuhon. Made in 1989, Kaizo Hayashi's second film (his first was *To Sleep So As to Dream*) confirms his talent for unique and memorable movies. A magical story (filmed in black-and-white) which mixes gangsters with the circus, flowing effortlessly to the excit-

ing, beautifully photographed and directed chase climax. [FDM]

Cast: Hiroshi Mikami (Jinta), Moe Kamura (Omacha), Michiru Akiyoshi (Maria), Yuki Assyama (Sayoko), Yoshio Harada (Yoshimoto), Sanshi Katsura (Sakejima). Dir and Screenplay: Kaizo Hayashi. Ex Pro: Hisamitsu Hida and Yoichi Sakurai. Co-Pro: Hayashi and Ryuzo Shirawaka. Ph: Yuichi Nagata. Ed: Osamu Tanaka. Pro Des: Takeo Kimura and Hidemitsu Yamaziki. M: Hidchiko Urayama and Yoko Kumagai. Sound: Ichiro Kawashima. (CBS/Sony Group Pro–ICA.) Rel: floating; first shown London (ICA) 14 June 1991. 106 mins. No cert.

Class Action. San Francisco – now. Gene Hackman is Jedediah Tucker Ward, a crusading civil liberties lawyer, an obstinate man who will fight for the underdog so long as it'll get him on the cover of *Time* magazine. Mary Elizabeth Mastrantonio is Margaret Ward, his daughter and a brilliant up-and-coming lawyer with a distaste for her father's ego. The inevitable happens when father and daughter end up on opposite sides in a case that looks impossible for Hackman to win – particularly when some vital evidence is buried. Intelligent courtroom thriller, supported by excellent performances and first-rate craftsmanship. [JC-W]

Also with: Colin Friels (Michael Grazier), Joanna Merlin (Estelle Ward), Larry Fishburne (Nick Holbrook), Donald Moffat (Quinn), Jan Rubes (Pavel), Matt Clark, Fred Dalton Thompson, Jonathan Silverman, Joan McMurtrey, Tim Hopper, Judge John Dearman, Carolyn Shelby. Dir: Michael Apted. Pro: Ted Field, Scott Kroopf and Robert W. Cort. Co-Pro: Carolyn Shelby and Christopher Ames. Screenplay: Shelby, Ames and Samantha Shad. Ph: Conrad L. Hall. Ed: Ian Crafford. Pro Des: Todd Hallowell. M: James Horner. Costumes: Rita Ryack; Giorgio Armani. Sound: Michael Evje. (Interscope Communications–Fox.) Rel: 21 June 1991. 109 mins. Cert 15.

Cold Dog Soup. A black comedy about a dead dog which starts out funny enough, but soon runs out of steam. Randy Quaid, who hangs around black comedies like the plague (cf. *Parents, Out Cold*, etc.) plays a taxi driver of the apocalypse who convinces yuppie Frank Whaley that he can sell his girlfriend's deceased pooch. Label this one a moribund *After Hours* – or, more accurately, a stiff dog. [JC-W]

Cast includes: Randy Quaid (Jack Cloud), Frank Whaley (Michael Latchmer), Christine Harnos (Sarah Hughes), Sheree North (Mrs Hughes), Nancy Kwan (Madame Chang), Pierre Epstein, Jeff Chayette, Nick LaTour, Clifford Shegog, Brent Hinkley, Michael DeLorenzo. Dir: Alan Metter. Pro: Richard G. Abramson, William E. McEuen and Thomas Pope. Ex Pro: George Harrison and Denis O'Brien. Screenplay: Pope; based on the book by Stephen Dobyns. Ph: Frederick Elmes. Ed: Kaja Fehr. Pro Des and Assoc Pro: David L. Snyder. M: Michael Kamen. Sound: Robert Anderson. (Hand-Made Films/Aspen Film Society–Palace.) Rel: 15 February 1991. 85 mins. Cert 15.

Cold Justice. Oddball drama with Dennis Waterman as an English priest in Chicago solving everybody's problems – at least, for a while. But is Father Jim really a priest? When he encourages has-been boxer Roger Daltrey to return to the ring – to disastrous results – some suspect the Limey stranger may be nothing more than a conman. Apart from the must-see attraction of Dennis Waterman in a dog collar in Chicago, this detached, unsympathetic drama has little else to offer. Unreleased in central London and formerly known as *Father Jim*. [CB]

Also with: Roger Daltrey (Keith Gibson), Ron Dean, Ralph Foody, Robert Carricart, Bert Rosario, Penelope Milford, Matthew Wuertz, Ernest Perry Jr, Bridget O'Connell, Larry Brandenburg, Bonnie Sue Arp, John Mohrlein. Dir & Screenplay: Terry Green. Pro: Ross Cameron and Dennis Waterman. Ex Pro: Paul and Carey Shakespeare. Line Pro: Robert Hudecek. Ph: Dusty Miller. Ed: Tom Morrish. Pro Des: Bill Arnold. Sound: Glenn Williams. Stunt Co-Ord: Rick Lefevour. (River First.) Rel: 8 March 1991. Cert 15.

Cold Light of Day. The chilling yet fascinating story of real-life homosexual killer Jordan March. This mild-looking fellow cared for one of his fellow bedsitters with kindness and understanding, while callously killing and then dissecting *fifteen* young men whose parts he hid around the place, even boiling the head of one of his victims on the stove. This British grisly is handled by a woman, Fhiona Louise, in her debut as writer-director. Not recommended for viewing before, during or after meals. [FDM]

Cast includes: Bob Flag (Jordan March), Geoffrey Greenhill (Inspector Simmons), Martin Byrne-Quinn (Joe), Andrew Edmans, Bill Merrow, Clare King, Mark

Come See the Paradise – *or visit hell on earth? The Kawamura family await their fate in the Californian desert.* Left to right: *Akemi Nishino, Ronald Yamamoto, Naomi Nakano, Stan Egi, Shizuko Hoshi, Tamlyn Tomita, Elizabeth Gilliam and Brady Tsurutani; and* (inset) *Dennis Quaid and Tamlyn Tomita embrace the gap between East and West in this Fox release.*

Hawkins, Jackie Cox. Dir and Screenplay: Fhiona Louise. Pro: Richard Driscoll. Ph: Nigel Axworthy. Ed: Leroy Stamps. Pro Des: Ski Newton. Sound and Music: Paul Stuart Davies. (Creative Artists–ICA.) Rel: floating; first shown London (ICA) 3 August 1990. 81 mins. No cert.

Come See the Paradise. Fascinating subject, this: the position of the American-Japanese following the bombing of Pearl Harbor, which Alan Parker has swept up into a romantic saga spanning several years. Dennis Quaid stars as Jack McGurn, a sweatshop lawyer 'full of rage', who flees to California to escape a bad reputation in New York. Taking a job as a projectionist of Japanese films, McGurn falls in love with Lily Kawamura, the boss's daugh-

29

Natasha Richardson and Rupert Everett find that their second honeymoon in Venice is far from the ideal that they had hoped – in Paul Schrader's mannered The Comfort of Strangers *(Rank).*

ter. Needless to say Jack encounters a wall of Japanese (and Californian) prejudice, and so the couple elope to Seattle where they can be legally married. World War II and Jack's involvement in trade union activities intrude on the couple's happiness and the film suddenly lurches into an epic documentary about the internment of the Japanese-American people in desert camps. As ever with Parker, the time and place of the film are superbly evoked and the mood is the thing. [JC-W]

Also with: Tamlyn Tomita (Lily Kawamura), Sab Shimono (Mr Kawamura), Shizuko Hoshi (Mrs Kawamura), Stan Egi (Charlie Kawamura), Ronald Yamamoto (Harry Kawamura), Akemi Nishino, Naomi Nakano, Brady Tsurutani, Pruitt Taylor Vince, John Finnegan, Robert Colesberry. Dir and Screenplay: Alan Parker. Pro: Robert F. Colesberry. Ph: Michael Seresin. Ed: Gerry Hambling. Pro Des: Geoffrey Kirkland. M: Randy Edelman. Costumes:

Molly Maginnis. Sound: Danny Michael. (Fox.) Rel: 30 November 1990. 131 mins. Cert 15.

The Comfort of Strangers. Eccentric romantic thriller adapted by Harold Pinter from the Ian McEwan novel. A young English couple are on holiday in Venice, sharing a hotel room, sleeping in separate beds. They pass their time in a nondescript way, on the edge of discord, far from ecstatic. She has two children back in Hastings, he has none. They hold hands and are followed by an enigmatic stranger in a white suit. And so this puzzling, stilted drama unfolds, languishing in its own longueurs. Part bizarre black comedy, part erotic mystery, *The Comfort of Strangers* lacks the quality of acting that could have made all this at least vaguely interesting. [JC-W]

Cast includes: Christopher Walken (Robert), Rupert Everett (Colin), Natasha Richardson (Mary), Helen Mirren (Caroline), Manfredi Aliquo, David Ford, Daniel Franco, Mario Cotone. Dir: Paul Schrader. Pro: Angelo Rizzoli. Ex Pro: Mario Cotone. Screenplay: Harold Pinter; based on the novel by Ian McEwan. Ph: Dante Spinotti.

Ed: Bill Pankow. Pro Des: Gianni Quaranta. M: Angelo Badalamenti. Costumes: Mariolina Bono. Sound: Drew Kunin. (Sovereign Pictures/Reteitalia–Rank.) Rel: 30 November 1990. 105 mins. Cert 18.

Coming Out. East German (apparently the last film to be made there before the Wall came tumbling down) study of a young man torn between his girlfriend and his growing desire for a boyfriend of his own. A tricky triangle. Too long, too slow and too agonised. [FDM]

Cast: Mathias Freihof (Philip), Dagmar Manzel (Tanja), Dirk Kummer (Mathias), Michael Grisdeck, Werner Dissel, Gudrun Ritt, Walfriede Schmitt, Axel Wandtke. Dir: Heiner Carow. Pro: Horst Hartwig. Screenplay: Wolfram Witt. Ph: Martin Schlesinger. Ed: Evelyn Cariw. Pro Des: George Wratsch. M: Stefan Carow. (DEFA–Studio/Group Babelsberg–Metro.) Rel: floating; first shown London (Metro) 15 March 1991. 109 mins. Cert 18.

Communion. Whitley Strieber, the author of *Wolfen* and *The Hunger*, claimed in his autobiographical bestseller *Communion* that he was visited by non-human intelligent life forms. His book, an articulate examination of our fear of the unknown, wrestled with the improbability of an alien presence on earth. All Strieber knew, for sure, is that we are not all that there is. The film, which the author scripted, veers away from the sensational aspects of the genre, but is saddled by an unrealistic, manic performance from Christopher Walken as Strieber (*is* he mad?) and by some rubbery monsters. Stick to the book. [JC-W]

Also with: Lindsay Crouse (Anne Strieber), Joel Carlson (Andrew), Frances Sternhagen (Dr Janet Duffy), Andreas Katsulas (Alex), Terri Hanauer (Sara), Basil Hoffman (Dr Friedman), John Dennis Johnston, Dee Dee Rescher, Irene Forrest, Vince McKewin, Sally Kemp, Maggie Egan, Paul Clemons. Dir and Co-Pro: Philippe Mora. Co-Pro: Dan Allingham. Ex Pro: Paul Redshaw and Gary Barber. Co-Pro and Screenplay: Whitley Strieber. Assoc Pro: Richard Strieber. Ph: Louis Irving. Ed: Lee Smith. Pro Des: Linda Pearl. M: Allan Zavod; main theme by Eric Clapton. Costumes: Malissa Daniel. (Pheasantry Films/Allied Vision/The Picture Property Company–Vestron.) Rel: 12 October 1990. 109 mins. Cert 15.

The Company of Strangers. A very promising debut by director (and co-scripter) Cynthia Scott. This delightful and unusual Canadian film is about seven elderly ladies (amateur actresses all) forced into close proximity when their coach breaks down and they are marooned with their driver in a *Golden Pond*side mansion. Slow, wordy and better suited to the small than the large screen, it will delight the old but probably bore young moviegoers to death. A collector's piece. [FDM]

Cast includes: Alice Diabo, Constance Garneau, Winifred Holden, Cissy Meddings, Mary Meigs, Catherine Roche, Michelle Sweeney, Beth Webber. Dir: Cynthia Scott. Pro: David Wilson. Ex Pro: Colin Neale, Rina Fraticelli and Peter Katadotis. Screenplay: Scott, Gloria Demers, David Wilson and Sally Bochner. Ph: David de Volpi. Ed: David Wilson. M: Marie Bernard. Sound: Jacques Drouin. (National Film Board of Canada–Electric/Contemporary.) Rel: floating; first shown London (Barbican) 3 May 1991. 100 mins. Cert PG.

Le Cop 2 – Les Nouveaux Ripoux. A welcome return to the two loveable

corrupt cops of the 18th *arrondisement* in Paris. Young François (Thierry Lhermitte) still intends to go straight, and is even plotting to become lieutenant, but veteran René (Philippe Noiret) will have none of it. What good is an honest cop, he argues, when the whole

Christopher Walken faces an intellectual nightmare in Philippe Mora's off-centre film version of Whitley Strieber's Communion *(Vestron).*

Immoral to a fault: Philippe Noiret and Thierry Lhermitte abuse the law in Claude Zidi's charming Le Cop 2 *(Gala).*

Dudley Moore surrounded by fellow inmates (David Paymer, Dick Cusack, Paul Bates, Danton Stone, Bill Smitrovich, Alan North and Floyd Vivino) in UIP's hopeless but not entirely unfunny comedy Crazy People.

of Paris is corrupt? To prove it, René takes in the first innocent bystander he sees, arrests him and forces the poor man to confess. However, when François triumphantly returns some stolen loot to its rightful owner, René's sins catch up with them both. The partners are suspended, and a new pair of ruthless cops move in on their lucrative territory – much to the horror of the local crime fraternity. Noiret and Lhermitte play their odd couple with relish in this sequel that dares to be more than a remake. A little long-winded at times, but always compulsive entertainment. [JC-W]

Also with: Guy Marchand (Inspector Brisson), Grace De Capitani (Natacha), Michel Aumont (Commissaire Bloret), Jean-Pierre Castaldi (Inspector Portal), Jean-Claude Brialy (banker), Jean Benguigui (Cesarini), Line Renaud (Simone), Bernard Freyd (Inspector-General Guichard). Dir: Claude

Zidi. Screenplay: Zidi, Simon Michael and Didier Kaminka. Ph: Jean-Jacques Tarbes. Ed: Nicole Saunier. M: Francis Lai. Sound: Jean-Louis Ughetto. (Films 7/Orly Films/Sedif/TFI Films Prod–Curzon/Gala.) Rel: 31 May 1991. 108 mins. Cert 12.

Crazy People. Dudley Moore, as yet another Englishman in New York, is Emory Leeson, a stressed-out adman behind schedule and out of luck in love. His slogans are not of the slick 'All because the lady loves . . .' variety, but more like (for an airline) 'Most of our passengers arrive alive.' After being dispatched to an asylum for the mentally unstable, Emory's copy is mistakenly (and miraculously) printed up and placed in magazines and newspapers all over North America. Paramount's *The Freak*, which claims, 'This movie won't just scare you . . . it will fuck you up for life,' is breaking box-office records, and Emory is required back at the office. Too late, Emory has fallen in love with fellow inmate Kathy Burgess (Daryl Hannah). *Crazy People*, originally a vehicle for John Malkovich (who stormed off the set), is a simplistic and overly sentimental comedy. It dis-

plays neither the wit of *How to Get Ahead in Advertising* nor the endearing lunacy of *The Dream Team* and its emotional heart is non-existent. That it is occasionally very funny is due more to Dudley Moore's innate silliness ('What a day, first I'm thrown into a mental institution, now it's raining') than to any inspired sense of human comedy. [JC-W]

Also with: Paul Reiser (Stephen), Mercedes Ruehl (Dr Liz Baylor), J. T. Walsh (Drucker), Ben Hammer (Dr Koch), Bill Smitrovich, Alan North, David Paymer, Danton Stone, Paul Bates, Dick Cusack, Doug Yasuda, Floyd Vivino, David Packer, Joyce L. Bowden, Randell Haynes, Mitch Markowitz, J. J., Larry King. Dir: Tony Bill. Pro: Thomas Barad. Ex Pro: Robert K. Weiss. Screenplay: Mitch Markowitz. Ph: Victor J. Kemper. Ed: Mia Goldman. Pro Des: John J. Lloyd. M: Cliff Eidelman, J. S. Bach. Costumes: Mary E. Vogt. Sound: David Ronne. (Paramount–UIP.) Rel: 14 September 1990. 92 mins. Cert 15.

Crimes and Misdemeanors. With this, his nineteenth film as writer and director, Woody Allen returns to the profound light comedy. A titillating menu of characters come and go, tragedy rears its ugly head, embarrassed comedy bursts forth here and there (Woody: 'The last time I was inside a woman was when I visited the Statue of Liberty'). Martin Landau stars as an eye doctor with a mistress (Anjelica Huston) he can't get rid of; Woody is a small-scale 'serious' documentary filmmaker who cannot find financing; Alan Alda is his brother-in-law, a New York success story, who gives Allen the chance of a lifetime; and so on. All this is impeccably put together and layered like rich gateau, but in the end is somehow neither funny enough nor that significant. [JC-W]

Cast includes: Caroline Aaron (Barbara), Alan Alda (Lester), Woody Allen (Cliff Stern), Claire Bloom (Miriam Rosenthal), Mia Farrow (Halley Reed), Joanna Gleason (Wendy Stern), Anjelica Huston (Dolores Paley), Martin Landau (Judah Rosenthal), Jenny Nichols (Jenny), Jerry Orbach (Jack Rosenthal), Sam Waterston (Ben), Bill Bernstein, Martin Bergmann, Frances Conroy, Daryl Hannah, Nora Ephron. Dir and Screenplay: Woody Allen. Pro: Robert Greenhut. Ex Pro: Jack Rollins and Charles H. Joffe. Ph: Sven Nykvist. Ed: Susan E. Morse. Pro Des: Santo Loquasto. M: Schubert and various songs. Costumes: Jeffrey Kurland. Sound: James Sabat. (Orion–Rank.) Rel: floating; first shown London (Odeon Haymarket) 27 July 1990. 104 mins. Cert 15.

Criminal Law. Present-day Boston. Ben Chase is a brilliant lawyer and has just got handsome, clean-cut rich boy Martin Thiel off a murder rap. But when the murder and its gory calling card are repeated, Chase suspects that his client *is* the serial killer – but can find neither evidence nor motive. Gary Oldman is surprising casting as the smart, straight Boston defence attorney and acquits himself well enough with an American accent. Director and co-Brit Martin Campbell (BBC's *Edge of Darkness*) piles on the rain-soaked atmosphere but is defeated by a script that refuses to gain momentum. A slow, heavy-handed drama which looks better than it is. [JC-W]

Also with: Kevin Bacon (Martin Thiel), Karen Young (Ellen Faulkner), Joe Don Baker (Detective Mesel), Tess Harper (Detective Stillwell), Elizabeth Sheppard (Dr Thiel), Michael Sinelnicoff (Prof. Clemens), Ron Lea, Karen Woollridge, Ter-

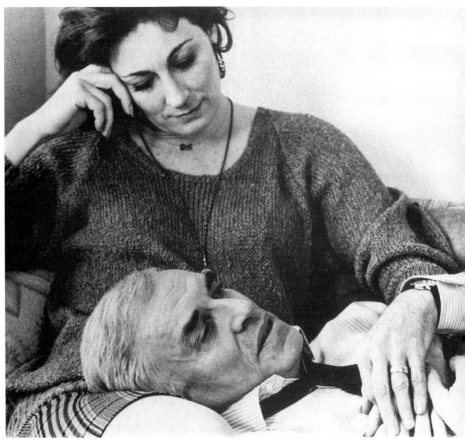

rence Labrosse, Jennie Walker, Rob Boy, Sean McCann, Paul Stewart. Dir: Martin Campbell. Pro: Robert MacLean and Hilary Heath. Ex Pro: John Daly and Derek Gibson. Screenplay: Mark Kasdan (brother of Lawrence Kasdan). Ph: Philip Meheux. Ed: Christopher Wimble. Pro Des: Curtis A. Schnell. M: Jerry Goldsmith. Sound: Peter Shewchuk. (Hemdale.) Rel: 16 November 1990. 117 mins. Cert 18.

Love and death and the whole damn thing: Martin Landau plots against Anjelica Huston in Woody Allen's Crimes and Misdemeanors *(Rank).*

The brilliant lawyer and the psychopath: Gary Oldman and Kevin Bacon switch personas in Martin Campbell's moody Criminal Law *(Hemdale).*

Anne Brochet as Roxane, in love with the soul of Cyrano de Bergerac *(Gerard Depardieu), who is in love with his cousin's beauty – from Artificial Eye.*

✓**Cry-Baby.** Teen comedy like many others from director John Waters; lots of loud music, loud fun and fighting in the story of a delinquent youngster whose parents end up sitting in the electric chair – an event commemorated in a tattoo on his chest! Waters does have a saving sense of humour, though, even if it is somewhat unusual. [FDM]

Cast: Johnny Depp (Cry-Baby), Amy Locane (Allison), Susan Tyrrell (Ramona), Polly Bergen (Mrs Vernon-Williams), Iggy Pop (Belvedere), Ricki Lake (Pepper), Traci Lords (Wanda), Kim McGuire (Hatchet Face), D. E. Burrows (Milton). Dir and Screenplay: John Waters. Pro: Rachel Talalay. Ex Pro: Jim Abrahams and Brian Grazer. Ph: David Insley. Ed: Janice Hampton. Pro Des: Vincent Peranio. Art: Delores Deluxe. Costumes: Van Smith. Sound: Richard Angelella and Dwayne Dell. M: Patrick Williams. (Imagine Entertainment-Universal–UIP.) Rel: floating; first shown London (Empire 2, several Cannons and UCI) 20 July 1990. 93 mins. Cert 12.

✓**Cyrano de Bergerac.** Magnificent, moving film version of the Edmond Rostand classic about a noble French captain cursed with a spectacular nose. A brilliant swordsman (who thinks nothing of tackling a hundred opponents at once) and legendary poet, Cyrano (Gerard Depardieu) is a fine idealist who cannot see beyond his own nose. He secretly worships his beautiful cousin, Roxane, but disguises his passion in brilliant love letters composed for a more suitably handsome suitor. Based on Rostand's 1897 play, itself inspired by the real-life seventeenth-century poet, *Cyrano* is a timeless tale of true love, honour and the shallow gift of physical beauty, superbly mounted on a sumptuous £10 million budget (making this the most expensive French film ever made). Sticking to the play's original verse form, this version has English subtitles supplied by the almighty Anthony Burgess. Depardieu won the best actor award at Cannes for his role. [JC-W]

Also with: Anne Brochet (Roxane), Vincent Perez (Christian de Neuvillette), Jacques Weber (Comte de Guiche), Roland Bertin, Philippe Morier-Genoud, Pierre Maguelon, Josiane Stoleru, Anatole Delalande, Philippe Volter. Dir: Jean-Paul Rappeneau. Pro: René Cleitman and Michel Seydoux. Screenplay and adaptation: Jean-Paul Rappeneau and Jean-Claude Carrière; based on the play by Edmond Rostand. Ph: Pierre Lhomme. Ed: Noelle Boisson. Pro Des: Ezio Frigerio. M: Jean-Claude Petit. Costumes: Franca Squarciapino. Sound: Jean Goudier. Fencing master: William Hobbs. English subtitles: Anthony Burgess. (Hachette Premiere & Cie/Camera One/Films A2/DD Productions/UGC–Artificial Eye.) Rel: 11 January 1991. 135 mins. Cert U.

Daddy's Dyin' . . . Who's Got the Will? In small-town Texas, a divided family uneasily gathers to find out who has been left what by dotty old dad. An amusing and lively comedy. [FDM]

Cast: Beau Bridges (Orville), Beverly D'Angelo (Evalita), Tess Harper (Sara Lee), Judge Reinhold (Harmony), Amy Wright (Lurlene), Patrika Darbo (Marlene), Molly McClure (Mama Wheelis), Bert Remsen (Daddy), Keith Carradine (Clarence). Dir: Jack Fisk. Pro: Sigurjon Sighvatsson, Steve Golin and Monty Montgomery. Ex Pro: Bobbie Edrick, Del Shores, Michael Kuhn and Nigel Sinclair. Screenplay: Shores; based on his stage play. Ph: Paul Elliott. Ed: Edward Warschilka. Pro Des: Michelle Minch. Sound: Darrel Henke. M: David McHugh. (Propaganda Films–Palace.) Rel: floating; first shown London (Cannon, Tottenham Ct Rd and Chelsea) 25 January 1991. 96 mins. Cert 12.

✓**Dances with Wolves.** Beautifully filmed, moving portrait of the Sioux Indians living in South Dakota. Union hero Lt John Dunbar (Kevin Costner) is given *carte blanche* to choose his own post and opts for *the* most remote fortress – so that he can 'see the frontier before it vanishes'. Left alone at a ramshackle settlement he is visited by Indians who initially regard him with understandable curiosity and fear. Gradually, a mutual respect is engendered and eventually Dunbar is accepted into the Sioux way of life and renamed 'Dancing With Wolves'. Dunbar sees his new family as a people 'eager to laugh, devoted to family and dedicated to each other', a noble race that has learned to live *with* the land. So why does the white man hate them so? Why does he steal their land, burn their homes and kill their women and children? Dunbar has no answer, but knows that the inevitable tragedy must

Scenes from Dances with Wolves *(Guild), Kevin Costner's masterful adaptation of Michael Blake's novel. Never has the American Indian (the Sioux) been treated on film with such respect, tenderness and humour. Above: Costner and Mary McDonnell; (right) Graham Greene and Rodney A. Grant sampling the joys of coffee for the first time.*

unfold. Directed and co-produced by Costner himself, this is a lesson that should be attended by all students of American history, if not all students of humanity itself. It is a shame that the Union soldiers are depicted as disgusting caricatures, as the rest of the film is so intelligently balanced. And full marks to Costner for a directorial debut that doesn't show off. All technical credits are top notch, and the buffalo stampede unforgettable. Although *Dances* ran into trouble during production, and was subsequently nicknamed *Kevin's Gate*, it was a huge box-office success which, for a three-hour Western, is little short of a miracle. [JC-W]

Also with: Mary McDonnell (Stands With a Fist), Graham Greene (Kicking Bird), Rodney A. Grant (Wind In His Hair), Floyd Red Crow Westerman (Ten Bears), Tantoo Cardinal, Robert Pastorelli, Charles Rocket, Maury Chaykin, Nathan Lee (Chasing His Horse). Dir and Co-Pro: Kevin Costner. Pro: Jim Wilson. Screenplay: Michael Blake; based on his novel. Ph: Dean Semler. Ed: Neil Travis. Pro Des: Jeffrey Beecroft. M: John Barry. Costumes: Elsa Zamperelli. Sound: Russell Williams and Mary Jo Devenney. (Tig–Guild.) Rel: 8 February 1991. 179 mins. Cert 12.

Dark Angel. A series of unexplained deaths is throwing the Houston police department into chaos. But it's not so much the sheer number of homicides as the murder weapon itself that is baffling

vice cop Jack Caine (Dolph Lundgren). Whatever it is, it can kill several armed men simultaneously and has the dexterity of a surgeon's scalpel. Now, extraordinary as this may sound, Caine suspects foul play from outer space. Add a soured romance, an unwanted police partner and a corrupt police captain, and we're into well-ploughed territory, but the film's sense of throwaway humour and visual style lift this well above the level of many bigger budgeted fantasy cop thrillers. [JC-W]

Also with: Brian Benben (Laurence Smith), Betsy Brantley (Diane Pollone), Mathias Hues (Talec), Jon Bilas (Azeck), Michael J. Pollard (Boner), Mark Lowenthal (Bruce), Sam Anderson, Sherman Howard, Jim Haynie, David Ackroyd. Dir: Craig Baxley. Pro: Jeff Young. Ex Pro: Mark Damon and David Saunders. Screenplay: Jonathan Tydor and Leonard Mass Jnr. Ph: Mark Irwin. Ed: Mark Helfrich. Pro Des: Phillip M. Leonard. M: Jan Hammer. Costumes: Joseph Porro. Sound: Bud Maffett. (Vision P.D.G.–Entertainment.) Rel: 13 July 1990. 92 mins. Cert 18.

Beware the man with the long white hair and eight-foot build: Mathias Hues in Entertainment's enjoyably corny Dark Angel.

And (below) *revenge has a face: Liam Neeson as* Darkman, *running for his lair in Sam Raimi's slick, sick chiller – from UIP.*

√**Darkman**. Horrific, visually stunning variation of the *Phantom of the Opera* story. Liam Neeson plays Dr Peyton Westlake, a brilliant American scientist on the verge of inventing synthetic skin. When he and his laboratory are burned beyond recognition by thugs, he plots a terrible revenge. With the advantage of science and the miraculous acquisition of new equipment, Peyton's place is reconstructed – along with a series of extraordinary facial disguises. A truly sickening thriller seeping with evil, with some of the most inventive visuals and special effects you're likely to be subjected to. From the creator of *The Evil Dead*. [JC-W]

Also with: Frances McDormand (Julie Hastings), Colin Friels (Louis Strack Jr), Larry Drake (Robert G. Durant), Nelson Mashita (Yakitito), Theodore Raimi (Rick), Jesse Lawrence Ferguson, Rafael H. Robledo, Danny Hicks, Dan Bell, Nicholas Worth, Aaron Lustig, Arsenio 'Sonny' Trinidad, William Dear, Julius W. Harris, John Landis (physician), John Cameron, William Lustig, Jenny Agutter (physician), Bruce Campbell (final shemp [sic]). Dir: Sam Raimi. Pro: Robert Tapert. Screenplay: Chuck Pfarrer, Sam Raimi, Ivan Raimi, Daniel Goldin and Joshua Goldin; from a

Top Car: Tom Cruise as Cole Trickle in the oil-slick Days of Thunder *(UIP).*

story by Sam Raimi. Ph: Bill Pope. Ed: Bud Smith and Scott Smith. Pro Des: Randy Ser. M: Danny Elfman. Costumes: Grania Preston. Sound: Terry Rodman. (Universal –UIP.) Rel: 16 November 1990. 91 mins. Cert 15.

Dark Habits – Entre Tiniebias. This early work of Spanish director Pedro Almodóvar might as well have been called Naughty Nuns in a Curious Convent. The gay little band indulge themselves with men, drugs and each other, though they retain an air of innocence throughout. But when a drug-addicted singer takes refuge with them she stirs things up and finally brings about the end of their order. Despite flashes of directorial promise, there's not a lot to hold your attention here. [FDM]

Cast: Christina S. Pascual (troublemaker Yolanda), Marisa Paredes (Sister Manure), Mari Carrillo (Marquesa), Lina Canalejas (Sister Snake), Carmen Maura (Sister Damned), Chus Lampreave (Sister Rat), Julieta Serrano (Mother Superior). Dir and Screenplay: Pedro Almodóvar. Pro: Luis Calvo. Pro Sup: Tadeo Villalba. Ph: Angel

L. Fernandez. Ed: Jose Salcedo. Pro Des: Pin Morales and Roman Arango. M: Cam Espana. (Tesauro–Metro Pictures.) Rel: floating; first shown London (Metro) 24 August 1990. 95 mins. Cert 15.

√**Days of Thunder.** Streamlined as a bullet, the first half of *Days of Thunder* gleams like a well-oiled machine. But then the brake fluid clogs the works. Tom Cruise (charging $8m this time round) stars as Cole Trickle, a rookie stock-car driver born with the right stuff. A fan of racing on TV, Cole's dream is to win the Daytona title and he's got crew chief Robert Duvall to help him claim it. Duvall acts as if he's in a better movie, Cruise simpers behind his Ray-Bans and the racing is the best you're likely to see on celluloid. [JC-W]

Also with: Robert Duvall (Harry Hogge), Randy Quaid (Tim Daland), Nicole Kidman (Dr Claire Lewicki), Cary Elwes (Russ Wheeler), Michael Rooker (Rowdy Burns), Fred Dalton Thompson (Big John), John C. Reilly (Buck Bretherton), J. C. Quinn (Waddell), Don Simpson (Aldo Benedetti), Stephen Michael Ayers, Donna Wilson, Chris Ellis, Peter Appel, Mike Slattery, Dr Jerry Punch, Neil Bonnett, Harry P. Gant,

Rusty Wallace. Dir: Tony Scott. Pro: Don Simpson and Jerry Bruckheimer. Ex Pro: Gerald R. Molen. Screenplay: Robert Towne; from a story by Towne and Cruise. Ph: Ward Russell. Ed: Billy Weber and Chris Lebenzon. Art: Benjamin Fernandez and Thomas E. Sanders. M: Hans Zimmer; guitar solos by Jeff Beck; songs performed by The Spencer Davis Group, Tina Turner, Cher, Chicago, Elton John, John Waite, Guns 'n' Roses, Joan Jett etc. Costumes: Susan Becker. Sound: Charles Wilborn. (Paramount–UIP.) Rel: 10 August 1990. 107 mins. Cert 12.

Death Warrant. Sadistic thriller with Jean-Claude Van Damme as the undercover kick-boxing cop who is assigned the task of finding out why so many jail inmates are being murdered. Fast-paced, well-produced, but very brutal. [FDM]

Also with: Robert Guillaume (Hawkins), Cynthia Gibb (Amanda), George Dickerson (Vogler), Art LaFleur (Sgt Degarf), Patrick Kilpatrick (the Sandman), Joshua Miller, Hank Woessner, George Jenesky, Jack Bannon, Abdul Salaam El Razzac. Dir: Deran Sarafian. Pro: Mark DiSalle. Screenplay: David Goyer. Ph: Russell Carpenter. Ed: Gregg McLaughlin and John Barton. Pro Des: Curtis Schnell. Art: Robert E. Lee.

A narrative of landscapes: a typical scene from Thaddeus O'Sullivan's resonant December Bride *(BFI).*

(Mark DiSalle Pro–UIP.) Rel: floating; first shown London (Cannon, Panton St) 7 December 1990. 88 mins. Cert 18.

December Bride. Pictorially arresting, authentically rural tale set in a remote corner of Ireland at the turn of the century. Hamilton Echlin (Donal McCann) is a hard-working, basically good-hearted farmer who for the most part resists 'the three curses of Ireland': England, religion and the drink. He cannot, however, resist the charms of his new servant, Sarah (Saskia Reeves), and neither can his brother. When Sarah becomes pregnant and cannot name the father, the community turns against the Echlin brothers. A decidedly small-scale film, and very leisurely paced at that, *December Bride* is nevertheless a significant accomplishment. The beauty of the old Irish dialogue is adequately matched by Jurgen Knieper's score and by the stark, brooding landscape. Winner of the 1990 Mon-

treal Critics' prize for best film 'out of competition'. [JC-W]

Also with: Ciaran Hinds (Frank Echlin), Patrick Malahide (Sorleyson), Brenda Bruce (Martha), Michael McKnight (Fergus), Geoffry Golden (Echlin), Frances Lowe (Victoria), Dervla Kirwan, Peter Capaldi, Cathleen Delaney, Gabrielle Reidy, Catherine Gibson, Karl Hayden. Dir: Thaddeus O'Sullivan. Pro: Jonathan Cavendish. Ex Pro: James Mitchell. Screenplay: David Rudkin; from the novel by Sam Hanna Bell. Ph: Bruno de Keyzer. Ed: Rodney Holland. Pro Des: Adrian Smith. M: Jurgen Knieper. Costumes: Consolata Boyle. Sound: Peter Lindsay. (Film Four International/CTE and British Screen–BFI.) Rel: 8 February 1991. 87 mins. Cert PG.

Defending Your Life. Following a fatal car crash on his birthday, Daniel Miller (Albert Brooks) finds himself in a wheelchair being pushed down a long corridor. Confused and inexplicably tired, he notices he is surrounded by old people likewise in wheelchairs. He is on his way to Judgement City, a holding port for the recently deceased. There, Daniel will have his life exam-

ined by a court, with key scenes of his existence revealed for inspection. Defending counsel Rip Torn pinpoints Daniel's moments of moral courage, while prosecutor Lee Grant shows him up as a coward. If Life proves to have made him a better soul he will pass on to a higher plane – if not, he goes back to earth to try again. A devastatingly romantic parable, *Defending Your Life* is a funny, warm and thought-provoking addition to the genre that has already brought us *Heaven Can Wait*, *Made in Heaven* and *Wings of Fame*. [JC-W]

Also with: Meryl Streep (Julia), Rip Torn (Bob Diamond), Lee Grant (Lena Foster), Buck Henry (Dick Stanley), Maxine Elliott (elderly woman on bus), Leonard O. Turner (Sam), Shirley MacLaine (as herself), Michael Durrell, James Eckhouse, Gary Beach, Peter Schuck, Time Winters, Marilyn Rockafellow, Art Frankel, Ernie Brown, George D. Wallace, Lillian Lehman, S. Scott Bullock, Carol Bivins, Gary Ballard, Toshio Shikami, Susan Walters, Hal Landon, Ida Lee, James Manis. Dir and Screenplay: Albert Brooks. Pro: Michael Grillo. Ex Pro: Herbert S. Nanas. Ph: Allen Daviau. Ed: David Finfer. Pro Des: Ida

But is it art? Danny Gerard and Mimi Rogers brace themselves for Mickey Rourke's next outburst in Michael Cimino's galloping remake of Desperate Hours (from Fox).

Random. M: Michael Gore; 'Something's Coming' sung by Barbra Streisand. Costumes: Deborah L. Scott. Sound: Thomas Causey. (Geffen–Warner.) Rel: 8 June 1991. 112 mins. Cert PG.

Delta Force 2: The Colombian Connection. All-action piece for Chuck Norris fans. Chuck heads a squad of US Marines who fly into the Colombian capital (here called San Carlos) and destroy the cocaine trade, rubbing out the top drug baron in a spectacular finale. Plenty of pace, sweat and gunfire. [FDM]

Also with: Billy Drago (Coda), Bobby Chavez (Paul), John R. Ryan (Gen. Taylor), Richard Jaeckel (Page), Begonia Plaza (Conquina), Mateo Gomez (Ernesto). Dir: Aaron Norris. Pro: Yoram Globus and Christopher Pearce. Screenplay: Lee Reynolds. Ph: Joao Fernandes. Ed: M. J. Duthie. M: Frederic Talgorn. (Cannon Films–UIP.) Rel: floating; first shown London (Cannon, Panton St) 4 January 1991. 105 mins. No cert.

Desperate Hours. Frenetic siege thriller with Mickey Rourke as a psychotic killer who takes over a wealthy, comfortable Utah household while he waits for his girlfriend to turn up. All is not as domestically cosy with the besieged Cornell family as at first would appear, but there's nothing like an upset to bring Mr and Mrs together again. Michael Cimino directs with a sledgehammer, building the suspense to a bloody climax, drowned by David Mansfield's score. A remake of the 1955 Humphrey Bogart thriller, in turn based on the 1954 novel and Broadway play by Joseph Hayes. FBI agent Brenda Chandler is played (way over the top) by Lindsay Crouse, wife of David Mamet, who, interestingly, scripted the 1989 *We're No Angels*, itself a remake of a 1955 Bogart vehicle. Mere coincidence? [JC-W]

Also with: Mickey Rourke (Michael Bosworth), Anthony Hopkins (Tim Cornell), Mimi Rogers (Nora Cornell), Kelly Lynch (Nancy Breyers), Elias Koteas (Wally Bosworth), David Morse (Albert), Shawnee Smith (May Cornell), Danny Gerard (Zack Cornell), Gerry Bamman, Matt McGrath,

John Christopher Jones, Dean Norris, John Finn, Christopher Curry, Stanley White, Mike Nussbaum. Dir: Michael Cimino. Pro: Cimino and Dino de Laurentiis. Ex Pro: Martha Schumacher. Screenplay: Lawrence Konner, Mark Rosenthal and Joseph Hayes. Ph: Doug Milsome. Ed: Peter Hunt. Pro Des: Victoria Paul. M: David Mansfield. Costumes: Charles De Caro. Mickey Rourke's wardrobe: Giorgio Armani. Sound: Keith A. Wester. (Fox.) Rel: 29 March 1991. 105 mins. Cert 15.

✓**Dick Tracy** is arguably the most proficient translation to screen of a comic strip yet, complete with animated backdrops and grotesquely made-up villains. Warren Beatty stars (and directs) as the square-jawed dick battling crime lord Big Boy Caprice (an unrecognisable, over-the-top and tiresome Al Pacino). Glenne Headley (replacing Sean Young at the last minute) co-stars as Dick's dame Tess Trueheart, but Madonna as Breathless Mahoney hots up the action with lashings of sexual innuendo and revealing costumes. There's plenty to go round, with the added attraction of cameos from Dustin Hoffman, James Caan and Dick Van

Left: *Warren Beatty as the man in charge, and* below: *Madonna as the chanteuse in the middle of the gunplay, in Beatty's homage to the gangster comic-strip* Dick Tracy, *from Warner.*

Dyke, but somehow *Dick Tracy* suffers from its own overkill. The characters are caricatures, the plot is familiar and the slam-bang action ultimately numbing. Enjoy the trailer. [JC-W]

Also with: Charlie Korsmo (The Kid/Dick Tracy Jr), Dustin Hoffman (Mumbles/Robert Evans), William Forsythe (Flattop), Charles Durning (Chief Brandon), Mandy Patinkin (88 Keys), Paul Sorvino (Lips Manlis), Dick Van Dyke (DA Fletcher), R. G. Armstrong (Pruneface), Stig Eldred, Ed O'Ross, Seymour Cassel, Allen Garfield, John Schuck, Charles Fleischer, Jack Kehoe, Marshall Bell, Tom Signorelli, James Tolkan, Kathy Bates, Hamilton Camp, Catherine O'Hara, Henry Silva, James Caan, Bert Remsen, Frank Campanella, Bing Russell, Michael J. Pollard, Estelle Parsons, Ian Wolfe, Mary Woronov, Henry Jones. Dir and Pro: Warren Beatty. Ex Pro: Barrie M. Osborne, Art Linson and Floyd Mutrux. Screenplay: Jim Cash and Jack Epps, Jr; based on characters created by Chester Gould. Ph: Vittorio Storaro. Ed: Richard Marks. Pro Des: Richard Sylbert. M: Danny Elfman; original songs by Stephen Sondheim. Costumes: Milena Canonero. Sound: Dennis Drummond. Special character make-up: John Caglione Jr and Doug Drexler. (Touchstone/Silver Screen Partners–Warner.) Rel: 6 July 1990. 103 mins. Cert PG.

√**Die Hard 2** – or *Airport '90*. Former New York cop John McClane (Bruce Willis) is at Dulles airport, Washington DC, to collect his wife for a Christmas of reconciliation. After what they went through in LA, Mr and Mrs McClane have rediscovered their love and John ain't gonna let *anything* get in its way. Bad news for terrorist Col. Stuart (William Sadler), who holds the airport to ransom in order to extradite South American drug lord Esperanza (Franco Nero). Jokey, violent and staggeringly expensive sequel to the megahit of '88, *Die Hard 2* feels like a James Bond film with a centre of gravity. Engrossing stuff. Number three will be set at sea. [JC-W]

Also with: Bonnie Bedelia (Holly McClane), William Atherton (Thornberg), Reginald VelJohnson (Al Powell), Franco Nero (Esperanza), John Amos (Grant), Dennis Franz (Carmine Lorenzo), Art Evans (Barnes), Fred Dalton Thompson (Trudeau), Tom Bower (Marvin), Sheila McCarthy (Samantha Copeland), Don Harvey, Tony Ganios, Peter Nelson, Robert Patrick, Pat O'Neal, Michael Francis Clarke, Sherry Bilsing, Jeanne Bates, Colm Meaney, Amanda Hillwood, Dominique Jennings, Robert Costanzo, Lauren Letherer, Connie Lillo-Thieman, John Cade, David Willis Sr etc. Dir: Renny Harlin. Pro: Lawrence Gordon, Joel Silver and Charles Gordon. Ex Pro: Lloyd Levin and Michael Levy. Screenplay: Steven E. de Souza and Doug Richardson. Ph: Oliver Wood. Ed: Stuart Baird. Pro Des: John Vallone. M: Michael Kamen; 'I've got my love to keep me warm' sung by Doris Day and Billie Holiday. Costumes: Marilyn Vance-Straker. Sound: Tim Cooney. (Fox.) Rel: 17 August 1990. 120 mins. Cert 15.

Django. A brutal Western – somewhat preceding the celebrated Spaghetti Westerns – which was completely banned in this country in the 1960s and is now getting its first showing. [FDM]

With Franco Nero. Dir: Sergio Corbucci. (BFI.) Rel: floating; first shown London (Scala) 4 June 1991. 95 mins. Cert details not available.

The Doors. Oliver Stone's long-awaited biography of Jim Morrison is both factually and atmospherically accurate in its voyeuristic, self-important dissection of sex, drugs and rock 'n' roll. No stone is left unturned as the director pushes and cajoles his camera up every metaphorical orifice of Morrison, the megalomaniac victim of success. Val Kilmer, inheriting the Morrison crown from the previously announced John Travolta and Timothy Hutton, looks, sings and staggers the part in a selfless exhibition of narcissism. There is a dark humour, too, amongst the violent psychedelia, as Morrison rambles on about his visionary Shaman, death and the whole damn thing. At a press reception, the legendary singer tells his audience, 'Actually, I don't remember being born – it must have happened during one of my blackouts.' A disturbing trip. [JC-W]

Also with: Meg Ryan (Pamela Courson Morrison), Kyle MacLachlan (Ray Manzarek), Frank Whaley (Robby Krieger), Kevin Dillon (John Densmore), Kathleen Quinlan (Patricia Kennealy), Sean Stone (young Jim), Will Jordan (Ed Sullivan), Jennifer Rubin (Edie Sedgewick), Crispin Glover (Andy Warhol), Billy Idol, Dennis Burkley, Josh Evans, Michael Madsen, Michael Wincott, John Densmore, Floyd Red Crow Wes-

Val Kilmer as the shaman poet Jim Morrison – in Oliver Stone's powerful, confused The Doors *(from Guild).*

terman, Harmonica Fats, Kelly Ann Hu, Fiona, John Capodice, Eric Burden, Mark Moses, Mimi Rogers, Paul Williams, Ashley Stone, Bill Graham, Rodney Grant, Patricia Kennealy, Annie McEnroe, Kelly Leach, Richard Rutowski, Oliver Sonte. Dir: Oliver Stone. Pro: Bill Graham, Sasha Harari and A. Kitman Ho. Ex Pro: Mario Kassar, Nicholas Clainos and Brian Grazer. Screenplay: Stone and J. Randal Johnson. Ph: Robert Richardson. Ed: David Brenner and Joe Hutshing. Pro Des: Barbara Ling. M and songs: Jim Morrison and The Doors, Harmonica Fats, Val Kilmer, The Velvet Underground, Carl Orff etc. Costumes: Marlene Stewart. Sound: Tod A. Maitland. (Carolco–Guild.) Rel: 26 April 1991. 141 mins. Cert 18.

Dr M. Strange and horrific French-Italian-German co-production, inspired by Fritz Lang's four *Dr Mabuse* fantasies, originally made between 1922 and 1962. Alan Bates is miscast as the mad media baron of the title who feasts off other people's sufferings, his latest gimmick being to induce mass suicide.

This time his control is not through hypnosis but through manipulation of television and video advertising, using the beauty of Jennifer Beals to lure the innocent to their deaths (!). Claude Chabrol, former master of the *film noir* thriller, directs with some visual flair but is too often tripped up by unintentionally hilarious dialogue. And although set in the future, the film feels terribly dated. Wolfgang Preiss, who appeared in the last Lang film, *The Thousand Eyes of Dr Mabuse*, makes a sentimental appearance. [JC-W]

Cast includes: Alan Bates (Marsfeldt), Jennifer Beals (Sonja Vogler), Jan Niklas (Hartmann), Hanns Zischler (Moser), Benoit Regent (Stieglitz), William Berger, Alexander Radszun, Peter Fitz, Wolfgang Preiss, Andrew McCarthy. Dir: Claude Chabrol. Pro: Ingrid Windisch. Ex Pro: François Duplat and Hans Brockmann. Screenplay: Chabrol, Sollace Mitchell and Thomas Bauermeister; based on a story by Bauermeister. Ph: Jean Rabier. Ed: Monique Fardoulis. Pro Des: Wolfgang Hundhammer and Dante Ferretti. M: Paul Hindemith and Mekong Delta. Costumes: Egon Strasser. Sound: Axel Arft. (NEF Filmproduktion/ Vertriebs GmbH/ZDF/La Sept/ELLEPI Film/CLEA Prod–HoBo.) Rel: 30 November 1990. 115 mins. Cert 18.

won the Silver Sakura Young Cinema award at the 1989 Tokyo Film Festival. [FMS]

Cast: Kumiko Akiyoshi (Miyako), Masao Kusakari (Sotomura), Kiwako Harada (Harumi). Dir: Shunichi Nagasaki. Pro: Toshiro Kamata and Kei Sasaki. Screenplay: Goro Nakajima. Ph: Makato Watanabe. M: Satosi Kadokura. (Fuji Television Pro–ICA.) Rel: floating; first shown London (ICA) 19 October 1990. 109 mins. No cert.

Everybody Wins is a good-looking, well-directed mystery, the first screenplay from Arthur Miller since his 1961 *The Misfits*. Unfortunately, there is a theatrical artificiality that pervades the film and makes the characters less than credible. Nick Nolte plays Tom O'Toole, a private investigator who is called into a peaceful, Connecticut town to sort out the guilty from the innocent in a closed murder case. The town whore, Angela Crispini (Debra Winger), is a schizophrenic nymphomaniac, but is the only person willing to feed O'Toole his leads – albeit a thread at a time. Quite why O'Toole is so improbably fascinated with this psychotic is unclear. However, Will Patton (*No Way Out, Stars and Bars*) makes an intriguing villain, and Miller's screenplay offers some nice touches of eccentricity. [JC-W]

Reisz pudding: Debra Winger and Nick Nolte act their socks off in Karel Reisz's disappointing Everybody Wins *(from Virgin Vision).*

The Emperor's Naked Army Marches On. Five years in the making, then left on the shelf because no exhibitor would touch it, before running for a year when it finally got an airing, this very Japanese film is a portrait of Okuzaki Kenzo, who created an outrage by firing four pachinko balls at the Emperor in 1969. More outrageously, the film contends that shortly after the Japanese surrender in 1945, a number of soldiers were shot to provide meat for their own officers. [FDM]

Dir: Hara Kazuo, based on an idea by Imamura Shoehei. Rel: floating; first shown London (ICA) 14 September 1990. 123 mins. No cert.

The Enchantment. Japanese film about a complicated relationship between a Tokyo psychologist who becomes fascinated by one of his (female) patients. His secretary-mistress becomes so infuriated by this that she eventually starts an affair with the patient herself. All too clearly made on a shoestring budget, and short on pace, the film nevertheless maintains steady interest, thanks largely to three good performances and the Tokyo locations. Director Shunichi Nagasaki is one of Japan's promising new talents, and the film

George C. Scott faces an awesome power in William Peter Blatty's 'official' sequel, The Exorcist III *(Fox).*

Cast includes: Will Patton (Jerry), Judith Ivey (Connie), Jack Warden (Judge Harry Marks), Kathleen Wilhoite (Amy), Frank Converse (Charley Haggerty), Frank Military (Felix), Steven Skybell, Mert Hatfield, Peter Appel, Sean Weil. Dir: Karel Reisz. Pro: Jeremy Thomas. Ex Pro: Terry Glinwood and Linda Yellen. Screenplay: Arthur Miller. Ph: Ian Baker. Ed: John Bloom. Pro Des: Peter Larkin. M: Mark Isham and Leon Redbone. Costumes: Ann Roth. Sound: Ivan Sharrock. (Recorded Picture Co–Virgin Vision.) Rel: 3 May 1991. 96 mins. Cert 15.

The Exorcist III. Georgetown, Washington DC, 1990. Suitably chilling and repellent sequel to the most successful horror film of all time. George C. Scott takes over the role of Police Lt Kinderman, originated by the late Lee J. Cobb (in the first film). Kinderman's best friend, Father Kevin Dyer (Ed Flanders), has been murdered in his hospital bed with all his blood neatly sucked out of him. The body also has the sign of the Gemini twins carved into its hand and has one finger chopped off, the trademark of a serial killer executed fifteen years earlier. As Kinderman pieces the mystery together, he realises this and other grisly murders are not the work of one man, although they appear identical. William Peter Blatty directs from his own screenplay (based on his novel *Legion*), injecting a good deal of humour (and some inappropriate in-jokes), but is tripped up by some hokey effects that weaken the film from the start. Still, there are some classic moments and a nice sense of claustrophobic menace. [JC-W]

Also with: Brad Dourif (the Gemini Killer), Jason Miller (Patient X), Nicol Williamson (Father Morning), Scott Wilson (Dr Temple), Nancy Fish, George DiCenzo, Don Gordon, Lee Richardson, Grand L. Bush, Mary Jackson, Viveca Lindfors, Tracy Thorne, Barbara Baxley, Zohra Lampert, Harry Carey Jr, Jodi Long. Dir and Screenplay: William Peter Blatty; from his novel *Legion*. Pro: Carter DeHaven. Ex Pro: James G. Robinson and Joe Roth. Ph: Gerry Fisher. Ed: Todd Ramsay and Peter Lee-Thompson. Pro Des: Leslie Dilley. M: Barry Devorzon. Costumes: Dana Lyman. Sound: Richard L. Anderson. (Morgan Creek–Fox.) Rel: 23 November 1990. 109 mins. Cert 18.

Fear. Few people believe in her powers, but the police cannot afford to ignore pretty psychic Cayse Bridges

Richard Harris giving the performance of his life (seen here with Sean Bean) in Jim Sheridan's powerful rural tale of The Field *(Enterprise).*

(Ally Sheedy). Able to enter the minds of serial killers, Cayse can supply vital clues to their whereabouts and has become something of a celebrity. However, she meets her match when she is zoned in on by the most dangerous of men: a murderer with psychic powers himself, nicknamed 'The Shadowman'. Nifty little chiller, this, which doesn't abuse the perimeters of the supernatural and doles out the frights in good measure. Intriguing, creepy and adult stuff. [JC-W]

Also with: Lauren Hutton (Jessica Moreau), Michael O'Keefe (Jack Hays), Dina Merrill (Catherine Tarr), Stan Shaw (Thomas Webber), Keone Young (William Wu), Pruit Taylor Vince, Dean Goodman, Don Hood, Marta DuBois, Jonathan Prince, John Agar, Raina Manuel, Helen Brown, Cyndi Strittmatter. Dir and Screenplay: Rockne S. O'Bannon. Pro: Richard Kobritz. Ex Pro: Mitchell Cannold and Diane Nabatoff. Ph: Robert Stevens. Ed: Kent

Beyda. Pro Des: Joseph Nemec III. M: Henry Mancini. Sound: Richard Lightstone. (Vestron.) Rel: 8 March 1991. 95 mins. Cert 18.

The Field. Ireland, 1939. Richard Harris, striking a pose somewhere between Moses and John Huston, gives the performance of his life as Bull McCabe, an Irish farmer obsessed with a field he rents. Transforming it from a rocky three acres to a green pasture with years of backbreaking toil and tons of seaweed, McCabe is determined to buy the field when it is put up for auction. But the land is not his only obsession, as we discover when this powerful, muscular story moves to its dramatic conclusion. McCabe is determined to see his family name continued and is piling his hopes on his son, the quiet, simplistic Tadgh (Sean Bean). Director-writer Jim Sheridan (*My Left Foot*) scores another success with this engaging, beautifully photographed and superbly acted drama. Richard Harris was nominated for an Oscar for his role, his first since 1963 (for *This Sporting Life*). [JC-W]

Also with: John Hurt (Bird O'Donnell), Brenda Fricker (Maggie McCabe), Frances Tomelty (young widow), Tom Berenger (Peter, the American), John Cowley, Jenny Conroy, Sean McGinley, Ruth McCabe. Dir and Screenplay: Jim Sheridan; from the play by John B. Keane. Pro: Noel Pearson. Ex Pro: Steve Morrison. Ed: Jack Conroy. Ed: J. Patrick Duffner. Pro Des: Frank Conway. M: Elmer Bernstein. Costumes: Joan Bergin. Sound: Kieran Horgan. (Granada--Enterprise.) Rel: 15 February 1991. 110 mins. Cert 12.

Filofax (US: *Taking Care of Business*). Charles Grodin is Spencer Barnes, a successful, meticulous business executive who organises his life through his Filofax. James Belushi is Jimmy Dworski, a loveable, impulsive slob who steals cars. Escaping prison to see the Chicago Cubs play the World Series, Jimmy picks up Spencer's mislaid Filofax and takes over his life. Spencer, meanwhile, is stranded in Los Angeles on a business trip without an identity. Although Grodin the actor speculates that 'people enjoy seeing a clean person get dirty,' this critic found it unbearable to watch Spencer's miserable decline – after all, he *had* worked hard for his life. A morally outrageous movie, *Filofax* suffers further from a flabby plotline and a line-up of grotesque caricatures. [JC-W]

A beautiful day to die: Kiefer Sutherland and Kevin Bacon explore the afterlife in Joel Schumacher's stylish Flatliners, *from Columbia.*

Also with: Anne DeSalvo (Debbie), Mako (Sakamoto/'Big Sak'), Veronica Hamel (Elizabeth), Hector Elizondo (Warden), Loryn Locklin (Jewel Bentley), Stephen Elliott (Walter Bentley), Gates McFadden (Diane), J. J. (LeBradford Brown), John de Lancie, Thom Sharp, Ken Foree, Andre Rosey Brown, Terrence E. McNally, Tom Nolan, Marjorie Bransfield, Joe Lerer, Elisabeth Barrett, Baldo Dal Ponte, Dr Ruth Weistmuller. Dir: Arthur Hiller. Pro: Geoffrey Taylor. Ex Pro: Paul Mazursky. Screenplay: Jill Mazursky and Jeffrey Abrams. Ph: David M. Walsh. Ed: William Reynolds. Pro Des: Jon Hutman. M: Stewart Copeland; numbers performed by Bachman-Turner Overdrive, T-Bone Walker, Party Posse. Costumes: Marilyn Matthews. Sound: John Leveque. (Hollywood Pictures/Silver Screen Partners IV–Warner.) Rel: 17 May 1991. 108 mins. Cert 12.

The First Power. Third-class supernatural horror-thriller marking the debut of writer-director Robert Resnikoff. Judging from this, he has a long way to go before he hits the big time. All the action hinges on the duel between LA cop Lou Diamond Phillips and a killer made immortal by Satan. [FDM]

Rest of cast: Tracy Griffith (Tess Seaton), Jeff Kober (Patrick Channing), Mykel T. Williamson (Det. Oliver Franklin), Elizabeth Arlem (Sister Marguerite), Dennis Lipscomb (Commander Perkins), Carmen Argenziano, Julianna McCarthy, Nada Despotovich, Sue Giosa, Clayton Landey,

Hansford Rowe, Philip Abbott, David Gale, Patrick MacNamara, Grand L. Bush, Melanie Shatner. Dir and Screenplay: Robert Resnikoff. Pro: David Madden. Ex Pro: Ted Field, Robert W. Cork and Melinda Jason. Ph: Theo van de Sande. Ed: Michael Bloecher. Pro Des: Joseph T. Garritz. Art: Pat Tagliaferro. Wardrobe: Marilyn Vance-Straker. M: Stewart Copeland. (Nelson Entertainment/Interscope Communications-Orion–Castle Premier.) Rel: floating; first shown London (Cannon, Chelsea, Haymarket and Oxford St) 21 September 1990. 98 mins. Cert 18.

✓ **Flatliners.** Glaring moodily across Lake Michigan, Chicago medical student Nelson Wright (Kiefer Sutherland) announces, 'Today is a good day to die.' Nelson has encountered enough survivors of near-death experiences to want a piece of the action himself. Under the strict supervision of four fellow students, Nelson has his heart stopped, registering a 'flat line' on the EKG and EEG monitors. Shortly afterwards he is brought round, but brings a part of the death experience back with him. One by one, the students all experiment with oblivion, but as they trespass on the after-life, so the Beyond invades their waking days. And they all have a price to pay. *Flatliners* is a brave, thought-provoking thriller that trips over its own ambitions. At once a serious, intellectual examination of real-life near-death experiences (interestingly, Keifer's own father, Donald, died briefly of acute meningitis), it also attempts to entertain as a flash horror film. Its conclusions are embarrassingly simplistic (the students' worst feelings of guilt materialise as physical threats, their absolution coming solely from within themselves), and at its worst the film is a scary ride through the taboo stretches of the imagination. Jan De Bont's atmospheric photography is too self-conscious for its own good (nocturnal graveyards exude steaming dry ice), but James Newton Howard's sinister score is suitably effective. A memorable, stylish experiment that could have been unparalleled cinema. N.B. Do not try this at home. [JC-W]

Also with: Julia Roberts (Rachel), Kevin Bacon (Labraccio), William Baldwin (Joe), Oliver Platt (Steckle), Kimberly Scott (Winnie Hicks), Joshua Rudoy, Benjamin Mouton, Aeryk Egan, Hope Davis, Deborah Thompson, Susan French, Beth Grant, Cage S. Johnson. Dir: Joel Schumacher. Pro: Michael Douglas and Rick Bieber. Ex

Signs of the times: a dirty Victorian backstreet in Christine Edzard's captivating small-scale epic, The Fool *(from HoBo Films).*

Pro: Scott Rudin, Michael Rachmil and Peter Filardi. Screenplay: Filardi. Ph: Jan de Bont. Ed: Robert Brown. Pro Des: Eugenio Zanetti. M: James Newton Howard; 'Party Town' performed by Dave Stewart. Costumes: Susan Becker. Sound: Charles L. Campbell and Richard Franklin. (Stonebridge Entertainment–Columbia.) Rel: 9 November 1990. 114 mins. Cert 15.

The Fool. Boasting the resonance of a richly detailed, acutely satirical adaptation of Dickens, this is in fact an original screenplay inspired by the diaries of Henry Mayhew, co-founder of *Punch* magazine. Set in the London of 1857, *The Fool* is a colourful look at the peeling, stinking poverty of the time, as well as the self-satisfaction and puffed-up idiocy of an upper class even richer than its counterpart is today. Strolling between these two worlds is Mr Frederick (Derek Jacobi), a timid 'pounds, shillings and pence man' working at a London theatre, who takes on the persona of the mysterious Sir John, a man of enormous grace and capital. An imposter in both worlds, Mr Frederick/Sir John is a delightful guide through a bygone era. A superb production, and a good deal more palatable than the same team's earlier *Little Dorrit*. [JC-W]

Also with: Cyril Cusack (the ballad seller), Maria Aitken (Lady Amelia), Irina Brook (Georgiana Shillibeer), Paul Brooke (Lord Paramount), Jim Carter (Mr Blackthorn), Jonathan Cecil (Sir Martin Locket), Ben Aris, Brenda Bruce, Richard Caldicot, James Cairncross, Maria Charles, Richard Clifford, Ron Cook, Marty Cruikshank, Rosalie Crutchley, Sally Faulkner, Michael Feast, Julian Firth, Graham Fletcher Cook, Jack Gittings, Christopher Good, Dilys Hamlett, Roger Hammond, Patricia Hayes, Don Henderson, Janet Henfrey, Michael Hordern, Stratford Johns, Darlene Johnson, Hugh Lloyd, Preston Lockwood, Norman Lumsden, Miriam Margolyes, Petra Markham, John McEnery, Michael Medwin, Murray Melvin, Ruth Mitchell, Patricia Napier, Emma Piper, Corin Redgrave, Miranda Richardson, Graham Seed, Joan Simms, John Tordoff, Frederick Treves, Alec Wallis, Bill Wallis, Jo Warne, Jane Wymark. Dir: Christine Edzard. Pro: Edzard and Richard Goodwin. Screenplay: Edzard and Olivier Stockman; based on interviews conducted by Henry Mayhew in 1851 and chronicled in *London Labour and the London Poor*. Ph: Robin Vidgeon. Ed: Olivier Stockman. Pro Des: Sands Films. M: Michel Sanvoisin. Sound: Paul Carr and Brian Paxton. (Sands Films–HoBo.) Rel: 18 January 1991. 137 mins. Cert U.

Forever Mary – Mary Per Sempre. A new teacher (Michele Placido – the only professional actor in the film) faces up to the tough boys at a reform school in Palermo (played by the actual schoolkids). Routine treatment of a familiar subject. [FDM]

Dir: Marco Risi. Pro: Claudio Bonevento. Screenplay: Sandro Petraglia and Stefano Ralli. Ph: Mauro Marchetti. Ed: Claudio di Mauro. Art: Massimo Spano. M: Giancarlo Bigazzi. (Sacis-Intra Films Numero Uno International-BFI.) Rel: floating; first shown London (NFT) 23 May 1991. 100 mins. No cert.

Freedom Is Paradise – SER. Bleakly atmospheric, unsentimental story of a 13-year-old juvenile delinquent who

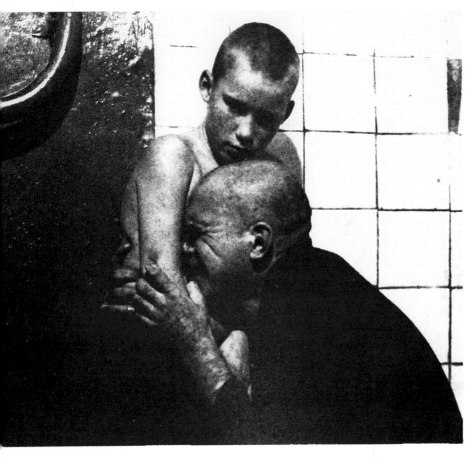

Volodya Kozyrev and Alexander Bureyev in Freedom Is Paradise: *little paradise in Sergei Brodov's compelling portrait of contemporary Russia as seen through the eyes of a 13-year-old boy (from Artificial Eye).*

Marlon Brando reprises an earlier role with Matthew Broderick as The Freshman, *in Columbia's slick, enjoyable parody.*

habitually escapes from reform school in Soviet Central Asia. More victim than oppressor, the empty-faced Sasha (played by real-life reform school inmate and motorcycle thief Volodya Kozyrev), wants only to see the father he has never met. Against the odds, he breaks out of the inhumane institution he knows as home and travels cross-country to the Archangel prison where his father is in solitary confinement. Director Sergei Bodrov, who didn't meet his own father until he was 30, attempts to offer hope in a world he sees as unremittingly depressing. And he has done so – with a film that doesn't have to explain itself, employ trickery or indulge in melodrama or sentimentality. This is a brutally honest, heart-breaking picture, evocative of a contemporary USSR still trapped in the Third World. Winner of the Grand Prix (best film) award at the 1989 Montreal Film Festival. [JC-W]

Also with: Alexander Bureyev (father), Svetlana Gaitan (Klava), Vitautas Tomkus (military commander). Dir and Screenplay: Sergei Bodrov. Pro: Mosfilm Studios. Ph: Youri Skirtladze. Pro Des: Valery Kostrin. M: Alexander Raskatov. (Mosfilm–Artificial Eye.) Rel: 19 April 1991. 75 mins. Cert 12.

The Freshman. This is the film that tempted Marlon Brando off his Tahitian island because he was such an admirer of comedy writer-director Andrew Bergman. 'You know', says Brando, 'when people laugh, their bodies produce endorphins, and I would like to be responsible for producing an endorphin or two.' Later, Brando slagged off the production, but then changed his mind after a little legal pressure. Paramount Pictures, too, queued up at the complaints counter, upset by the actor's parody of *The Godfather*. Of course, Brando is the sole reason to see this movie, a routine caper about a New York college kid, Clark Kellogg (Matthew Broderick), caught up working for a Mafia don. Worse still, Kellogg becomes involved with the notorious Gourmet Club, a gastronomic society that charges over $200,000 a meal – so that its millionaire patrons can sample the meat of endangered species (in this case a Komodo dragon). Amiable, but nothing to write home about. [JC-W]

Also with: Marlon Brando (Carmine Sabatini), Bruno Kirby (Victor Ray), Penelope Ann Miller (Tina Sabatini), Frank Whaley (Steve Bushak), Paul Benedict (Arthur Fleeber), Kenneth Welsh (Dwight Armstrong), Maximilian Schell (Larry London), Jon Polito, Richard Gant, Pamela Payton-Wright, B. D. Wong, Leonard Cimino, Gianni Russo. Dir and Screenplay: Andrew Bergman. Pro: Mike Lobell. Ph: William A. Fraker, Ed: Barry Malkin. Pro Des: Ken

Nightmares of the living dead: Patrick Swayze dreams he's still alive, with widow Demi Moore – in UIP's megahit Ghost.

Adam. M: David Newman; numbers performed by Tony Bennett, Nat King Cole, Grandmaster Flash, Bert Parks etc. Costumes: Julie Weiss. Sound: Michael Kirchberger. (Columbia Tri-Star.) Rel: 2 November 1990. 103 mins. Cert PG.

The Garden. Derek Jarman's latest effort forfeits any real story, and settles for a bombardment of graphic images, mixing scenes of present-day Britain with dream sequences of the time of Christ, loosely mirroring the Passion. Most moviegoers will probably find the symbolism and repetition confusing and eventually boring. Definitely for Jarman's admirers only. [FDM]

Cast: Kevin Collins, Roger Cook, Jody Graber, Peter Lee-Wilson, Philip Macdonald, Johnny Mills, Tilda Swinton. Dir and Screenplay: Derek Jarman. Pro: James McKay. Ph: Christopher Hughes. Ed: Peter Cartwright. M: Simon Fisher Turner. (Bazilist Prods-Channel 4–British Screen-ZDF-Uplink Pro–Artificial Eye.) Rel: floating; first shown London (Camden Plaza) 4 January 1991. 92 mins. Cert 15.

Ghost. The surprise hit of 1990, *Ghost* is a perfectly crafted romantic thriller. Patrick Swayze is improbably cast as Sam Wheat, a New York banker, who stumbles across a spare $4 million in the computer. The discovery leads to his death in a back alley and threatens the life of his romantic partner, Molly Jensen, played by the beautiful Demi Moore. But Sam and Molly were inseparable in life and Sam's death isn't going to come between them. Besides, Sam has his murder to solve. Enter Oda Mae Brown (Whoopi Goldberg), a crank who thinks she's a fake medium. Wrong. *Ghost*, invisibly propelled by director Jerry Zucker (*Airplane!*, *Ruthless People*), is genuinely funny, touching and moving, with a good story to boot. Sheer entertainment. [JC-W]

Also with: Tony Goldwyn (Carl Bruner), Rick Aviles (Willie Lopez), Phil Leeds, Vincent Schiavelli, Armelia McQueen, Gail Boggs, Stephen Root, Laura Drake, Vivian Bonnell, Derek Thompson, Charlotte Zucker, Bruce Jarchow, Sondra Rubin. Dir: Jerry Zucker. Pro: Lisa Weinstein. Ex Pro: Steven-Charles Jaffe. Assoc Pro and Screenplay: Bruce Joel Rubin. Ph: Adam Greenberg. Ed: Walter Murch. Pro Des: Jane Musky. M: Maurice Jarre; 'Unchained Melody' and 'Since I Fell For You' sung by The Righteous Brothers. Costumes: Ruth Morley. Sound: Leslie Shatz. (Paramount–UIP.) Rel: 5 October 1990. 126 mins. Cert 12.

The Gift. Re-edited, condensed version of the six-part children's television serial about suspense and the supernatural. Fourteen-year-old Davy and his kid sister are sent to Wales when their parents' squabbles reach boiling point. Once there, the boy is touched by the occult . . . [FDM]

Cast: Tat Whalley (Davy), Jodhi May (his sister). Dir: Marc Evans and Red Saunders; based on the book by Peter Dickinson. M: Michael Storey. (ICA Children's Cinema.) Rel: floating; first shown London (ICA) 15 December 1990. 102 mins. No cert.

The Girlfriend – La Amiga. 1988 Argentine/West German co-production: one of the several movies made

Al Pacino and Richard Bright strike a familiar pose in the third instalment of Francis Ford Coppola's immoral trilogy, The Godfather Part III *(from UIP).*

Love-locked: Chris Haywood strokes his golden flame in Paul Cox's offbeat romance, Golden Braid *(from Artificial Eye).*

and subject to diabetic fits. He is also attempting to go legitimate, although his $100 million donation to the Vatican is highly suspect. The storyline is pretty thin, and the pace decidedly sluggish, but Andy Garcia makes a memorable impression as Vincent Mancini, Michael's hot-headed nephew who brings murder and respect back to the Corleone dynasty. There's a romantic subplot, in which Vincent falls in love with Michael's daughter, Maria, providing a major role for the director's own daughter, Sofia Coppola (who took over from Winona Ryder at the eleventh hour). The film's artistry is spectacular, and there's an unforgettable coda at a Sicilian performance of Mascagni's opera *Cavalleria Rusticana*, but otherwise this sequel is a plodding indulgence in nostalgia. Scripted by Coppola and Mario Puzo during bouts of gambling in Reno. [JC-W]

Also with: Diane Keaton (Kay Adams), Talia Shire (Connie Corleone Rizzi), Eli Wallach (Don Altobello), Joe Mantegna (Joey Zasa), George Hamilton (B. J. Harrison), Raf Vallone (Cardinal Lamberto), Franc D'Ambrosio (Anthony Corleone), Donal Donnelly (Archbishop Gilday), Vittorio Duse (Don Tommasino), Al Martino (Johnny Fontane), Tere L. Baker (Teresa Hagen), Bridget Fonda, Richard Bright, Helmut Berger, Don Novello, John Savage, Franco Citti, Michele Russo, Don Costello, Al Ruscio, Rick Aviles, Michael Bowen, Brett Halsey, John Abineri, Catherine Scorsese. Dir and Pro: Francis Ford Coppola. Ex Pro: Fred Fuchs and Nicholas Gage. Screenplay: Coppola and Mario Puzo. Ph: Gordon Willis. Ed: Barry Malkin, Lisa Fruchtman and Walter Murch. Pro Des: Dean Tavoularis. M: Carmine Coppola; additional themes by Nino Rota. Costumes: Milena Canonero. Sound: Richard Beggs. (Paramount–UIP.) Rel: 8 March 1991. 160 mins. Cert 15.

around that time about the 'Mothers of the Plaza de Mayo', the women who waited for sons and lovers recruited into the Argentine army but who never returned. [FDM]

Cast includes: Liv Ullmann, Cipe Lincovsky, Federico Luppi, Victor Laplace, Harry Baer, Lito Cruz, Grager Hansen, Nicholas Frei, Cristina Murta, Amancay Espindola. Dir: Jeanine Meerapfel. Assoc Pro: Jeffrey Steiner and Hans-Gerhard Stahl. Screenplay: Meerapfel and Alcides Chiesa. Ph: Axel Block. Ed: Julia de Lorenz. M: Jose Luis Casteneira de Dios. (Journal Film Klaus Volkerborn, Berlini-Jorge Estrada Mora Pro, Buenos Aires-Alma Film Pro– ICA.) Rel: floating; first shown London (ICA) 10 May 1991. 108 mins. No cert.

The Godfather Part III. The Corleones are back, courtesy of Francis Ford Coppola, who cloaks the familiar violence with religion, opera and lavish production design. It is 1979, and Michael Corleone (Al Pacino) is greying

Golden Braid. Chris Haywood has played some strange characters in his time, but none weirder than Bernard, an Australian clock repairman who falls in love with a braid of golden hair. Obsessed by the past, Bernard fills his house with antiques and old clocks, prompting his mistress, Therese (Gosia Dobrowolska), to mutter, 'I've had enough eternity to last me a lifetime.' When the clockmaker discovers the braid behind a secret panel in an ancient cabinet, Therese is relegated to the bottom drawer. Although decidedly odd, *Golden Braid* is both touching and gently humorous, another unique episode from the eccentric Dutch-born filmmaker Paul Cox (*Man of Flowers, Lonely Hearts*). [JC-W]

Also with: Paul Chubb (Joseph), Norman Kaye (psychiatrist), Marion Heathfield (cleaning woman), Monica Maughan (antique shop owner), Robert Menzies (Ernst), Jo Kennedy, Sheila Florance, George Fairfax, Harold Baigent, Margaret Mills. Dir: Paul Cox. Pro: Cox, Paul Ammitzboll and Santhana Naidu. Ex Pro: William T. Marshall. Screenplay: Cox and Barry Dickins; inspired by Guy de Maupassant's short story *La Chevelure* (The Head of Hair). Ph: Nino G. Martinetti. Ed: Russell Hurley. Pro Des: Neil Angwin. Sound: Livia Ruzic. (The Australian Film Commission / Film Victoria / Illumination Films– Artificial Eye.) Rel: 29 March 1991. 91 mins. Cert 15.

✓**GoodFellas**. New York, 1955–80. Once again Martin Scorsese illustrates why he is America's premier filmmaker with this perfectly crafted, violent true-life gangster epic. The story of Henry Hill (Ray Liotta) and his rise through the tight Mafia of Sicilian gangsters is as poetic and entertaining as it is chilling and repugnant. 'To me, being a gangster was better then being president,' Henry relates in the voice-over narrative; 'you were treated like a film star.' In the central role, Liotta (*Something Wild, Field of Dreams*) confirms his stature as a front-ranking leading man, while Robert De Niro makes an unglamorous supporting contribution as Jimmy Conway – his seventh gangster part. A masterpiece for strong stomachs. Formerly known as *Wiseguys*. [JC-W]

Also with: Joe Pesci (Tommy DeVito), Lorraine Bracco (Karen Hill), Paul Sorvino (Paul Cicero), Mike Starr (Frenchy), Frank Vincent (Billy Batts), Chuck Low (Morris Kessler), Gina Mastrogiacomo (Janice Rossi), Catherine Scorsese (Tommy's mother), Suzanne Shepherd (Karen's mother), Welker White (Lois Byrd), Christopher Serrone (Young Henry), Robbie Vinton (Bobby Vinton), Frank Sivero, Tony Darrow, Frank DiLeo, Henry Youngman, Charles Scorsese, Debi Mazar, Margo Winkler, Jerry Vale, Elaine Kagan, Beau Starr, Kevin Corrigan, Michael Imperioli, John Williams, Joseph D'Onofrio, Frank Adonis, Katherine Wallach, Marianne Leone, Samuel L. Jackson, Paul Herman, Edward McDonald, Edward Hayes, Anthony Powers, Paul Mougey, Stella Kietel, Dominique DeVito. Dir: Martin Scorsese. Pro: Irwin Winkler. Ex Pro: Barbara De Fina.

Gerard Depardieu and Andie MacDowell in a marriage of inconvenience, in Peter Weir's delightful Green Card *(from Warner).*

Screenplay: Nicholas Pileggi and Martin Scorsese; based on Pileggi's book *Wiseguy*. Ph: Michael Ballhaus. Ed: Thelma Schoonmaker. Pro Des: Kristi Zea. M: Songs performed by Tony Bennett, Johnny Mathis, The Crystals, Bobby Vinton, The Shangri-Las, Dean Martin, Donovan, Aretha Franklin, Bobby Darin, The Rolling Stones, Cream, The Who, George Harrison, Muddy Waters, Sid Vicious etc. Costumes: Richard Bruno. Titles: Saul and Elaine Bass. Sound: Skip Lievsay. (Warner.) Rel: 26 October 1990. 146 mins. Cert 18.

✓**Graveyard Shift**. Remember *Ben*? All those fat rats are back in work, trying to inject a shiver into this distinctly unshivery tale of the monster in the mill with a taste for the mill's employees. One for video, surely, rather than the cinema. [FDM]

Cast includes: David Andrews (John Hall), Kelly Wolf (Jane Wisconsky), Stephen Macht (Warwick), Brad Dourif (the Exterminator), Andrew Divoff, Vic Polizof, Ilona Margolis, Jimmy Woodard. Dir and Co-Pro:

Ralph F. Singleton. Co-Pro: W. J. Dunn. Ex Pro: Bonnie and Larry Sugar. Screenplay: John Esposito; based on the short story by Stephen King. Ph: Peter Stein. Ed: Jim Gross and Randy Jon Morgan. Pro Des: Gary Wissner. M: Anthony Marinelli and Brian Banks. (Columbia–Tri-Star.) Rel: floating; first shown London (Cannons, Panton St and Oxford St) 31 May 1991. 86 mins. Cert 18.

✓**Green Card**. Georges Faure is an overweight, down-to-earth, working-class Frenchman who wants to gain residency in the United States. Brontë Parrish is a beautiful, obsessive and aristocratic New Yorker who needs a husband to qualify for the apartment of her dreams. The easy solution is for Georges and Brontë to marry and then part company. This they do, to the satisfaction of both parties. But when two Immigration officials investigate Brontë's marriage, she and George are forced to undergo a crash course in each other's lives. The outcome is predictable – but only up to a point. This is a delightful, sophisticated and often unexpected romantic comedy, both hilarious and moving, with Gerard Depar-

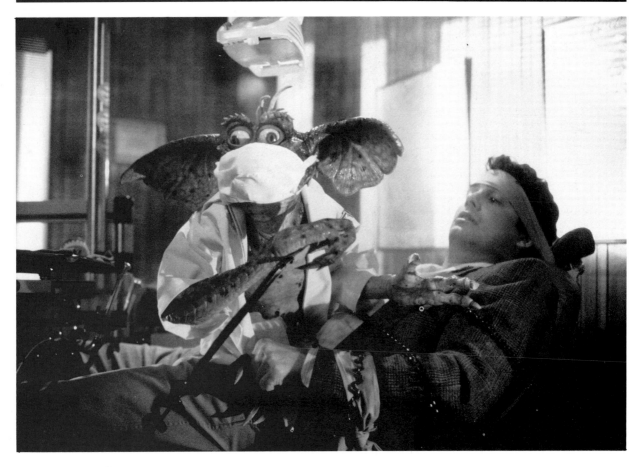

Is it safe? This Gremlin mocks Laurence Olivier in Marathon Man *as it checks for plaque on Zach Galligan; while another Arcimboldiesque monstrosity brings a new meaning to salad days for Dick Bucktus – in Warner's hilarious* Gremlins 2 – The New Batch.

dieu excelling himself in his first English-speaking role. [JC-W]

Also with: Andie MacDowell (Brontë), Bebe Neuwirth (Lauren), Gregg Edelman (Phil), Robert Prosky (Brontë's lawyer), Lois Smith (Mrs Parrish, Brontë's mother), Conrad McLaren (Mr Parrish, Brontë's father), Danny Dennis (Oscar), Jessie Keosian, Ethan Phillips, Mary Louise Wilson, Ronald Guttman, Stephen Pearlman, Victoria Boothby, Ann Wedgeworth, Vasek Simek, Rick Aviles, Larry Wright. Dir, Pro and Screenplay: Peter Weir. Ex Pro: Edward S. Feldman. Ph: Geoffrey Simpson. Ed: William Anderson. Pro Des: Wendy Stites. M: Hans Zimmer; Mozart, The Beach Boys, ENYA, *Holdin' On* sung by Soul II Soul, etc. Sound: Pierre Gamet. (Touchstone–Warner.) 1 March 1991. 107 mins. Cert 12.

√**Gremlins 2 – The New Batch**. It is five years later and Billy Peltzer and Kate Beringer (Zach Galligan and Phoebe Cates) have moved to New York to work for the giant Clamp organisation. Incredibly, Billy stumbles across Gizmo in the genetics lab at Clamp's – and all hell is let loose when the furry little Mogwai is subjected to a dose of H_2O. This time the malevolent, versatile Gremlins wreak havoc on one building, obviously modelled on the Trump colossus in New York, and the sour taste left by the first film is happily banished. The humour here is just as sick, but less cruel and punctuated with a plethora of in-jokes, from the obvious to the obscure. A film buff's dream, but one that should entertain almost everybody. [JC-W]

Also with: John Glover (Daniel Clamp), Robert Prosky (Grandpa Fred), Robert Picardo (Forster), Christopher Lee (Dr Catheter), Haviland Morris (Marla Bloodstone), Kathleen Freeman (Microwave Marge), Howie Mandel (the voice of Gizmo), Tony Randall (the voice of the 'Brain' Gremlin), Dick Miller, Jackie Joseph, Gedde Watanabe, Keye Luke, Heather Haase, Jason Presson, Jerry Goldsmith, Rick Ducommun, John Capodice, Belinda Balaski, Paul Bartel, Kenneth Tobey, Page Hannah, Charlie Haas, John Astin, Henry Gibson, Leonard Maltin, Hulk Hogan, Dick Butkus, Bubba Smith. Dir: Joe Dante. Pro: Michael Finnell. Ex Pro: Steven Spielberg, Kathleen Kennedy and Frank Marshall. Co-Pro: Rick Baker. Screenplay: Charlie Haas; based on characters created by Chris Columbus. Ph: John Hora. Ed: Kent Beyda. Pro Des: James Spencer. M: Jerry Goldsmith. Costumes: Rosanna Norton. Gremlin and Mogwai F/X supervised by Rick Baker. Sound: Ken King and Douglas Vaughan. (Amblin/Warner.) Rel: 27 July 1990. 107 mins. Cert 12.

√ **The Grifters**. Style-conscious update of Jim Thompson's murky pulp novel about three con artists, or 'grifters'. Roy Dillon is a fresh-faced, 25-year-old small-timer dating Myra Langtree, an older woman who tricks desperate millionaires out of their savings. And then there's Lily Dillon, Roy's 39-year-old mother who 'works' the racetrack for her sadistic boss. With three characters this scheming in the same town, something's gotta give. Sex, death and incest wrestle for centre stage in this smart-ass tribute to '50s *film noir*, which looks too slick for its own good. By opening out Thompson's steamy, claustrophobic novel, director Stephen Frears has lost a lot of his story's nervy edge. Still, Anjelica Huston and Annette Bening both won awards from America's National Society of Film Critics for their roles as mother and mistress. [JC-W]

Also with: John Cusack (Roy Dillon), Pat Hingle (Bobo Justus), Henry Jones (Simms), Michael Laskin, Eddie Jones, J. T. Walsh, Charles Napier, Stephen Tobolowsky, Xander Berkeley, Michael Greene, John Barrymore, Sandy Baron, Lou

Oedipus with a gun: John Cusack and Anjelica Huston as son and mother making deals in Jim Thompson's shady, Martin Scorsese-produced The Grifters *(Palace).*

Hancock, Steve Buscami, Sy Richardson. Dir: Stephen Frears. Pro: Martin Scorsese, Robert Harris and James Painten. Co-Pro: Peggy Rajski. Ex Pro: Barbara De Fina. Screenplay: Donald Westlake; based on the novel by Jim Thompson. Ph: Oliver Stapleton. Ed: Mick Audsley. Pro Des: Dennis Casner. M: Elmer Bernstein. Sound: John Sutton. (Palace.) Rel: 1 February 1991. 119 mins. Cert 18.

Grim Prairie Tales. A couple of old Western characters sit around the camp fire and brighten up the evening with several creepy old stories. [FDM]

Cast: James Earl Jones (Morrison), Brad Dourif (Farley), Will Hare, Marc McClure, Michelle Joyner, William Atherton, Lisa Eichhorn, Wendy Cooke. Dir and Screenplay: Wayne Coe. Pro: Richard Hahn. Ex Pro: Ricky Blumenthal and Larry Haber. Ph: Janusz Minsky. Ed: Earl Chaffari. Sound: Beau Franklin. Pro Des: Anthony Zierhut. Art: Angela Levy. M: Steve Dancz. (East/West Film Partners–BBC.) Rel: float-

ing; first shown London (NFT) 8 June 1991. 94 mins. No cert.

√ **The Guardian**. Not a documentary about a Fleet Street newspaper, but a ludicrous shocker concerning a baby-devouring tree. Jenny Seagrove branches out as a Druid babysitter who sacrifices infants to this living, breathing Californian oak, conjuring up fond memories of the talking trees in *The Wizard of Oz*. Wooden performances all round, conjured up by a tired, lacklustre William Friedkin (he who directed *The Exorcist*). Barking mad. [CB]

Cast includes: Jenny Seagrove (Camilla), Dwier Brown (Phil), Carey Lowell (Kate), Brad Hall (Ned Runcxie), Miguel Ferrer (Ralph Hess), Natalie Nogulich (Molly Sheridan). Dir: William Friedkin. Pro: Joe Wizan. Ex Pro: David Salven. Screenplay: Steven Volk, Dan Greenburg and William Friedkin; based on Greenburg's story *The Nanny*. Ph: John A. Alonzo. Ed: Seth Flaum. Pro Des: Gregg Fonseca. M: Jack Hues. Costumes: Denise Cronenberg. Sound: James R. Alexander and Tom Causey. (Universal–UIP.) Rel: 31 August 1990. 93 mins. Cert 18.

Robert De Niro and old associate Martin Scorsese share a scene in Irwin Winkler's intelligent look at the McCarthy witchhunts, with the latter playing a director modelled on the late Joseph Losey – in Warner's Guilty by Suspicion.

Guilty by Suspicion. 1951–2, Los Angeles. David Merrill (Robert De Niro) is Hollywood's golden boy, a one-time decorated naval officer and now Darryl Zanuck's number one director. Returning from scouting locations in Europe for his next film, Merrill finds the doors closing on him when he refuses to cooperate with the House Un-American Activities Committee. Merrill is no communist, but he's not about to point the finger at his friends and associates. His honour costs him the most important thing in his life – his career. Irwin Winkler, who produced De Niro in *New York, New York, Raging Bull, True Confessions* and *GoodFellas*, makes his directing debut here with the finesse of an accomplished filmmaker. *Guilty by Suspicion* is adult, absorbing and above all authentic, and delivers its punches without melodrama. [JC-W]

Also with: Annette Bening (Ruth Merrill), George Wendt (Robert 'Bunny' Baxter), Patricia Wettig (Dorothy Nolan), Sam Wanamaker (Felix Graff), Luke Edwards (Paulie Merrill), Chris Cooper (Larry Nolan), Ben Piazza (Darryl Zanuck), Martin Scorsese (Joe Lesser; based on Joseph Losey), Barry Primus, Gailard Sartain, Robin Gammell, Brad Sullivan, Tom Sizemore, Roxann Biggs, Stuart Margolin, Barry Tubb, Gene Kirkwood, Margo Winkler, Allan Rich, Al Ruscio, Adam Baldwin, Joan Scott, Dianne E. Reeves, Kevin Page. Dir and Screenplay: Irwin Winkler. Pro: Arnon Milchan. Ex Pro: Steven Reuther. Co-Pro: Alan C. Blomquist. Ph: Michael Ballhaus. Ed: Priscilla Nedd. Pro Des: Leslie Dilley. M: James Newton Howard; numbers performed by Nat King Cole, Marilyn Monroe, Billie Holiday, Louis Armstrong, Duke Ellington, Dianne E. Reeves and George Shearing. Costumes: Richard Bruno. Sound: Richard Lightstone. (Warner.) Rel: 24 May 1991. 105 mins. Cert 15.

The Hairdresser's Husband – Le Mari de la Coiffeuse. Asked by his father what he wants to be when he grows up, young Antoine answers, 'a hairdresser's husband'. His dream comes true many decades later when he proposes to the beautiful, voluptuous Mathilde while having his hair cut. A most unusual film from the director of *Monsieur Hire, The Hairdresser's Husband* mixes anecdote with a free-flowing cross-narrative of past and present. Little is explained (least of all Antoine's source of income), but this has never mattered less, particularly in the context of this sublime, sensuous fairy tale. Excellent use of close-ups and the undervalued art of silence. [JC-W]

Also with: Roland Bertin (Antoine's father), Maurice Chevit (Agopian), Henry Hocking (12-year-old Antoine), Julien Bukowski (gloomy man), Youssef Hamid (Tunisian customer), Thomas Rochefort (Little Edouard), Philippe Clevenot, Jacques Mathou, Claude Aufaure, Michele Laroque, Pierre Meyrand, Yveline Ailhaud, Christophe Pichon. Dir: Patrice Leconte. Pro: Thierry De Ganay. Line Pro: Monique Guerrier. Screenplay: Leconte and Claude Klotz. Ph: Eduardo Serra. Ed: Joelle Hache. Art: Ivan Maussion. M: Michael Nyman. Costumes: Cecile Magnan. Sound: Pierre Lenoir and Jean Goudier. (Lambart Prods/T .F.1 Films/Soficas Investimage 2 et 3 et Creations/ CNC–Palace.) Rel: 7 June 1991. 80 mins. Cert 15.

Hamlet. A spirited, colourful version of Shakespeare's tragedy, with Mel Gibson a very physical Prince of Denmark. Franco Zeffirelli returns to the Shakespearean stage after an absence of 22 years (he directed *Romeo and Juliet* in 1968, and *The Taming of the Shrew* in 1967) and shows that he's lost none of his zest. Gibson is surprisingly effective as a Hamlet of the Errol Flynn school, with full control of his vowels, and is backed up by a first-rate cast. Art direction, costumes and music are all top-notch, bringing a fresh glamour to the dusty pages of this oft-played classic. Other film Hamlets include Laurence Olivier (1948), Kishore Sahu (1954), Maximilian Schell (1960), Innokenti Smoktunovski (1964), Richard Burton (1964), Nicol Williamson (1969), Richard Chamberlain (TV, 1970), Anthony and David Meyer (1976), Pirkka-Pekka Petelius (1987), and, briefly, Iain Glen in *Rosencrantz and Guildenstern Are Dead* and Steven Grives in *Highlander II*. [JC-W]

Gertrude & Son recognise some painful home truths in Guild's spirited version of Hamlet, *with Glenn Close and Mel Gibson.*

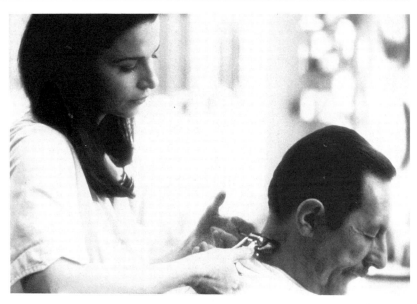

Anna Galiena seduces Jean Rochefort with her clippers in Patrice Leconte's life-affirming, would-be autobiographical The Hairdresser's Husband *(Palace).*

Also with: Glenn Close (Gertrude), Alan Bates (Claudius), Paul Scofield (the ghost), Ian Holm (Polonius), Helena Bonham-Carter (Ophelia), Stephen Dillane (Horatio), Nathaniel Parker (Laertes), Sean Murray (Guildenstern), Michael Maloney (Rosencrantz), Trevor Peacock (the gravedigger), John McEnery (Osric), Richard Warwick (Bernardo), Christien Anholt (Marcellus), Dave Duffy (Francisco), Vernon Dobtcheff (Reynaldo), Pete Postlethwaite (player king), Christopher Fairbank (player queen), Sarah Phillips, Justin Case, Roy Evans. Dir: Franco Zeffirelli. Pro: Dyson Lovell. Ex Pro: Bruce Davey. Screenplay: Zeffirelli and

Lamb to the slaughter: a fertile Offred (Natasha Richardson) is supplied to the Commander (Robert Duvall) to keep the master race going – in Virgin Vision's stilted The Handmaid's Tale.

Michael J. Fox and James Woods battle the scum of the New York subway in John Badham's periodically hilarious The Hard Way *(from UIP).*

at the end of the twentieth century. All women are divided into wives (most of whom have been rendered sterile by pollution) and cattle-prod wielding 'aunts' who, in turn, command the remaining fertile and HIV negative 'handmaids'. The last named are forced to bear children for the ruling elite, a militant, racist, sexist and God-fearing government of a country called Gilead. All very unconvincing, and sometimes downright embarrassing, even with the presence of such heavyweights as Robert Duvall and Faye Dunaway. Elizabeth McGovern, as a rebellious lesbian (penalised for her 'gender treachery'), burgles the acting honours. [JC-W]

Cast includes: Natasha Richardson (Kate), Faye Dunaway (Serena Joy), Aidan Quinn (Nick), Elizabeth McGovern (Moira), Victoria Tennant (Aunt Lydia), Robert Duvall (Commander), Blanche Baker, Traci Lin, Zoey Wilson, Kathryn Doby, Julian E. Bell, Randall Haynes. Dir: Volker Schlondorff. Pro: Daniel Wilson. Ex Pro: Wolfgang Glattes. Screenplay: Harold Pinter; based on the novel by Margaret Atwood. Ph: Igor Luther. Ed: David Ray. Pro Des: Tom Walsh. M: Ryuichi Sakamoto. Costumes: Colleen Atwood. Sound: Danny Michael. (Virgin Vision.) Rel: 2 November 1990. 108 mins. Cent 18.

Christophe De Vore. Ph: David Watkin. Ed: Richard Marden. Pro Des: Dante Ferretti. M: Ennio Morricone. Costumes: Maurizio Millenotti. Sound: David Stephenson. (Carolco–Guild.) Rel: 19 April 1991. 133 mins. Cert U.

The Handmaid's Tale. Self-important adaptation of Margaret Atwood's celebrated novel about a simplistic dystopia

The Hard Way. James Woods is at his wiry, edgy best as John Moss, a reckless New York cop on the trail of a serial killer. A muscular Stephen Lang (with cropped, peroxide hair) is The Party Crasher, a magnificent villain who enjoys blowing away coke dealers in crowded discos. And Michael J. Fox is the movie idol Nick Lang, a pint-sized Indiana Jones clone (and personal friend of Steven Spielberg) who wants to become a serious actor. To study for his part as a cop, Lang fastens on to Moss, puts on a false moustache and views the inner city like a Disneyland for dedicated actors. But real life keeps getting in the way. *The Hard Way* starts off on a winning wicket, making fun of Hollywood and paying homage to the New York cop movie, but eventually crystallises into the very thing it is sending up. Daniel Pyne's and Lem Dobbs's screenplay makes the most of the initial set-up (Woods's hatred of Fox, Fox's naivety and eagerness to learn), but the film cannot sustain the tension of the opening scenes or let us believe in Woods and Fox as more than just stereotypes. [JC-W]

Also with: Annabella Sciorra (Susan), Delroy Lindo (Capt. Brix), John Capodice, Luis Guzman, LL Cool J, Mary Mara, Conrad Roberts, Christina Ricci, Penny Marshall, George Cheung, Sharrieff Pugh, Bill Cobbs, John Costelloe, Jan Speck, William Truesdale, Bryant Gumbel. Dir: John Badham. Pro: William Sackheim and Rob Cohen. Screenplay: Daniel Pyne and Lem Dobbs; from a story by Dobbs and Michael Kozoll. Ph: Don McAlpine and Robert Primes. Ed: Frank Morriss and Tony Lombardo. Pro Des: Philip Harrison. M: Arthur B. Rubinstein; numbers performed by LL Cool J, Dion, Frankie Valli and The Four Seasons etc. Costumes: Mary Vogt. Sound: William L. Manger. 2nd Unit Director: Rob Cohen. (Universal–UIP.) Rel: 3 May 1991. 111 mins. Cert 15.

The end of William Hootkins as we know him: Victim No. 2 in Richard Stanley's chilling, style-conscious Hardware *(Palace).*

Hardware. Depending on how you care to look at it, this is either a highly original and surreal thriller or an incredibly pretentious load of scrap. Mark 13 is a cyborg built to destroy the 'enemy' and capable of both repairing and recharging itself from any energy source available. Discovered in a radioactive desert by a brain-dead nomad, the head of Mark 13 finds its way (as a bizarre Christmas present) into the apartment of a beautiful sculptress. There, in a stylised, nihilistic nightmare, cyborg meets metal modern art, and it's a stirring confrontation. Heavy metal music and a certain radioactive humour fill in

'Of all the gin joints in all the towns in all the world . . .': a rakish Robert Redford in the colossal, sluggish Havana *(from UIP).*

the chinks in the armour. Largely shot at London's old Roundhouse theatre for, reputedly, £800,000. [JC-W]

Cast includes: Dylan McDermott (Mo), Stacey Travis (Jill), John Lynch (Shades), William Hootkins (Lincoln), Iggy Pop (Angry Bob), Mark Northover (Alvy), Oscar James, Paul McKenzie, Carl McCoy, Lemmy (taxi driver). Dir and Screenplay: Richard Stanley. Pro: Joanne Sellar and Paul Trybits. Ex Pro: Nik Powell, Stephen Woolley and Trix Worrell. Ph: Steve Chivers. Ed: Derek Trigg. Pro Des: Joseph Bennett. M: Simon Boswell. Costumes: Michael Baldwin. Sound: Jonathan Miller and Kate Hopkins. (British Screen/BSB/Wicked Films–Palace.) Rel: 5 October 1990. 95 mins. Cert 18.

Havana. Robert Redford lays on the star power as a beautiful, rugged gambler who has 'been a lot of places, and liked every one of them – even Vegas'. It is 1959 and the youthful 54-year-old Jack Wild has come to Havana, Cuba, to play cards, bed women and make a

Fred Ward and Uma Thurman as Henry and June, *as seen through the eyes of erotic diarist Anaïs Nin – from UIP.*

lot of money. What he hadn't bargained on was falling in love with the 'seriously beautiful' Bobby Duran, a *Vogue*-cover revolutionary. The critics dug their knives into this $40 million *Casablanca* transplant, an old-fashioned saga of love and greed in high places, and it's easy to see why. After the movie finally, *finally* ends, you feel like you've just put down a very heavy, glossy magazine. And only Redford could actually get away with dialogue like 'Something happened to me last week, Joe – I realised I wasn't going to die young.' [JC-W]

Also with: Lena Olin (Bobby Duran), Alan Arkin (Joe Volpi), Raul Julia (Arturo Duran), Tomas Milian (Menocal), Daniel Davis (Marion Chaigwell), Tony Plana (Julio Ramos), Betsy Brantley, Lise Cutter, Richard Farnsworth, Mark Rydell, Vasek Simek, Fred Asparagus, Richard Portnow, Dion Anderson, Bernie Pollack, Owen Roizman, Hugh Kelly. Dir: Sydney Pollack. Pro: Pollack and Richard Roth. Ex Pro: Ronald L. Schwary. Screenplay: Judith

Rascoe and David Rayfiel; from a story by Rascoe. Ph: Owen Roizman. Ed: Frederic Steinkamp and William Steinkamp. Pro Des: Terence Marsh. M: Dave Grusin; songs performed by Frank Sinatra, Perry Como, Doris Day, The Andrews Sisters, Fats Domino, Frankie Lymon, Dean Martin, Bobby Darin etc. Costumes: Bernie Pollack. Sound: Peter Handford. (Universal–UIP.) Rel: 25 January 1991. 145 mins. Cert 15.

Heart Condition. Disagreeable black comedy about a racist, junk food-devouring, chain-smoking LA vice cop who inherits the black heart of his *bête noire*. Bob Hoskins is the cussing, panting cop Jack Mooney, Denzel Washington the suave, attractive, slick lawyer Napoleon Stone who accompanies the disbelieving, irritable Mooney on his errands. In the year of the ghost epidemic (*Always, Ghost, Ghost Dad, Ghosts Can't Do It – ad nauseam*), *Heart Condition* was one addition we could have done without. Sentimental, violent, sexist, racist, clichéd . . . [JC-W]

Also with: Chloe Webb (Crystal Gerrity), Jeffrey Meek (Graham), Kieran Mulroney

(Dillnick), Ray Baker (Harry Zara), Roger E. Mosley (Captain Wendt), Alan Rachins (Dr Posner), Lisa Stahl, Ja'net Dubois. Dir and Screenplay: James D. Parriott. Pro: Steve Tisch. Ex Pro: Robert Shaye. Co-Pro: Marie Cantin and Bernie Goldmann. Ph: Arthur Albert. Ed: David Finfer. Pro Des: John Muto. M: Patrick Leonard. Costumes: Louise Frogley. (Enterprise.) Rel: 12 October 1990, 100 mins. Cert 15.

Heavy Petting. Director Obie Benz spent years researching material for this documentary about the silly side of sex and the even sillier way America has treated it. The extracts from old films, children's sex-instruction movies and other gems are hilarious. To add to the fun Benz assembles a nice line-up of people to relate their sexual experiences: people like Josh Mostel, David Byrne, Laurie Anderson and Allan Ginsberg etc. Fun! [FDM]

Dir and Pro: Obie Benz. Co-Pro: Carol Noblitt. Co-Dir: Josh Waletzky. Ph: Sandi Sissel. Ed: Waletzky and Judith Sobol. (Fossil Films–ICA.) Rel: floating; first shown London (ICA) 14 December 1990. 80 mins. No cert.

Forever Ireland: Maurice Roeves is abducted in broad daylight in Ken Loach's brilliant, controversial attack on the British government of Northern Ireland, in Hidden Agenda *(from Enterprise).*

Henry and June. Paris, 1931. Picturesque telling of the passionate, intellectual and illicit affair between the penniless Henry Miller and the wealthy French diarist Anaïs Nin. Fred Ward (signed up after Alec Baldwin backed out) is unlikely casting as the controversial novelist, but lends an earthy, masculine air to the man who accused D. H. Lawrence of being a prude. Portuguese actress Maria De Medeiros (*La Lectrice*) bears an uncanny resemblance to Nin, a small, frail figure in the Edith Piaf mould. But for all the film's artistic pretensions and fine acting, it will be best remembered for being a thorn in the side of the American censor. Such was the controversy surrounding the picture's X-rating, that a new certificate – the NC17 – was created for the film's American release. (See the September entry in this edition's Film World Diary.) [JC-W]

Also with: Uma Thurman (June Miller), Richard E. Grant (Hugo), Kevin Spacey (Osborn), Jean-Philippe Ecoffey (Eduardo), Bruce Myers, Jean-Louis Bunuel, Feodor Atkine, Sylvie Huguel, Artus De Penguern, Pierre Edernac, Gaetan Bloom. Dir: Philip Kaufman. Pro: Peter Kaufman. Screenplay: Philip Kaufman and Rose Kaufman; based on the book by Anaïs Nin. Ph: Philippe Rousselot. Ed: Vivien Hillgrove, William S. Scharf and Dede Allen. Pro Des: Guy-Claude François. M: Mark Adler. Costumes: Yvonne Sassinot De Nesle. Sound: Alan Splet. (Universal–UIP.) Rel: 23 November 1990. 136 mins. Cert 18.

Hidden Agenda. Articulate, controversial thriller in which a senior English police official, Peter Kerrigan (Brian Cox), is asked to investigate the murder of an American lawyer in Belfast. Unafraid to bash his way through the thickest red tape, Kerrigan exposes a police cover-up that extends to the highest levels of British government. Brian Cox, in his first starring film role, delivers a powerful *tour de force* in Ken Loach's uncharacteristically slick thriller. Still, the working-class, gritty anger of the director of *Kes* and *Father-*

land is thankfully evident, making this a compelling, uncompromising look at the war in Ireland. Although blatantly one-sided, *Hidden Agenda* does provide a feast of food for thought. A powerful, important film, winner of the Jury Prize at Cannes. [JC-W]

Also with: Frances McDormand (Ingrid), Brad Dourif (Paul), Mai Zetterling (Moa), Maurice Roeves (Harris), Bernard Archard (Sir Robert Neil), Robert Patterson, Bernard Bloch, George Staines, Michelle Fairley, Brian McCann, Des McAleer, Patrick Cavanagh, John Benfield, John Keegan, Jim Norton, Jack McElhinney, Maureen Bell. Dir: Ken Loach. Pro: Eric Fellner. Co-Pro: Rebecca O'Brien. Ex Pro: John Daly and Derek Gibson. Screenplay: Jim Allen. Ph: Clive Tickner. Ed: Jonathan Morris. Pro Des: Martin Johnson. M: Stewart Copeland. Costumes: Daphne Dare. Sound: Simon Okin. (Initial Film and Television–Enterprise.) Rel: 11 January 1991. 108 mins. Cert 15.

Highlander II – The Quickening. Whizz-bang, pop videoesque sequel to the cult 1986 fantasy epic that injected some flair into the time-worn theme of time travel, if not the predicted box-

Chic trash and high dramatics: Christopher Lambert and Michael Ironside slug it out in Russell Mulcahy's entertaining sequel High-lander II – The Quickening *(Entertainment).*

office muscle. Christophe(r) Lambert is back as the immortal Scot with the French accent, now an old man living on earth in 2024. Thanks to his invention (25 years earlier) of a global shield to replace the ozone layer, the world is a stuffy, irritable place suffering from a constant 97° humidity. Worse still, the shield is in the hands of greedy businessman 'Blake' (John C. McGinley), who is holding the world to ransom – with the help of the even nastier General Katana (Michael Ironside), from the planet Zeist. Time for some of that old-fashioned magic and a return from the past for the wisecracking, sword-wielding Sean Connery. All very silly, played with enormous elan by Ironside, Connery and the special effects department. Witty, stylish and entertaining trash. [JC-W]

Cast includes: Christopher Lambert (Connor MacLeod), Virginia Madsen (Louise Marcus), Sean Connery (Juan Villa-Lobos Ramirez), Allan Rich (Alan Neyman), Steven Grives (Hamlet), Eddie Trucco, Peter Buccossi, Peter Antico, Phil Brock, Rusty Schwimmer. Dir: Russell Mulcahy. Pro: Peter S. Davis and William Panzer. Ex Pro: Guy Collins and Mario Sotela. Screenplay: Peter Bellwood; from a story by Brian Clemens and William Panzer. Ph: Phil Meheux. Ed: Hubert C. De La Bouillerie, John Rathbourne and Anthony Redman. Pro Des: Roger Hall. M: Stewart Copeland. Costumes: Deborah Everton. Sound: Ed White. (Lamb Bear Entertainment–Entertainment). Rel: 12 April 1991. 100 mins. Cert 15.

Home Alone. The McCallister family (all fifteen of them) are preparing for their Christmas vacation in Paris. When a power cut makes them late for the airport, they leave 8-year-old Kevin behind in the rush. Not that he cares – he hates his squabbling, chaotic family and can now 'eat junk food and watch rubbish' to his heart's content. Still, Kevin has some growing up to do, particularly when two burglars target the McCallister home for an easy break-in. John Hughes, Hollywood's Chicago-based expert on celluloid Christmases-with-the-family, hit pay dirt when this took the US box office by storm. A modern-day live-action cartoon, *Home Alone* is essentially a fairy tale with enough messages to stock a children's encyclopaedia (don't be afraid of the dark, junk food is *not* nutritious, Mummy didn't mean it). Charming, funny, sentimental and ideal entertainment for the *whole* family. One of the best Christmas movies to come out of Hollywood in aeons. [JC-W]

Cast includes: Macaulay Culkin (Kevin), Joe Pesci (Harry), Daniel Stern (Marv), John Heard (Peter McCallister), Roberts Blossom (Marley), Catherine O'Hara (Kate McCallister), Angela Goethals, Devin Ratray, Gerry Bamman, Hillary Wolf, John Candy (Gus Polinski), Larry Hankin, Michael C. Maronna, Kristin Minter, Kieran Culkin, Jeffrey Wiseman, Bill Erwin. Dir: Chris Columbus. Pro and Screenplay: John Hughes. Ex Pro: Mark Levinson, Scott Rosenfelt and Tarquin Gotch. Ph: Julio Macat. Ed: Raja Gosnell. Pro Des: John Muto. M: John Williams; numbers performed by Mel Tormé, The Drifters, Brenda Lee, Chuck Berry etc. Costumes:

Jay Hurley. Sound: Jim Alexander. (Fox.)
Rel: 7 December 1990. 103 mins. Cert PG.

The Hot Spot. Sluggish, sultry, erotic
drama from Dennis Hopper, set in the
boondocks of Texas. Don Johnson
plays the stranger in town, Harry
Madox, a good-looking drifter who
immediately starts making himself at
home. On his first day he secures a job
as a car salesman and then starts picking out the good-looking women – Virginia Madsen, married to his boss, and
19-year-old Jennifer Connelly, his
boss's secretary. Behaving like he's got
'a grudge against the world', Madox
soon meets his match when the town's
darker elements sift to the surface.
Adultery, robbery and blackmail erupt
in a town where 'there's only two things
to do . . . and if you don't have a TV,
you're down to one.' Compelling stuff,
if you're prepared to fidget through the
longueurs. [JC-W]

Also with: Virginia Madsen (Dolly Har-
shaw), Jennifer Connelly (Gloria Harper),
Charles Martin Smith (Lon Gulik), William
Sadler (Frank Sutton), Jerry Hardin (George
Harshaw), Barry Corbin, Leon Rippy, Jack
Nance, Virgil Frye, John Hawker. Dir:
Dennis Hopper. Pro: Paul Lewis. Ex Pro:
Bill Gavin, Derek Power and Stephen
Ujlaki. Co-Pro: Deborah Capograsso.
Screenplay: Nona Tyson and Charles Wil-
liams; based on the novel *Hell Hath No Fury*
by Williams. Ph: Ueli Steiger. Ed: Wende
Phifer Mate. Pro Des: Cary White. M: Jack
Nitzsche, with songs performed by Billy
Squier, Hank Williams Jr, k. d. lang etc.
Costumes: Mary Kay Stolz. Sound: Jim
Tanenbaum. (Orion–Rank.) Rel: 7
December 1990. 130 mins. Cert 18.

House Party. Minor but quite entertaining comedy which follows in the
footsteps of the white teenager Beach
Party movies of the '60s. This time it's
the black kids who defeat the bullies
and the spoil-sport adults. Comedy,
dancing and rhythm. [FDM]

Cast includes: Christopher Reid (Kid),
Robin Harris (Pop), Christopher Martin
(Play), Martin Lawrence (Bilal), Tisha
Campbell (Sidney), A. J. Johnson (Shar-
ane), Paul Anthony, Bowlegged Lou, B.
Fine, Edith Fields, Kelly Jo Minter, Clifton
Powell, Verda Bridges, Desi Arnez Hines
II, Lou D. Washington, Kimi-Sung. Dir
and Screenplay: Reginald Hudlin. Pro:
Warrington Hudlin. Ex Pro: Gerald Olson.

Ph: Peter Deming. Ed: Earl Watson. Pro
Des: Bryan Jones. Art: Susan Richardson.
Sound: Oliver Moss. M: Marcus Miller.
(Hudlin Bros-New Line Cinema–Enterpr-
ise.) Rel: floating; first shown London
(Odeon Mezzanine; Cannon, Panton St,
Oxford St, Chelsea) 31 August 1990. 95
mins. Cert 15.

*Kevin McCallister (Macaulay Culkin) faces
the adult facts in John Hughes's enchanting
moral comedy,* Home Alone *(Fox).*

*Lust in the boondocks: Don Johnson and Vir-
ginia Madsen – in Dennis Hopper's sultry, sluggish* The Hot Spot *(from Rank).*

Dreams are made of this: Jean-Pierre Leaud romances Margi Clarke in the pub in Aki Kaurismaki's Keatonesque comedy, I Hired a Contract Killer *(from Electric).*

Hush-a-Bye-Baby. Unwanted pregnancy and the moral issues of abortion are at the heart of this Northern Irish film about a group of schoolgirls living in a Catholic housing estate in Derry. Made with very modest resources, there's a lot of promise here from several newcomers, in front of and behind the cameras, including first-time director Margo Harker and young actress Emer McCourt. [FDM]

Cast also includes: Michael Liebmann, Sinéad O'Connor. Dir: Margo Harker. Pro: Tom Collins. M: Sinéad O'Connor. (The Derry Film and Video Workshop–ICA.) Rel: floating; first shown London (ICA) 27 July 1990. 72 mins. No cert.

I Bought a Vampire Motor Cycle. 'We started out to write the most frightening, horrifying and disgusting film we could think of,' explains producer-scripter Mycal Miller, 'but for some

reason, whatever we wrote made people laugh.' Not everybody. The completed film was banned from a horror festival on the grounds of indecency, and horror maestro Sam Raimi found the whole concept 'really horrible', or so the production notes tell us. There is some kind of plot, concerning the blood lust of a Norton motorbike possessed by a demonic force. Sucking the blood out of Hell's Angels and traffic wardens, it seems indestructible until faced by the garlic breath of Michael Elphick's Inspector Cleaver. Mmmm. With lines like 'Let's go and kick some bottom,' you can appreciate how infantile all this is. Filmed in the back streets of Birmingham. [CB]

Also with: Neil Morrissey (Noddy), Amanda Noar (Kim), Anthony Daniels (priest), Andrew Powell, George Rossi, Midge Taylor, Daniel Peacock, David Daker, Burt Kwouk, Brendan Donnison, Ann Casson, Douglas Campbell, Ed Devereaux, Jim Allan, Alan Frank, Colin Campbell, Esta Charkham. Dir: Dirk Campbell. Pro and Screenplay: Mycal Miller and John Wolskel. Assoc Pro: Jim Allan. Ph: Tom Ingle. Ed: Mycal Miller. Art: Jose Furtado. M: Dean Friedman. Costumes:

Denver Hall. Sound: Steve Phillips. (Dirk Prods–HoBo.) Rel: 6 July 1990. 104 mins. Cert 18.

I Hired a Contract Killer. When Her Majesty's Waterworks in London is privatised, Henri Boulanger (Jean-Pierre Léaud) finds himself out of work. Checking his address book, he discovers he has only two telephone numbers: one for his deceased aunt, the other for the company that has just fired him. For Henri, suicide is the only option. Unfortunately, his attempts at killing himself are foiled by fate, so the sad little Frenchman takes out a contract on his own life. Shortly afterwards he falls in love with Margaret (Margi Clarke), a flower girl. Riveting commedy-drama from cult Finnish film-maker Aki Kaurismaki (*Ariel, Leningrad Cowboys Go America*), *I Hired a Contract Killer* is an old story approached with a fresh simplicity. Léaud, Truffaut's former *alter ego*, produces a superb portrait of controlled pathos (in the tradition of Buster Keaton) while Karismaki paints a London of graffiti and decay. But, ultimately, it is the attention to character and detail that makes this film so richly rewarding. [JC-W]

Also with: Kenneth Colley (the killer), Tony Rohr (Frank), Serge Reggiani (Vic), Trevor Bowen, Imogen Clare, Angela Walsh, Nicky Tesco, Charles Cork, Michael O'Hagan, Walter Sparrow, Joe Strummer, Roberto Pla, Ette Eliot. Dir, Pro, Screenplay and Ed: Aki Kaurismaki. Ph: Timo Salminen. Pro Des: John Ebden. Sound: Timo Linnasalo and Jouko Lumme. (Villealfa Filmprods/Swedish Film Institute/Channel 4–Electric.) Rel: 15 February 1991. 80 mins. Cert 15.

I Love You to Death. Off-beat black comedy (based on the true story of Frances and Tony Toto) about a cheated wife who plots to kill her husband. Considering the talents involved, this should have been a lot funnier – but it does have some hysterical moments. John Kostmayer's script is encrusted with verbal gems ('If we keep shooting Joey, don't you think he'll start to get suspicious?') and Joan Plowright steals the show as a Yugoslav amateur mechanic. Tracey Ullman makes her American film debut as the provoked wife – after Meryl Streep turned the part down. [JC-W]

Cast includes: Kevin Kline (Joey), Tracey Ullman (Rosalie), River Phoenix (Devo), Joan Plowright (Nadja), William Hurt (Harlan), Keanu Reeves (Marlon), James Gammon, Jack Kehler, Victoria Jackson, Miriam Margolyes, Alisan Porter, Jon Kasdan, Heather Graham, Michelle Joyner, John Kostmayer, Kathleen York, Phoebe Cates. Dir: Lawrence Kasdan. Pro: Jeffrey Lurie and Ron Moler. Ex Pro: Charles Okun and Michael Grillo. Screenplay: John Kostmayer. Ph: Owen Roizman. Ed: Anne V. Coates. Pro Des: Lilly Kilvert. M: James Horner. Costumes: Aggie Guerard Rodgers. Sound: Robert Grieve. (Tri-Star–Columbia.) Rel. 21 September 1990. 98 mins. Cert 15.

√ **The Icicle Thief – Ladri di Saponette**. Crazy Italian satirical send-up of TV commercials: the device of a film within a film parodies *Bicycle Thieves*, the de Sica classic which launched neo-realism. The 'Icicle' of the title is a glass chandelier, the theft of which leads to some very complicated fun and games. [FDM]

Cast includes: Maurizio Nichetti (Nichetti/Antonio), Caterini Sylos Labini (Maria), Federico Rizzo (Bruno), Renato Scarpa (Don Italo), Heidi Komarex (model), Carlina Torta, Massimo Sacilotto, Claudio Fava, Lella Costa, Marco Zanoni, Annamaria Torniai, Clara Droetto, Enesto Calindri, Matteo Augnardi. Dir and (with Mauro Monti) Screenplay: Maurizio Nichetti. Pro: Ernesto di Sarro. Pro Sup: Andrea Martinazzi. Ph: Maria Battistoni. Ed: Rita Rossi and Anna Misoni. Pro Des: Ada Legori. M: Manuel De Sica and Franco Godi. (Bambu in assoc with Reitalia–Metro Pictures.) Rel: floating; first shown London (Metro) 16 November 1990. 90 mins. Cert PG.

Impromptu. 1836–8, France. Thoroughly entertaining, witty and articulate account of George Sand's passion for Chopin (both the man and his music). Described by Mandy Patinkin as 'a 19th-century *Big Chill*', *Impromptu* is, in the words of its writer, 'a free association on a series of themes. So the history of George Sand and Chopin is my theme and the events of the script are my impromptu. Of course', she continues, 'my hope is that I know both characters so well that my free associations have the ring of truth about them.' Seldom has a film this funny looked so good, sounded so intelligent or been so touching. An all-star cast inhabit their real-life characters with gusto, hitting the balance just right between the plodding gloss of a Hal B.

Wallis costumer and the absurd excesses of a Ken Russell biography. [JC-W]

Cast includes: Judy Davis (George Sand), Hugh Grant (Frederic Chopin), Mandy Patinkin (Alfred de Musset), Bernadette Peters (Marie d'Agoult), Julian Sands (Franz Liszt), Ralph Brown (Eugene Delacroix),

William Hurt and Keanu Reeves as Harlan and Marlon, the would-be killers in Lawrence Kasdan's sporadically hilarious I Love You to Death *(from Columbia Tri-Star).*

All-star soap from the past: Judy Davis as George Sand and Mandy Patinkin as Alfred de Musset in James Lapine's stylish and witty Impromptu *(from Rank).*

Tom Hanks and Meg Ryan face the volcano and its various implications in John Patrick Shanley's meandering joyride, Joe Versus the Volcano, *from Warner.*

Georges Corraface (Felicien Mallefille), Anton Rodgers (Duke d'Antan), Emma Thompson (Duchess d'Antan), Anna Massey (George Sand's mother), David Birkin, Sylvie Herbert, Annette Milsom, John Savident, Lucy Speed, Elizabeth Spriggs, Fiona Vincente. Dir: James Lapine. Pro: Stuart Oken and Daniel A. Sherkow. Ex Pro: Jean Nachbaur. Screenplay: Sarah Kernochan. Ph: Bruno de Keyzer. Ed: Michael Ellis. Art: Gerard Daoudal. M: Chopin; supervised by John Strauss. Costumes: Jenny Beavan. Sound: Peter Glossop. (Sovereign/Governor Prods/Les Films Ariane–Rank.) Rel: 12 April 1991. 107 mins. Cert 12.

Interrogation. Krystyna Janda (*Man of Marble, Man of Iron*) deservedly won the best actress award at Cannes for her role as a bit actress who is inexplicably arrested by the Polish police and put through a series of harrowing 'interrogations'. Gradually Tonia (Janda) realises that her imprisonment and ritualistic sexual abuse is no mistake, and

the human drama turns into a battle of wills between her and her captors. Set in 1951 at the time of the Stalinist terror, the film was actually made in 1981 – but banned for eight years under martial law in Poland. A remarkable, challenging film that stands up to the test of time. [CB]

Cast includes: Krystyna Janda (Antonia Dziwisz), Adama Ferencego (Morawski), Agnieszka Holland (Witowska), Janusz Gajos (Zawada), Anna Romantowska, Bozena Dykiel, Olgierda Lukaszewicza. Dir and (with Janusza Dymka) Screenplay: Ryszard Bugajski. Pro Ex: Tadeuse Dreng. Ph: Jacek Petrycky. Ed: Katarzyna Maciejko. Art: Janusz Sosnowski. M: various songs. Costumes: Jolanta Jackowska and Jolanta Gerneralczyk. Sound: Danuta Zankowska and Tadeusz Wosinski. (Zespoly Filmowe/Unit X–Gala.) Rel: floating; first shown London (Cannon Premiere) 20 July 1990. 117 mins. Cert 18.

Jetsons: The Movie. Hanna and Barbera bring their animated cartoon series from TV to the big screen with only so-so results. Not much here for grown-ups, but children may possibly enjoy this space-age sitcom. [FDM]

With the voices of: George O'Hanlon (George Jetson), Mel Blanc, Penny Singleton, Tiffany, Patric Zimmerman, Don Messick, Jean Van Der Pyl, Ronnie Schell etc. Dir and Pro: William Hanna and Joseph Barbera. Screenplay: Dennis Marks. M: John Debney. (Hanna/Barbera Studios in assoc with Wang Films Pro and Cuckoos Nest Studios-Universal–UIP.) Rel: floating; first shown London (Cannon, Oxford St) 22 March 1991. 82 mins. Cert U.

√**Joe Versus the Volcano.** Old-fashioned, rambling morality tale with Tom Hanks as a nobody trapped in an Orwellian nightmare on Staten Island. You know: lousy job, crumbling apartment, friendless existence. Life couldn't get any worse, could it? Wrong. The doctor (Robert Stack) tells Joe he's got a 'brain cloud' and only six months to live. It's the news Joe needed to wake himself up. Occasionally magical, occasionally plodding misfire that harks back to Capra & Co., complete with a chain of telling cameos. Directorial debut for *Moonstruck* scripter John Patrick Shanley. Great soundtrack. [JC-W]

Cast includes: Tom Hanks (Joe Banks), Meg Ryan (DeDe/Angelica/Patricia), Lloyd Bridges (Graynamore), Robert Stack (Dr Ellison), Abe Vigoda (Chief of the Waponis), Dan Hedaya (Mr Waturi), Barry McGovern (luggage salesman), Amanda Plummer (Dagmar), Ossie Davis (Marshall), James Haynes, Darrell Zwerling, Jim Ryan. Dir and Screenplay: John Patrick Shanley. Pro: Teri Schwartz. Ex Pro: Steven Spielberg, Kathleen Kennedy and Frank Marshall. Ph: Stephen Goldblatt. Ed: Richard Halsey. Pro Des: Bo Welch. M: Georges Delerue; songs performed by Eric Burdon, The Ink Spots, Elvis Presley, Ray Charles, Tom Hanks etc. Costumes: Colleen Atwood. Sound: Keith A. Wester. (Amblin –Warner.) Rel: 6 July 1990. 102 mins. Cert PG.

Ju Dou. Set in a dye factory, with a dazzlingly beautiful use of the rich colours available, this Zhang Yi-mou directed Chinese-Japanese co-production is an artistic triumph. (Zhang also helmed the Golden Bear Berlin Festival winner *Red Sorghum*.) The story may be old (old man, young and unfaithful wife . . .), but it holds one's attention right the way through to the melodramatic ending. [FDM]

Cast includes: Gong Li (Ju Dou), Li Bao-tian (Yang Tian-quing), Zhang Yi, Zhen Ji-an. Dir: Zhang Yi-mou with Yang Feng-liang. Pro: Zhang Wen-ze, Yasuyoshi Tokuma and Hu Jian. Screenplay: Lui Heng. Ph: Gu Chang-Wei and Yang Lun. Ed: Du Yuan. Pro Des: Cao Jiu-Ping and Rujin. M: Zhao Ji-ping. (China Film/Tokuma Shoten Publishing and Communications/Ex and Import Corp, co-pro with Xi-An Film Studio–ICA.) Rel: floating; first shown London (ICA) 22 March 1991. 95 mins. No cert.

Kamikaze Hearts. Naked lesbians frolic and cavort their way through a script composed almost entirely of four-letter words. In what is claimed to be 'part fiction, part fact' Mitch and Tigr live out their dreams and frustrations against a backdrop of the desperate eroticism of the porn world. Rubbish masquerading as art. [FDM]

Cast includes: Tigr Mennett, Sharon Mitchell, Jon Martin, Sparky Vasque, Jerry Abrahams, Robert McKenna, Jorge, Mantra, Jenifer Blowdryer. Dir: Juliet Bashore. Screenplay: Bashore, Tigr Mennett and John Knoop. Pro: Heinz Legler, Sharon Hennessey and Bob Rivkin. Ex Pro: Heinz Legler. Ph: David Golia. Ed: John Knoop. Art: Hans Fuss. M: Paul M. Young and

Walter Fowler. (Metro Pictures Ltd.) Rel: floating; first shown London (Metro) 20 July 1990. 80 mins. No cert.

Kickboxer 2: The Road Back. Lacking *Kickboxer 1*'s star attraction Jean-Claude Van Damme (and a lot else besides), this flimsily plotted actioner seems unlikely to win kickboxing any new fans. [FDM]

Cast includes: Sasha Mitchell (Sloan), Peter Boyle (Justin), Dennis Chan (Xian Chow), Cary-Hiroyuki Tagawa, John Diehl, Michel Qissi, Heather McComb, Vince Murducco, Mathias Hues. Dir: Albert Pyun. Pro: Tom Karnowski. Screenplay: David Goyer. Ph: Mark Emery Moore. Ed: Alan E. Baumgarten. Art: Nicholas T. Prevolos. M: Tony Riparetti and James Saad. (Kings Road Entertainment–Entertainment Dist.) Rel: floating; first shown London (Cannon, Panton St and Oxford St) 1 February 1991. 90 mins. Cert 18.

Kid. Listen to this dialogue: 'What are you doing here?' asks the native. 'I've come for the ocean air,' replies the stranger. 'But the nearest ocean is two states away.' 'Somebody lied.' *Kid* is this corny, although the film somehow keeps our interest. C. Thomas Howell

You have been warned: C. Thomas Howell as the Kid who shaves, in Entertainment's cod Western.

turns up in Whitebrush, Arizona, the hub of Nowhere, and in spite of his boyish looks proves to be all man. A serial killer at heart, the Kid just has a few scores to settle, squints into the sunset and wins our sympathy because everybody else is *really* nasty. Part thriller, part love story and even occasionally amusing, *Kid* is basically a work-manlike Western in modern clothes. Look out for young Brian Austin Green as a good-natured heavy metal freak – he could go far. [JC-W]

Cast includes: C. Thomas Howell (the Kid), Sarah Trigger (Kate), Brian Austin Green (Metal Louie), R. Lee Ermey (Luke Clayton), Dale Dye (Garvey), Michael Bowen (Harlan), Damon Bowen (Pete), Lenore Kasdorf (Alice), Michael Cavanaugh, Tony Epper, Don Collier, Don Baker, Don Starr, Fred Sugarman, Heather McNair. Dir: John Mark Robinson. Pro: Robert L. Levy, Peter Abrams and Natan Zahavi. Ex Pro: J. P. Guerin. Screenplay: Leslie Bohem. Ph: Robert Yeoman. Ed: Natan Zahavi. Pro Des: Sharon Seymour. M: Tim Truman. Costumes: Cynthia Bergstrom. Sound: Don A. Sanders. (Tapestry–Medusa.) Rel: 2 November 1990. 92 mins. Cert 18.

The Killer. Technically excellent, highly melodramatic and very bloody Hong Kong production about a hit man who 'wants out' but finds his way there strewn with corpses. Breathless action. [FDM]

Cast includes: Chow Yun-Fat (Jeffrey), Sally Yeh (Jenny), Danny Lee (Det. Lee), Kenneth Tsang (Det. Randy), Chu Kong, Shing Fui-on. Dir and Screenplay: John Woo. Pro: Tsui Hark. Ph: Won Wing-Hang. M: Lowell Lowe. (Film Workshop-Golden Princess-Marnum–ICA.) Rel: floating; first shown London (ICA) 10 August 1990. 110 mins. No cert.

Kindergarten Cop. Efficient formula vehicle for Arnold Schwarzenegger, who once again plays a ruthless undercover cop. Sporting dark glasses and free-swinging raincoat, Arnie is John Kimble, a wisecracking killing machine who blasts his way through LA with a big gun. Assigned to trace the 6-year-old son of a ruthless murderer, Kimble is forced undercover as a kindergarten teacher in a soporific corner of Colorado. The kids prove more troublesome than your average low-life, providing plenty of laughs and playpens of sentimentality. You know what's going to

Vork dis vay: Arnold Schwarzenegger brings mayhem to the classroom in Ivan Reitman's predictably amusing Kindergarten Cop *(UIP).*

happen, but the enjoyment of getting there is half the fun. The dialogue crackles, and Pamela Reed is good value as Kimble's food-obsessed partner. [JC-W]

Also with: Penelope Ann Miller (Joyce), Pamela Reed (Phoebe), Linda Hunt (Miss Schlowski), Richard Tyson (Crisp), Carroll Baker (Eleanor Crisp), Cathy Moriarty (Sylvester's mother), Jayne Brook (Zach's mother), Richard Portnow (Captain Salazar), Joseph Cousins, Christian Cousins, Park Overall, Tom Kurlander, Alix Koromzay, Betty Lou Henson, Heidi Swedberg, Stephen Root, John Hamil, Michael Chapman, Kenneth Chapman, Catherine Reitman, Jason Reitman, Justin Page, Peter Rakow, Sarah Rose Karr, Marissa Rosen. Dir: Ivan Reitman. Pro: Reitman and Brian Grazer. Ex Pro: Joe Medjuck and Michael C. Gross. Screenplay: Murray Salem, Herschel Weingrod and Timothy Harris; from

Christopher Walken, as Frank White, surveys his realm – in Abel Ferrara's forceful thriller, 'King of New York' (Rank).

King Ralph *Jones (John Goodman) entertains his royal guests at Buck House with a sampling of 'Good Golly, Miss Molly' – in David S. Ward's right royal cock-up. From UIP.*

a story by Salem. Ph: Michael Chapman. Ed: Sheldon Kahn and Wendy Greene Bricmont. Pro Des: Bruno Rubeo. M: Randy Edelman. Costumes: Gloria Gresham. Sound: Gene S. Cantamessa. (Imagine/Universal–UIP.) Rel: 1 February 1991. 111 mins. Cert 12.

'King of New York'. Stylish and extremely violent gangster film, with Christopher Walken as the cold-blooded don just released from prison. While ensconced in a luxurious Manhattan hotel, drinking champagne and surrounded by beautiful bodyguards, Frank White methodically arranges to have his rival drug kings terminated. The police are a nuisance, and will be dealt with, but Frank's prime concern is raising the $6 million needed to keep open the South Bronx hospital of his old neighbourhood. Walken plays the calm, benign killer with enormous

strength and dignity – even when snatching some nookie on a moving subway train. Director Abel Ferrara (*Driller Killer, China Girl*) lays on the atmosphere with a paint brush. A powerful good-looking addition to the gangster genre, released two years too late. Filmed in 1989. [JC-W]

Also with: David Caruso (Dennis Gilley), Larry Fishburne (Jimmy Jump), Victor Argo (Lt Roy Bishop), Wesley Snipes (Thomas Flanigan), Janet Julian (Jennifer), Joey Chin (Larry Wong), Frank Gio (Arty Clay), Jay Julien (Abraham Cott), Freddy Jackson (as himself), Giancarlo Esposito, Paul Calderon, Steve Buscemi, Theresa Randle, Leonard Lee Thomas, Roger Smith, Carrie Nygren, Ernest Abuba, Frank Adonis, Vanessa Angel, Erica Gimpel, Susannah Julien, James Lorinz, Gerald Murphy, Marty Pesci, Ariane, Peter Hamill, Sari Chang. Dir: Abel Ferrara. Pro: Mary Kane. Ex Pro: Jay Julien and Vittorio Squillante. Screenplay: Nicholas St John. Ph: Bojan Bazelli. Pro Des: Alex Tavoularis. M: Joe Delia; Vivaldi; numbers performed by Party Posse, Schooly D, Haywood Gregory, Freddy Jackson. Costumes: Carol Ramsey. Sound: Drew Kunin. (Reteitalia SPA/Scena Int. SRL–Rank.) Rel: 21 June 1991. 104 mins. Cert 18.

King Ralph. When the 'entire' British royal family is electrocuted during a family portrait, Las Vegas slob John Goodman is made King of England. It's not his idea but, hell, he needs a job. What Ralph Jones lacks in the social graces and a knowledge of English history (and geography), is made up for by a superb cricket batting hand and – well, he's a decent bloke. Occasionally this outrageous $21m comedy throws up sparks, due more to an excellent cast than any pomp or circumstance. Goodman is at his loveable best, Peter O'Toole repeats his royal tutor bit from *The Last Emperor* and John Hurt has fun with his accent as the treacherous Lord Graves (you have to admire those vowel movements). Based on Emlyn Williams's novel *Headlong*, and filmed at various stately homes around England. [JC-W]

Also with: Peter O'Toole (Cedric Willingham), Camille Coduri (Miranda), Richard Griffiths (Duncan Phipps), Joely Richardson (superbly funny as Princess Anna of Finland), Julian Glover (King Gustav), Judy Parfitt (Queen Katherine), Rudolph Walker (King Mulambon), Leslie Phillips (Gordon),

Over the top: Matt Dillon disposes of fiancée Sean Young in James Dearden's self-consciously artificial thriller, A Kiss Before Dying (UIP).

James Villiers (Prime Minister Hale), Niall O'Brien, Ed Stobart, Gedren Heller, Ann Beach, Jack Smethurst, Roger Ashton Griffiths, Cameron Blakely, Tim Seely (King of England), Gareth Forwood, Alan McMahon. Dir and Screenplay: David S. Ward. Pro: Jack Brodsky. Ex Pro: Sydney Pollack and Mark Rosenberg. Co-Pro: Julie Bergman and John Comfort. Ph: Kenneth Macmillan. Ed: John Jympson. Pro Des: Simon Holland. M: James Newton Howard. Costumes: Catherine Cook. Sound: Ivan Sharrock. (Mirage/JBRO/Universal–UIP.) Rel: 29 March 1991. 95 mins. Cert PG.

✓**A Kiss Before Dying**. After an excruciating opening in which mean Matt Dillon pushes student (and fiancée) Sean Young off the top storey of a skyscraper, *A Kiss Before Dying* settles down to unveil its intriguing story. A remake of the 1956 romantic thriller with Robert Wagner (itself based on the Ira Levin novel), this *Kiss* often feels more dated than its predecessor. British director James Dearden spices up the action with dollops of sex and gore, but otherwise coats his film in a stylistic glow punctuated with studied nods to Hitchcock (including a clip from *Vertigo*). Filmed at Lee International Studios in London and on location in New York and Virginia. [JC-W]

Cast includes: Matt Dillon (Jonathan Corliss), Sean Young (Ellen/Dorothy Carlsson), Max Von Sydow (Thor Carlsson), Diane Ladd (Mrs Corliss), James Russo (Dan Corelli), Martha Gehman (Patricia Farren), Joy/Joie Lee (Cathy), Ben Browder, Sam Coppola, Elzbieta Czyzewska, Jim Fyfe, Adam Horovitz (Jay Faraday), Freddy Koehler, Leslie Lyles, Shane Rimmer, Sarah Keller. Dir and Screenplay: James Dearden; from the novel by Ira Levin. Pro: Robert Lawrence. Ex Pro: Eric Fellner. Ph: Mike Southon. Ed: Michael Bradsell. Pro Des: Jim Clay. M: Howard Shore; numbers performed by Miles Davis, Blood Brothers, Simon Stokes etc. Costumes: Marit Allen. (Initial/Universal–UIP.) Rel: 14 June 1991. 92 mins. Cert 18.

Korczak. The first film to be made in five years in his native Poland, this depressing black-and-white story of a Polish wartime hero is well below Andrzej Wajda's best. Korczak was a doctor who stayed in the Warsaw ghetto to try and protect the orphans there, finally accompanying them to the gas chambers of Treblinka. [FDM]

Cast includes: Wojtec Pszoniak (Korczak), Ewa Dalkowska (Stefa), Piotr Kozlowski (Heniek), Marzena Trybala (Estera), Wojciech Klata, Adam Siemion, Karolina Czernicka, Agnieszka. Dir: Andrzej Wajda.

Wojtek Pazoniak as Korczak (Artificial Eye), Andrzej Wajda's biopic about the wartime Polish doctor who sacrificed his life for the children of the Warsaw ghetto.

Pro: Regina Ziegler, Janusz Morgenstern and Daniel Toscan du Plantier. Screenplay: Agnieszka Holland. Ph: Robby Muller. Ed: Ewa Smal. Art: Allan Starski. (Filmstudio Perspektywa/Regina Ziegler Film-produktion/Telmar Film Int./Erato Films/ ZDF/BBC Films co-pro-Artificial Eye.) Rel: floating; first shown London (Camden Plaza and Curzon Phoenix) 26 October 1990. 113 mins. Cert PG.

Last Images of the Shipwreck – Ultimas Imagenes del Naufragio. Difficult, confusing and imaginative Spanish-Argentine film – a multi-prizewinner on the film festival circuit, where it won general acclaim – which maybe says something about how a writer's characters can take on a life of their own . . . A film full of nuggets, some gold, some dross. [FDM]

Cast includes: Lorenzo Quinteros (Roberto), Noemi Frenkel (Estela), Hugo Soto (Claudio), Pablo Richya (José), Sara Benitez (mother), Andres Tiengo (Mario), Alicia Aller (wife), Alfredo Stuart (Cristo), Alfredo Alcon (Cristo's voice), Maria Ferrari, Viviana Tellas. Dir: Eliseo Subielo. Pro: Hugo Lauraia. Ex Pro: Enrique Marti. Screenplay: Eliseo Subiela. Ph: Alberto Basail. Ed: Marcela Saenz. Pro Des: Abel Facello. M: Pedro Aznar. (Cinequanom, Buenos Aires/ TVE Television Espanola, Madrid/developed in assoc with The Sundance Institute USA–Palace Pictures.) Rel: floating; first shown London (ICA) 23 November 1990. 127 mins. No cert.

LA Story. Personal valentine from writer-actor Steve Martin to his kind of town. Trapped in an irritating relationship, whacky TV weatherman Harris K. Telemacher finds love with a loopy visiting journalist from the London *Times*. There are complications and plenty of irritations, but – thanks to the weather – Telemacher's crazy life is transformed for the better. Martin is always at his funniest (and most sentimental) when he writes his own scripts, and even though some jokes evaporate, *LA Story* is a warm, feel-good and frequently hilarious comedy. Martin's real-life wife, Victoria Tennant, plays his romantic interest, Sara McDowel, while Richard E. Grant and Patrick Stewart also appear – all under (the British) Mick Jackson's inventive direction. Oh yes, and Rick Moranis makes a cameo appearance as a Cockney gravedigger. Steve Martin may love LA, but he's an Anglophile at heart. [JC-W]

California Scheming: Steve Martin at his wacky best in Guild's LA Story.

Also with: Richard E. Grant (Roland Mackey), Marilu Henner (Trudi), Sarah Jessica Parker (SanDeE★), Susan Forristal (Ariel), Kevin Pollack (Frank Swan), Sam McMurray (Morris Frost), Patrick Stewart (Maitre d' at L'Idiot), Andrew Amador, Gail Crate, Eddie DeHarp, Frances Fisher, Iman, Tommy Hinkley, Larry Miller, Anne Crawford, Samantha Caulfield, Aaron Lustig, George Plimpton. Dir: Mick Jackson. Pro: Daniel Melnick and Michael Rachmil. Ex Pro: Mario Kassar and Steve Martin. Screenplay: Martin. Ph: Andrew Dunn. Ed: Richard A. Harris. Pro Des: Lawrence Miller. M: Peter Melnick; numbers performed by Enya, Manfred Mann, Big World, Fats Domino, Stephane Grappelli and Django Reinhardt etc. Costumes:

Rudy Dillon. Sound: Jim Webb. (Carolco-- Guild.) Rel: 17 May 1991. 95 mins. Cert 15.

Leatherface: The Texas Chainsaw Massacre III. In 1974 Tobe Hooper set out to make a film full of horror for its own sake, and *The Texas Chain Saw Massacre* succeeded beyond his expectations. Made for a modest $140,000 the picture garnered over $50 million at the box office. His sequel of 1986 didn't do well simply because it was a spoof. The third in the series, directed by Jeff Burr, is a partial return to the spirit of the original and contains the usual decapitation, mutilation, impalement, bisection and stabbing. So – you know what to expect and have been duly warned. Two youngsters driving across America settle on a lonely gas

Life is a domestic crisis. Above, Claire Skinner and Jane Horrocks as the terrible twins; and, left, Alison Steadman and Jim Broadbent as Mum and Dad, in Mike Leigh's hilarious Middlesex melodrama Life Is Sweet *(from Palace).*

station in Texas, home for a weird family of cannibals – including the chainsaw-wielding Leatherface. Based on real-life mass murderer Ed Gein, Leatherface makes masks out of human skin and 'playthings' from other human parts and organs. Although some of the ensuing bloodletting is performed, as it were, tongue in cheek, this second sequel is by no means a send-up. As I say, you have been warned . . . [MD]

Cast includes: Kate Hodge (Michelle), Viggo Mortensen (Tex), William Butler (Ryan), Ken Foree (Benny), Joe Unger (Tinker), Tom Everett (Alfredo), Toni Hudson (Sara), Miriam Byrd-Nethery (Mama), R. A. Mihailoff (Leatherface), David Cloud, Beth Depatie, Dwayne Whitaker, Jennifer Banko. Dir: Jeff Burr. Pro: Robert Engelman. Screenplay: David J.

Schow; based on characters created by Kim Henkel and Tobe Hooper. Ph: James L. Carter. Ed: Brent A. Schoenfeld. Pro Des: Mick Strawn. M: Jim Manzie and Pat Regan. Costumes: Joan Hunter. Sound: Robert Janiger. (New Line.) Rel: 30 September 1990 (Scala, London). 81 mins. No cert.

Life Is Cheap . . . But Toilet Paper Is Expensive. Deliberately shocking, unashamedly quirky and offensive and boring by turns, *Life Is Cheap . . .* started as a documentary and went downhill from there. Wayne Wang, director of the gently domestic *Dim Sum* and *Eat a Bowl of Tea*, visited his birthplace of Hong Kong and tried to capture the spirit of the colony. The result is a series of monologues to camera, interposed with shots of extreme violence and smut. The plot line is both daft and impenetrable, while Hong Kong remains an enigma. Avoid. [JC-W]

Cast includes: Spencer Nakasako (The-Man-With-No-Name), Victor Wong (the blind man), Cora Miao (Money), Lo Wai (the Big Boss), Chan Kim Wan, Cheng

Kwan Min, Allen Fong, Cinda Hui, Yu Chien, Lo Lieh. Dir: Wayne Wang. Pro: Winnie Fredriksz. Ex Pro: John Koon-chung Chan and Wayne Wang. Screenplay: Spencer Nakasako; from a story by Wang, Nakasako and Amir M. Mokri; Chinese dialogue by John Koon-chung Chan. Ph: Amir M. Mokri. Ed: Chris Sanderson and Sandy Nervig. Art: Collette Koo. M: Mark Adler. English subtitles: Tony Rayns. Narration: Dennis Dun. (ICA.) Rel: 24 May 1991. 88 mins. Cert 18.

Life Is Sweet. As near to an indigenous London filmmaker as we've got, Mike Leigh is celebrated for his painfully observant social caricatures. This time he sets his scene in Enfield, Middlesex, in the home of Andy and Wendy. Andy (Jim Broadbent) is chef for a large local company and could be DIY genius, if only fate would let him. Wendy (Alison Steadman) teaches disco dancing to young girls and tries to cope with her twin 21-year-old daughters, Natalie and Nicola. Natalie (Claire Skinner) is a plumber's mate and dreams of visiting America; Nicola (Jane Horrocks) is a reclusive sexually deviant anorexic. Other characters/caricatures encircle their lives, invariably to disastrous effect. These are wonderful people, with problems we recognise but recoil from, ordinary working-class types who are all bizarrely unique. They are superbly performed by an ensemble cast, each of whom contributed substantially to the creation of his or her role. [JC-W]

Also with: Stephen Rea (Patsy), Timothy Spall (Aubrey), David Thewlis (Nicola's lover), Moya Brady, David Neilson, Harriet Thorpe, Paul Trussel, Jack Thorpe Baker. Dir and Screenplay: Mike Leigh. Pro: Simon Channing-Williams. Ph: Dick Pope. Ed: Jon Gregory. Pro Des: Alison Chitty. M: Rachel Portman. Sound: Malcolm Hirst. (Thin Man Prods/Film Four International/ British Screen–Palace.) Rel: 22 March 1991. 102 mins. Cert 15.

Listen to Me. Forget football, baseball and ice hockey: the kids at California's Kenmont College want to compete with a whiplash tongue and ferocious logic. Yes, *Listen to Me* is the first film to chronicle the college sport of 'debating'. A grizzled Roy Scheider is the coach who really cares about his players, putting them through their paces and genning them up on abortion, AIDS, the handicapped, capital pun-

Ariel rescues her Prince Charming in Disney's enchanting story of miscegenation, The Little Mermaid.

ishment, promiscuity, rape and divorce – you wanna hear about it, *Listen To Me* will preach. The film is so eager to cover everything under the sun in two hours that it resembles an entire soap opera stuck on the fast-forward button. Eloquent, unusual, a little *too* earnest, but compulsively enjoyable nonetheless. [JC-W]

Cast includes: Kirk Cameron (Tucker Muldowney), Jami Gertz (Monica Tomanski), Roy Scheider (Charlie Nichols), Amanda Peterson (Donna Lumis), Tim Quill (Garson McKellar), George Wyner (Dean Schwimmer), Anthony Zerbe (Senator McKellar), Christopher Atkins (Bruce Arlington), Quinn Cummings, Timothy Dang, Peter De Luise, Jason Gould, Jon Matthews, Christopher Rydell, Moon Zappa, Dottie Archibald, Rance Howard, Nancy Valen, Dylan Stewart, Don Galloway. Dir and Screenplay: Douglas Day Stewart. Pro: Marykay Powell. Ph: Fred J. Koenekamp. Ed: Anne V. Coates. Pro Des: Gregory Pickrell. M: David Foster. Costumes: Durinda Rice Wood. Sound: Tom Causey. (Weintraub–Columbia Tri-Star.) Rel: 6 July 1990. 117 mins. Cert 15.

√**The Little Mermaid**. Genuinely enchanting 'free' adaptation of the Hans Christian Andersen fairy tale about the mermaid Ariel, who falls in love with a land-locked prince. The 28th full-length animated feature from

Walt Disney, *The Little Mermaid* boasts an array of hilarious villains, some witty dialogue ('Look what the catfish dragged in!') and seven splendid songs from the creators of the *Little Shop of Horrors* musical. At times the animation borders on the grotesque, but on the whole

this has more charm than a Disney outing for some time. The 'Under the Sea' and 'Kiss the Girl' sequences are modern classics of their kind. Winner of two Oscars, for Alan Menken's score and for best song ('Under the Sea'). [CB]

With the voices of: René Auberjonois (Louis), Christopher Daniel Barnes (Eric), Jodi Benson (Ariel), Pat Carroll (Ursula), Paddi Edwards (Flotsam & Jetsam), Buddy Hackett (Scuttle), Jason Marin (Flounder), Kenneth Mars (Triton), Edie McClurg (Carlotta), Will Ryan (Seahorse), Ben Wright (Grimsby), Samuel E. Wright (Sebastian), Hamilton Camp, Phillip Ingram, Anne Lockhart, Robert Weil, Nancy Cartwright, Sherry Lynn etc. Dir and Screenplay: John Musker and Ron Clements. Pro: Musker and Howard Ashman. Ed: John Carnochan. Art: Michael A. Peraza and Donald A. Towns. M: Alan Menken; songs by Menken and Howard Ashman. (Silver Screen Part-

Listen to him: star pupils Jami Gertz and Kirk Cameron listen to the debating advice of coach Roy Scheider, in Douglas Day Stewart's extraordinary Listen to Me, *from Columbia Tri-Star.*

Laughing all the way to the bank: John Travolta and Kirstie Alley are joined by young newcomers Megan Milner and Lorne Sussman, in the painful re-make Look Who's Talking Too *(from Columbia Tri-Star).*

ners/Walt Disney–Warner.) Rel: 19 October 1991. 82 mins. Cert U.

Longshot. Lian is a would-be singer with a death fixation, on drugs and the edge of insanity. When her weird roommate persuades her to make a home movie, Lian winds up dead. [FDM]

Cast includes: Liam Amber and Dennis Matthews. Dir: Lynn Hersham. (ICA Cinematheque). Rel: floating; first shown London (ICA) 7 December 1990. 62 mins. No cert.

Look Who's Talking Too. Sloppy, hurried sequel to the surprise 1989 hit *Look Who's Talking*. Once again Bruce Willis supplies the voice of baby Mikey, son of paranoid New York accountant Kirstie Alley, now married to cab driver John Travolta. The twist here is that Mikey has a baby sister,

Julie, while Kirstie's brother (Elias Koteas) moves into their apartment and JT indignantly moves out. The script, without fail, takes a dive for the most obvious joke available, the storyline is non-existent and the entire cast eminently dislikeable. And when there's nothing else to do, a musical interlude is wedged in to pad out the sequel's meagre, excruciating 81 minutes. Roseanne Barr, as the voice of the foetal Julie, does win some laughs ('Don't you just hate it when you get your head caught in your placenta?'), although Richard Pryor was replaced (at the eleventh hour) by Damon Wayans as the vocal embodiment of little black playmate Eddie. [JC-W]

Cast includes: John Travolta (James), Kirstie Alley (Mollie), Olympia Dukakis (Rosie), Elias Koteas (Stuart), Twink Caplan (Rona), Mel Brooks (voice of Mr Toilet Man), Gilbert Gottfried, Lorne Sussman, Megan Milner, Georgia Keithley, Danny Pringle, Louis Heckerling, Neal Israel, Lesley Ewen, Paul Shaffer, Rick Avery, Mollie Israel. Dir: Amy Heckerling. Pro: Jonathan D. Krane. Screenplay: Heckerling and Neal Israel. Ph: Thomas Del Ruth. Ed: Debra Chiate. Pro Des: Reuben

Freed. M: David Kitay. Costumes: Molly Maginnis. Sound: Jay Kamen and Larry Mann. Sperm Wrangler(!): Blair Clark. (Columbia Tri-Star.) Rel: 22 March 1991. 80 mins. Cert 12.

Lord of the Flies. Nightmarish updating of Golding's novel, about 25 US military school cadets – aged between 7 and 12 – stranded on a mountainous, tropical island. Balthazar Getty (great-grandson of the oil tycoon) stars as Ralph, who attempts to take charge, introducing rules and discipline – but is overthrown by the more basic forces of nature. A metaphor for society as a whole, this is a dynamic, painterly adaptation with a very cruel streak. Executive producer Lewis Allen previously produced the 1963 black-and-white version helmed by Peter Brook. This one was filmed in Jamaica by another English director, Harry Hook (*The Kitchen Toto*). [JC-W]

Also with: Chris Furrh (Jack), Danuel Pipoly (Piggy), Badgett Dale (Simon), Andrew Taft, Edward Taft, Gary Rule, Bob Peck, Michael Greene. Dir and Ed: Harry Hook. Pro: Ross Milloy. Ex Pro: Lewis Allen and Peter Newman. Screenplay: Sara Schiff; based on the 1954 novel by Sir William Golding. Ph: Martin Fuhrer. Supervising Ed: Tom Priestly. Pro Des: Jamie Leonard. M: Philippe Sarde. Costumes: Doreen Watkinson. Sound: Douglas B. Arnold. (Nelson Entertainment/Castle Rock–Palace.) Rel: 6 July 1990. 95 mins. Cert 15.

Love at Large. Labyrinthine detective romance with Tom Berenger as Harry Dobbs, a low-rent dick from Portland, Oregon. Assigned to follow the boyfriend of rich, beautiful Miss Gwendoline Dolan (Anne Archer), he tags on to the wrong man, whom he discovers is a polygamist. Meanwhile, Dobbs's girlfriend Doris (Ann Magnuson) becomes suspicious of his unsocial hours. She hires her own detective, Stella Wynkowski (Elizabeth Perkins), who promptly falls in love with him. Director Alan Rudolph presents a moody comedy of love, showing that no romance comes without alternative attachments. Tom Berenger growls like an ageing Paul Newman, Perkins is becoming indistinguishable from Elizabeth McGovern, while Annette O'Toole – as a cheated wife – gives an hilarious impersonation of Meryl

Detectives in love – Tom Berenger and Elizabeth Perkins in Love at Large *(Rank).*

Streep. If only the film was as amusing. [JC-W]

Also with: Kate Capshaw (Ellen McGraw), Annette O'Toole (Mrs King), Ted Levine (Frederick King/James McGraw), Kevin J. O'Connor (Art), Neil Young (Rick), Ruby Dee, Barry Miller, Meegan Lee Ochs, Gailard Sartain, Robert Gould, Dirk Blocker, Bob Terhune, Michael Wilson. Dir and Screenplay: Alan Rudolph. Pro: David Blocker. Ph: Elliot Davis. Ed: Lisa Churgin. Pro Des: Steven Legler. M: Mark Isham; numbers performed by Leonard Cohen, Anne Archer, Grady Walker etc. Costumes: Ingrid Ferrin. Sound: Richard King. (Orion–Rank.) Rel: 2 November 1990. 97 mins. Cert 15.

Love Hurts. Described as 'a big comedy about life's little heartaches', *Love Hurts* is a mildly amusing,

Jeff Daniels and Cynthia Sikes: Paul Weaver faces up to his ex-wife's brutal intransigence in Vestron's Love Hurts.

occasionally touching drama about the traumas of divorce that collide with a wedding. Paul Weaver (Jeff Daniels) is the divorcee, a 37-year-old New York insurance salesman who cannot communicate with his young daughter or control his libido. His sister Karen Weaver (Amy Wright) is getting cold feet as her wedding day approaches and she weighs the pros and cons of her fiancé (she likes 70 per cent of him, but cannot reconcile herself to the remaining 30 per cent). Obviously written from experience and the heart, *Love Hurts* sifts through all the debris of marriage and comes up smiling (although the female of the species has the edge; Q: 'What is the difference between marriage and prison?' A: 'In prison somebody else does the cooking.'). [JC-W]

Also with: Judith Ivey (Susan Volcheck), Cynthia Sikes (Nancy Weaver), John Mahoney (Boomer), Cloris Leachman (Ruth Weaver), Amy Wright (Karen Weaver), Mary Griffin (Sarah Weaver), Thomas Allen (David Weaver), Jo Livingston (Harold Whipkey), Annabelle Weenick, Matthew

A good cop in a bad mood: Steven Seagal in the totally offensive Marked for Death *(from Fox).*

Carlton, Eve Smith, Jack Willis, Brady Quaid, Ken Paige. Dir and Pro: Bud Yorkin. Co-Pro: Doro Bachrach. Ex Pro: Mitchell Cannold and Steven D. Reuther. Screenplay: Ron Nyswaner. Ph: Adam Greenberg. Ed: John C. Horger. Pro Des: Armin Ganz. M: Burt Bacharach. Costumes: Elizabeth McBride. Sound: John Pritchett. (Vestron.) Rel: 30 November 1990. 101 mins. Cert 15.

The Mad Monkey – El Mono Loco. An American writer in Paris is unsure about the film script he's been asked to write. His doubts vanish when he meets the sexy young star of the piece, until he finds himself caught up in mystery, drug addiction and incest. Sounds promising, but *The Mad Monkey* is likely to leave many moviegoers pretty mad too. This Franco-Spanish co-production leads us artfully up a neatly designed garden path of intriguing mystery – and then leaves us with nothing but loose ends and unresolved questions. Some really good sequences along the way make it all the more frustrating to be left in mid-air. [FDM]

Cast includes: Jeff Goldblum (the writer), Miranda Richardson (his agent), Liz Walker (the girl), Dexter Fletcher (the director), Anemone (Marianne Gillis), Daniel Caccaldi

(Legrand), Jerome Natalie, Arielle Dombasle, Mickey Sebastian, Asuncion Balaguer. Dir and (with Manolo Matji) Screenplay: Fernando Trueba; based on the novel *The Dream of the Mad Monkey* by Christopher Frank. Pro: Andres Vincente Gomez. Assoc Pro: Emmanuel Schlumberger. Ph: Jose Luis Alcaine. Ed: Carmen Frias. Art: Pierre-Louis Thevenet. M: Antoine Duhamel. (Iberoamerica Films in assoc with Emmanuel Schlumberger--HoBo.) Rel: floating; first shown London (Cannon, Piccadilly and Tottenham Ct Rd) 9 November 1990. 108 mins. Cert 18.

Madhouse. Generally unpleasant so-called comedy about a young couple who move into their new home and are immediately invaded by a crew of repulsive pals who won't leave. I foresee greater success for new director Tom Ropelewski if he cuts out such dubious fun as a vomiting cat. [FDM]

Cast includes: John Larroquette (Mark), Kirstie Alley (Jessie), Alison LaPlaca (Claudia), John Diehl (Fred), Jessica Lundy (Bernice), Bradley Gregg, Dennis Miller, Robert Ginty. Dir and Screenplay: Tom Ropelewski. Pro: Leslie Dixon. Co-Pro: D. C. Klune. Ph: Denis Lewiston. Ed: Michael Jablow. Pro Des: Dan Leigh. Art: C. J. Simpson. M: David Newman. Costume Des: Jim Lapidus. Sound: Peter Bentley. (Boy of the Year Pro.-Orion Pictures –Rank.) Rel: floating; first shown London (Odeon Mezzanine) 16 November 1990. 90 mins. Cert 15.

The Mahabharata. Tongue-twistingly titled British/French/American co-production. Peter Brook helmed this gargantuan effort based on the Indian book (and Brook's own stage adaptation of it which lasted, incidentally, for nine hours). The original is fifteen times longer than the Bible and relates the entire history of the world from Creation to Destruction, and eventually to Redemption. Although this is a remarkable, marathon entertainment, it's obviously better suited to stage than screen and would probably work best on TV, where its massive length could be accommodated by serial production. [FDM]

Cast includes: Robert Langton-Lloyd (Vyasa), Bruce Myers (Krishna), Vittorio Mezzogiorno (Arjuna), Antonin Stahly-Vishwanadan (boy), Andrzej Seweryn, Mamadou Dioume, Jean-Paul Denizon, Mahmoud Tabrizi-Zadeh. Dir: Peter Brook. Pro: Michel Propper. Co-Pro: Ed Myerson,

Kati Outinen, tragic heroine of The Match Factory Girl, *does the family's ironing in this Electric/Contemporary release.*

Rachel Tabori, Micheline Rozan and William Wilkinson, Channel 4, Brooklyn Academy of Music and Mahabharata Ltd. Ex Pro: Michael Birkett, Michael Kustow and Harvey Lichtenstein. Screenplay: Jean-Claude Carrière. Ph: William Lubtchansky. Ed: Nicholas Gaster. Pro Des: Chloe Obolensky. Art: Emmanuel de Chauvigny and Raul Gomez. Costumes: Pippa Cleator. Sound: Daniel Brisseu. M: Toshi Tsuchitori, Djamchid Cheminari, Kudsi Erguner, Kim Menzer and Mahmoud Tabrizi-Zadeh. (Les Productions du 3ème Etage Pro.–Virgin.) Rel: floating; first shown London (Barbican and Notting Hill Gate) 26 December 1990. 110 mins. Cert PG.

Maniac Cop 2. *Maniac Cop 1* was a cinema flop and a video success, and its makers have smartened up their act: this sequel is a distinct improvement, with a satisfactory *film noir* atmosphere and a dash of class in the horror-action. The resurrected non-human cop is now well and truly on the side of the villains as he makes a pal of another killer. Touches of wit; some good performances and a spectacular climax. [FDM]

Cast includes: Robert Davi (detective), Claudia Christian (police psychologist), Bruce Campbell (cop Jack Forrest), Michael Lerner (Doyle), Robert Z'Dar (title role), Laurence Landon, Clarence Williams III, Leo Rossi, Lou Bonacki, Paula Trickey, Charles Napier, Claude Earl Jones. Dir: William Lustig. Pro and Screenplay: Larry Cohen. Ph: James Lemmo. Ed: David Kerr. Pro Des: Gene Abel and Charles LaGola. Sound: Craig Felburg. M: Jay Chattaway. (Movie House Sales Co Ltd/Fadd Enterprises–Medusa.) Rel: floating; first shown London (Cannon, Panton St) 25 January 1991. 88 mins. Cert 18.

Marked for Death. After killing a naked prostitute in a gun battle, renegade cop stereotype John Hatcher (Steven Seagal) retires from the force. But no sooner has he enlisted as Family Man in suburban Chicago than his life – and family – are threatened by a bloodthirsty Jamaican drug cartel. Thus stirred, Hatcher brushes up on his martial arts skills and goes into action. A Z-grade B-movie on an A-budget, *Marked for Death* manages to offend at every turn. Racist, misogynistic and xenophobic, it plagiarises every cop movie in existence and even steals the occasional line of dialogue.

Otherwise it's just confusing and sickeningly violent. I hated it. Previously known as *Screwface*. [JC-W]

Also with: Keith David (Max), Basil Wallace (Screwface), Elizabeth Gracen (Melissa), Bette Ford (Kate Hatcher), Tony Di Benedetto (Jimmy Fingers), Jimmy Cliff (as himself), Tom Wright, Joanna Pacula, Danielle Harris, Al Israel, Arlen Dean Synder, Victor Romero Evans, Kevin Dunn, Peter Jason, Richard Delmonte, Stanley White. Dir: Dwight H. Little. Pro: Michael Grais, Mark Victor and Steven Seagal. Co-Pro: Peter MacGregor-Scott. Screenplay: Grais and Victor. Ph: Ric Waite. Ed: O. Nicholas Brown. Pro Des: Robb Wilson King. M: James Newton Howard; numbers performed by Def Jef, Kenyatta, Tone Loc, Jimmy Cliff, Steven Seagal, Mellow Man Ace etc. Costumes: Isabella Van Soest Chubb. Sound: John Pritchett. (Fox.) Rel: 7 June 1991. 93 mins. Cert 18.

The Match Factory Girl – Tulitikkutehtaan Tytto. Finnish film about a born loser who finally reaches the end of her tether and commits four murders, only to revert to submissive type when the police come for her. Owing something to Hans Christian Andersen (story) and to Robert Bresson (style),

Stockard Channing and Ed Begley Jr as a pair of Brazilian bugs trying valiantly to be all-American, in Michael Lehmann's misfire, Meet the Applegates *(from Castle Premier).*

this could be merely grim, but it's lifted by the shining work of Kati Outïnen, who turns in a moving performance in the title role. [FDM]

Rest of cast: Elina Salo (mother), Esco Nikkari (stepfather), Vesa Vierikko (lover), Reijo Taipale, Silu Seppälä, Outi Mäenpää, Marja Packalén, Richard Reitinger, Helga Viljanen, Kurt Siilas, Ismo Keinanen, Klaus Heydemann. Dir, Pro and Screenplay: Aki Kaurismaki. Ex Pro: Klas Olofsson and Katinka Farago. Ph: Timo Salminen. Ed: Kaurismaki. Pro Des: Risto Karilula. Sound: Jouko Lumme. M: modern pop songs. (Villealfa Film-productions, Helsinki/Swedish Film Institute, Stockholm–Electric Pictures/Contemporary.) Rel: floating; first shown London (Electric) 19 October 1990. 70 mins. Cert 15.

✓**Meet the Applegates**. Inventive ecological black comedy that deteriorates into farcical grotesquerie. The Applegates aspire to be the average American family to hide their true identity. In reality, Dick and Jane – and their children, Johnny and Sally – are giant Brazilian bugs disguised as *homo sapiens*. Their mission is to nuke the United States in order to stop the destruction of their rain forest. Unfortunately, the bugs become so averagely American that Jane succumbs to consumerism, Dick to lust, Johnny to drugs and Sally to, er, lesbianism. Director/co-writer Michael Lehmann (*Heathers*) brews up

a welter of intriguing ideas, but then dissipates them with manic abandon. [JC-W]

Cast includes: Ed Begley Jr (Dick Applegate), Stockard Channing (Jane Applegate), Dabney Coleman (Aunt Bea), Bobby Jacoby (Johnny Applegate), Cami Cooper (Sally Applegate), Glenn Shadix (Greg Samson), Susan Barnes (Opal Withers), Savannah Smith Boucher (Dottie), Roger Aaron Brown (Sheriff Heidegger), Adam Biesk, Lee Garlington, Phillip Arthur Ross, Steven Robert Ross, Joe Van Slyke, Barbara Lehmann, Kiki Huygelen, John Escobar, Rick Snyder. Dir: Michael Lehmann. Pro: Denise Di Novi. Ex Pro: Christopher Webster and Steve White. Screenplay: Lehmann and Redbeard Simmons. Ph: Mitchell Dubin. Ed: Norman Hollyn. Pro Des: Jon Hutman. M: David Newman. Costumes: Joseph Porro. Sound: Douglas Axtell. (New World–Castle Premier.) Rel: 22 February 1991. 89 mins. Cert 15.

Memphis Belle. A surprisingly formulaic, 'Boy's Own' war film from the producer who brought us such serious masterpieces as *Chariots of Fire*, *The Killing Fields* and *The Mission*. David Puttnam, like Steven Spielberg before him, has attempted to revive the Saturday matinee adventure film, and on the whole has succeeded. The 'Memphis Belle' of the title, a B–17 Flying Fortress, is the legendary English-based

A load of rubbish: Keith David, Charlie Sheen, Darrell Larson (binned) and Emilio Estevez fight for laughs in Entertainment's Men at Work.

bomber – crewed by ten young Americans – that flew 25 missions over Nazi Germany. The film focuses on the plane's final and most dangerous mission, and is replete with fascinating (and accurate) detail and as many clichés. Inspired by the 1944 documentary of the same name, directed by William Wyler. [JC-W]

Cast includes: Matthew Modine (Dennis), Eric Stoltz (Danny), John Lithgow (Col Bruce Derringer), Tate Donovan (Luke), D. B. Sweeney (Phil), Billy Zane (Val), Sean Astin (Rascal), Harry Connick Jr (Clay), Reed Edward Diamond (Virge), Courteney Gains (Eugene), Neil Giuntoli (Jack), David Strathairn (commanding officer), Jane Horrocks (Faith). Dir: Michael Caton-Jones. Pro: David Puttnam and Catherine Wyler. Screenplay: Monte Merrick. Ph: David Watkin. Ed: Jim Clark. Pro Des: Stuart Craig. M: George Fenton. Costumes: Jane Robinson. Sound: David John. (Enigma–Warner.) Rel: 7 September 1990. 107 mins. Cert 12.

Men at Work. Redondo Beach, California; today. When garbage collector and Peeping Tom Carl Turner (Charlie Sheen) witnesses (as he sees it) a lovers' brawl between a beautiful neighbour and a male aggressor, he shoots an anonymous air-gun pellet into the rear end of the latter. And that's an end to it. But when he and his best buddy, James St James (Emilio Estevez), find the same guy's body in the trash the following day, Turner suspects himself of murder. Worse still, the body

belongs to the city commissioner. What might have been a wry observation of real men at work (besides cops, lawyers or daredevil pilots) deteriorates into a comedy so stupid and simple-minded that it would seriously offend the sensibilities of a 5-year-old. An idiot's paradise. For the record, Emilio Estevez, older brother of Charlie Sheen, also wrote and directed. [JC-W]

Also with: Leslie Hope (Susan Wilkins), Keith David (Louis Fedders), Dean Cameron (pizza man), John Getz (Maxwell Potterdam III), Darrell Larson (Jack Berger), Hawk Wolinski, John Lavachielli, Geoffrey Blake, Cameron Dye, John Putch, Tommy Hinkley. Dir and Screenplay: Emilio Estevez. Pro: Cassian Elwes. Co-Pro: Barbara Stordahl. Ex Pro: Irwin Yablans. Ph: Tim Suhrstedt. Ed: Craig Bassett. Pro Des: Dins Danielsen. M: Stewart Copeland; numbers performed by UB40, 2 Live Crew, Technotronics, Ziggy Marley, Blood Brothers etc. Costumes: Keith Lewis. Sound: Craig S. Clark. (Epic/Elwes/Euphoria–Entertainment.) Rel: 15 February 1991. 90 mins. Cert 12.

Men Don't Leave. Unexceptional weepy with Jessica Lange as the bereaved wife who moves to the big city of Baltimore to bring up her two sons. There, she discovers just how dependent women are on their men and has trouble raising her own. Trendy musician Arliss Howard moves into her life and tries to help out, but mad Jessica is beyond the pale. However, you know everything will work out in the end as this looks like a perfectly normal TV movie. A disappointingly bland drama, particularly as scripter Barbara Bendedek previously brought us *The Big Chill* and *Immediate Family*. Filmed in Chicago and Baltimore. [JC-W]

Cast includes: Jessica Lange (Beth Macauley), Arliss Howard (Charles Simon), Joan Cusack (Jody), Kathy Bates (Lisa Coleman), Tom Mason (John Macauley), Chris O'Donnell (Chris Macauley), Charlie Korsmo (Matt Macauley), Corey Carrier (Winston Buckley), Belita Moreno, Jim Haynie, Shannon Moffett, Kevin Corrigan, David Cale, Constance Shulman, Mark Hardwick, Lora Zane, Rick Rubin, Richard Wharton, Jane Morris, Tom Irwin, Jesse James, Wandachristine, Seka. Dir and Ex Pro: Paul Brickman. Pro: Jon Avnet. Screenplay: Brickman and Barbara Benedek; from a story by Benedek. Ph: Bruce

Jessica Lange and Arliss Howard sort through the debris of shattered families in Paul Brickman's solid, uninspired Men Don't Leave *(Warner).*

Surtees. Ed: Richard Chew. Pro Des: Barbara Ling. M: Thomas Newman; numbers performed by Frankie Laine, The Inkspots and Stevie Ray Vaughan. Costumes: J. Allen Highfill. Sound: Curt Frisk. (Geffen–Warner.) Rel: 3 August 1990. 114 mins. Cert 15.

√**Mermaids**. Massachusetts, 1963. Dramatic comedy about a nomadic single mother and her two daughters. Cher looks ill-at-ease as Mrs Flax, the impulsive, 'let's-have-a-party' man-eater, at loggerheads with her elder daughter, Charlotte, 15, who wants to be a nun (and goes by the sobriquet of Joan Arc). Again Winona Ryder, as Charlotte, steals the film from the adults – as another funereal youth coming of age

Baby workout: Winona Ryder (second from right) faces the daunting task of pregnancy in Richard Benjamin's quirky Mermaids *(from Rank).*

Games of love and strip poker: Bryan Leder, Edward Clements, Isabel Gillies, Dylan Hundley, Christopher Eigeman and Allison Rutlede-Parisi deal the cards in Whit Stillman's delightful Metropolitan, *from Mainline.*

with a vamp for a mother. At times *Mermaids* strives too hard to be cute and often the comedy feels forced. Only in the film's more dramatic passages does it come into its own, providing Winona with a platform to let the sparks fly. Originally, both Lasse Halstrom and Frank Oz were hired to direct, with Emily Lloyd cast as Charlotte. For her role, Winona Ryder was voted best supporting actress by The National Board of Review. [JC-W]

Also with: Bob Hoskins (Lou Landsky), Michael Schoeffling (Joe), Christina Ricci (Kate Flax), Caroline McWilliams, Jan Miner, Betsey Townsend, Richard McElvain, Paula Plum. Dir: Richard Benjamin. Pro: Lauren Lloyd, Wallis Nicita and Patrick Palmer. Screenplay: June Roberts; based on the novel by Patty Dann. Ph: Howard Atherton. Ed: Jacqueline Cambas. Pro Des: Stuart Wurtzel. M: Jack Nitzsche; numbers performed by Peggy Lee, Jackie

Wilson, Shelley Fabares, The Four Seasons, The Miracles, Rosemary Clooney, Leslie Gore, Marvin Gaye, Jimmy Soul, Cher etc. Costumes: Marit Allen. Sound: Richard Lightstone. (Orion–Rank.) Rel: 24 May 1991. 110 mins. Cert 15.

Metropolitan. Deep in the heart of East Manhattan an octet of young New Yorkers – calling themselves the urban haute bourgeoisie – fulfil their social obligation by dressing up and hanging out on 'group dates'. An initially reluctant addition to the set, Tom Townsend (Edward Clements), is invited into the social vortex by accident, particularly curious in view of his self-proclaimed 'committed socialism'. He talks of his love for the elusive debutante Serena Slocum (Elisabeth Thompson), and argues literary criticism with his escort-of-convenience, Audrey Rouget (Carolyn Farina). An insensitive bore at heart, Tom learns more than he bargained for from his new set of preppy friends. A pleasantly amusing comedy of manners, *Metropolitan* is a low-budget miracle, executed with intelligence and restraint and winning enor-

mous praise at various festivals. Also refreshing is the fact that all eight of the leading actors are making their film debuts. [JC-W]

Also with: Christopher Eigeman (Nick Smith), Taylor Nichols (Charlie Black), Allison Rutledge-Parisi (Jane Clarke), Dylan Hundley (Sally Fowler), Isabel Gillies (Cynthia McLean), Bryan Leder (Fred Neff), Will Kempe (Rick von Sloneker), Stephen Uys, Alice Connorton, Linda Gillies, John Lynch, Caroline Bennett. Dir, Pro and Screenplay: Whit Stillman. Co-Pro: Peter Wentworth. Line Pro: Brian Greenbaum. Ph: John Thomas. Ed: Christopher Tellefsen. M: Mark Suozzo and Tom Judson. Costumes: Mary Jane Fort. (Westerly Films–Mainline.) Rel: 23 November 1990. 98 mins. Cert 15.

Miami Blues. Frederick J. Fenger Jr is an ex-con who reckons the good life is there for the taking. Literally. Newly arrived in Miami, he turns on the charm, picks up a girlfriend and steals his way to a quiet, comfortable life. His *pièce de résistance* is beating up a cop and taking on the guy's identity. Perfect. Very black, wickedly immoral comedy with wit, bonhomie and some unexpectedly gruesome vignettes. Alec Baldwin, as 'Junior', takes to his part like a hyena to the slaughter. Good fun – if you can take it. Director George Armitage's last film seen in Britain was *Vigilante Force* – made in 1976! [JC-W]

Also with: Fred Ward (Sgt Hoke Moseley), Jennifer Jason Leigh (Susie Waggoner), Nora Dunn (Ellita Sanchez), Charles Napier (Sgt Bill Henderson), Obba Babatunde (Blink Willie), Jose Perez (Pablo), Gary Goetzman, Martine Beswick, Kenneth Utt, Bobo Lewis, Paul Gleason, Gary Klar, Shirley Stoler. Dir and Screenplay: George Armitage; from the novel by Charles Willeford. Pro: Jonathan Demme and Gary Goetzman. Ex Pro: Edward Saxon and Fred Ward. Ph: Tak Fujimoto. Ed: Craig McKay. Pro Des: Maher Ahmad. M: Gary Chang; numbers performed by Freddie McGregor, Desmond Dekker & The Aces, Norman Greenbaum, Highway 101 etc. Costumes: Eugenie Bafaloukos. Sound: Michael Tromer. (Tristes Tropiques/Orion–Rank.) Rel: 14 December 1990. 97 mins. Cert 18.

Mignon Has Left – Mignon e Partita. Winner of five David awards, this Italian domestic comedy concerns itself with the story of a sullen 14-year-old who is forced to stay in the crowded home of relatives. Mamma Forbicioni (Stefania Sandrelli) rules the unruly roost with desperate smiles while Celine Beauvallet as Mignon is most unappealing. Which shows you how much Italy knows about its own quality – this trifle won more local adulation than the magnificent *Cinema Paradiso*. Directed by 27-year-old newcomer Francesca Archibugi who, with two other women, also penned the screenplay. [C B]

Also with: Jean-Pierre Duriez (Federico), Leonardo Ruta (Giorgio), Francesca Antonelli (Chiara), Lorenzo De Pasqua, Eleonara Sambiagio, Daniele Zaccaria, Micheline Presle (Miss Girelli). Dir: Francesca Archibugi. Pro: Leo Pescarolo. Screenplay: Archibugi, Gloria Malatesta and Claudia Sbarigia. Ph: Luigi Verga. Ed: Alfredo Muschietti. M: Roberto Gatto and Battista Lena. Costumes: Paola Marchesin. Sound: Giancarlo Tiburzi. (Ellepi/Chrysalide– Metro.) Rel: 17 August 1990. 90 mins. Cert 12.

✓ **Miller's Crossing.** Complex, intricate homage to the gangster movie of the '30s, which neatly mixes caricature

with a hard, dark edge. It is 1929 in an unnamed American city where a bloody power struggle is being waged between two political leaders. Gabriel Byrne takes the central role as Tom Reagan, a cold-hearted, smart-ass anti-hero human enough to vomit when his own life is at stake. When his clandestine

In the worst possible taste: Alec Baldwin wins female hearts and critics' praise for his portrayal of a magnetic, brutal ne'er-do-well in the Jonathan Demme-produced Miami Blues *(Rank).*

Defending his realm: Albert Finney as Leo, a crime boss with a knack for staying alive. But for how long? A scene from the Coen brothers' remarkable Miller's Crossing *(Fox).*

Michel Piccoli enjoying the quiet life in Louis Malle's marvellous Milou in May, *from Curzon.*

affair with gangster's moll Verna (Marcia Gay Harden, perfect) is discovered by Irish crime lord Leo (Albert Finney), Tom is forced to switch allegiances. But not without complications. Even if the characters are one-dimensional, the plot of *Miller's Crossing* is as layered as puff pastry and the dialogue crackles. Stylish, quirky, funny and chilling entertainment for connoisseurs of dark cinema. (The Miller's Crossing of the title refers to the stretch of woodland where the gangsters bring their prisoners to be shot.) [JC-W]

Also with: John Turturro (Bernie Bernbaum), Jon Polito (Johnny Caspar), J. E. Freeman (Eddie Dane), Steve Buscemi (Mink), Mike Starr, Al Mancini, Richard Woods, Thomas Toner, Olek Krupa, Jeanette Kontomitras, Danny Aiello III, Hilda McLean, Monte Starr, Salvatore H. Tornabene, Sam Raimi and (uncredited) Frances McDormand. Dir: Joel Coen. Pro: Ethan Coen. Co-Pro: Mark Silverman. Ex

Pro: Ben Barenholtz. Screenplay: Coen and Coen. Ph: Barry Sonnenfeld. Ed: Michael Miller. Pro Des: Dennis Gassner. M: Carter Burwell. Costumes: Richard Hornung. Sound: Allan Byer. (Circle Films–Fox.) Rel: 15 February 1991. 115 mins. Cert 18.

Milou in May – Milou en Mai (US: *May Fools*). 1968, the Loire Valley. A delectable black comedy from Louis Malle, a sort of rural *Discreet Charm of the Bourgeoisie* (both, incidentally, co-scripted by Jean-Claude Carrière). When Madame Vieuzac dies in the act of frying onions, the family descends on her country estate to carve up the spoils. Attracting offbeat strangers like flies to a corpse, the house opens its doors to a growing horde – a lesbian ballerina, a lecherous truck driver, a pair of pompous neighbours (to the manor born) and a lovelorn solicitor. Viewing the squabbles, lechery and ultimate panic is the calm spectre of Madame Vieuzac herself, who seems more than a little amused by what her death has caused. To make matters worse, the national strike of 1968 is in full swing and the country is at a standstill. Even the gravediggers are on

strike! In the midst of this maelstrom, Milou (Michel Piccoli) – the 60-year-old bohemian son and remaining occupant of the estate – must recover his balance and opts for the Voltaire solution: 'I decided to be happy – because it's healthier.' A richly textured, poetic, earthy, political and observant comedy of bad manners. [JC-W]

Also with: Miou-Miou (Camille), Michel Duchaussoy (Georges), Dominique Blanc (Claire), Harriet Walter (Lily), Bruno Carette (Grimaldi), Martine Gautier (Adele), Paulette Dubost (Madame Vieuzac), Renaud Danne (Pierre-Alain), François Berleand, Rozenn Le Tallec, Jeanne Herry-Leclerc, Marcel Bories, Etienne Draber, Valerie Lemercier. Dir: Louis Malle. Ex Pro: Vincent Malle. Screenplay: Malle and Jean-Claude Carrière. Ph: Renato Berta. Ed: Emmanuelle Castro. Set Design: Willy Holt. M: Stephane Grappelli; Mozart, Debussy. Costumes: Catherine Leterrier. Sound: Jean-Claude Laureux and Dominique Hennequin. (Curzon/Gala). Rel: 31 August 1990. 106 mins. Cert 15.

The Miracle. After four films away from his native Ireland, writer-director Neil Jordan returns to his home town of Bray in County Wicklow. There, he leisurely unfolds the story of two 15-year-olds – Rose (Lorraine Pilkington) and Jimmy (Niall Byrne). The pair spend their days on the beach idly concocting stories to fit the people they watch. But one such victim of their gaze, a glamorous American blonde, turns out to be stranger than their fiction. Jordan's concept is great, and he has framed it in an eloquent, stylish film, while coaxing bright performances from his young leads. But then he flogs his horse prostrate, labouring the point to our extreme irritation and padding out his narrative with disruptive dream sequences. Cut down by 35 minutes this would have made an exceptional TV play. A nice ending, though, and a great sax score played by Courtney Pine. [JC-W]

Also with: Beverley D'Angelo (Renee Baker), Donal McCann (Sam), J. G. Devlin, Cathleen Delaney, Tom Hickey, Shane Connaughton, Mikkel Gaup, Sylvia Teron, Ruth McCabe, Johnny Devlin, Stephen Brennan, Martin Dunne. Dir and Screenplay: Neil Jordan. Pro: Stephen Woolley and Redmond Morris. Ex Pro: Nik Powell. Co-Ex Pro: Bob and Harvey Weinstein. Ph: Philippe Rousselot. Ed: Joke Van Wijk. Pro Des: Gemma Jackson. M: Anne Dudley. Costumes: Sandy Powell. Sound: Colin Nicholson. (Film Four International/British Screen/Promenade–Palace.) Rel: 12 April 1991. 95 mins. Cert 15.

Miracle Mile. Miracle Mile, Los Angeles; the near future. If you knew you had 75 minutes to live until the nuclear holocaust, what would you do? Glenn Miller wannabe Harry Washello (Anthony Edwards) just wants to find his brand new girlfriend, whom he's barely kissed. With the minutes ticking by, Washello runs all over town, trying to get his act together, refusing to tell his new paramour what's going on and behaving like he's in a Blake Edwards farce. *Miracle Mile* is an extraordinary film, a self-proclaimed romantic thriller, that is both a tender and wildly pessimistic hymn to American humanity. A collector's item. [JC-W]

Also with: Mare Winningham (Julie Peters), Denise Crosby (Landa), John Agar, Lou Hancock, Mykel T. Williamson, Kelly Minter, Kurt Fuller, Robert Doqui, O-Lan Jones, Claude Earl Jones, Alan Rosenberg, Danny De La Paz, Brian Thompson, Peter Berg. Dir and Screenplay: Steve DeJarnatt.

Lorraine Pilkington and Niall Byrne fantasise away their days in Neil Jordan's heavy-handed home movie, The Miracle *(from Palace).*

Pro: John Daly and Derek Gibson. Ph: Theo Van De Sande. Ed: Stephen Semel and Kathie Weaver. Pro Des: Christopher Horner. M: Tangerine Dream. Sound: Morteza Rezvani. (Hemdale.) Rel: 18 January 1991. 87 mins. Cert 15.

✓**Misery**. Paul Sheldon (James Caan) is a romantic novelist imprisoned by his own fame and in particular by his 19th-century heroine, Misery Chastain, the

star of his eight best-sellers. Having completed his first serious novel, *Untitled*, Sheldon crashes with the precious manuscript into a snowdrift in the middle of a Colorado blizzard. Rescued by a local nurse, Annie Wilkes, Sheldon is told he has fractured his tibia and fibula and discovers that he is a prisoner in her isolated home. There, she declares she is his 'number one fan',

Kathy Bates in her Oscar-winning performance as the redoubtable Annie Wilkes, with Misery *the pig, in Rob Reiner's superbly crafted, seat-wetting* Misery *(First Independent).*

A good man in Africa: Maynard Eziashi helps Pierce Brosnan build a road to the future, in Bruce Beresford's disappointing Mister Johnson *(from Fox).*

but is outraged by the profanity in his latest manuscript. Worse still, when Annie realises he has killed Misery off, she forces him to write a new novel, bringing Misery back to life. His life depends on it. One of the best screen adaptations of a Stephen King story yet, *Misery* is elevated to credible suspense by Kathy Bates's eerie interpretation of Annie Wilkes. Sweet and coy one moment, and dangerously psychotic the next, this fan is no loony, but a clever, scheming schizophrenic trapped in her own fantasy world. Bette Midler and Warren Beatty were originally set to star. [JC-W]

Also with: Richard Farnsworth and Frances Sternhagen (as Buster and Virginia, both excellent), Lauren Bacall (Macia Sindell), Graham Jarvis, Jerry Potter. Dir: Rob Reiner. Pro: Reiner and Andrew Scheinman. Screenplay: William Goldman. Ph: Barry Sonnenfeld. Ed: Robert Leighton. Pro Des: Norman Garwood. M: Marc Chai-

man. Costumes: Gloria Gresham. Sound: Charles L. Campbell and Donald J. Malouf. (Castle Rock/Nelson Entertainment–First Independent.) Rel: 10 May 1991. 107 mins. Cert 18.

Mister Frost. They say the devil has all the best lines and certainly Jeff Goldblum as Old Nick is the only one with any decent dialogue here. When Inspector Felix Detweiler (Alan Bates) sneers, 'you disgust me,' Mr Frost answers with the utmost civility, 'You're too kind – you really didn't have to.' Frost (first name unknown) is taken to the St Clair mental hospital after torturing seven children and seventeen adults to death and burying them in his front lawn. Frost will only talk to Dr Sarah Day (Kathy Baker) and only through her belief in him can his evil powers become stronger. Goldblum is charming as the devil, Baker acts as if she's in a better movie and Bates looks utterly bewildered. However, for an Anglo-French co-production it's – *interesting*. Previously known as *The Deadly Mr Frost*. [JC-W]

Also with: Roland Giraud (Raymond Reynhardt), Jean-Pierre Cassel (Inspector Corelli), Daniel Gelin (Simon Scolari), François Negret (Christopher Kovac), Maxime Leroux, Boris Bergman, Henry Serre, Charlie Boorman. Dir: Philip Setbon. Pro: Xavier Gelin. Ex Pro: Stephane Marsil, Claude Ravier and Michael Holzman. Screenplay: Setbon and Brad Lynch. Ph: Dominique Brencuier. Ed: Ray Lovejoy. Set Design: Max Berto. M: Steve Levine. Costumes: Judy Shrewsbury. Sound: Bernard Rochui. (Hugo Films/OMM–Blue Dolphin.) Rel: 7 December 1990. 103 mins. Cert 15.

Mister Johnson. Disappointing screen adaptation of Joyce Cary's novel about the influence of the English in West Africa in the early 1920s. Mister Johnson, a cheerful, Anglophile native, works as a clerk for district officer Harry Rudbeck (Pierce Brosnan). However, in spite of his (relatively) high wages, Johnson is constantly in debt and unable even to pay for his wife's services. And therein lies his tragedy. In the words of scenarist William Boyd, 'Mr Johnson, the most enthusiastic herald of the new day, is fated to be its first victim.' The picture's humour has a certain quaintness and London-born Maynard Eziashi struggles manfully in the title role, but there is an international gloss (Australian director, Irish star, American producer) that ultimately distances the film from its audience. [JC-W]

Also with: Edward Woodward (Sargy Gollup), Beatie Edney (Celia Rudbeck), Denis Quilley (Bulteen), Femi Fatoba (The Waziri), Kwabena Manso (Benjamin), Bella Enaharo, Nick Reding, Steve James. Dir: Bruce Beresford. Pro: Michael Fitzgerald. Ex Pro: Bill Benenson. Co-Pro: Penelope Glass. Screenplay: William Boyd. Ph: Peter James. Ed: Humphrey Dixon. Pro Des: Herbert Pinter. M: Georges Delerue. Costumes: Rosemary Burrows. Sound: Leslie Hodgson. (Fox.) Rel: 29 March 1991. 102 mins. Cert 12.

Mo' Better Blues. Endless, self-indulgent 'Spike Lee joint' set in the world of New York jazz. Denzel Washington flexes his charismatic dimples as Bleek Gilliam, a jazz trumpeter obsessed by his music since a little boy. Sex is OK, particularly with the spirited Indigo Downes (Joie Lee, Spike's little sister) and the gorgeous Clarke Bentancourt (newcomer Cynda Williams) – but 'mo' better' (Bleek's euphemism for nookie) must take second place to music practice. Director Lee (who also writes, produces and co-stars) flaunts his size-

What could be mo' better than the sultry Cynda Williams? Denzel Washington serenades his love in Spike Lee's tortured Mo' Better Blues, *from UIP.*

able budget with a new-found confidence, experimenting with camera moves, angles and filters to his heart's content. He could even become a master craftsman – if somebody would control his excesses. Previously known as *Love Supreme* and *Variation of the Mo' Better Blues*. [JC-W]

Also with: Spike Lee (Giant), Wesley Snipes (Shadow Henderson), Giancarlo Esposito (Left Hand Lacey), John Turturro (Moe Flatbush), Dick Anthony Williams (Big Stop Gilliam), Abbey Lincoln (Lillian Gilliam), Robin Harris, Bill Nunn, Nicholas Turturro, Jeff 'Tain' Watts, Samuel L. Jackson, Leonard Thomas, Ruben Blades, Bill Lee. Dir, Pro and Screenplay: Spike Lee. Co-Pro: Monty Ross. Ph: Ernest Dickerson. Ed: Sam Pollard. Pro Des: Wynn Thomas. M: Bill Lee; numbers performed by Branford Marsalis Quartet, Denzel Washington, Wesley Snipes, John Coltrane, Miles Davis, Terence Blanchard, Cynda Williams etc. Costumes: Ruth E. Carter. Sound: Skip Lievsay. (Universal–UIP.) Rel: 28 September 1990. 129 mins. Cert 15.

Moon 44. 2038 – and a pretty nasty future is on offer. Wars rage, and the only source of energy left for the world is the chemicals mined on other planets and fought over by giant commercial corporations. The End might come at any moment . . . [FDM]

Cast includes: Michael Pare (Felix Stone), Lisa Eichhorn (Major Morgan), Malcolm McDowell (Capt. Lee), Brian Thompson, Stephen Geoffreys, Dean Devlin, Leon Rippy, John March, Mehmet Yilmaz, Drew Lucas, Jochen Nickel, Calvin Burke, David

Joanne Woodward in her award-winning role as India Bridge, in James Ivory's accomplished Mr and Mrs Bridge *(from Palace).*

Williamson. Dir: Roland Emmerich. Pro: Dean Heyde and Emmerich. Assoc Pro: Carsten Lorenz. Ex Pro: Michael A. P. Scording. Screenplay: Heyde and Emmerich. Ph: Karl Walter Lindenlaub. Ed: Tony Wigand. (Spectrum Entertainment-Centropis Film–Medusa.) Rel: floating; first shown London (Cannon, Haymarket, Fulham Rd and Oxford St) 6 July 1990. 99 mins. Cert 15.

Mr and Mrs Bridge. Kansas City, 1919 –44. Paul Newman and Joanne Woodward star in James Ivory's elegant platform for America's premier acting couple. Walter G. Bridge (Newman) is a successful attorney with rigid Victorian values, a cold fish occasionally revealing subterranean emotions. India Bridge (Woodward) is a doting, irritating doormat in search of love and a good psychiatrist. The three Bridge children are variously carefree and rebellious, but all anchored by their parents' values. The film is little more than a fictional family album, chronicling the ups and downs, occasional tragedies and halcyon moments of domestic middle-class America. But the acting is so forceful, and the direction so fluid, that you can't help being swept up by it all – in spite of a somewhat

Jose van Dam as the opera star who gives up his career to become The Music Teacher *(Mainline).*

unsatisfactory ending. Her performance won Joanne Woodward the New York Critics' award for Best Actress (in spite of an uncanny vocal similarity to Eric Idle doing his American dowager turn). [JC-W]

Also with: Robert Sean Leonard (Douglas Bridge), Margaret Welsh (Carolyn Bridge), Kyra Sedgwick (Ruth Bridge), Blythe Danner (Grace), Simon Callow (Dr Sauer), Malachy McCourt, Austin Pendleton, Diane Kagan, Sandra McClain. Dir: James Ivory. Pro: Ismail Merchant. Ex Pro: Robert Halmi. Screenplay: Ruth Prawer Jhabvala; based on two novels by Evan S. Connell. Ph: Tony Pierce-Roberts. Ed: Humphrey Dixon. Pro Des: David Gropman. M: Richard Robbins. Costumes: Carol Ramsey. Sound: Ed Novick. (Palace.) Rel: 22 February 1991. 124 mins. Cert PG.

The Music Teacher – Le Maître de Musique. Outstandingly successful in its native Belgium, *The Music Teacher* made an impact at the 1988 Montreal Film Festival. In this delightful and polished blend of film, opera, and music, a star of the opera suddenly bows out of the limelight in order to train two pupils whose voices he recognises to be outstanding. A magnificent musical treat. [FDM]

Cast includes: Jose van Dam (Joachim Dalyrac, the teacher), Anne Roussel and Phillipe Volter (Sophie and Jean, the pupils), Sylvie Fennec (Estelle), Johan Leysen (François),

Patrick Bauchau (Prince Scotti). Dir: Gerard Corbiau. Pro: Jacqueline Pierreux. Screenplay: Gerard and Andrée Corbiau, Patrick Iratni, Christine Watton and Jacqueline Pierreux. Ph: Walther Vanden Ende. M: Mahler, Verdi, Bellini, Mozart, Schubert etc. Vocals: Van Dam, Dinah Bryant and Jerome Pruett. Sound: André Defossez. Set Designs: Zouc Lanc. Costumes: Catherine Frognier. With the Nouvel Orchestre Symphonique of ATBF dir. by Ronald Zollman. (ATBF and K2 One, Belgian TV–Mainline.) Rel: floating; first shown London (Barbican) 12 October 1990. 98 mins. Cert U.

My Blue Heaven. Loose-limbed comedy in which a Mafia hood is relocated to a suburban middle-American 'paradise' in a federal witness programme. There, he wreaks havoc on the local community and proves a nightmare for his FBI babysitter. Steve Martin swaggers through his role as Vinnie Antonelli in an uncharacteristically over-the-top performance, while Rick Moranis plays straight man as agent Barney Coopersmith. Moranis, nerdy but low-key, steals most of the show, and is ably matched by Joan

Cusack as a prim assistant DA. This is high comedy on an off day, but the supporting cast are all so good that the film should serve as a pleasant enough diversion for a rainy afternoon. Goldie Hawn is executive producer. [JC-W]

Also with: Joan Cusack (Hannah), Melanie Mayron (Crystal), William Irwin (Kirby), Carol Kane (Shaldeen), William Hickey (Billy Sparrow), Deborah Rush (Linda/Terrie), Daniel Stern, Jesse Bradford, Corey Fisher, Seth Jaffe, Robert Miranda, Ed Lauter, Julie Bovasso, Colleen Camp, Gordon Currie, Raymond O'Connor, Arthur Brauss. Dir: Herbert Ross. Pro: Ross and Anthea Sylbert. Ex Pro: Goldie Hawn, Nora Ephron and Andrew Stone. Screenplay: Ephron. Ph: John Bailey. Ed: Stephen A. Rotter and Robert Reitano. M: Ira Newborn; numbers performed by Fats Domino, The Beach Boys, Tony Bennett etc. Costumes: Joseph G. Aulisi. Sound: Al Overton. (Warner.) Rel: 9 November 1990. 96 mins. Cert PG.

The nerd and the bird: Rick Moranis and Joan Cusack steal the acting honours in Herbert Ross's stylised My Blue Heaven *(from Warner).*

Joris Molinas and Julien Giamaca smoke clematis sticks in the hills of Provence – in Yves Robert's bewitching My Father's Glory, *from Palace.*

My Father's Glory – La Gloire de Mon Père. The memoirs of Marcel Pagnol, the novelist who brought us *Jean de Florette* and *Manon des Sources*, are brought magically to life in this rich, entertaining tapestry about Pagnol's childhood in Provence. Pagnol was the eldest son of a Marseilles schoolteacher, a boy so precocious that he learned to read years before his father's pupils. Afraid his brain will explode, Marcel's mother banishes books from her son's life, only to find him surreptitiously poring over her cookery manuals. Transported to the country, Marcel discovers a magical world of rugged terrain, wild animals and hunting, but his new-found happiness is soon marred by his father's

humiliation at the hands of Uncle Jules. The French have a knack for this kind of thing, and Yves Robert pulls off his cinematic poetry with aplomb. It took the director years to secure the rights to Pagnol's past, but for us it was a delay worth waiting for. A minor classic. To be followed by *My Mother's Castle*. [JC-W]

Cast includes: Philippe Caubère (Joseph), Nathalie Roussel (Augustine), Didier Pain (Uncle Jules), Thérèse Liotard (Aunt Rose), Julien Ciamaca (Marcel, aged 11), Joris Molinas (Lili des Parpaillouns), Benoît Martin (Marcel, aged 5), Benjamin Detriche (Marcel, aged 3), Jean-Pierre Darras (the voice of Marcel), Paul Crauchet, Pierre Maguelon, Victor Garrivier. Dir: Yves Robert. Pro: Alain Poiré. Screenplay: Robert, Jerome Tonnerre and Louis Nucera; from the book by Marcel Pagnol. Ph: Robert Alazraki. Ed: Pierre Gillette. Pro Des: Jacques Dugied. M: Vladimir Cosma. Costumes: Agnès Nègre. Sound: Alain Sempé. (Gaumont/Productions de la Gue-ville/TF1 Films/Centre National de la Cine-

matographie–Palace.) Rel: 14 June 1991. 105 mins. Cert U.

The Naked Gun 2½ – The Smell of Fear. Frank Drebin, fearless police lieutenant and deadpan idiot, is once again essayed by Leslie Nielsen as the cop permanently surprised by the havoc he has unknowingly wreaked. This time he's pitted against the slimy Quentin Hapsburg (Robert Goulet), a crooked businessman out to sabotage a plan to provide environmentally friendly energy. Worse still, Hapsburg is dating the luscious, curvaceous, red-headed Jane Spencer (Priscilla Presley), a babe Drebin still lusts for himself. Something has to give. High expectations sabotage this sequel to the original dotty comedy (which was itself based on the unsuccessful TV sitcom *Police Squad*). There are fewer jokes this time around, and even fewer verbal quips, but there *are* some splendid set

Leslie Nielsen and Priscilla Presley are reunited in a merciless world of corruption in high places and sudden death, in The Naked Gun 2½ – The Smell of Fear *(UIP).*

pieces – not least the one in which Drebin attempts to eat a whole lobster at a White House dinner. [JC-W]

Also with: George Kennedy (Captain Ed Hocken), O. J. Simpson (Nordberg), Richard Griffiths (Dr Meinheimer/the other Dr Meinheimer), Jacqueline Brookes (Commissioner Brumford), Anthony James (Savage), Lloyd Bochner, Tim O'Connor, Peter Mark Richman, Ed Williams, John Roarke (George Bush), Margery Ross (Barbara Bush), Mel Torme, Zsa Zsa Gabor (woman with handbag), Weird Al Yankovic (as the man who says, 'you pigs . . . say your prayers'), Charlotte Zucker, David Zucker, Robert Weil, Robert K. Weiss, Burton Zucker. Dir: David Zucker (brother of the director of *Ghost*). Pro: Robert K. Weiss. Ex Pro: Jerry Zucker, Jim Abrahams and Gil Netter. Screenplay: David Zucker and Pat Proft. Ph: Robert Stevens. Ed: James Symons and Chris Greenbury. Pro Des: John L. Lloyd. M: Ira Newborn; 'Unchained Melody' performed by The Righteous Brothers. Costumes: Taryn Dechellis. Sound: Richard Bryce Goodman. (Paramount–UIP.) Rel: 28 June 1991. 81 mins. Cert 12.

Narrow Margin. Gripping, fast-paced chase thriller set on a train hurtling through breathtaking scenery towards Vancouver. Carol Hunnicutt (Anne Archer) is the sole witness to a Mafia killing and deputy DA Robert Caulfield (Gene Hackman) wants her to testify – risking his life by shielding her from the Mob. Excellent photography, tight editing and a smarmy turn from James B. Sikking as the villain help speed his classy suspenser to its somewhat anti-climactic finale. 'Based' on the 1952 B-movie classic *The Narrow Margin*. [JC-W]

Also with: James B. Sikking (Nelson), J. T. Walsh (Michael Tarlow), M. Emmet Walsh (Sgt Dominick Benti), Susan Hogan (Kathryn Weller), Nigel Bennett (Jack Wootton), J. A. Preston, B. A. 'Smitty' Smith, Codie Lucas Wilbee, Antony Holland and Harris Yulin (Leo Watts). Dir and Screenplay: Peter Hyams; based on the RKO picture *The Narrow Margin*. Pro: Jonathan A. Zimbert. Ex Pro: Mario Kassar and Andrew Vajna. Assoc Pro: Mary Eilts. Ph: Hyams. Ed: James Mitchell. Pro Des: Joel Schiller. M: Bruce Broughton. Sound: Ralph Parker. (Carolco–Guild.) Rel: 18 November 1990. 97 mins. Cert 15.

The Nasty Girl – Das Schreckliche Madchen. Unusual, stylised film about a schoolgirl from a small West German town who is given an essay to write, entitled 'My Home Town During the Third Reich'. Meeting a corridor of closed doors, Sonja's curiosity is piqued and her essay turns into a life-long crusade to expose her community's dark secrets and Nazi guilt. Starting out as a gently amusing satire of small-town life, *The Nasty Girl* builds into a drama with some teeth. However, the film's stagy gimmicks (black-and-white backdrops, studio sets etc) finally engulf it, de-fanging the whole before the final curtain. Inspired by the true story of Anja Rosmus, *The Nasty Girl* was a festival favourite the world over and won Lena Stolze the best actress award at both the Chicago Film Festival and the German version of the Oscars. [JC-W]

Also with: Monika Baumgartner (mother), Michael Gahr (father), Robert Giggenbach

Love amongst the corruption: Lena Stolze and Robert Giggenbach in Michael Verhoeven's The Nasty Girl *(Mainline).*

(Martin), Hans-Richard Müller (Dr Juckenack), Fred Stillkrauth, Elisabeth Bertram. Dir and Screenplay: Michael Verhoeven. Ph: Axel del Roche. Ed: Barbara Hennings. M: Mike Herting and Elmar Schloter. (Mainline.) Rel: 4 January 1991. 94 mins. Cert PG.

Navy Seals. Episodic, clunking B-movie tribute to America's naval elite, the offensive, silent and almost invisible 'seals'. At heart just good ol' boys, the off-duty seals act like hooligans, letting steam off from killing Arabs ('ragheads') in Beirut. Even some good action scenes and effective location work cannot elevate this mundane actioner out of the routine. Joanne Whalley-Kilmer, as a Washington journalist, is totally wasted as an all-too-brief romantic foil. [JC-W]

Gene Hackman lending weight to a stylish B-movie, Narrow Margin *(from Guild).*

Cast includes: Charlie Sheen (Hawkins), Michael Biehn (Curran), Joanne Whalley-Kilmer (Claire), Dennis Haysbert (Graham), Nicholas Kadi (Ben Shaheed), S. Epatha Merkerson (Jolena), Rick Rossovich, Cyril O'Reilly, Bill Paxton, Paul Sanchez, Ron Joseph, Richard Venture, Ron Faber, William Knight. Dir: Lewis Teague. Pro: Brenda Feigen and Bernard Williams. Screenplay: Chuck Pfarrer and Gary Goldman. Ph: John A. Alonzo. Ed: Don Zimmerman. Pro Des: Guy J. Comtois and Veronica Hadfield. M: Sylvester Levay; numbers performed by Lisa Hartman, Bon Jovi, Ritchie Havens, Vicki Thomas, Mr Big etc. Costumes: Brad Loman. Sound: Ed White. (Orion–Rank.) Rel: 28 June 1991. 113 mins. Cert 15.

✓The Neverending Story II: The Next Chapter. Despite its illogicality and papered-over holes, this lavish German-made sequel to the 1984 hit film of Michael Ende's classic novel has a lot going for it. The young hero Bastian buys a copy of Ende's book and – rather

Charlotte Gainsbourg and Julian Sands as madwoman and saint in this strange, rural tale, Night Sun *(from Artificial Eye).*

like Alice – literally falls into one of its illustrations, landing in the strange world of Fantasia, where he has been summoned to defeat the evil machinations of the sorceress Xayide. A delightful example of the importance of memory and imagination, this is fun for adults as well as children. [FDM]

Cast: Jonathan Brandis (Bastian Bux), Kenny Morrison (Atreyu), Clarissa Burt (Xayide), Alexandra Johnes (the Childish Empress), Martin Umbach (Nimbly), John Wesley Shipp (Barney Bux), Helena Michell (Mrs Bux), Chris Burton (Tri Face), Thomas Hill (Koreander), Patricia Fugger, Birge Schade, Claudio Maniscalco, Andreas Borcherding, Ralf Weikinger, Colin Gilder, Rob Morton, Frank Lenart, Victoria Searle. Dir: George Miller. Ex Pro: Tim Hampton. Ex in charge of Pro: Gisela Hahn. Pro: Dieter Geissler. Co-Pro: Bodo Scriba. Screenplay: Karin Howard; based on the novel *The Neverending Story* by Michael Ende. Ph: Dave Connell. Ed: Peter Hollywood and Chris Blunden. Pro Des: Bob Laing and Gotz Weidner. Art: O. Jochen Schmidt. M: Robert Folk (songs by Giorgio Moroder). Sound: Chris Price. Costumes: Heidi Weber. (The Never Ending Story Film Co. for Warner Bros/Soriba and Deyhle–Warner.) Rel: 21 December 1990. 90 mins. Cert U.

Night Sun – Il Sole Anche di Notte. Julian Sands forsakes his role as the romantic Englishman to play a baron-turned-monk-turned-hermit in 18th-century Italy. The fourth screen adaptation of Leo Tolstoy's short story 'Father Sergius', *Night Sun* displays the lyricism and narrative economy we have come to expect and admire from the brothers Paolo and Vittorio Taviani. Sands, dubbed into Italian by Giancarlo Giannini, is surprisingly effective as the man in search of inner peace and is in good company with Charlotte Gainsbourg and Nastassja Kinski as his earthly distractions. An Italian-Franco-German co-production. [JC-W]

Cast includes: Julian Sands (Sergio Giuramondo), Charlotte Gainsbourg (Matilda), Nastassja Kinski (Cristina), Massimo Bonetti (Prince Santobuono), Margarita Lozano (Sergio's mother), Patricia Millardet (Aurelia), Rudiger Vogler (King Charles III), Pamela Villoresi, Geppy Gleijeses, Sonia Gessner, Matilde Piana. Dir and Screenplay: Paolo and Vittorio Taviani; 'freely' adapted from Tolstoy's 'Father Sergius', in collaboration with Tonino Guerra. Pro: Giuliani G. De Negri. Pro Ex: Grazia Volpi. Ph: Giuseppe Lanci. Ed: Roberto Perpignani. Art: Gianni Sbarra. M: Nicola Piovani. Costumes: Lina Nerli Taviani. Sound: Frank Jahn. (Filmtre/RAI-TV/Capoul/Interpool/Sara Films/Direkt Film–Artificial Eye.) Rel: 10 May 1991. 112 mins. Cert 12.

Nightbreed. A mixture of the imaginative and the downright silly; but director/writer Clive Barker emerges with a lot of credit from this version of his own tricky story about murders most foul, and a killer who claims he comes from Midian, where the Nightbreed live. [FDM]

Cast: Craig Sheffer (Aaron Boone), Anne Bobby (Lori Winston), David Cronenberg (yes, *that* David Cronenberg, playing Dr Decker), Charles Haid (Capt. Eigerman), Hugh Quarshie (Det. Joyce), Hugh Ross (Narcisse), Doug Bradley, Catherine Chevalier, Malcolm Smith, Bob Sessions, Oliver Parker, Debora Weston, Nicholas Vince, Simon Bamford, Kim and Nina Robertson, Christine McCorkindale, Tony Bluto, Vincent Keane, Bernard Henry, Richard Van Spall, David Young, Valda Aviks, Mac McDonald, Richard Bowman. Dir and Screenplay: Clive Barker; based on his novel *Cabal*. Pro: Gabriella Martinelli. Ex Pro: James G. Robinson and Joe Roth. Assoc Pro: David Barron. Ph: Robin Vidgeon,

Wally Byatt and Steven Fierberg. Ed: Richard Marden and Mark Goldblatt. Pro Des: Steve Hardie and Mark Haskins. Art: Ricky Etres. M: Danny Elfman. (Morgan Creek Pro–Fox.) Rel: floating; first shown London (Odeon, West End) 27 September 1990. 102 mins. Cert 18.

Nikita. Four punks stride down a deserted Paris street at night, one dragging what appears to be a corpse. The latter is Nikita, a 19-year-old junkie craving a fix, which may or may not explain her murder of a gendarme shortly afterwards. Everything is unexpected in this epic thriller – part Orwellian nightmare, part black comedy – that ends in a moment of overwhelming tenderness as two men discover that the woman they have moulded has gone forever. The wildly talented, 31-year-old director Luc Besson (*Subway, The Big Blue*) conceived *Nikita* as a showcase for the remarkable talents of the actress Anne Parillaud, whom he later married. His film is an extraordinary achievement, and several movies in one. [JC-W]

Cast includes: Anne Parillaud (Nikita), Jean-Hugues Anglade (Marco), Tcheky Karyo (Bob), Jeanne Moreau (Amande), Jean Reno (Viktor, the cleaner), Jean Bouise (Chief of Intelligence), Roland Blanche. Dir and Screenplay: Luc Besson. Ph: Thierry Arbogast. Ed: Olivier Mauffroy. Pro Des: Dan Weil. M: Eric Serra. Costumes: Anne Angelini. Sound: Pierre Befve and Gerard Lamps. (Gaumont–Palace.) Rel: 12 October 1990. 116 mins. Cert 18.

Not Without My Daughter. 1985, Iran. All-American housewife Betty Mahmoody (Sally Field) reluctantly accompanies her Iranian-born husband to Tehran for a two-week holiday. Once there, he decides to remain, forcing Betty and their 5-year-old daughter to stay with him. Under Iranian law, there is nothing Betty can do. And, under the dictates of Islam, she cannot go anywhere alone without written permission. She is not even allowed to show one strand of her hair in public. Overnight, Betty Mahmoody has become a prisoner in a foreign country she knows little about. If this story weren't true, it would still be dramatic cinematic meat. Based on fact, it is a fascinating, harrowing tale of human suffering and spirit. English director

Brian Gilbert thankfully refrains from directorial gimmickry, and Sally Field gives yet another performance of outstanding strength and verisimilitude. Filmed in Israel. [JC-W]

Also with: Alfred Molina (Moody), Sheila Rosenthal (Mahtob), Roshan Seth (Mouss-

Down but not out: Anne Parillaud defending her experience in Luc Besson's extraordinarily riveting Nikita *(from Palace).*

Sally Field and daughter Sheila Rosenthal find themselves engulfed by a turbulent foreign culture in Brian Gilbert's moving, disturbing Not Without My Daughter *(UIP).*

ein), Sarah Badel (Nicole), Soudabeh Far-rokhnia (Nasserine), Mony Rey, Georges Corraface, Michael Morim, Gili Ben-Ozilio, Racheli Chaimian, Judith Robinson. Dir: Brian Gilbert. Pro: Harry J. Ufland and Mary Jane Ufland. Screeplay: David W. Rintels; based on the book by Betty Mahmoody and William Hoffer. Ph: Peter Hannan. Ed: Terry Rawlings. Pro Des: Anthony Pratt. M: Jerry Goldsmith; *Tosca* by Puccini. Costumes: Nic Ede. Sound: Eli Yarkoni. (Pathe Entertainment/MGM–UIP.) Rel: 21 June 1991. 115 mins. Cert 12.

Out Cold. Following his pork practices in *A Private Function*, English director Malcolm Mowbray crosses the Atlantic to a butcher's shop in Northern California. There, mild-mannered meat-seller Dave Geary (John Lithgow) thinks he has killed his partner, Ernie, by accidentally locking him in the freezer overnight. However, it is Ernie's battered, scheming wife Sunny (Teri Garr) who is behind the murder, and she teams up with the guilt-torn Geary to dispose of the corpse. Unfortunately,

Judge Reinhold and Elizabeth Perkins struggle to find a suitable resting place for Maureen Mueller in First Independent's spectacularly unfunny Over Her Dead Body.

John Lithgow as the nobody with a body on his hands just isn't funny, while Mowbray's direction crawls along at the speed of frozen meat thawing. [JC-W]

Also with: Randy Quaid (Lester Atlas), Bruce McGill (Ernie Cannald), Frederick Coffin (Sgt Haroldson), Robert Schenkkan (Sgt Roberts), Lisa Blount, Alan Blumenfeld, Morgan Paull, Barbara Rhoades, Tom Byrd, Fran Ryan, Richard Embardo, Carmen Alvarez Block, Carole Goldman, Deborah Lamb, Marvin J. McIntyre. Dir: Malcolm Mowbray. Pro: George G. Braunstein and Ron Hamady. Ex Pro: John Daly and Derek Gibson. Screeplay: Leonard Glasser and George Malko. Ph: Tony Pierce-Roberts. Ed: Dennis M. Hill. Pro Des: Linda Pearl. M: Michel Colombier. Costumes: Linda Bass. Sound: Robert Eber. (Hemdale.) Rel: 17 August 1990 (not London). 89 mins. Cert 15.

Over Her Dead Body (US: *Enid Is Sleeping*). June (Elizabeth Perkins) accidentally kills her sister, Enid (Maureen Mueller), when Enid discovers June in bed with her husband Harry (Judge Reinhold). The trouble with Harry is that he's a cop in the soporific town of Las Moscas, New Mexico, and

his partner, Floyd (the manic Jeffrey Jones), is desperate for a smidgen of crime to turn up. So June is left to dispose of the body, a task which proves to be increasingly complicated. Although the location may be different, allowing for a chorus of hick accents, this is very tired territory indeed (cf. *The Trouble with Harry, Weekend at Bernie's, Out Cold, Cold Dog Soup* etc.). Elizabeth Perkins, normally an adept comedienne, is wasted here as a bleating dumb blonde, a service performed for her boyfriend, the director and co-writer Maurice Phillips. [JC-W]

Also with: Rhea Perlman (Mavis), Michael J. Pollard, Brion James, Charles Tyner. Dir: Maurice Phillips. Pro: John A. Davis and Howard Malin. Ex Pro: Mitchell Cannold, Dori Berinstein and Adam Platnick. Screenplay: Phillips, A. J. Tipping and James Whaley. Ph: Affonso Beato. Ed: Malcolm Campbell. Pro Des: Paul Peters. M: Craig Safan; 'Stand By Your Man' sung by Tammy Wynette. Costumes: Lisa Jensen. (Vestron/Davis Entertainment–First Independent.) Rel: 17 May 1991. 101 mins. Cert 15.

Pacific Heights. Young, desperately-in-love Patty Palmer and Drake Goodman (Melanie Griffith, Matthew Modine) invest their savings in a run-down property in central San Francisco. Together they do the place up, move into the top apartment and rent off the bottom two to help ends meet. Insisting on an application form from each prospective tenant, neither Patty nor Drake can quite understand how Carter Hayes (Michael Keaton), an apparently respectable businessman, has managed to move in downstairs. But his sudden materialisation is only the beginning of their nightmares. Before Hayes, a professional con man, has finished with his inexperienced landlords, he has them owing *him* money – when he hasn't paid one cent of his rent. John Schlesinger directs with a nod to Hitchcock, utilising all the expected thriller devices, from disorientating camera work to the unexpected appearance of the cat at a moment of extreme tension. Scripter Daniel Pyne's unbearable 'what if?' premise was actually derived from personal experience. [JC-W]

Also with: Mako (Toshio Watanabe), Nobu McCarthy (Mira Watanabe), Laurie Metcalf (Stephanie MacDonald), Carl Lumbly, Dorian Harewood, Luca Bercovici, Tippi

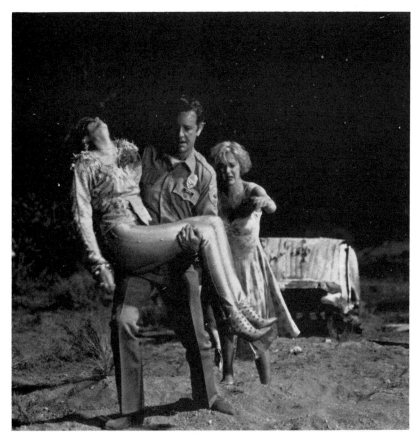

Tentative tenant: Michael Keaton in John Schlesinger's efficient, if occasionally clichéd, Pacific Heights (from Fox).

Hedren, Sheila McCarthy, Guy Boyd, Jerry Hardin, Dan Hedaya, Miriam Margolyes, Nicholas Pryor, O-Lan Jones, Tom Nolan, J. P. Bumstead, Hal Landon Jr, Hy Anzell, Tracey Walter, D. W. Moffett, Barbara Bush. Dir: John Schlesinger. Pro: Scott Rudin and William Sackheim. Ex Pro: James G. Robinson and Joe Roth. Screenplay: Daniel Pyne. Ph: Amir Mokri. Ed: Mark Warner. Pro Des: Neil Spisak. M: Hans Zimmer. Costumes: Ann Roth and Bridget Kelly. Sound: Robert Grieve. (Morgan Creek–Fox.) Rel: 22 February 1991. 102 mins. Cert 15.

Paper Mask. Slick, compulsive English thriller in which a hospital porter decides on a better life. 'When Alexander the Great was my age he was invading Tunisia,' marvels Matthew Harris. And before you can whisper 'metamor-

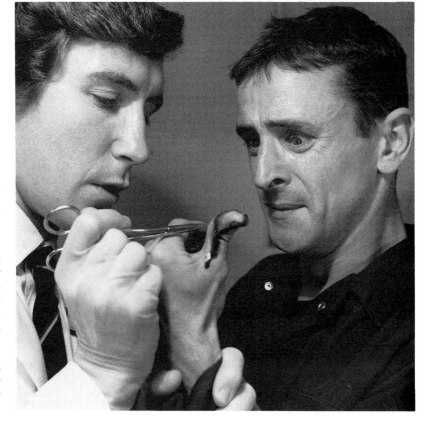

You won't feel a thing: Dr Simon Hennessey (Paul McGann) at your service (with patient Glyn Pritchard) in Enterprise's neat little thriller Paper Mask.

The Perfectly Normal *Michael Riley and the eccentric Robbie Coltrane entertain their dinner guests with the love duet from Bellini's* Norma *(from Palace).*

ski wrote the script with Paul Quarrington from his own (semi-autobiographical) idea, but is largely undermined by Yves Simoneau's tricksy direction. Still, this is a vaguely compelling eccentricity, co-financed by the late, great BSB and the Ontario Film Development Corp. [JC-W]

Cast includes: Robbie Coltrane (Alonzo Turner), Michael Riley (Renzo Parachi), Deborah Duchene (Denise), Eugene Lipinski ('Hopeless'), Kenneth Welsh (Charlie Glesby), Jack Nichols (Duane Bickle), Peter Millard (Bunden), Patricia Gage, Elizabeth Harpur, Kristina Nicoll, Bryan Foster, Ellen Ray Hennesey. Dir: Yves Simoneau. Pro: Michael Burns. Screenplay: Eugene Lipinski and Paul Quarrington. Ph: Alain Dostie. Ed: Ronald Sanders. Pro Des: Anne Pritchard. M: Richard Gregoire; with Prokofiev, Bellini, Verdi, Mahler, Puccini, Richard Strauss and Berlioz. Costumes: Margaret M. Mohr. Sound: David Evans, Wayne Griffin and Tony Currie. (Telefilm Canada/Ontario Film Development/BSB/British Screen–Palace.) Rel: 10 May 1991. 105 mins. Cert 15.

phosis', Harris exchanges identities with the recently deceased Dr Simon Hennessey (and only his patients seem duly concerned). The premise is pretty hard to swallow, but is nevertheless a worrying indictment of the British National Health Service. Scripted by former doctor John Collee. [JC-W]

Cast includes: Paul McGann (Matthew Harris/Simon Hennessey), Amanda Donohoe (Christine Taylor), Frederick Treves (Dr Mumford), Tom Wilkinson (Dr Thorn), Jimmy Yuill (Alec Moran), Barbara Leigh-Hunt, Mark Lewis Jones, John Warnaby, Alexander Mathie, Oliver Ford Davies. Dir and Pro: Christopher Morahan. Co-Pro: Sue Austen. Screenplay: John Collee. Ph: Nat Crosby. Ed: Peter Coulson. Pro Des: Caroline Hanania. M: Richard Harvey. Costumes: Amy Roberts. Sound: Tony Jackson. (Film Four–Enterprise.) Rel: 14 September 1990. 103 mins. Cert 15.

Perfectly Normal. Odd little Canadian film, this, part-comedy, part-love story and part-morality tale. Robbie Coltrane dominates the proceedings as a giant, opera-loving human sponge who moves into the bland life of Michael Riley. It is Riley, however, who is the central

thread of the film, a 'dull person' who operates the machinery at a local brewery, drives a taxi at night and plays ice hockey in his spare time. His life is an escape from stress and danger, but he is forced to reassess his values when Coltrane proposes opening an opera-themed restaurant – La Traviata – with Riley's money. Co-star Eugene Lipin-

Martin Priest as Harry, with Ben Lang, in The Plot Against Harry *(Contemporary), a Jewish comedy left on the shelf since completion in 1969 until now.*

The Plot Against Harry. A museum piece, this black-and-white Jewish comedy has been on the shelf since it was placed there by its pessimistic and hard-up production company in 1969. Now it emerges as a fast-paced, over-plotted and cast-crowded but amusing memento of the past. So *this* was life in the 'sixties! Well worth resurrecting. [FDM]

Cast: Martin Priest (Harry Plotnick), Ben Lang (Leo Perlmutter), Maxine Woods

Great acting writ large: Meryl Streep and Shirley MacLaine battle the domestic blahs against the glamorous background of showbiz – in Postcards from the Edge *(Columbia Tri-Star).*

(Kay Skolnik), Henry Nemo (Max), Jacques Taylor (Jack), Jean Leslie (Irene), Ellen Herbert (Mae), Sandra Kazan (Margie), Ronald Coralian (Mel), Ruth Roemer (Linda), Max Ulman (Sidney), Margo Solin, Paul Guskin, Zviah Ralnag, Sarah Christie, Jack Hirsch, Jeanette Wilkins, Nicholas Ponzini, José Ocasio, Paul Zayas, Stephen Cheng, Ernesto Gonzales, Sylvia Glickman, Angela Deluca. Dir, Screenplay and (with Robert Young) Pro: Michael Roemer. Ph: Robert Young. Ed: Terry Lewis and Georges Klotz. Art: Howard Mandel. M: Frank Lewin. Sound: Peter Vollstadt and Paul Jaeger. Costumes: Lily Partridge. (King Screen–Electric Pictures/Contemporary.) Rel: floating; first shown London (Everyman) 5 October 1990. 81 mins. Cert PG.

✓**The Pope** (formerly *The Pope Must Die*). A spelling mistake propels bumbling country priest and part-time car mechanic Dave Albinizi into the hallowed vestments of the Pope. He knows there must be some mistake, but while he's in the Vatican Dave attempts to sort out some of the Papal corruption. Borrowing a time-worn concept (a commoner plonked into a position of power – cf. *King Ralph, Moon Over Parador* etc.), *The Pope* offers no new insights into the genre. Robbie Coltrane is endearing enough as His Holiness and the photography is lovely, but otherwise this is obvious, corny farce. Balthazar Getty – as an English rock star in Rome – is intriguing casting, and had his voice dubbed for the occasion. [JC-W]

Also with: Beverly D'Angelo (Veronica Dante), Herbert Lom (Corelli), Alex Rocco (Cardinal Rocco), Balthazar Getty (Joe Don Dante), Peter Richardson ('Bish'), Khedija Sassi (Luccia Corelli), Paul Bartel, Salvatore Coscio, William Hootkins, Robert Stephens, Annette Crosbie, Steve O'Donnell, John Sessions, Adrian Edmondson, Jeff Beck, Ernest Clark, Niall Tobin, Ralph Brown. Dir: Peter Richardson. Pro: Stephen Woolley. Ex Pro: Michael White and Nik Powell. Screenplay: Pete Richens. Ph: Frank Gell. Ed: Katherine Wenning. Pro Des: John Ebden. M: Anne Dudley and Jeff Beck. Costumes: Sandy Powell. (Miramax/British Screen/Film Four International –Palace.) Rel: 21 June 1991. 97 mins. Cert 15.

✓**Postcards from the Edge**. Carrie Fisher takes an affectionate, satirical swipe at the excesses of Hollywood that shaped her starlet years. Meryl Streep is cast against type (isn't she always?) as the spoilt daughter of legendary singer Doris Mann/Debbie Reynolds, played with relish by Shirley MacLaine. 'I came from nothing and made something out of my life,' Doris declares, 'and you' – to Suzanne Vale/Fisher/Streep – 'came from something and made nothing of yours.' In between the in-jokes, Ms Streep digs under the nail varnish and exorcises some painful ghosts. Mike Nichols directs with the aplomb of a master craftsman, winning first-class performances from his cast, particularly Streep and MacLaine, and Gene Hackman as a tough, caring film director. Based on Fisher's *roman à clef*, *Postcards from the Edge*. [JC-W]

Also with: Dennis Quaid (Jack Falkner), Gene Hackman (Lowell), Richard Dreyfuss (Dr Frankenthal), Rob Reiner (Joe Pierce), Mary Wickes (Grandma), Conrad Bain (Grandpa), Annette Bening (Evelyn Ames), Simon Callow (Simon Asquith), Robin Bartlett (Aretha), Gary Morton, C. C. H. Pounder, Anthony Heald, Dana Ivey, Oliver

One man and his gun: Danny Glover faces the odds in the footsteps of Arnie – in Stephen Hopkins's muscular, familiar Predator 2 *(Fox).*

Platt, Michael Ontkean, Pepe Serna, Scott Frankel. Dir: Mike Nichols. Pro: Nichols and John Calley. Ex Pro: Neil Machlis and Robert Greenhut. Screenplay: Carrie Fisher; based on her novel. Ph: Michael Ballhaus. Ed: Sam O'Steen. Pro Des: Patrizia Von Brandenstein. M: Carly Simon. Costumes: Ann Roth. Sound: Stan Bochner. (Columbia Tri-Star.) Rel: 25 January 1991. 104 mins. Cert 15.

Predator 2. Energetic if cliché-riddled sequel to the monster Schwarzenegger vehicle of 1987. Last time the giant, frequently invisible Thing (which looks like a Rastafarian Bigfoot) had to contend with the former Mr Universe in a Central American jungle. This time it's 1997 in Los Angeles, and the Creature from the Black Lagoon is enjoying itself tearing the innards out of Colombian drug soldiers. Detective-Lieutenant Mike Harrigan (Danny Glover), himself something of a human tank, is on the trail of the invisible monster – much

to the concern of the 'authorities', who know better. Great production design and effects abound, but otherwise this is tasteless, monstrous, sledgehammer escapism. [JC-W]

Also with: Gary Busey (Keyes), Ruben Blades (Danny), Maria Conchita Alonso (Leona), Bill Paxton (Jerry), Calvin Lockhart (King Willie), Kevin Peter Hall (the Predator), Robert Davi, Adam Baldwin, Kent McCord, Morton Downey Jr, Steve Kahan, Henry Kingi, Elpidia Carrillo (Anna), Nick Corri, Tom Finnegan. Dir: Stephen Hopkins. Pro: Lawrence Gordon, Joel Silver and John Davis. Ex Pro: Michael Levy and Lloyd Levin. Screenplay: Jim Thomas and John Thomas; based on their characters. Ph: Peter Levy. Ed: Mark Goldblatt. Pro Des: Lawrence G. Paull. M: Alan Silvestri: numbers written and performed by Papa Dee. Costumes: Marilyn Vance-Straker. Creature created by: Stan Winston. (Fox.) Rel: 3 May 1991. 107 mins. Cert 18.

Presumed Innocent. Rusty Sabich (Harrison Ford) is a hard-working, well-respected Detroit prosecutor. When his colleague, the beautiful Carolyn Polhemus (Greta Scacchi) is found

bound, raped and murdered, he is asked to investigate the case – against his wishes. He has his reasons for avoiding the investigation, not least his clandestine extramarital affair with the deceased. As the evidence piles up, the finger of suspicion points at Sabich himself. Based on the international bestseller by ex-attorney Scott Turow, the film is an intelligent examination of the American judicial system – although to appreciate the details fully a crash course in law would help. Alan J. Pakula directs with a strong feeling for credibility and avoidance of melodrama, and is well served by Bonnie Bedelia as Sabich's pathetic wife and Paul Winfield as the no-bull presiding judge. [JC-W]

Also with: Brian Dennehy (Raymond Morgan), Raul Julia (Sandy Stern), Bonnie Bedelia (Barbara Sabich), Paul Winfield (Judge Larren Lyttle), John Spencer (Detective Lipranzer), Joe Grifasi (Tommy Molto), Tom Mardirosian (Nico Della Guardia), Anna Maria Horsford, Sab Shimono, Christine Eastabrook, Michael Tolan, Ron Frazier, David Wohl. Dir: Alan J. Pakula. Pro: Sydney Pollack and Mark Rosenberg. Ex Pro: Susan Solt. Screenplay: Frank Pier-

Court in the act: Raul Julia, Bonnie Bedelia and Harrison Ford on the side of the accused in Alan J. Pakula's cunning Presumed Innocent, *from Warner.*

son and Alan J. Pakula; based on the novel by Scott Turow. Ph: Gordon Willis. Ed: Evan Lottman. Pro Des: George Jenkins. M: John Williams. Costumes: John Boxer. Sound: James Sabat. (Mirage–Warner.) Rel: 28 September 1990. 126 mins. Cert 15.

✓**Problem Child.** Any film that ends with a close-up of a pig's rear end cannot be accused of subtlety. *Problem Child*, a cruel antidote to *Home Alone*, is a frenetic and obvious farce about an impossibly destructive 7-year-old. The film's first ten to fifteen minutes are actually spotted with laughs, but newcomer Michael Oliver is so uncharismatic in the title role that we quickly tire of his ludicrous antics. Beware of *Problem Child II*. [J C-W]

Cast includes: John Ritter (Ben Healy), Michael Richards (Martin Beck, the Bow Tie Killer), Gilbert Gottfried (Igor Peabody), Jack Warden (Big Ben Healy), Michael Oliver (Junior), Amy Yasbeck (Flo Healy), Peter Jurasik, Charlotte Akin, Anna

Marie Allred, Dennis Dugan, Corki Grazer, Helena Humann, Judy Jones, Melody Jones. Dir: Dennis Dugan. Pro: Robert Simonds. Ex Pro: James D. Brubaker. Screenplay: Scott Alexander and Larry Kar-

Maniac Cop with brains: Nick Nolte in Sidney Lumet's dark, familiar world as depicted in Q & A *(from Virgin Vision).*

aszewski. Ph: Peter Lyons Collister. Ed: Daniel Hanley and Michael Hill. Pro Des: George Costello. M: Miles Goodman; numbers performed by The Beach Boys (*Problem Child*), George Thorogood, Iggy Popp, Leslie Gore, and Steppenwolf. Costumes: Eileen Kennedy. Sound: Robert Allan Wald. (Imagine/Universal–UIP.) Rel: 24 May 1991. 80 mins. Cert 12.

Q & A. Once again director Sidney Lumet trudges back to New York to expose the police corruption of that city, much as he has already done in such films as *Serpico* and *Prince of the City*. Nick Nolte is the paunchy rogue cop, whose cold-blooded racist killings have to be repeatedly covered up. Timothy Hutton is the young lawyer with a conscience who refuses to conform to his superiors' blind-eye tactics. And Armand Assante is the noble and charismatic drug lord with the star wardrobe. This is tired, threadbare territory, shot in superb documentary style and thoroughly unpleasant. [JC-W]

Cast includes: Nick Nolte (Mike Brennan), Timothy Hutton (Al Reilly), Armand Assante (Bobby Texador), Patrick O'Neal

Bill Murray as the bank robber who corrects the grammar of his victims (seen here with Bob Elliott), in Quick Change *(from Warner).*

(Kevin Quinn), Jenny Lumet (Nancy Bosch), Lee Richardson (Leo Bloomenfeld), Luis Guzman (Luis Valentin), Charles Dutton (Sam Chapman), Paul Calderon (Roger Montalvo), Gloria Irizarry (Mrs Bosch), International Chrysis, Dominick Chianese, Leonard Cimino, Gustavo Brens, Martin E. Brens, John Capodice, Burtt Harris, Cynthia O'Neal. Dir and Screenplay: Sidney Lumet; from the book by Edwin Torres. Pro: Arnon Milchan and Burtt Harris. Ex Pro: Patrick Wachsberger. Ph: Andrzej Bartowiak. Ed: Richard Cirincione. Pro Des: Philip Rosenberg. M: Ruben Blades. Costumes: Ann Roth and Neil Spisak. Sound: Chris Newman. (Regency International/Odyssey Dist–Virgin Vision.) Rel: 5 April 1991. 132 mins. Cert 18.

Quick Change. Three loonies team up to rob a New York bank, masterminded by Bill Murray disguised as a circus clown. The robbery is a cinch, but getting out of New York with the loot proves to be an urban nightmare. Murray, having failed to attract such filmmakers as Martin Scorsese and Jonathan Demme, makes his directing debut here (in tandem with scripter Howard Franklin), and pulls off one of the funniest films of the year. As the deadpan ad-libber at odds with New York City, the actor has never been shown to better effect. The plot also works in the characters' favour – and is edge-of-the-seat stuff – while every scene throws out a memorable moment. In short, a comedy rich in cameo performances and hilarious detail, that entertains even when it's not trying to be funny. [JC-W]

Cast includes: Bill Murray (Grimm), Geena Davis (Phyllis), Randy Quaid (Loomis), Jason Robards (Chief Rotzinger), Richard Joseph Paul (Lt Jameson), Tony Shalhoub (cab driver), Victor Argo (Skelton), Philip Bosco (Lou, the bus driver), Kurtwood Smith (Russ Crane/Lombino), Bob Elliott, Brian McConnachie, Jack Gilpin, Jordan Cael, Barbara Flynn, Jamey Sheridan, Phil Hartman, Kathryn Grody, Gary Goodrow, Michael Chapman, Stanley Tucci, Paul Herman, Susannah Bianchi. Dir: Howard Franklin and Bill Murray. Pro: Murray and Robert Greenhut. Ex Pro: Frederic Golchan. Screenplay: Franklin; based on the book by Jay Cronley. Ph: Michael Chapman. Ed: Alan Heim. Art: Speed Hopkins. M: Randy Edelman and Howard Shore. Sound: Les Lazarowitz. (Devoted–Warner.) Rel: 26 April 1991. 89 mins. Cert 15.

Quigley Down Under. Matthew Quigley (Tom Selleck) dons stetson and spurs and heads – not West – but to Australia. Quigley is the best long-distance sharpshooter in the world, which is precisely why he's hired by rich landowner Elliott Marston (Alan Rickman snarling on overdrive). But no sooner has Quigley arrived Down Under than Marston reveals his real reason for the gunman's services: to pick off the local Aborigines. Quigley refuses, and, left for dead in the desert, turns his sights on Marston and his men. *Quigley Down Under*, for all its entertainment value, isn't sure what it wants to be; part jokey Western and part violent anthropological history lesson, the film leaves an odd taste in the mouth. The humour is broad, but the scenes of Aborigine genocide are horrific. Whither goest thou, Tom? [JC-W]

Also with: Laura San Giacomo (Crazy Cora), Chris Haywood (Major Ashley Pitt), Ron Haddrick (Grimmelman), Tony Bonner, Jerome Ehlers, Conor McDermottroe, Roger Ward, Ben Mendelsohn, Steve Dodd, William Zappa, Evelyn Krape. Dir: Simon Wincer. Pro: Stanley O'Toole and Alexandra Rose. Co-Pro: Megan Rose. Screenplay: John Hill. Ph: David Eggby. Ed: Adrian Carr. Pro Des: Ross Major. M: Basil Poledouris. Sound: Lloyd Carrick. (Pathe Entertainment–UIP.) Rel: 5 April 1991. 120 mins. Cert 12.

The Reflecting Skin. A real hybrid of a movie: British – the work of a new director with a distinctly odd sense of humour – but set in America in the '50s and made in Canada. All the characters are more or less off their trolley, including an unendearing lead who gets his kicks by inflating frogs and then exploding them. His Ma is obsessed with smells and Dad is a pederast who is falsely accused of a murder – in fact the work of a gang of perverts. And a jolly good time is had by all! [FDM]

Cast: Viggo Mortensen (Cameron Dove), Lindsay Duncan (Dolphin Blue), Jeremy Cooper (Seth), Sheila Moore (Ruth), Duncan Fraser (Luke), David Longworth, Robert Koons, David Bloom. Dir and Screenplay: Philip Ridley. Pro: Dominic Anciano and Ray Burdis. Ex Pro: Jim Beach. Ph: Dick Pope. Ed: Scott Thomas. Sound: George Tarrant. Art: Rick Roberts. (Fugitive Films–Virgin Vision.) Rel: floating; first shown London (Cannon, Tottenham Ct Rd and Piccadilly; Gate, Notting Hill) 16 November 1990. 95 mins. Cert 15.

Repossessed. Cack-handed parody of *The Exorcist* that takes sidelong swipes at TV evangelism, fitness centres, homosexuals and very large breasts. Leslie Nielsen, once a reliable, straight-faced actor in such spoofs as *Airplane!* and *The Naked Gun*, is here reduced to epileptic mugging as a retired exorcist with a yellow streak. All in the worst possible taste. [JC-W]

Cast includes: Linda Blair (Nancy Aglet), Ned Beatty (Wily Weller), Leslie Nielsen (Father Mayii), Anthony Starke (Father Brophy), Lana Schwab (Fanny Weller), Robert Fuller (Dr Hackett), Chuck Kovacic (Ollie North), Thom J. Sharp, Ben J. Thall, Dove Dellos, Jacqueline Masche, Melissa Moore, May Quigley, Roger Scott, Jake Steinfeld, Charlotte Helkamp, Army Archerd, Jack Lalanne, Wally George, Jesse Ventura, Gene Okerlund. Dir and Screenplay:

Christien Anholt and Samuel West enjoy a short-lived, but lifelong friendship in Jerry Schatzberg's reflective Reunion, *from Rank.*

Bob Logan. Pro: Steve Wizan. Co-Pro: Jean Higgins and Ernest Losso. Ph: Michael Margulies. Ed: Jeff Freeman. Pro Des: Shay Austin. M: Charles Fox. Costumes: Timothy D'Arcy. Sound: Clancy T. Troutman. (New Line Cinema–Guild.) Rel: 30 November 1990. 85 mins. Cert 15.

Reunion. Atmospheric, eloquent drama set in the shadow of the Holocaust. Crusty old Jason Robards holidays in Stuttgart, obviously with some ghosts to exorcise. Then it's flashback time to an era of unblemished Germany, of hopes for the future, of eternal friendships. Young aristocrat Count Konradin von Loehenburg is new in town and befriends Hans Strauss, his Jewish classmate. The boys become inseparable, exchanging ideas, ideals and hopes for the future. Meanwhile, the threat of a militant new Germany rears its ugly head. Although *Reunion* arrived on the coat-tails of *Enemies, a Love Story*, *Music Box* and *Triumph of the Spirit*, this is less an examination of the horrors and effects of war than an affectionate homage to the power of childhood friendship. Harold Pinter scripted from the Fred Uhlman novel. [JC-W]

Cast includes: Jason Robards (Henry), Christien Anholt (Hans Strauss), Samuel West (Konradin), Françoise Fabian (Grafin Von Lohenburg), Maureen Kerwin (Lisa, Henry's daughter), Barbara Jefford (Mrs Strauss), Bert Parnaby (Herr Strauss), Struan Rodger (excellent, as Pompetski), Roland Schaefer (Judge Freisler), Frederick Warder (gym instructor), Tim Barker, Gideon Boulting, Jacques Brunet, Gerhard Fries, Amelie Pick. Dir: Jerry Schatzberg. Pro: Anne François. Ex Pro: Vincent Malle. Screenplay: Harold Pinter. Ph: Bruno De Keyser. Ed: Martine Barraque. Pro Des: Alexandre Trauner. M: Philippe Sarde. Costumes: David Perry. Sound: Karl Laabs. (Sovereign–Rank.) Rel: 6 July 1990. 110 mins. Cert 12.

Reversal of Fortune. Slick, efficient retelling of the Claus Von Bulow trial, told from the viewpoint of defending lawyer Alan Dershowitz (Ron Silver). A European aristocrat, Von Bulow

Jeremy Irons in his Oscar-winning role as the ambiguous Claus von Bulow, in Barbet Schroeder's workmanlike film version of the notorious court case, Reversal of Fortune *(from Rank).*

(Jeremy Irons) is tried and sentenced (to 30 years) for the attempted murder of his wife, Sunny, who is now in a coma. Determined to prove his innocence, Von Bulow hires Jewish New York lawyer Dershowitz (on whose book this film is based). *Reversal of Fortune* is not so much a courtroom drama as a detective case – as Dershowitz explains, 'Remember, most cases are won in the field, not in the court.' The lawyer hires a small posse of students and starts sifting through the loopholes. Director Barbet Schroeder (*Barfly*) presents an elegant, well-written drama, like an intellectual game of 'truth and lies'. But ultimately the film lacks warmth and excitement, in spite

of the fine performances from its two male stars. Jeremy Irons won the Oscar and the best actor award from the Los Angeles Film Critics Association. [JC-W]

Also with: Glenn Close (Sunny Von Bulow), Annabella Sciorra (Sarah), Uta Hagen (Maria), Fisher Stevens (David Marriott), Jack Gilpin (Peter Macintosh), Christine Baranski, Stephen Mailer, Christine Dunford, Felicity Huffman, Mano Singh, Johann Carlo, Keith Reddin, Alan Pottinger, Mitchell Whitfield, Tom Wright, John David Cullum, Jad Mager, Sarah Fearon, Dir: Barbet Schroeder. Pro: Edward R. Pressman and Oliver Stone. Ex Pro: Michael Rauch. Screenplay: Nicholas Kazan; based on the book by Alan Dershowitz. Ph: Luciano Tovoli. Ed: Lee Percy. Pro Des: Mel Bourne. M: Mark Isham; Mozart, Haydn etc. Costumes: Judianna Makovsky. Sound: Tom Nelson. (Sovereign Pictures/ Shochiku Fuji–Rank.) Rel: 11 January 1991. 111 mins. Cert 15.

Riff-Raff. Ken Loach (maker of the classic *Kes*) focuses on a building site and working-class characters in this made-for-TV 'slice of life'. A great success at the 1991 London Film Festival, it also won a quite considerable British cinema release. Nonetheless, I wish Loach could recapture the innocent simplicity and charm of his *Kes* days. [FMS]

Cast includes: Robert Carlyle (Stevie), Emer McCourt (Susan), Jimmy Coleman (Shem), George Moss (Mo), Nicky Tomlinson (Larry), Daid Finch (Kevin), Richard Belgrave, Ade Sapara, Derek Young, Bill Moores, Luke Kelly, Garrie J. Lammin. Dir: Ken Loach. Pro: Sally Hibbin. Screenplay: Bill Jesse. Ph: Barry Ackroyd. Ed: Jonathan Morris. Pro Des: Martin Johnson. Art: Jonathan Lee. M: Stewart Copeland. (Parallax Pictures for Channel 4–BFI.) Rel: floating; first shown London (NFT) 19 April 1991. 95 mins. Cert 15.

The Road Home (US: *Lost Angels*). Sincere but far too slick examination of teenage delinquency in Los Angeles. Tim Doolan is a middle-class kid from a broken home who just wants to fit in. Unfortunately, he is led astray by his 'bad ass' friends and ends up in an institution dependent on fat insurance handouts. Only Donald Sutherland's Dr Charles Loftis shows an ounce of concern, but he has his own demons to fight. Adam Horovitz of The Beastie Boys fame, is surprisingly natural as Tim – avoiding both sentimentality and smouldering aggression – but cannot overcome the lack of gut emotion in Hugh Hudson's direction. [JC-W]

Also with: Amy Locane (Cheryl Anderson), Don Bloomfield (Andy Doolan), Graham Beckel (Richard Doolan), Patricia Richardson (Mrs Anderson), Celia Weston, Ron Frazier, Joseph d'Angerio, William O'Leary, Kevin Corrigan, Leonard Portar Salazar, David Herman, Max Perlich, Gino De Mauro, Nina Siemaszko, Shana O'Neil, Dana Behr, Mary Greening, Kevin Tighe, John C. McGinley, Jane Hallaren, Peter Maloney, Frances Fisher, Jack Gold, Keone Young, Park Overall. Dir: Hugh Hudson. Pro: Howard Rosenman and Thomas Baer. Screenplay: Michael Weller. Ph: Juan Ruiz-Anchia. Ed: David Gladwell. Pro Des: Assheton Gorton. M: Philippe Sarde, Edward Elgar; *San Fernando Valley* sung by Bing Crosby. Costumes: Judianna Makovsky. Sound: Edward Tise. (Orion–Rank.) Rel: 15 March 1991. 116 mins. Cert 15.

Patrick Bergin makes a dashing, vivacious Robin Hood in the first of two big-budget productions, this one from Twentieth Century-Fox.

Robin Hood. Lively, historically credible romp through the legend of England's Green hero. Patrick Bergin is a noble Sir Robin Hood – a.k.a. the Earl of Huntingdon – investing the role with swagger and humanity, while genuine foreigners Jurgen Prochnow and Jeroen Krabbe play the thick-accented Norman oppressors like Hollywood villains. Production design, music and particularly the photography are all first rate, although the editing and make-up betray the speed with which this film was assembled to beat Kevin Costner's Robin to the wickets. Warning: although the film is essentially light-hearted, and often downright comedic, some scenes may seriously upset younger children. [JC-W]

Also with: Uma Thurman (Maid Marian), Jurgen Prochnow (Sir Miles Folcanet), Edward Fox (Prince John), Jeroen Krabbe (Baron Daguerre), Owen Teale (Will Scarlet), David Morrissey (Little John), Alex Norton (Harry), Barry Stanton (Miter), Jeff Nuttall (Friar Tuck), Daniel Webb (Much the Miller), Gabrielle Reidy, Cecily Hobbs, Conrad Asquith, Anthony O'Donnell, Carolyn Backhouse, Phelim McDermott. Dir: John Irvin. Pro: Sarah Radclyffe and Tim Bevan. Ex Pro: John McTiernan. Screenplay: Mark Allen Smith and John McGrath. Ph: Jason Lehel. Ed: Peter Tanner. Pro Des: Austen Spriggs. M: Geoffrey Burgon. Costumes: Emma Porteous. Sound: Leslie Wiggins. (Fox.) Rel: 17 May 1991. 104 mins. Cert PG.

RoboCop 2. Ultra-violent sequel with Peter Weller returning as the Tin Man programmed to serve the public trust, protect the innocent and uphold the law. This time the villain is a highly addictive drug, Nuke, that has Detroit by the arteries. Meanwhile, the power-hungry OCP Corporation is buying the city wholesale and is creating its own omnipotent law enforcer: the apocalyptic RoboCop 2. Lacking the exhilarating style of the original, this mega-budgeted sequel has its share of sick humour (illustrated in the futuristic violence-prevention commercials) and unrelenting action. Gripping stuff – if you can take it. Filmed in Houston. [JC-W]

Cast includes: Nancy Allen (Anne Lewis), Tom Noonan (Cain), Willard Pugh (Mayor Kuzak), Felton Perry (Donald Johnson), Dan O'Herlihy (the old man), Belinda Bauer (Juliette Faxx), John Glover, Gabriel Damon, Galyn Gorg, Robert Do'qui, Yogi Baird, Jerry Nelson, Christopher Quinten. Dir: Irvin Kershner. Pro: Jon Davison. Ex Pro: Patrick Crowley. Screenplay: Frank Miller and Walon Green; from a story by Miller. Ph: Mark Irwin. Ed: William Anderson. Pro Des: Peter Jamison. M: Leonard Rosenman. Costumes: Rosanna Norton. Sound: Edward Tise. (Orion–Rank.) Rel: 12 October 1990. 116 mins. Cert 18.

Rocky V. The Italian Stallion has brain damage and retires from the ring, and due to a financial blunder (c/o brother-in-law Paulie), the Balboas have to sell their manse and move to a squalid neighbourhood in Philadelphia. So Rocky's back to his roots. And it's time now to pay attention to his 13-year-old son, Rocky Jr (Stallone Jr). But no sooner have the Balboas come to accept their fate, than in steps Tommy 'Machine' Gunn, a hungry, inexperienced boxer with a sledgehammer technique. Rocky takes him under his wing, carefully nurturing him for the

The late great Alex J. Murphy (Peter Weller) is reunited with co-crime fighter Anne Lewis (Nancy Allen) in Irvin Kershner's powerful sequel, RoboCop 2 (from Rank).

Rocky & Son cope with the realities of brain damage and poverty in the last – really – Rocky episode: Sylvester and Sage Stallone in Rocky V *(from UIP).*

big time and treating him like a son. Which goes down like a seven-stone heavyweight with Rocky Jr. But we all know Rocky's got one last fight in him and Sylvester Stallone builds up his story (several, actually) to a predictable, adrenalin-pumping finale. John G. Avildsen, who won an Oscar for directing the first film, returns for the final bout, although writer-star Stallone had final cut. Tommy Morrison as Tommy Gunn is an unglamorous heavy (unlike Mr T and Dolph Lundgren), but does have the added interest of being a real-life undefeated brick wall. [JC-W]

Also with: Talia Shire (Adrian Balboa), Burt Young (Paulie), Sage Stallone (Rocky Jr), Burgess Meredith (Mickey), Richard Gant (George W. Duke), Tony Burton (Tony), James Gambina, Delia Sheppard, Michael Sheehan, Micheal [sic] Williams, Kevin Connolly, Elisabeth Peters, Chris Avildsen, Jonathan Avildsen, Tony Munafo, Lloyd Kaufman, Michael Pataki. Dir: John G. Avildsen. Pro: Irwin Winkler and Robert Chartoff. Ex Pro: Michael S. Glick. Assoc Pro: Tony Munafo. Screenplay: Sylvester Stallone. Ph: Steven Poster. Ed: Avildsen and Michael N. Knue. Pro Des: William J. Cassidy. M: Bill Conti. Sound: David B. Cohn. (United Artists–UIP.) Rel: 25 January 1991. 104 mins. Cert PG.

Roger Corman's Frankenstein Unbound. Roger Corman, maestro of the '50s and '60s low-budget quickie, returns to directing after a hiatus of nineteen years. Not that you would notice. This tired piece of schlock looks as tacky as anything Corman 'knocked out' in '65 or '66. Clambering around the cardboard sets is the unlikely appar-

The bumpy road to happiness: Daniel Auteuil and Firmine Richard make strange roommates in Coline Serreau's delightful Romuald & Juliette *(from Gala).*

ition of John Hurt as Dr Joseph Buchanan, a brilliant scientist from the year 2031. While attempting to create a weapon that 'makes things disappear', the good doctor falls through 'a time slip' and ends up in nineteenth-century Europe. There he bumps into a whole string of celebrities – Mary Godwin and future husband Percy Shelley, Dr Frankenstein and his monster and the great Lord Byron. While Corman has some fun with these meetings of remarkable men, his film soon generates into a low-budget *Back to the Future* meets *Frankenstein*, both genres which are well beyond their sell-by date. A sequel is in the works. [JC-W]

Also with: Raul Julia (Dr Victor Frankenstein), Bridget Fonda (Mary Godwin Shelley), Nick Brimble (Monster), Jason Patric (Lord Byron), Michael Hutchence (Percy Shelley), Catherine Rabett (Elizabeth), Grady Clarkson, Geoffrey Copleston, Myriam Cyr, Mickey Knox. Dir: Roger Corman. Pro: Corman, Thom Mount and Kobi Jaeger. Assoc Pro: Laura Medina and Jay Cassidy. Screenplay: Corman, F. X. Feeney and Ed Neumeier; based on the novel by Brian W. Aldiss. Ph: Armando Nannuzzi and Michael Scott. Ed: Jay Cassidy. Pro Des: Enrico Tovaglieri. M: Carl Davis. Costumes: Franca Zucchelli. Sound: Gary Alper. (Mount Co.–Blue Dolphin.) Rel: 11 January 1991. 86 mins. Cert 18.

Romuald & Juliette. A successful, happily married chairman of a yoghurt company is framed for corruption and hides out with his black office cleaner. As *'Trop Belle Pour Toi!'* was contrived and pretentious, so *Romuald & Juliette* is brimming with warmth and ingenuity. And although rooted in fantasy, this human comedy exposes a very real world and offers few compromises – it's both a joy and an education. After being spotted in a restaurant by the casting director, office worker Firmine Richard made her film debut as the responsible, hard-working and no-bull Juliette. A remarkable performance. [JC-W]

Also with: Daniel Auteuil (Romuald), Pierre Vernier (Blache) Maxime Leroux (Cloquet), Gilles Privat, Muriel Combeau, Catherine Salviat, Alexandre Basse. Dir and Screenplay: Coline Serreau. Pro: Jean-Louis Piel and Philippe Carcassonne. Ph: Jean-Noel Ferragut. Ed: Catherine Renault. M: various. Costumes: Monique Perrot. Sound: Joelle Dufour. (Cinea Enilog Films FR3–Gala.) Rel: 10 August 1990. 107 mins. Cert 12.

The Rookie. Routine Clint Eastwood vehicle, a present to Warner Bros for letting him direct *White Hunter, Black Heart*. Once again Eastwood is a tough, unsociable and indestructible cop, on the trail of a murderous car thief. Enter Charlie Sheen as the rookie of the title, a preppie, squeaky-clean cop signed up to replace Eastwood's murdered partner. Something's got to give. Corny, stunt-heavy and occasionally rather nasty actioner, with the usual quota of throwaway dialogue, car stunts and despicable villains. A box-office dud, which should cause Warners to reassess their Eastwood formula. [JC-W]

Cast includes: Clint Eastwood (Nick Pulovski), Charlie Sheen (David Ackerman), Raul Julia (Strom), Sonia Braga (Liesl), Tom Skerritt (Eugene Ackerman), Lara Flynn Boyle (Sarah), Pepe Serna (Lt Ray Garcia), Marco Rodriguez, Pete Randall, Donna Mitchell, Xander Berkeley, Tony Plana, Seth Allen. Dir: Clint Eastwood. Pro: Howard Kazanjian, Steven Siebert and David Valdes. Screenplay: Boaz Yakin and Scott Spiegel. Ph: Jack N. Green. Ed: Joel Cox. Pro Des: Judy Cammer. M: Lennie Niehaus. Sound: Don Johnson. (Malpaso–Warner.) Rel: 18 January 1991. 115 mins. Cert PG.

Rosencrantz and Guildenstern Are Dead. Budget-conscious screen version of Tom Stoppard's celebrated stage burlesque, inspired by two minor Shakespearean characters, the courtiers Rosencrantz and Guildenstern, friends of Hamlet. Mysteriously summoned to Elsinore castle, R & G find Fate in a strange mood. They pass the time playing word games and discussing the imponderables of life, while Rosencrantz, less intellectual than his colleague, verges on making a series of remarkable discoveries and inventions (the displacement of water, the first executive toy, the bi-plane etc.). Meanwhile, the tragedy of *Hamlet* unfolds around them. Although heavy-going at times, the film is blessed by a reappraisal of Stoppard's ingenious dialogue, positively bursting with thought-provoking puns. Self-indulgent, maybe, but a most unusual and ultimately rewarding film. Filmed in Yugoslavia by Stoppard himself, making an assured directorial debut. [JC-W]

Cast includes: Gary Oldman (Rosencrantz), Tim Roth (Guildenstern), Richard Dreyfuss (the player), Joanna Roth (Ophelia), Iain Glen (Hamlet), Donald Sumpter (Claudius),

Men will play with guns: Clint Eastwood is promised a filling from Raul Julia in Warner's decidedly below-par The Rookie.

Joanna Miles (Gertrude), Ian Richardson (Polonius), Ljubo Zecevic, Sven Medvesck, John Burgess. Dir and Screenplay: Tom Stoppard. Pro: Michael Brandman and Emanuel Azenberg. Ex Pro: Louise Stephens and Thomas J. Rizzo. Co-Pro: Iris Merlis and Patrick Whitley. Ph: Peter Biziou. Ed: Nicolas Gaster. Pro Des: Vaughan Edwards. M: Stanley Myers. Costumes: Andreane Neofitou. Sound: Louis

Kramer. (Brandenberg Int.–HoBo.) Rel: 24 May 1991. 117 mins. Cert PG.

The Russia House. Classy, top-drawer production of John Le Carré's *glasnost* spy novel. Sean Connery is Barley Blair, a witty, gruff 'unmade bed' of a British publisher who is coerced by

Danes at sea: Richard Dreyfuss, Tim Roth and Gary Oldman in Tom Stoppard's delicious Rosencrantz and Guildenstern Are Dead *(from HoBo).*

Glasnost with gloss: a charismatic Sean Connery baits and courts your common-or-garden Russian hausfrau Michelle Pfeiffer – in UIP's The Russia House.

British Intelligence into discovering the identity of a Russian scientist. Blair goes along with the plan, in spite of his attraction to the scientist's go-between, Katya – 'Russia's answer to the Venus di Milo'. Michelle Pfeiffer is surprisingly effective as the Russian housewife (although unbelievably beautiful for the part), fighting the chains of moral pain, but Connery has all the best lines. And the film has so much else to recommend it – the authentic Moscow (and Leningrad) locations, Tom Stoppard's sparkling script, Jerry Goldsmith's sweeping score and a superb turn from James Fox as the bemused head of British Intelligence. Unfortunately, its many good elements do not compensate for a surprisingly dull film. Shoot the editor? [JC-W]

Also with: Roy Scheider (Russell), James Fox (Ned), Klaus Maria Brandauer (Dante), John Mahoney, Michael Kitchen, J. T. Walsh, Ken Russell, David Threlfall, Mac

McDonald, Nicholas Woodeson, Martin Clunes, Ian McNiece, Denys Hawthorne, Nikolai Pastukhov, Jay Benedict, Martin Wenner, Charlotte Cornwell, Gennady Venov, David Ryall. Dir: Fred Schepisi. Pro: Schepisi and Paul Maslansky. Screenplay: Tom Stoppard; from the novel by John Le Carré. Ph: Ian Baker. Ed: Peter Honess. Pro Des: Richard MacDonald. M: Jerry Goldsmith. Costumes: Ruth Myers. Sound: Chris Munro. (MGM/UA/Pathé Entertainment–UIP.) Rel: 22 February 1991. 123 mins. Cert 15.

The Salute of the Jugger. Ultra-violent, post-apocalyptic twaddle about a nomadic band of battle-scarred gladiators. Wearing chains and segments of rubber tyre, this crew of misfits compete in a bloody game not unlike American gridiron football, using a dog's skull instead of a ball. And they called *Rollerball* sadistic! For the record, a jugger is a participant of this 'sport', with no apparent profit other than the joy of winning. Filmed in South Australia by first-time director David (Webb) Peoples, scripter of *Blade Runner, Predator* and *Leviathan*. [JC-W]

Cast includes: Rutger Hauer (Sallow), Joan Chen (Kidda), Vincent Phillip D'Onofrio (Young Gar), Anna Katarina (Big Cimber), Delroy Lindo (Mbulu), Max Fairchild (Gonzo), Hugh Keays-Byrne (Lord Vile), Gandhi MacIntyre, Justin Monju, Lia Francisa, Steve Rackman. Dir and Screenplay: David Peoples. Pro: Charles Roven. Ex Pro: Bryan Rosen. Ph: David Eggby. Ed: Richard Francis-Bruce. Pro Des: John Stoddart. M: Todd Boekelheide. Sound: Jay Boekelheide and Lloyd Carrick. (Kings Road Entertainment–Virgin Vision.) Rel: 19 October 1990. 92 mins. Cert 18.

Scenes from a Mall. Los Angeles, Christmas Eve – a day in the life of a couple celebrating their 16th wedding anniversary. Deborah Fifer (Bette Midler) is a successful psychologist and author of the best-selling marriage guide *I Do! I Do! I Do!*. Nick Fifer (Woody Allen) is a top-echelon sports lawyer. While wandering around LA's illustrious Beverly Center they discover some painful truths about one another. Interesting to see Bette Midler and Woody Allen on such intimate terms, but this is pretty hackneyed territory. There are a few bright moments (a reconciliation during a screening of *Salaam Bombay*), but not enough considering the talent involved. [JC-W]

Also with: Bill Irwin (Mime), Daren Firestone (Sam), Rebecca Nickels (Jennifer), Paul Mazursky (Dr Hans Clava). Dir and Pro: Paul Mazursky. Screenplay: Mazursky and Roger L. Simon. Ph: Fred Murphy. Ed: Stuart Pappé. Pro Des: Pato Guzman. M: Marc Shaiman. Costumes: Albert Wolsky. Sound: Les Lezarowitz. (Silver Screen Partners IV/Touchstone–Warner.) Rel: 26 April 1991. 88 mins. Cert 15.

Secret Wedding – Boda Secreta. Argentine/Dutch/Canadian co-production about a romance set against a political background. More romance than politics, though. [FDM]

Cast includes: Tito Haas (Fermin), Mirtha Busnelli (Tota), Sergio Poves Campos (Pipi), Nathan Pinzon (priest). Dir and Screenplay: Alejandro Agesi. Ex Pro: J. Collini, K. Dasander, D. Wigman and Andre Bennett. Ph: Ricardo Rodriguez. Ed: Rene Weigman. M: Paul M. Van Brugge. (Allarts Enterprises/Cinephile/Movie Center–Metro.) Rel: floating; first shown London (ICA) 4 January 1991. 95 mins. No cert.

✓**The Sheltering Sky**. 1947, Morocco/Algeria/Niger. Powerful intelligent screen adaptation of Paul Bowles's celebrated novel, a journey through the Sahara to self-discovery. John Malkovich and Debra Winger play Porter and Kit Moresby, composer and playwright respectively, and self-styled American 'travellers', joined by dilettante George Turner (Campbell Scott), who is in love with Kit. In the blazing heat of North Africa, their lives are transformed. Bernardo Bertolucci, who won an Oscar for directing *The Last Emperor*, turns in arguably his *magnum opus*, capturing the sweat, dust and flies of Africa with an unerring eye. Fiercely atmospheric, enigmatic and superbly crafted, *The Sheltering Sky* makes *Lawrence of Arabia* look like a mere movie. [JC-W]

Also with: Jill Bennett (Mrs Lyle), Timothy Spall (Eric Lyle), Eric Vu-An (Balqassim), Paul Bowles (narrator), Amina Annabi, Sotigui Kouyate, Philippe Morier-Genoud, Ben Smail, Carolyn De Fonseca, Veronica Lazar. Dir: Bernardo Bertolucci. Pro: Jeremy Thomas. Ex Pro: William Aldrich. Screenplay: Bertolucci and Mark Peploe; from the book by Paul Bowles. Ph: Vittorio Storaro. Ed: Gabriella Cristiani. Pro Des: Gianni Silvestri. M: Ryuichi Sakamoto and

Woody Allen and Bette Midler try to have a quiet drink in Paul Mazursky's marital trifle, Scenes from a Mall *(Warner).*

Richard Howowitz. Costumes: James Acheson. Sound: Don Sharpe. (Palace.) Rel: 30 November 1990. 138 mins. Cert 18.

She's Out of Control. Dad suddenly finds daughter Ami Dolenz has come into full, worrying sexual flower. Billed as a 'true-life comedy about every teenager's fantasy and every father's nightmare', this minor comedy's major appeal is probably the 25 musical numbers. Tony Danza is pleasant enough. Undemanding stuff. [FDM]

Also with: Wallace Shawn, Dick O'Neill, Laura Mooney, Derek McGrath, Dana Ashbrook, Matthew Perry, Lance Wilson-White, Michael Maimo, Marcie Barkin, Diana Barrows, Jan Bina. Dir: Stan Dragoti. Pro: Stephen Deutsch. Assoc. Pro: Bill

John Malkovich and Debra Winger star in Bernardo Bertolucci's The Sheltering Sky, *a film of enormous power and mystery, a stunning cross between* Lawrence of Arabia *and* Last Tango in Paris *– from Palace.*

comic performance as the cop dying to be killed and manages to keep the lid on his histrionics. A neat idea, directed at a decent clip by first-time director Gregg Champion (son of the Broadway choreographer Gower Champion). Could have been a lot funnier, though. [JC-W]

Also with: Matt Frewer (Ernie Dills), Teri Garr (Carolyn Simpson), Barry Corbin (Captain), Xander Berkeley (Stark), Kaj-Erik Eriksen (Dougie Simpson), Joe Pantoliano, Rob Roy, Tony Pantages, Wes Tritter, Kim Kondrashoff, Paul Jarrett, Paul Batten, Kevin McNulty. Dir: Gregg Champion. Pro: Todd Black. Ex Pro: Joe Wizan and Mickey Borofsky. Screenplay: John Blumenthal and Michael Berry. Ph: John Connor. Ed: Frank Morriss. Pro Des: Michael Bolton. M: Ira Newborn. Costumes: Christopher Ryan. Sound: Larry Sutton. (Gladden–Rank.) Rel: 8 February 1991. 97 mins. Cert 12.

Sibling Rivalry. Slyly plotted comedy about two chalk-and-cheese sisters who fall for two widely different brothers. There's a body in there, too, to take the edge off the sweetness, although Bill Pulman's performance as a nerdy blind salesman (a sort of 'Crispin Glover meets Robin Williams' affair) shifts the film into reverse gear. Unfortunately, Carl Reiner directs his cast with a bullwhip – subtlety would have made this well-scripted diversion a lot, lot funnier. However, Kirstie Alley has come a long way since she played the Vulcan pilot in *Star Trek II* – she is, arguably, America's most successful, accomplished and beautiful comedienne. [JC-W]

Cast includes: Kirstie Alley (Marjorie Turner), Bill Pullman (Nicholas Meany), Carrie Fisher (Iris Turner-Hunter), Jami Gertz (Jeanine), Scott Bakula (Harry Turner), Sam Elliott (Charles Turner Jr), Ed O'Neill (Wilbur Meany), Frances Sternhagen (Rose Turner), John Randolph (Charles Turner Sr), Paul Benedict, Bill Macy, Matthew Laurance. Dir: Carl Reiner. Pro: David Lester, Don Miller and Liz Glotzer. Ex Pro: George Shapiro and Howard West. Screenplay: Martha Goldhirsh. Ph: Reynaldo Villalobos. Ed: Bud Molin. Pro Des: Jeannine C. Oppewall. M: Jack Elliott; numbers performed by Dwight Yoakam, Joan Armatrading, Estelle Reiner etc. Costumes: Durinda Wood. Sound: Richard Goodman. (Castle Rock/Nelson Entertainment–First Independent.) Rel: 31 May 1991. 88 mins. Cert 15.

No sex for the wicked: Kirstie Alley attempts to seduce her boring husband (Scott Bakula) in First Independent's promising farce Sibling Rivalry.

Wilson. Ex Pro: Robert Kaufman. Co-Pro: J. G. Wilson. Screenplay: Seth Winston and Michael J. Nathanson. Ph: Donald Peterman. Ed: Dov Hoenig. Pro Des: David L. Snyder. Art: Joe Wood. Costumes: Maria France. M: Alan Silvestri. M Sup: Tim Sexton. (Weintraub Entertainment Group–Columbia/Tri-Star.) Rel: floating; first shown London (Odeon, West End) 13 July 1990. 94 mins. Cert 12.

A Shock to the System. Morally dubious black comedy-thriller with Michael Caine as a New York advertising executive ('a sorcerer' who 'can fix anything') who accidentally kills a vagrant on the subway. Finding that the episode leaves him with no feelings of guilt, he proceeds to tidy up his life with a little murder here and there. Elizabeth McGovern as his unwitting accomplice is somewhat under-used, but then this is primarily a vehicle for Caine and his slimy charisma. Fun while it lasts. [JC-W]

Cast includes: Michael Caine (Graham Marshall), Elizabeth McGovern (Stella Anderson), Peter Riegert (Robert Benham), Swoosie Kurtz (Leslie Marshall), Will Patton (Lt Laker), Jenny Wright (Melanie O'Connor), John McMartin (George Brewster), Barbara Baxley, Haviland Morris, Philip Moon, Kent Broadhurst, David Schramm, Christopher Durang, Mia Dillon, Mike Starr. Dir: Jan Egelson. Pro: Patrick McCormick. Ex Pro: Leslie Morgan. Assoc Pro: Alice Arlen. Screenplay: Andrew Klavan; based on the novel by Simon Brett. Ph: Paul Goldsmith. Ed: Peter C. Frank and William A. Anderson. Pro Des: Howard Cummings. M: Gary Chang. Costumes: John Dunn. Sound: Danny Michael. (Corsair–Medusa.) Rel: 26 October 1990. 87 mins. Cert 15.

Short Time. Burt Simpson has spent thirty years on the Seattle police force and has eight days left. When he discovers he is dying of a rare blood disease (Wexler's Curtain), he realises his son can only claim his life insurance if he is killed in the line of duty. Determined to stop a fatal bullet, Burt Simpson has eight days to become a hero. Dabney Coleman turns in another fine

The Silence of the Lambs *(Rank): Jodie Foster (far right) watches as Tracey Walter (left) and a forensic medic check for vital clues in the mouth of a murder victim. Below: Foster faces master criminal Dr Hannibal Lecter (Anthony Hopkins) in a bid to find clues to the identity of a serial killer.*

Side Out. Mediocre movie about beach volleyball. Will 'hero' C. Thomas Howell throw the Big Game to please his ex-girlfriend (Harley Jane Kozak)? And do you really want to see it to find out? (Lots of delightfully brown beach girls, though.) [FDM]

Also with: Peter Horton (Zack Barnes), Courtney Thorne-Smith (Samantha), Christopher Rydell (Wiley Hunter), Terry Kiser (Uncle Max), Randy Stoklos (Rollo Vincent). Dir: Peter Israelson. Pro: Gary Foster. Ex Pro: Jay Weston. Screenplay: David Thoreau. Ph: Ron Garcia. Ed: Conrad Buff. Pro: Dan Lomino. Sound: Vince Gutierrez. Art: Bruce Krone. M: Jeff Lorber. (Columbia Tri-Star.) Rel: floating; first shown London (Odeon Mezzanine) 4 January 1991. 100 mins. Cert 12.

√**The Silence of the Lambs**. Dr Hannibal Lecter is a brilliant psychiatrist, pre-eminent in his field. Unfortunately, he also has a psychotic need to kill and eat parts of his victims. Fortunately, he is incarcerated in maximum security in an asylum for the insane. And he is the only man who can provide a lead to the identity of a serial killer nicknamed 'Buffalo Bill'. Jodie Foster is the FBI student used to infiltrate Lecter's mind but it is Lecter's eery intelligence, and Anthony Hopkins's manifestation of it, that supplies this chilling, intelligent thriller with its trump card. Although Lecter instantly sees through the FBI's plan, he plays along for his own amusement until Foster announces triumphantly, 'Your anagrams are showing, doctor.' A gripping examination of the criminal mind, *The Silence of the Lambs* moves at a cracking pace and triumphs on almost every level. Based on the best-seller by Thomas Harris, author of *Black Sunday* and *Red Dragon* (the latter filmed as *Manhunter*, with Brian Cox cast as Hannibal Lecter). [JC-W]

Also with: Jodie Foster (Clarice Starling), Scott Glenn (Jack Crawford), Ted Levine (James Gumb), Kasi Lemmons (Ardelia Mapp), Anthony Heald (Dr Frederick Chilton), Brooke Smith (Catherine Martin), Diane Baker (Senator Ruth Martin), Stuart Rudin, Leib Lensky, Pat McNamara, Tracey Walter, Kenneth Utt, Dan Butler, Paul Lazar, Obba Babatunde, Roger Corman, Ron Vawter, Charles Napier, Jim Dratfield, Danny Darst, Cynthia Ettinger, Brent Hinkley, Chris Isaak, Josh Broder, Harry Northup. Dir: Jonathan Demme. Pro: Edward Saxon, Kenneth Utt and Ron Bozman. Ex Pro: Gary Goetzman. Screenplay: Ted Tally. Ph: Tak Fujimoto. Ed: Craig McKay. Pro Des: Kristi Zea. M: Howard Shore; numbers performed by Tom Petty and The Heartbreakers, Book of Love etc. Costumes: Colleen Atwood. Sound: Kevin Lievsay. (Orion/Strong Heart–Rank.) Rel: 31 May 1991. 119 mins. Cert 18.

Silent Scream. True-life story of Larry Winters, a Scottish paramilitary sentenced to life imprisonment for the killing of a Soho barman. The film attempts to get under Winters's skin, examining his childhood and adolescence through a series of flashbacks. Ambitiously, it also explores the workings of his mind, scrambled by drugs and choked with memories and visions. The final effect is to produce an excruciating eighty-six minutes, not because we suffer for Winters under the injustice of the Scottish penal system, but because the film presents its hero as a theatrical gimmick frittered away in a zigzag narrative. Some might dismiss this as pretentious cinema. Winner of the best actor award (for Iain Glen) at the 1990 Berlin Film Festival. [JC-W]

Cast includes: Iain Glen (Larry Winters), Tom Watson (Patrick), Anne Kristen (Mary Winters), Alexander Morton (Don Winters), Paul Samson, John Murtagh, David Hayman, Julie Graham, Vincent Friell, Harry Jones, Michael McDonald. Dir: David Hayman. Pro: Paddy Higson. Ex Pro: Colin McCabe and Ben Gibson. Screenplay: Bill Beech and Jane Beech. Ph: Denis Crossan. Ed: Justin Krish. Pro Des: Andy Harris. M: Callum McNair. Costumes: Trisha Biggar. Sound: Cameron Crosby. (Film Four International/Scottish

Iain Glen in his award-winning role as the creative convict Larry Winters – in David Hayman's confusing and over-directed Silent Scream *(from the BFI).*

Would you marry this man? Julia Roberts sleeps on the bed she has made with Patrick Bergin in Joseph Ruben's sadly vacuous thriller, Sleeping with the Enemy *(from Fox).*

Film Production Fund–BFI.) Rel: 19 October 1990. 86 mins. Cert 15.

Sleeping with the Enemy. Handsome but disappointingly one-dimensional thriller about a battered wife who escapes from her husband to start a new life. Julia Roberts as the young victim is lovely to look at, but Patrick Bergin's psycho is merely an unexplained cipher. Worse still, the music telegraphs the events to come, many of which lack any logic. Kim Basinger was linked to the project for a year, but backed out when the studio couldn't find a male star to suit her. Bergin fits the part physically (looking uncannily like Kevin Kline without a sense of humour), but the script gives him little to chew on. [JC-W]

Cast includes: Julia Roberts (Sara/Laura Burney), Patrick Bergin (Martin Burney), Kevin Anderson (Ben Woodward), Eliza-

beth Lawrence (Chloe), Kyle Secor, Claudette Nevins, Tony Abatemarco, Marita Geraghty, Harley Venton, Nancy Fish. Dir: Joseph Ruben. Pro: Leonard Goldberg. Ex Pro: Jeffrey Chernov. Screenplay: Ronald Bass; from the novel by Nancy Price. Ph: John Lindley. Ed: George Bowers. Pro Des: Doug Kraner. M: Jerry Goldsmith. Costumes: Richard Hornung. Sound: Susumu Tokunow. (Fox.) Rel: 12 April 1991. 100 mins. Cert 15.

Spaced Invaders. Disney jumps on the overflowing bandwagon of films about cute little characters arriving from other planets. Confused by a radio broadcast of *War of the Worlds*, a Martian spaceship lands on Earth instead of the planet they're supposed to be helping invade. It's easy to see that the debuting director comes from the special effects department, as that's what he relies on here. Just as well there's something to distract from the obnoxious kids. [FDM]

Cast includes: Douglas Barr (Sam), Royal Dano (Wrenchmuller), Ariana Richards (Kathy), J. J. Anderson, Gregg Berger, Wayne Alexander, Kevin Thompson. Dir:

Sean Penn deals out some tough justice in Phil Joanou's gritty, well-acted gangster drama State of Grace *(Rank).*

Patrick Read Johnson. Pro: Cingolani. Ex Pro: George Zekevic. Screenplay: John and Scott Lawrence Alexander. Ph: James L. Carter. Ed: Seth Gavan and Daniel Gross. Pro Des: Tony Tremblay. Art: Alexander. M: David Russo (Smart Egg Pictures-Luigi Cingolani-Touchstone Pictures in assoc with Silver Screen Partners 4–Medusa.) Rel: floating; first shown in London (Cannon, Haymarket) 3 August 1990. 100 mins. Cert PG.

State of Grace. Well-acted but slow-moving gangster film set in Hell's Kitchen, on the West Side of Manhattan. Sean Penn stars as Terry Noonan, an Irish-American who returns to New York after a mysterious absence (in prison?). There, he is reunited with his childhood friend Jackie Flannery (Gary Oldman on top form) and Jackie's sister, Kathleen (Robin Wright), Terry's erstwhile sweetheart. But fings ain't what they used to be, as Jackie's older brother, Frankie (Ed Harris), attempts to form a partnership with the Mafia. Inspired by the real-life misadventures of the Irish gang 'the Westies', who ruled Hell's Kitchen in the 'seventies. Make it fun – guess the order in which the characters die. [JC-W]

Also with: John Turturro (Nick), John C. Reilly (Stevie), R. D. Call, Joe Viterelli, Burgess Meredith, Dierdre O'Connell, Marco St John, Thomas G. Waites. Dir: Phil Joanou. Pro: Ned Dowd, Randy Ostrow and Ron Rotholz. Screenplay: Dennis McIntyre and David Rabe. Ph: Jordan Cronenweth. Ed: Claire Simpson. Pro Des: Patrizia Von Brandenstein and Doug Kraner. M: Ennio Morricone. Costumes: Aude Bronson-Howard. Sound: Peter A. Ilardi. (Cinehaus-Orion–Rank.) Rel: 14 June 1991. 134 mins. Cert 18.

Staying Together. Sentimental domestic drama set in the small town of Ridgeway, South Carolina. Three young brothers work at 'McDermott's Famous Chicken' diner and dream of turning the place into a family conglomerate – selling 'chicken, condoms and running shoes'. When the father sells the place to developers without telling the boys, sparks begin to fly. An ensemble cast act the socks off Monte Merrick's mundane screenplay, while a slushy score conspires to sell the film up river. *Mystic Pizza* without the edge. [JC-W]

Cast includes: Sean Astin (Duncan McDermott), Stockard Channing (Nancy Trainer), Melinda Dillon (Eileen McDermott), Jim Haynie (Jake McDermott), Dermot Mulroney (Kit McDermott), Tim Quill (Brian McDermott), Keith Szarabajka (Kevin Burley), Daphne Zuniga (Beverly Young), Levon Helm, Dinah Manoff, Sheila Kelley, Ryan Hill, Rick Marshall. Dir: Lee Grant. Pro: Joseph Feury. Ex Pro: John Daly and Derek Gibson. Screenplay: Monte Merrick. Ph: Dick Bush. Ed: Katherine Wenning. Pro Des: Stuart Wurtzel. M: Miles Goodman; songs performed by Paul Cotton, Kevin Savigar, Levon Helm, Melinda Dillon etc. Costumes: Carol Oditz. Sound: Jan Erik Brodin. (Hemdale.) Rel: 8 February 1991. 91 mins. Cert 15.

✓**Stella.** Glutinous re-make of the 1937 weepie with Barbara Stanwyck (*Stella Dallas*), the story of a mother's selfless love for her only child. To give Bette Midler her due, she was appalled by the idea of playing the vulgar, working-

Love means never having to comb your own hair: Trini Alvarado and Bette Midler in the mawkish Stella, *from Rank.*

class mother but was persuaded by Disney (with whom she has a long-term contract) to do so. Barmaid Stella Claire (whose motto, 'it's a great life – if you don't weaken', gets her into a multitude of scrapes), brings up her daughter, Jenny, by her own rules. This produces a rollercoaster ride of emotions, but only the last five minutes of the film begin to make the trip worthwhile. However, Trini Alvarado, as Jenny, is a stand-out. [JC-W]

Also with: John Goodman (Ed Munn), Stephen Collins (Stephen Dallas), Marsha Mason (Janice Morrison), Eileen Brennan (Mrs Wilkerson), Linda Hart (Debbie Whitman), Ben Stiller (Jim Uptegrove), William McNamara (Pat Robbins), John Bell, Rex Robbins, Ron White, Matthew Cowles, Jayne Eastwood, Charles Gray. Dir: John Erman. Pro: Samuel Goldwyn Jr. Ex Pro: David V. Picker. Co-Pro: Bonnie Bruckheimer-Martell. Screenplay: Robert Getchell. Ph: Billy Williams. Ed: Jerrold L. Ludwig. Pro Des: James Hulsey. M: John Morris; songs performed by The Mamas & The Papas, Percy Sledge, The David Rose

Orchestra, The Box Tops etc. Costumes: Theadora Van Runkle. Sound: Bruce Carwardine. (Samuel Goldwyn/Touchstone–Rank.) Rel: 7 September 1990. 114 mins. Cert 15.

Stepfather 2: Make Room for Daddy. 'Jerry Blake likes to look after the family – *any* family,' was the selling line for the original *Stepfather*, in which Jerry, a psychotic real-estate salesman, was stabbed and shot to death at the film's end. This unconvincing but darkly enjoyable sequel opens with Jerry – now Dr Gene Clifford – having a nightmare about his own demise. Do we hear cries of 'Cheat!' from the back benches? Clifford (Terry O'Quinn again), incarcerated in a criminal mental hospital, escapes and starts a new life as a personal guidance counsellor. Holding therapy groups with local women, the good doctor soon gets to realise his dream of being a family man again. This is a workmanlike sequel, or re-make, well acted by the entire cast, with the one-liners reminding us not to take the gore too seriously. From the director of *Leatherface: The Texas Chainsaw Massacre III*. [CB]

Also with: Meg Foster (Carol Grayland), Caroline Williams (Matty Crimmins), Jonathan Brandis (Todd Grayland), Henry Brown (Dr Joseph Danvers), Mitchell Laurance, Leon Martell, Renata Scott, John O'Leary, Eric Brown. Dir: Jeff Burr. Pro: Darin Scott and William Burr. Ex Pro: Carol Lampman. Screenplay: John Auerbach; based on characters created by Carolyn Lefcourt, Brian Garfield and Donald E. Westlake. Ph: Jacek Laskus. Ed: Pasquale A. Buba. Pro Des: Bernadette Disanto. M: Jim Manzie and Pat Regan. Costumes: Julie Carnahan. (ITC Entertainment.) Rel: London (Scala) 8 March 1991. 88 mins. No cert.

Stockade. Loner Franklin Bean Junior (Charlie Sheen – here directed by father Martin) has an 'attitude' problem: faced with the alternative of jail or the army, he joins up but is still a rebel. When he's thrown into the army jail (The Stockade) he comes to a fateful decision – and maturity. [FDM]

Cast: Charlie Sheen (Bean), Martin Sheen (Sgt McKimmey), F. Murray Abraham (Garcia), Larry Fishburne (Stokes), Blu Mankuma (Spoonman), Michael Beach (Webb), Harry Stewart, John Toles-Bey, James Marshall, Ramon Estevez, Jay Bra-

Charlie Sheen (left) is a loner facing up to his personality problem in army jail in Entertainment's Stockade.

zeau, Samantha Langevan, Ken Douglas, Weston McMillion, David O'Neill, Alan Lysell, Don Davis, Roark Critchlow, Alec Burden, Steve Hilton, Joe Lowry. Dir and (with Dennis Shyrack) Screenplay: Martin Sheen; based on the novel by Gordon Weaver. Pro: Richard Davis. Ex Pro: Peter E. Strauss and Frank Giustra. Co-Pro: Glennis Liberty. Ph: Richard Leiterman. Ed: Martin Hunter. Pro Des: Ian Thomas. M: Georges Delerue. (Entertainment.) Rel: floating; first shown London (Prince Charles) 23 November 1990. 98 mins. Cert 12.

Tatie Danielle. Wickedly funny black comedy about an 82-year-old dear who lives in the Yonne region of France. There Auntie Danielle leads a peaceful

In a class of her own: Tsilla Chelton as Tatie Danielle *(Palace), octogenarian ogress of the year.*

existence, tormenting her ailing house-keeper and setting her Doberman on the postman and unsuspecting smaller dogs. When the family arrives to visit, Danielle plays the frail, aged patient, while cursing humanity under her breath. She is too clever to let anybody catch her out, but sooner or later you know the old witch will meet her match. A real original, this, genuinely funny, occasionally touching and very

well played. From the director of *Life Is a Long Quiet River*. [JC-W]

Cast includes: Tsilla Chelton (Tatie Danielle), Catherine Jacob (Catherine Billard), Isabelle Nanty (Sandrine), Neige Dolsky (Odile), Éric Pratt (Jean-Pierre Nillard), Laurence Février (Jeanne Billard), Virginie Pradal, Mathieu Foulon, Gary Ledoux, André Wilms, Patrick Bouchitey. Dir: Étienne Chatiliez. Pro: Charles Gassot. Screenplay: Chatiliez and Florence Quentin. Ph: Philippe Welt. Ed: Catherine Renault. Pro Des: Geoffroy Larcher. M: Gabriel Yared; songs performed by Catherine Ringer. Costumes: Elisabeth Tavernier. Sound: Guillaume Dalmasso and Dominique Brémond. (Telema/FR3 Films/Les Productions du Champ Poirier–Palace.) Rel: 5 April 1991. 110 mins. Cert 15.

✓**Teenage Mutant Ninja Turtles**. The most bizarre marketing idea that became the most successful independent film ever made. For the record, turtles Leonardo, Raphael, Donatello and Michelangelo are accidentally dropped in a New York sewer where

Turtle cuisine: pizza – with no anchovies! A scene from the extraordinary Teenage Mutant Ninja Turtles *(from Virgin Vision).*

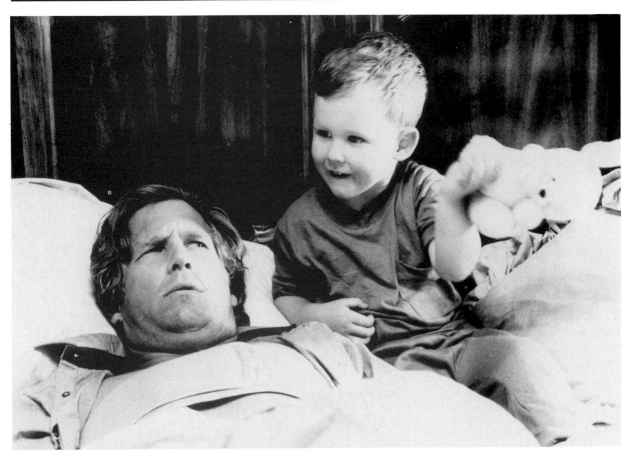

Thirty years on: Granddaddy Duane Jackson (Jeff Bridges) is picked on by his children's offspring (here, Ty Chambers) in Bogdanovich's extraordinary Texasville, *from Guild.*

they encounter a spillage of radioactive ooze. Growing to the size of small humans with the gift of speech, they are taught the martial arts by a similarly mutated rat, the ninja master 'Splinter'. If you want to know more, grab a kid. The film's wacky sense of humour, dotted with American street slang, makes this a refreshingly different and unpretentious kids' movie, while the violence is strictly of the cartoon variety. Judith Hoag (*Cadillac Man*) makes a comely leading lady, the sets are awesome and the story is complicated enough to fire the imagination of children everywhere. Incidentally, the turtles and Splinter were created by the late Jim Henson's Creature Shop and the director is England's very own Steve Barron. [JC-W]

Cast includes: Judith Hoag (April O'Neil), Elias Koteas (Casey Jones), Josh Pais (Raphael), Michelan Sisti (Michelangelo), Leif Tilden (Donatello), David Forman (Leonardo), Michael Turney (Danny Pennington), Jay Patterson (Charles Pennington), Raymond Serra (Chief Sterns), James Sato (The Shredder), Toshishiro Obata, Sam Rockwell, Kitty Fitzgibbon, and the voices of Robbie Rist (Michelangelo), Kevin Clash (Splinter), Brian Tochi (Leonardo), David McCharen (The Shredder), Corey Feldman (Donatello). Dir: Steve Barron. Pro: Kim Dawson, Simon Fields and David Chan. Ex Pro: Raymond Chow. Screenplay: Todd W. Langen and Bobby Herbeck; based on characters created by Kevin Eastman and Peter Laird. Ph: John Fenner. Pro Des: Roy Forge Smith. M: John du Prez. Costumes: John M. Hay. Sound: Lee Orloff, Steve Maslow, Michael Herbick and Gregg Landaker. (Golden Harvest/Limelight–Virgin Vision.) Rel: 23 November 1990. 93 mins. Cert PG.

Texasville is, perhaps, unique of its kind. Nineteen years after Peter Bogdanovich directed *The Last Picture Show*, he reassembled his original cast (save Ellen Burstyn) to take a fresh, lively look at Anarene, Texas, and its inhabitants. The film (this time in colour) opens on a flat, sagebrush landscape punctuated solely by an outsize satellite dish. We are immediately into the 'eighties ('84) – Ronald Reagan is having his colonoscopy, Duane Jackson (Jeff Bridges) has made it rich in oil and Jacy Farrow (Cybill Shepherd) has become a minor film star in Italy. With her return thirty years later, to coincide with the county's centennial celebrations, old wounds are opened and memories unleashed. This time, the film is less an ensemble, dramatic piece than a jocular, star vehicle for Bridges and Shepherd, with the healthy introduction of Annie Potts as Duane's steely, beautiful wife. The movie lags, inevitably, but is a fascinating exercise in small-town soap opera, with its all-star cast virtually intact after all these years. [JC-W]

Also with: Annie Potts (Karla Jackson), Cloris Leachman (Ruth Popper), Randy Quaid (Lester Marlow), Timothy Bottoms (Sonny Crawford), Eileen Brennan (Genevieve Morgan), William McNamara (Dickie Jackson), Pearl Jones (Minerva), Loyd Catlett (Lee Roy), Romy Snyder (Julie), Earl Poole Ball, Harvey Christiansen, Kay Pering, Allison Marich, Katherine Bongfeldt, Su Hyatt, Angie Bolling, Sharon Ullrick, Ty Chambers. Dir and Screenplay:

Peter Bogdanovich; from the novel by Larry McMurtry. Pro: Bogdanovich and Barry Spikings. Ph: Nicholas Von Sternberg. Ed: Richard Fields. Pro Des: Phedon Papamichael. M: various songs. Costumes: Rita Riggs. Sound: James Troutman, Kirk Francis and Michael Haines. (Nelson Films–Guild.) Rel: 7 December 1990. 126 mins. Cert 15.

These Foolish Things – Daddy Nostalgia. A tribute to his father, Bertrand Tavernier's tender, literate film is the story of an old man's last few days with his daughter. Dirk Bogarde, now 69, appears in his first film for twelve years, playing a 65-year-old Englishman recuperating in his home on the Cote d'Azur following a serious operation. His daughter Caroline (Jane Birkin) leaves her apartment in Paris to ply him with secret whiskies and cigarettes (behind his wife's back) and, for the first time, is let into his past. He talks of a once-perfect world, she accuses him of a selfish life. Together, peeling away the subtext, they unearth an enormous mutual love. An intelligent, if self-indulgent film, blessed with two outstanding performances, with Bogarde looking remarkable for his years. [JC-W]

Also with: Odette Laure (Miche), Emmanuelle Bataille (Juliette), Charlotte Kady (Barbara), Michele Minns, Andrée Duranson, Raymond Defendente, Louis Ducreux. Dir: Bertrand Tavernier. Pro: Adolphe Viezzi. Screenplay: Tavernier and Colo Tavernier O'Hagan. Ph: Denis Lenoir. Ed: Ariane Boeglin. Art: Jean-Louis Poveda. M: Antoine Duhamel; 'These Foolish Things' sung by Jane Birkin and Jimmy Rowles. Costumes: Christian Gasc. Sound: Michel Desrois. (Clea Prods/Little Bear/Solyfic/Eurisma–Gala.) Rel: 17 May 1991. 107 mins. Cert PG.

✓ **Three Men and a Little Lady.** Little Mary Holden's growing pains (learning to walk, potty training) are dispensed with during the picture's opening credits. And before you know it, Mary wants to know what a penis is – much to the embarrassment of her three fathers, Peter (Tom Selleck), Michael (Steve Guttenberg) and her biological dad, Jack (Ted Danson). Unlike most sequels, this follow-up to *Three Men and a Baby* is precisely that – a follow-up. It builds on the old story of the three ladykilling New York bachelors

(an architect, cartoonist and largely out-of-work actor) attempting to rear a baby on their own, and follows their misadventures with the child five years on. This time they're joined by Mary's English mother, stage actress Sylvia (Nancy Travis) – at least until she can find a *proper* father. When smarmy

Dirk Bogarde and Jane Birkin breathe intelligence into Bertrand Tavernier's literate, semi-autobiographical These Foolish Things *(from Gala).*

Growing up is fun in Disneyland: Tom Selleck and Robin Weisman in Emile Ardolino's agreeable sequel, Three Men and a Little Lady *(Warner).*

theatre director Edward (Christopher Cazenove) proposes to her, Sylvia accepts and a stately wedding in the English countryside is arranged. But Edward is a heel and the real man for Sylvia cannot bring himself to proclaim his undying love. The love story element is predictably mawkish and the final scenes in England descend into *St Trinian's*-style farce (Fiona Shaw's artful impersonation of a Joyce Grenfell schoolmarm – infatuated with Tom Selleck – is a classic): however, *Little Lady* has a good enough story to make this a most enjoyable sequel. There's also plenty of good jokes and buckets of charm. [JC-W]

Also with: Robin Weisman (Mary Holden), Sheila Hancock (Vera), John Boswall (Barrow), Jonathan Lynn (Vicar Hewitt), Sydney Walsh, Lynne Marta, Everett Wong, Bryan Pringle, Ian Redford. Dir: Emile Ardolino. Pro: Ted Field and Robert W. Cort. Ex Pro: Jean Francois Lepetit. Screenplay: Charlie Peters; from a story by Sara Parriott and Josann McGibbon. Ph: Adam Greenberg. Ed: Michael A. Stevenson. Pro Des: Stuart Wurtzel. M: James Newton Howard. Costumes: Louise Frog-

Oedipus of Africa: Rasmane Ouedraogo as the man in love with his stepmother, formerly his fiancée (played by Ina Cisse), in Artificial Eye's Tilai.

ley. Sound: C. Darin Knight. (Touchstone –Warner.) Rel: 8 February 1991. 104 mins. Cert PG.

Three Sisters – Paura e Amore. Pavia, Northern Italy, the early 'eighties. Inspired but not dictated by Chekhov's play, Margarethe von Trotta's theatrical conceit is an articulate wallow in love. The three unlikeliest sisters (teacher, housewife, medical student) experience the whole spectrum of amorous possibility – bereavement, boredom, adultery, separation, betrayal, *ad nauseam*. France's Fanny Ardant glows intelligence as the eldest, Velia; England's Greta Scacchi is lovely as Maria; and Italy's Valeria Golino steals the show as the impetuous, life-loving Sandra. However, the fine performances ultimately fail to conjure up either emotion or sympathy. [JC-W]

Also with: Peter Simonischek (Massimo), Sergio Castellitto (Roberto), Agnes Soral (Sabrina), Paolo Hendel (Federico), Gila Von Weitershausen (Erica), Jan-Paul Biczycki, Ralph Schicha, Guido Alberti. Dir: Margarethe von Trotta. Pro: Angelo Rizzoli. Ex Pro: Romano Cardarelli. Screenplay: von Trotta and Dacia Maraini. Ph: Guiseppe Lanci. Ed: Enzo Meniconi. Set Design: Giantito Burchiellaro. M: Franco Piersanti. Costumes: Nicoletta Ercole. Sound: Bruno Charrier. (Erre Produzioni/Reteitalia/Bioskop/Cinemax–Generale D'Im-

ages–Curzon.) Rel: 14 December 1990. 112 mins. Cert 12.

√ **Tie Me Up! Tie Me Down! – Atame!** Taking *The Collector* (remember that 1965 film?) a few dodgy steps further, this somewhat dubious 'bondage' film shocked the American censors, but in present-day terms hardly seems worth the fuss. A silly porno queen is abducted by a loving nutcase who ties her up (or down!) and gags her every time he goes out – bizarrely, this makes her decide she loves him. Dotty, or what? [FDM]

Cast includes: Victoria Abril (the girl), Antonio Banderas (her abductor), Loles Leon (the victim's sister), Francisco Rabal, Julieta Serrano, Maria Barranco, Ross de Palma, Lola Cardona, Montse G. Romeu, Emiliano Redondo, Oswaldo Delgado, Jose Maria Tasso, Victor Aparicio, Carlos G. Cambero, Angelina Llongueras, Concha Rabal. Dir and Screenplay: Pedro Almodóvar. Production Director: Esther Garcia. Ex Pro: Augustin Almodóvar. Ph: Jose Luis Alcaine. Ed: Jose Salcedo. M: Ennio Morricone. (El Deseo Pro–Enterprise Pictures.) Rel: floating; first shown London (Lumiere, Screen on the Hill and Gate) 6 July 1990. 102 mins. Cert 18.

Tilai (The Law). Arguably the greatest filmmaker to emerge from the West African country Burkina Faso, Idrissa Ouedraogo (*Yaaba*) captures the rural life of his country with a painterly eye. Although Ouedraogo's films exist in another world, *Tilai* is totally modern in its naturalism, humour and behaviourism, following a course of events rather than a storyline. The film's protagonist, Saga, has been away for two years, and returns home to find that his father has married his fiancée, Nogma. The law (or the *tilai*) dictates that Saga must accept his lot, but Nogma still loves Saga and love will out . . . This is leisurely, lyrical cinema, smiling with charm and awash in its own ingenuousness. Winner of the Grand Jury prize at Cannes '90. A French-Swiss-Burkina Faso co-production. [JC-W]

Cast includes: Rasmane Ouedraogo (Saga), Ina Cisse (Nogma), Roukietou Barry (Kuilga), Assane Ouedraogo (Kougri), Sibidou Sidibe (Poko), Moumouni Ouedraogo, Mariam Barry, Seydou Ouedraogo, Mariam Ouedraogo, and the inhabitants of Koumbri and Komsilga. Dir, Pro and Screenplay: Idrissa Ouedraogo. Ex Pro: Beatrice Korc.

Ph: Jean Monsigny and Pierre Laurent Chenieux. Ed: Luc Barnier. M (piano/flute/voice): Abdullah Ibrahim. Sound: Alix Comte and Dominique Hennequin. (Artificial Eye.) Rel: 22 February 1991. 81 mins. Cert PG.

Time of the Gypsies. If Emir Kusturica isn't the greatest Yugoslav filmmaker to emerge from that country in the last decade, then we have some very exciting cinema to look forward to. As original and masterful a story-teller as Fellini or Olmi, Kusturica won an Oscar nomination for his 1985 *When Father Was Away on Business* and snared the 1989 best director prize at Cannes for this film. Deservedly so. A story of magic, treachery and unrequited love, this epic saga runs to 142 minutes but is never less than watchable. An ungainly teenager, Perhan (Davor Dujmovic), is blessed with magical powers and the love of a good gypsy girl. Over the course of a decade or so, he comes to abuse both and to learn some uncomfortable truths. In the style of Latin American magic-realism, the film is rich in everyday detail and humour and never pulls its punches. An extraordinary feast for the eyes and ears, it casts a wondrous spell that lingers long after the film has ended. Filmed in the Romany language, making this the first feature with guaranteed subtitles – wherever in the world it is shown! [JC-W]

Also with: Bora Todorovic (Ahmed Dzida), Ljubica Adzovic (Baba, the grandmother), Husnija Hasimovic (Uncle Merdzan), Sinol-icka Trpkova (Azra), Zabit Memedov (Zabit, the neighbour), Elvira Sali (Daca, Perhan's sister), Suada Karisik (Dzamila), Mirsad Zulic, Ajnur Redzepi, Bedrije Halim. Dir: Emir Kusturica. Pro: Mirza Pasic. Screenplay: Kusturica and Gordan Mihic. Ph: Vilko Filac. Ed: Andrija Zafranovic. Pro Des: Miljen Kljakovic. M: Goran Bregovic. Costumes: Mirjana Ostojic. Sound: Ivan Zakic. (Forum Sarajevo/Television of Sarajevo–Enterprise.) Rel: 7 December 1990. 142 mins. Cert 15.

To Sleep So As to Dream – Yume Miruyoni Nemurital. Modest but witty 1988 black-and-white Japanese film by a new director, which reveals a love and respect for the old silent movies. A private eye and his assistant try to track down a kidnapped actress, known as The Princess. A collector's item. [FDM]

Ljubica Adzovic, Davor Dujmovic, Elvira Sali and Husnija Hasimovic lose their home in Emir Kusturica's haunting, magical Time of the Gypsies, *from Enterprise.*

Cast includes: Moe Kamura (Bellflower), Shiro Sano (Botsuka), Kojji Otake (Kobay-ashi), Fajiko Fukamizu (Cherry Blossom). Dir and Screenplay: Kaizo Hayashi. Pro: Hayashi and Takashige Ichiso. Ph and Ed: Yuichi Nagata. Art: Takeo Kimura. M: Hidchiko Urayama. (Eizo Tanteisha Pro–ICA.) Rel: floating; first shown London (ICA) 19 June 1991. 81 mins. No cert.

To Sleep with Anger. Gently satirical domestic sitcom set in a middle-class black household in Los Angeles. Nothing much happens until the arrival of Harry Mention, a relative from the South who sets a chain of mishaps in motion. Danny Glover acts a little too hard as Harry, an ambiguous catalyst who dangles temptation in the face of

A touch of whimsy: Danny Glover as the mysterious Harry Mention in Charles Burnett's To Sleep with Anger *(Metro).*

The literary critic becomes a vampire: A cockroach-chewing Nicolas Cage in Hemdale's Vampire's Kiss.

his God-fearing relatives. *To Sleep with Anger* is far too slow for its own good, as much a fault of our age of the pop video as of the film itself. Danny Glover executive-produced. [JC-W]

Also with: Paul Butler (Gideon), Mary Alice (Suzie), Richard Brooks (Babe Brother), Sheryl Lee Ralph (Linda), Carl Lumbly (Junior), Vonetta McGee (Pat), Ethel Ayler (Hattie), Devaughn Walter Nixon, Wonderful Smith, Sy Richardson, Julius W. Harris. Dir and Screenplay: Charles Burnett. Pro: Caldecot Chubb, Thomas S. Byrnes and Darin Scot. Ex Pro: Edward R. Pressman, Danny Glover and Harris E. Tulchin. Ph: Walt Lloyd. Ed: Nancy Richardson. Pro Des: Penny Barrett. M: Stephen James Taylor. (Capitol–Metro.) Rel: 15 February 1991. 102 mins. Cert 12.

√**Total Recall**. Ultra-violent comic-strip extravaganza with Arnold Schwarzenegger as Douglas Quaid, a happily married, well-paid construction worker who has recurring nightmares about living on Mars. When he checks into a mind travel agency and chooses a trip to the red planet, assassins appear out of the woodwork to eliminate him. Even his wife turns against him. So who *is* Douglas Quaid? An enormous popular hit, *Total Recall* works on several levels: as black comedy, as a

rollercoaster adventure and as an intriguing look into the future – complete with mirrored holograms and the privatisation of air. Ten years in pre-production, the film was variously planned to star Richard Dreyfuss, Dennis Quaid and Patrick Swayze. As the final choice, Arnie lends the spectacular an undeniable humour and charm – and muscle. Holland's Paul Verhoeven (*RoboCop*) directs with a sick sense of the absurd. [JC-W]

Also with: Rachel Ticotin (Melina), Sharon Stone (Lori), Ronny Cox (Cohaagen), Michael Ironside (Richter), Marshall Bell (George/Kuato), Mel Johnson (Benny), Michael Champion (Helm), Roy Brocksmith, Ray Baker, Rosemary Dunsmore, Debbie Lee Carrington, Erika Carlson, Paula McClure, Rebecca Ruth and Robert Picardo (voice of 'Minicab'). Dir: Paul Verhoeven. Pro: Buzz Feitshans and Ronald Shusett. Ex Pro: Mario Kassar and Andrew Vajna. Screenplay: Shusett, Dan O'Bannon and Gary Goldman; from a story by Shusett, O'Bannon and Jon Povill, inspired by the short story *We Can Remember It for You Wholesale* by Phillip K. Dick. Ph: Jost Vacano. Ed: Frank J. Urioste. Pro Des: William Sandell. M: Jerry Goldsmith. Costumes: Erica Edell Phillips. Sound: Nelson Stoll. Special Make-Up Effects: Rob Bottin. (Carolco–Guild.) Rel: 27 July 1990. 109 mins. Cert 18.

Vampire's Kiss. Not a horror film, but a stylish psychological black comedy

from first-time English director Robert Bierman. Nicolas Cage, in his bravest performance to date, plays Peter Loew, an eccentric literary agent and womaniser searching for love. Frustrated by his string of one-night stands, he picks on his secretary Alva (Maria Conchita Alonso), harassing her for a missing file that she cannot find. He plagues her to the point of lying to her and dragging her to the office from her house on the other side of New York. There is obviously something seriously wrong with Peter Loew, a condition usually confined to horror literature. A quirky, daring film, full of unexpected touches, but not to everybody's taste. The scene in which Cage chews up a live cockroach is for real – yuck. [JC-W]

Also with: Jennifer Beals (Rachel), Elizabeth Ashley (Dr Glaser), Kasai Lemmons (Jackie), Bob Lujan (Emilio), Jessica Lundy, John Walker, Michael Knowles, Marc Coppola, Rex Robbins, Robert Dorfman. Dir: Robert Bierman. Pro: Barbara Zitwer and Barry Shils. Screenplay: Joseph Minion. Ph: Stefan Czapsky. Ed: Angus Newton. Pro Des: Christopher Nowak. M: Colin Towns. Costumes: Irene Albright. Sound: Rolf Pardula. (Hemdale.) Rel: 30 November 1990. 103 mins. Cert 18.

Waiting for the Light refers to both a spiritual expectation and the anticipation of the atom bomb. It is the dark days of 1962, and America is in negotiations with the USSR to curb the Cold War. Meanwhile in Chicago single mother Kay Harris (Teri Garr) is trying to raise her two prank-playing children. And while they're fabricating spontaneous human combustion at school, Kay has to contend with her Aunt Zena (Shirley MacLaine), an eccentric, streetwise party magician. Unable to cope with this troublesome trio, Kay transplants her bizarre family to the country where they can inflict the least amount of harm and where she attempts to resurrect a closed-down cafe. And then some strange 'miracles' begin to happen. An unexpected, original comedy brimming with heart and lashings of charm: a rare delight. [JC-W]

Also with: Hillary Wolf (Emily), Colin Baumgartner (Eddie), Clancy Brown (Joe), Vincent Schiavelli (Mullins), John Bedford Lloyd (Reverend Stevens), Jack McGee (Slim Slater), Eric Helland (Bob), Peg Phillips (Iris). Dir and Screenplay: Christopher Monger. Pro: Ron Bozman and Caldecott Chubb. Ex Pro: Edward Pressman. Ph:

Gabriel Beristain. Ed: Eva Gardos. Pro Des: Phil Peters. M: Michael Storey. Costumes: Isabella Van Soest Chubb. Sound: Harry Cohen. (Epic Prods/Sarlui/Diamant–Entertainment.) Rel: 7 September 1990. 102 mins. Cert PG.

War Party. To help boost tourism in the area, the mayor of Binger, Montana, arranges a spectacular re-enactment of the Milk River Battle, fought a hundred years earlier between the Indians and the US cavalry. The Blackfeet from the local reservation and the young men of Binger join in the spectacle, which comes to a bloody climax when a redneck pulls a real gun and kills an Indian. The redneck is felled in turn by Sonny Crowkiller (Billy Wirth), who escapes with four of his friends before the police can intercept. On the run, the fugitive Blackfeet are tracked down by ruthless rednecks, whose innate racism is brought to boiling point. *War Party* is basically an old-fashioned Western brought up to date with a strong social message and attractive young stars (Billy Wirth from *The Lost Boys*, Kevin Dillon from *The Blob*). The Montana scenery is breathtaking (a cliché, but it is), and the story gallops to its predictable conclusion with the efficiency of a computer program. But, compared to *Dances with Wolves*, this is cartoon exploitation. [JC-W]

Also with: Kevin Dillon (Skitty Harris), Tim Sampson (Warren Cutfoot), Jimmy Ray Weeks (Jay Stivic), Kevyn Major Howard (Calvin Morrisey), Jerry Hardin (the sheriff), Bill McKinney (the mayor), M. Emmet Walsh (Colin Ditweiller), Rodney Grant (Peter the Crow), Peggy Lipton (Kelly Eastman, TV correspondent), Matthew E. Montoya (Louis Manshadow), Tantoo Cardinal, Guy Boyd, R. D. Call, William Frankfather, Jackie Old Coyote, Micole Mercurio, Cameron Thor. Dir: Franc Roddam. Pro: John Daly and Derek Gibson. Ex Pro: Roddam and Chris Chesser. Screenplay: Spencer Eastman. Ph: Brian Tufano. Ed: Sean Barton. Pro Des: Michael Bingham. M: Chaz Jankel. Costumes: Kathryn Morrison. Sound: Martin Evans. Horse painter: Robin Johnson. (Hemdale.) Rel: 19 April 1991. 96 mins. Cert 18.

Where Angels Fear to Tread. The English are abroad again and causing havoc in the Italian rural town of Monteriano. Lilia Herriton (Helen Mirren) has gone and married a 21-year-old Ital-

An Englishwoman abroad: Judy Davis superimposes her English cool on the heated Italian mentality in Forster's Where Angels Fear to Tread *(from Rank).*

ian 'boy', the son of a dentist, and refuses to come home. Her erstwhile brother-in-law, Philip Herriton (Rupert Graves, with moustache and floppy fringe), is despatched to Monteriano to make her see reason. Tragedy, farce and romance follow in various doses as once again the English are transformed by the power of Italy. Although we are once more in E. M. Forster territory, this outing lacks the power and edge of *A Room with a View*: the comparison is inevitable, as Forster is the author of both, and as Italy, Graves and Helena Bonham-Carter (playing Lilia's young companion) all

reappear. This is a pretty adaptation, but could've done with a stronger directorial style. Other Forster screen adaptations include *A Passage to India*, with Judy Davis; *Maurice*, with Rupert Graves; and the upcoming *Howard's End*, with Helena Bonham-Carter. Hmm . . . [JC-W]

Also with: Helena Bonham-Carter (Caroline Abbott), Judy Davis (Harriet Herriton), Giovanni Guidelli (Gino Carella), Barbara Jefford (Mrs Herriton), Sophie Kullmann (Irma), Thomas Wheatley, Siria Betti, Evelina Meghangi. Dir: Charles Sturridge. Pro: Derek Granger. Ex Pro: Jeffrey Taylor and Kent Walwin. Assoc Pro: Olivia Stewart. Screenplay: Granger, Sturridge and Tim Sullivan. Ph: Michael Coulter. Ed: Peter Coulson. Pro Des: Simon Holland. M: Rachel Portman. Costumes: Monica Howe. Sound: Peter Sutton. (Sovereign Pictures/ LWT/Stagescreen Prods–Rank.) Rel: 21 June 1991. 113 mins. Cert PG.

Ethan Hawke and Jed get to know each other amid the stunning scenery of America's 49th state – in Warner's ambitious White Fang.

Producer and director of The African Queen *(alias the moneyman and the 'creative' lunatic): George Dzundza and Clint Eastwood in Warner's* White Hunter, Black Heart.

White Fang. Workmanlike, decidedly unhurried and somewhat unconvincing version of Jack London's famous story. While greenhorn Jack Conroy (Ethan Hawke) struggles to make his way in the Klondike, half-wolf/half-dog White Fang (Jed) loses his mother and makes his way in an uncaring human world.

It takes forever for the two to meet and fall in love, by which time we're bloated with the Alaskan scenery and Basil Poledouris's sweeping orchestral score. *White Fang* is one of those films you feel you *ought* to like, and are not entirely sure why you don't. Previously filmed in 1972 with Franco Nero. [JC-W]

Also with: Klaus Maria Brandauer (wasted as Alex Larson), Seymour Cassell (Skunker), James Remar (Beauty Smith), Susan Hogan (Belinda), Bill Moseley, Clint B. Youngreen, Pius Savage, Aaron Hotch, Suzanne Kent, Bart the Bear. Dir: Randal Kleiser. Pro: Marykay Powell. Ex Pro: Mike Lobell and Andrew Bergman. Screenplay: Jeanne Rosenberg, Nick Thiel and David Fallon; based on the novel by Jack London. Ph: Tony Pierce-Roberts. Ed: Lisa Day. Pro Des: Michael Bolton. M: Basil Poledouris. Costumes: Jenny Beavan and John Bright. Sound: David Kelson. (Walt Disney–Warner.) Rel: 24 May 1991. 108 mins. Cert PG.

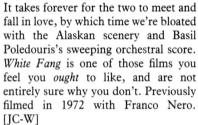

White Hunter, Black Heart. The most remarkable thing about this fictionalised look at the making of *The African*

The story of a younger man and a bolder woman: James Spader and Susan Sarandon in White Palace *(from UIP).*

Queen is Clint Eastwood's impersonation of John Huston. More than ever before Eastwood gets to 'act' away from his own monosyllabic persona, revealing a gangly man with a thin, reedy voice. Huston he ain't. However, *White Hunter, Black Heart* is primarily a character study, the story of an egocentric, fearless director less enamoured of filmmaking than of killing his first elephant. It is unfortunate, then, that Eastwood chose to cast himself in the role of the charismatic tyrant. Filmed in Zimbabwe. [JC-W]

Cast includes: Clint Eastwood (John Wilson), Jeff Fahey (Pete Verrill), George Dzundza (Paul Landers), Alun Armstrong (Ralph Lockhart), Marisa Berenson (Kay Gibson/Katharine Hepburn), Timothy Spall (Hodkins), Mel Martin (Mrs MacGregor), Richard Vanstone (Phil Duncan/Humphrey Bogart), Jamie Koss (Mrs Duncan/Lauren Bacall), Charlotte Cornwell (Miss Wilding), Norman Lumsden, Edward Tudor Pole, Roddy Maude-Roxby, Richard Warwick, John Rapley, Catherine Neilson, Geoffrey

Hutchings, Christopher Fairbank, Clive Mantle, Martin Jacobs, Alex Norton, Eleanor David, Boy Mathias Chuma, Conrad Asquith. Dir and Pro: Clint Eastwood. Ex Pro: David Valdes. Screenplay: Peter Viertel, James Bridges and Burt Kennedy; based on the novel by Peter Viertel. Ph: Jack N. Green. Ed: Joel Cox. Pro Des: John Graysmark. M: Lennie Niehaus. Costumes: John Mollo. Sound: Peter Handford. (Malpaso/Rastar–Warner.) Rel: 31 August 1990. 112 mins. Cert PG.

White Palace. St Louis, Missouri; today. Hard to believe, but good-looking, affluent yuppie James Spader, 27, falls head over his Guccis for lived-in hamburger waitress Susan Sarandon, 43. Sarandon is sensational as the uneducated, working-class floozie, but even she cannot make us believe Spader could fall for her. Mexican filmmaker Luis Mandoki (*Gaby – A True Story*) puts on a splendid show, but his characters are *too* extreme for even an ounce of credibility. This is an entertaining, adult fairy tale (complete with plugs for morality) that ultimately succumbs to the Hollywood formula. [JC-W]

Cast includes: Susan Sarandon (Nora Baker), James Spader (Max Baron), Jason Alexander (Neil), Kathy Bates (Rosemary), Eileen Brennan (Judy), Rachel Levin (Rachel), Renee Taylor (Edith Baron), Kim Myers (Ms Solomon), Spiros Focas, Gina Gershon, Steven Hill, Corey Parker, Jonathan Penner, Barbara Howard, Hildy Brooks, O-Lan Jones, Dir: Luis Mandoki. Pro: Mark Rosenberg, Amy Robinson and Griffin Dunne. Ex Pro: Sydney Pollack. Screenplay: Ted Tally and Alvin Sargent. Ph: Lajos Koltai. Ed: Carol Littleton. Pro Des: Jeannine C. Oppewall. M: George Fenton. Costumes: Lisa Jenson. Sound: Stephan Von Hase. (Mirage/Double Play/Universal–UIP.) Rel: 26 April 1991. 105 mins. Cert 18.

Why Me? American caper movie with Christopher Lambert as a con man who can open any safe. When he acquires a jewel with a curse on it, he becomes the prey of crooks, cops, terrorists and the Turkish authorities, all anxious to get the jewel and overlook the curse. Plenty of slapstick fun, if somewhat familiar – Robert Redford and George.

Christopher Lloyd and Kim Greist as father and daughter in the crime caper Why Me? *(Entertainment).*

C. Scott have previously starred in films based on the same story. [FDM]

Rest of cast: Christopher Lloyd (Bruno), Kim Greist (June), J. T. Walsh (Inspector Mahoney), Michael J. Pollard (Ralph), Tony Plana (Benjy), John Hancock (Tiny), Wendel Meldrum, Rene Assam, Greg Millar, Lawrence Tierney, Jill Terashita, Thomas Callaway. Dir: Gene Quintano. Pro: Marjorie Israel. Ex Pro: Irwin Yablans. Screenplay: Donald E. Westlake and Leonard Mass Jr; from Westlake's novel. Ph: Peter Deming. Ed: Alan Belsam. Pro Des: Woody Grocker. M: Basil Poledouris. (Epic Pictures/Sarlui Diamant/Caroline Pro–Entertainment.) Rel: floating; first shown London (Cannon, Haymarket, Oxford St and Chelsea) 5 September 1990. 87 mins. Cert 15.

Wild at Heart. If Jim Jarmusch (*Mystery Train, Down by Law*) was handed a large budget and told to remake *Raising Arizona* mixed with David Lynch's *Blue Velvet* he might well have come up with *Wild at Heart.* But it's Lynch himself who directed this self-indulgent, flabby road movie that captured the Palme d'Or at the 1990 Cannes Film Festival. Laura Dern is Lula Pace Fortune, a 20-year-old tearaway who tells her parole-jumping boyfriend, Sailor Ripley (Nicolas Cage): 'The whole world's wild at heart and weird on top.' And that's only the half of it. Lula and Sailor are on the run and in love and on fire, but Mother is a problem. Sailor holds a dark secret and Lula's mother is a part of it. So deep is this mystery that she wants Sailor dead. Diane Ladd, Laura Dern's real-life mother, hams up the drunken pyscho like Bette Davis on amphetamines, but there's a more effective turn from Willem Dafoe as a truly deranged piece of work. Some striking moments jostle with some very dull patches to make up an uneven work of sick originality. [JC-W]

Also with: Willem Dafoe (Bobby Peru), Crispin Glover (Dell), Diane Ladd (Marietta Pace), Isabella Rossellini (Perdita Durango), Harry Dean Stanton (Johnnie Farragut),

Weird on top: Nicolas Cage and Laura Dern struggle for the yellow brick road in David Lynch's Wild at Heart *(from Palace).*

Grace Zabriskie (Juana), J. E. Freeman (Marcello Santos), Morgan Shepherd, Bellina Logan, Glenn Walker Harris Jr, Freddie Jones, Calvin Lockhart, David Patrick Kelly, Tracey Walter, John Lurie, Jack Nance. Dir and Screenplay: David Lynch; from the novel by Barry Gifford. Pro: Monty Montgomery, Steve Golin and Joni Sighvatsson. Ph: Fred Elmes. Ed: Duwayne Dunham. Pro Des and Costumes: Patricia Norris. M: Angelo Badalamenti. Sound: John Huck. (Polygram/Propaganda –Palace.) Rel: 24 August 1990. 127 mins. Cert 18.

Wild Orchid. It's a wonder that Mickey Rourke, who has worked with such celebrated directors as Francis Coppola, Michael Cimino, Barry Levinson, Nicolas Roeg and Alan Parker, got himself lassoed into this meretricious mess – and that he volunteered to utter such risible dialogue. Once again he is an enigmatic stranger, this time luring sheltered lawyer Carré Otis into a world of decadence in Rio de Janeiro. Surprisingly, this uncut version underwent *forty* different snips on its American release. [JC-W]

Cast includes: Mickey Rourke (James Wheeler), Jacqueline Bisset (Claudia Lirones), Carré Otis (Emily Reed), Assumpta Serna (Hanna), Oleg Vidov (Otto), Bruce Greenwood (Jerome), Milton Goncalves, Antonio Da Silva, Michael Villella, Bernardo Jablonsky. Dir: Zalman King. Pro: Mark Damon. Ex Pro: David Saunders and James Dyer. Co-Pro: Tony Anthony. Screenplay: King and Patricia Louisianna Knop. Ph: Gale Tattersall. Art: Carlos Conti. M: Geoff MacCormack and Simon Goldenberg. Costumes: Marlene Stewart and Luciano Soprani. (Vision Int.–Entertainment.) Rel: 3 August 1990. 112 mins. Cert 18.

Wings of the Apache (US: *Firebirds*). Take *Top Gun*, switch the F–14s for killer helicopters and turn the girl into a rocket launcher-toting heroine and you have *Wings of the Apache* (*Top Rotor*?). Sort of. This time the enemy ain't Gorby and the Kremlin but a South American drug cartel selling coke on every American street corner. Justice must be served, and so superpilot Jake Preston ('I am the greatest!') is fine-tuned by tough, grizzly instructor Brad Little ('I'm a genius') and pointed at South America. The stunts are fantastic, the script and music on the corny side, but the story zips along at a heart-pounding clip. Although

Tommy Lee Jones shines as Little, the rest of the cast are overshadowed by the Apache of the title, a $10 million 'attack helicopter'. Phil Collins, who starred in director David Green's *Buster*, provides two songs, 'Do You Remember?' and 'Find a Way To My Heart'. [JC-W]

Also with: Nicolas Cage (Jake Preston), Sean Young (Billie Lee Guthrie), Bryan Kestner (Breaker), Dale Dye (A. K. McNeil), Mary Ellen Trainor (Janet Little), J. A. Preston, Peter Onorati, Charles Lanyer, Marshall Teague, Bert Rhine. Dir: David Green. Pro: William Badalato. Ex Pro: Arnold Kopelson and Keith Barish. Screenplay: Nick Thiel and Paul F. Edwards; from a story by Step Tyner, John K. Swensson and Dale Dye. Ph: Tony Imi. Ed: John Poll, Norman Buckley and Dennis O'Connor. Pro Des: Joseph T. Garrity. M: David Newman. Costumes: Ellis Cohen. Sound: Mark Ulano. (Inter-Ocean/Nova International–Medusa.) Rel: 19 October 1990. 89 mins. Cert 15.

Colin Firth and Peter O'Toole are rowed across the Styx (by Bernard Fontaine) to Hotel Paradiso – in the weird and woolly Wings of Fame *(from Gala).*

Wings of Fame. Bizarre allegorical fantasy about a film star (Peter O'Toole) who is shot and goes to a celestial resort for the temporarily famous. Ironically, his slain assassin (Colin Firth) is allowed the same privileges by becoming an overnight 'celebrity' in the shadow of his victim. However, the famous dead can only stay in luxury for as long as their renown continues on earth – when they are forgotten, it's over. As the self-centred megalomaniac star, Peter O'Toole is perfect casting and has seldom been better of late, while Colin Firth looks suitably bemused as his killer. Quite what the film is getting at – besides debunking the myth of celebrity – is a moot point, but as an exercise in naturalistic surreal comedy it almost succeeds. [JC-W]

Cast includes: Peter O'Toole (Cesar Valentin), Colin Firth (Brian Smith), Marie Trintignant (Bianca), Maria Becker (Dr Frisch), Walter Gotell (receptionist), Robert Stephens (Horace T. Merrick), Ellen Umlauf, Andréa Ferréol, Michiel Romeyn, Nicolas Chagrin, Gottfried John, Ken Campbell, Terry Raven, Mark Tandy, Pat Roach, David Doyle. Dir: Otakar Votocek.

The beautiful Linnea (Amanda Ooms) poses for 'art' in the mysterious and wonderful The Women on the Roof *(from Curzon).*

Pro: Laurens Geels and Dick Maas. Screenplay: Votocek and Herman Koch. Ph: Alex Thomson. Ed: Hans Van Dongen. Pro Des: Dick Schillemans. M: Paul M. Van Brugge. (Gala.) Rel: 26 April 1991. 109 mins. Cert 15.

The Women on the Roof. Strange little erotic mystery from Carl-Gustaf Nykvist, son of the celebrated cinematographer Sven Nykvist. As is to be expected, the film looks wonderful, and displays some directorial confidence, but fails to answer all the questions it dredges up. It is 1914 in Stockholm and an innocent photogenic waif, Linnea (the lens-catching Amanda Ooms), turns up out of nowhere. She is befriended by the equally enigmatic Anna (Helena Bergstrom), a bohemian neighbour who inveigles Linnea into her erotic photographic studies. As the story gradually unfolds, Linnea uncovers some startling truths about her new friend, but we are left infuriat-

ingly in the dark as to the history of the central protagonist. [JC-W]

Also with: Stellan Skarsgard (Willy), Percy Brandt (Fischer), Lars Ori Backstrom (Holger), Katarina Olsson (Gerda), Leif Andree (Oskar), Kalla Nykvist. Dir: Carl-Gustaf Nykvist. Pro: Katinka Farago and Waldemar Bergendahl. Screenplay: Carl-Gustav Nykvist and Lasse Summanen. Ph: Jorgen Persson and Ulf Brantas. Ed: Lasse Summanen. Set Design: Birgitta Brensen. M: Hakan Moller. Costumes: Inger Pehrsson. Sound: Owe Svensson and Lars Rechlin. (Curzon.) Rel: 14 September 1990. 89 mins. Cert 15.

A World Without Pity – Un Monde Sans Pitié. Quite impressive debut by new French director Eric Rochant: a part tragic, part amusing look at modern youth, drifting along without purpose or ambition. A pretty thin plot is made more interesting by the sometimes sympathetic, sometimes infuriating characters and the sensitive, beautifully on-key direction. Very much a love-it-or-hate-it movie. [FDM]

Cast includes: Hippolyte Giradot (Hippo), Mireille Perrier (Nathalie), Yvan Attal (Hal-

pern), Jean-Marie Rollin (Xavier), Cecile Mazan (Francine). Dir and Screenplay: Eric Pochant. Ex Pro: Alain Rocca. Ph: Pierre Novion. Ed: Michele Darmon. Pro Des: Thierry François. M: Gerard Torikian. Sound: Jean-Jacques Ferran. (Les Productions Lazennec–Artificial Eye.) Rel: floating; first shown London (Renoir) 7 December 1990. 104 mins. Cert 15.

Young Guns II – Blaze of Glory. Superior sequel to the 1988 Brat Pack Western which reunites Emilio Estevez, Kiefer Sutherland and Lou Diamond Phillips. This time out, Pat Garrett is played with silent strength by William Petersen (replacing Patrick Wayne), who is bribed to hunt down his old shooting mate William H. Bonney, a.k.a. Billy the Kid. As Billy, Estevez is even less likeable this time around, with a childish cackle that needs serious attention. If this Kid doesn't deserve to die, at the very least he needs a crucial spanking. The opening five minutes are a real twist, the photography and production design are superb, while Alan Silvestri's score is one of the best of the year. James

Coburn, who played Garrett in Sam Peckinpah's legendary *Pat Garrett and Billy the Kid*, takes a cameo as cattle rancher John Chisum. [JC-W]

Also with: Kiefer Sutherland (Doc Scurlock), Lou Diamond Phillips (Chavez Y Chavez), Christian Slater (Arkansas Dave Rudabaugh), Alan Ruck (Hendry William French), Balthazar Getty (Tom O'Folliard), R. D. Call (D. A. Ryerson), Jack Kehoe (Ashmun Upson), Robert Knepper (Deputy Carlyle), Jenny Wright (Jane Greathouse), Tom Kurlander, Viggo Mortensen, Leon Rippy, Tracey Walter, Brad Whitford, Scott Wilson, John Hammil, John Alderson, Don Simpson, Tony Frank, Danielle Blanchard, Alexis Alexander, Ginger Lynn Allen, John Fusco, Jon Bon Jovi. Dir: Geoff Murphy. Pro: Irby Smith and Paul Schiff. Ex Pro: James G. Robinson, Joe Roth and John Fusco. Screenplay: John Fusco. Ph: Dean Semler. Ed: Bruce Green. Pro Des: Gene Rudolf. M: Alan Silvestri; songs performed by Alan Silvestri. Costumes: Judy Ruskin. Sound: Louis L. Edemann and Donald J. Malouf. (Morgan Creek–Fox.) Rel: 2 November 1990. 104 mins. Cert 12.

Zandalee. Imagine Nicolas Cage as a quirky, violent guy with a rampant libido, throw in lots of steamy sex and set the whole thing in the damp, exotic French Quarter of New Orleans, and you have this daft erotic melodrama in one. Quite *why* filmmakers have gathered in Louisiana to expose the underbelly of American sexuality is one of the great mysteries of the universe. Add *Zandalee* to the pile already occupied by *The Big Easy*, *No Mercy*, *Two Moon Junction* and *Angel Heart*. Seldom has so much flesh been exposed in an American movie – or for that matter so much ludicrous dialogue (Cage: 'I want to shake you naked and eat you alive, Zandalee.') Tiresome, pretentious and predictable. Watch for New Orleans singer Aaron Neville (of The Neville Brothers) as Jack, an incongruous bartender. [JC-W]

Cast includes: Nicolas Cage (Johnny Collins), Judge Reinhold (Thierry Martin), Erika Anderson (Zandalee Martin), Joe Pantoliano (Gerri), Viveca Lindfors (Tatta), Marisa Tomei (Remy), Zach Galligan (Rog), Aaron Neville, Steve Buscemi, Ian Abercrombie, Jo-El Sonnier, Newell Alexander, Blaise Delacroix. Dir: Sam Pillsbury. Pro: William Blaylock and Eyal Rimmon. Co-Pro: Mari Kornhauser and Judge Reinhold. Ex Pro: Nicole Seguin and Staffan Ahrenberg. Screenplay: Kornhauser. Ph: Walt

Lloyd. Ed: Michael Horton. Pro Des: Michael Corenblith. M: Pray For Rain; numbers performed by Judge Reinhold, Giant Sand, Jump with Joey, Jo-El Sonnier etc. Costumes: Deena Appel. Sound: Bill Wistrom and Mace Matiosian. (ITC Entertainment–Rank.) Rel: 10 May 1991. 104 mins. Cert 18.

Emilio Estevez as a tiresome Billy the Kid in Young Guns II *(Fox).*

'I wanna shake you naked, Zandalee': Erika Anderson and Nicolas Cage indulge in a bit of extra-marital nookie in Sam Pillsbury's preposterous glob of erotica (from Rank).

Letter from Hollywood

ANTHONY SLIDE

The silent film is alive and well in Hollywood! January 1991 saw the reopening of the Silent Movie Theatre, which had closed 'temporarily' in 1980. Located on Fairfax Avenue, a bustling Jewish neighbourhood, the Silent Movie Theatre is a two-storey, stucco building opened in February 1942 by John Hampton. Originally called simply 'The Movie', the Silent Movie Theatre tried to recreate the silent filmgoing experience with programmes which nightly included a feature along with comedy and interest shorts. In 1951, distinguished critic Ezra Goodman rhapsodised, 'Here are pratfalls and passion; unabashed emotion and a kind of primitive grandeur; the clean rangy sharpness of pre-panchromatic photography; the sense of voyaging and discovery of those pioneering, halcyon days of Hollywood.'

The bulk of John Hampton's considerable silent film collection was sold in the late 1980s to David Packard. Hampton died in May 1990 at the age of 80. Shortly after his death, Hampton's widow, Dorothy, was approached by a film buff named Larry Austin, whose father, William Austin, had specialised in portraying effeminate young men in 1930s comedy shorts and features. Austin persuaded Dorothy to allow him to renovate and reopen the Silent Movie Theatre, screening exactly the same type of programmes for which the venue had become famous two nights a week. Attendances of 200 or more at each performance seem to indicate that the reopening is a success, and that the Silent Movie Theatre should have a long life.

The Silent Movie Theatre is not the only Los Angeles venue for silent film screenings. Since 1986, the Silent Society has been presenting the best possible prints of rare silent features on a regular basis at the Hollywood Studio Museum. Additionally, each summer the Silent Society has presented 'Silent Films under the Stars' in the open air at the Paramount Ranch, located just north of the city.

The guiding light and founder of the Silent Society is a young enthusiast named Randy Haberkamp. He recalls as the highlight of the Society's evenings a visit by Fritz Feld for a screening of the German classic *The Golem*. Although better known perhaps as a comedian, Feld had appeared as an actor in *The Golem* and other German silent films. When he arrived for the April 1990 presentation, Feld was showing his age, seeming timid and shy and concerned that people would not know who he was. But as the audience began to question him with enthusiasm, it was as if Feld lost forty years in as many seconds. He even went over to the piano and began to play songs from his past.

Other celebrities who have appeared at the Silent Society are Mary Brian, who autographed copies of my own 1990 book, *Silent Portraits*, and William Bakewell, who came along in May 1991 to autograph his autobiography, *Hollywood Be Thy Name*.

As well as organising the Silent Society, Randy Haberkamp was responsible for the annual Labor Day weekend Cinecon of the Society for Cinephiles. Held from 31 August to 3 September at the Hollywood Roosevelt Hotel, the Cinecon featured screenings of dozens of rare films, many in 35mm, and celebrity appearances by Evelyn Venable, Rose Hobart, Esther Ralston, Jackie Cooper, Buddy Rogers and many others. Lew Ayres and Ruby Keeler were guests of honour and awards recipients at a Sunday evening banquet, where honours also went to Robert Gitt (for his preservation activities) and David Packard (for funding such activities through the David and Lucile Packard Foundation).

Major issues facing Hollywood in the past year both came from outside the industry. Efforts in Congress either to destroy or at least restrict funding by the National Endowment for the Arts were opposed by many in the film community, culminating in the 7 June 1990 nationwide celebration of Arts Day USA. One actor conspicuously absent from the pro-National Endowment for the Arts happenings was Charlton Heston, who is never one to adopt popular causes or concern himself with criticism from liberal opponents. Heston resigned from Actors' Equity in protest against its objection to Jonathan Pryce starring in the Broadway production of *Miss Saigon*. He also shocked many in Hollywood by supporting the 1990 re-election campaign of the virulently anti-gay and anti-feminist Senator Jesse Helms, who had accused the National Endowment for the Arts of funding 'obscene art'.

The Gulf conflict had Hollywood celebrities virtually speechless. No one was willing to speak out against American actions in the Gulf. Most were anxious to go on record as supporting the troops in the Middle East, and on 10 February 1991, some one hundred stars from film, television, music and sport gathered at Warner Bros to record a music video entitled 'Voices That Care', the proceeds from which were to benefit the USO and the American Red Cross. Among those joining Bugs Bunny centrestage were Chevy Chase, Kevin Costner, Billy Crystal, Sally Field, Richard Gere, Whoopi Goldberg, Ali McGraw, Michelle Pfeiffer, William Shatner, Brooke Shields, Sissy Spacek, Meryl Streep and James

Lew Ayres and Ruby Keeler with their Society for Cinephiles awards

Woods. The British were represented by Dudley Moore.

A number of Hollywood celebrities, including Arnold Schwarzenegger, Angie Dickinson, Whitney Houston and Robin Williams, visited the Armed Forces Radio and Television Service to record audio or video greetings to the troops. Also participating were the casts of such popular television series as *Knots Landing* and *Golden Girls*. A few Hollywood 'names' actually made it to the Gulf, but found it difficult adequately to entertain the troops in view of the religious and moral requirements of the Saudi Arabian government. Bob Hope recorded yet another of his tedious television specials there, but I suspect the troops enjoyed more a visit from Steve Martin. Also in Saudi Arabia were Delta Burke, the star of the television series *Designing Women*, and her husband Gerald McRaney, star of the series about the US Marine Corps, *Major Dad*.

Hollywood's liberal voices were strangely silent on the conflict. The Los Angeles *Times* tried to contact various liberal activists but was refused comment by Barbra Streisand, Warren Beatty, Richard Dreyfuss, Michael Douglas and Paul Newman. Newman did however send 300,000 cases of his name-brand lemonade to the troops in the desert.

Jane Fonda, who gained the sobriquet 'Hanoi Jane' during the Vietnam War, has said nothing. Her fiancé Ted Turner was jubilant over the reporting of the war by his CNN network. CNN came in for criticism as too obviously serving the interests of Iraq in its reporting from Baghdad, and some conservative commentators were not slow in pointing out the close personal ties between Turner and Fonda.

Ed Asner expressed his opposition to the war, but at the same time pointed out he was not willing to stand alone and that he was too tired to be a leader. Notwithstanding, Asner did receive the newly-created Workers' Rights Committee's Golden Lunchbox Award for his outspoken defence of the rights of American workers from the American Civil Liberties Union. The major presentation at the ACLU's 17 January 1991 event, however, was that of the Bill of Rights Award to Gregory Peck. Peck revealed that he had not joined the ACLU until George Bush made membership an issue in his presidential campaign against Michael Dukakis – 'I joined, I carried the card,' Peck proudly told his audience.

As always, the number of awards presentations in Hollywood and its environs has been considerable. Admittedly, few actually take place in Hollywood, because Hollywood is a city in decay, and there is only one hotel (the Roosevelt) and one restaurant (the Columbia Bar and Grill) remaining with a semblance of glamour.

On 7 July 1990, the Psychotherapy Screening Guild (an organisation of 300-plus members concerned with the social and psychological impact of films) presented its sixth annual Helos awards. The gay-oriented feature *Longtime Companion* was the big winner, receiving the Triumph of the Human Spirit Award, the Courage in Filmmaking Award and the Psychodramatic Realism Award. At the end of the month, on 28 July, the eighth annual Golden Boots Awards raised some

$175,000 for the Motion Picture and Television Fund, with the biggest donation, of $50,000, coming from the Mary Pickford Foundation. Awards went to Burt Reynolds, Katharine Ross, Hal Needham, George Kennedy, Noah Beery Jr, Budd Boetticher and Sam Elliott. Gene Autry was inducted into the Hollywood Westerner Hall of Fame, and Denver Pyle auctioned a collection of guns.

Milos Forman received the fourth annual Eastman Kodak Second Century Award on 3 October 1990. Apart from his better-known career as a director, Forman has, for the past twelve years, been co-chairman of the film department at Columbia University's School of the Arts. Michael Douglas made the presentation to Forman, there were tributes from Jack Lemmon and Buck Henry, and Eastman Kodak donated $10,000 in Forman's name to Columbia.

The night of 21 October 1990 was a busy one in Hollywood. Richard Brooks received the first annual Lifetime Achievement Award presented jointly by the Writers' Guild of America and the Directors' Guild of America. He was lauded by Shirley Jones, Elizabeth Taylor (in a letter read by Robert Culp), Glenn Ford, Robert Blake and others. Brooks recalled a nameless railway employee he had met during the Depression who had told him, 'For every word you write, read a thousand. Maybe you'll make it.' Across town, Whoopi Goldberg and Lee Meriwether were honoured by Women in Show Business. In a speech critical of the Bush administration and the prosecution of the rap group 2 Live Crew in Florida, Goldberg remarked, 'We tell kids we don't want them to be involved in drugs. We want them to be thinking and intelligent human beings. Then, when their ideas are a little different than ours, we put them in jail.'

The prosecution of 2 Live Crew, and subsequent dismissal of charges against them, was the first of a number of major events which disturbed the American recording industry in the past year. The industry was shaken from within when Sinead O'Connor withdrew from the annual Grammy Awards, presented by the National Academy of Recording Arts and Sciences in New York on 20 February 1991. She objected to the music industry's focus on 'false and destructive materialistic values'.

On 1 November 1990, Bob Hope was presented with the second annual Hal Roach Entertainment Award from Loyola Marymount University. Hope's co-star Jane Russell acted as mistress of ceremonies and in a recorded message former President Ronald Reagan hailed Hope as 'our favourite clown', a somewhat questionable comment in that Hope has not been funny for years and his television specials rely all too heavily on canned laughter. The second major awards presentation of the month took place on 19 November, when James Earl Jones received the eighteenth annual Jean Renoir Humanitarian Award from the Los Angeles Film Teachers' Association.

Another black performer, Brock Peters, was honoured on 9 December with the 26th annual Achievement Award from the Screen Actors' Guild; it is the only national honour presented by SAG. A day later, the Hollywood Women's Press Club presented its Golden Apples (for top male and female stars of the year) to Patrick Swayze and Whoopi Goldberg. The Sour Apple of the Year Award went to Zsa Zsa Gabor. Upon learning she was not present, master of ceremonies Johnny Grant commented 'Good.'

On 19 January 1991, the American Society of Cinematographers honoured Billy Wilder at its annual awards dinner. Wilder acknowledged the three major cameramen in his career, Joseph LaShelle, John Seitz and Charles Lang Jr.

Two musical-related events took place in February. Debbie Reynolds and Onna White were honoured by the Professional Dancers' Society, which is trying to build a retirement home for dancers, or 'gypsies' as they are called in the profession. On hand for the luncheon ceremony were Cyd Charisse, Janet Blair, Janis Paige, Donald O'Connor, Milton Berle, Ann-Margret, Ann Miller, Carrie Fisher, Juliet Prowse, June Allyson and Bea Arthur. Frank Sinatra was the guest of honour at a posthumous tribute to composer Jimmy Van Heusen, organised by ASCAP (the American Society of Composers, Authors and Publishers). Unfortunately Sinatra forgot the lyrics to the Van Heusen songs he was supposed to perform! Matters improved with the on-stage arrival of Bob Hope, who revealed that Van Heusen had adopted his nom-de-plume after seeing

an advertisement for Van Heusen shirts. Others paying tribute were Angie Dickinson, Dudley Moore, Donald O'Connor and lyricist Sammy Cahn, who collaborated with Van Heusen on 'All the Way', 'Call Me Irresponsible' and 'The Second Time Around'.

Actor Kirk Douglas was the centre of attention early in 1991. In February, he survived a collision between the helicopter in which he was flying and a small plane. (The pilot of the helicopter, Noel Blanc, son of cartoon voice Mel Blanc, was seriously injured.) Douglas remembered the crash when he received the AFI Lifetime Achievement Award on 7 March 1991: 'They say that life flashes before you like a movie, but I was knocked out. I didn't see one thing. Thank God, I got a second chance to see it tonight.' Hosted by son Michael Douglas, the event included comments by Lauren Bacall, Karl Malden, Tom Cruise, Patricia Neal, Sylvester Stallone, Jean Simmons, and others.

Thirteen days later, Douglas received a special award from the Writers' Guild of America, honouring his efforts to end the McCarthy blacklisting era in 1960 by requiring that blacklisted writer Dalton Trumbo receive credit on *Spartacus*. As an added bonus for Douglas, *Spartacus* has been restored and received its repremiere in April. Douglas expressed only one regret during these celebrations – that he had never won an Academy Award.

If Kirk Douglas is the star of the year, MCA/Universal is the studio of the year. It was the star player in the number one deal, whereby it was purchased by the Japanese company, Matsushita, for $6.6 billion. The deal was arranged by high-powered agent Mike Ovitz, who made himself $50 million from the sale, and studio executives did not come out of it too badly either. David Geffen, who sold his record company to MCA in exchange for 9 million shares of the company's stock, walked away with $700 million. The American public fared less well. MCA/Universal was able to work out an arrangement which ensured that its top executives avoided paying too much in taxes on the profits from the sale. In addition, Americans woke up to discover that the concessions in their top national park, Yosemite, were now owned by a Japanese company. (The US Parks Service subsequently arranged for Matsushita to dispose of that part of its acquisition within a year.)

While the deal was going through, the Universal Studio lot was the site of a spectacular arson blaze on 6 November 1990. The fire, which caused millions of dollars' worth of damage, destroyed the sets for Sylvester Stallone's new feature, *Oscar*, (which coincidentally features Kirk Douglas as Stallone's father), and the actor was forced to complete shooting at Universal's Florida studio complex.

Los Angeles Mayor Tom Bradley declared 1991–2 as 'The Year of the Television Academy', in recognition of the move by the Academy of Television Arts and Sciences to its new headquarters in North Hollywood on 26 April 1991. However, it has been the older Academy of Motion Picture Arts and Sciences which has received attention in the last year.

The Academy's Samuel Goldwyn Theater was totally remodelled and renovated in 1990, and reopened on 14 December with a black-tie, invitation-only tribute to Irving Berlin, hailed by Academy president Karl Malden as 'the composer of some of the greatest songs ever written'. There were film clips featuring Fred Astaire, Bing Crosby, Judy Garland and Ginger Rogers (including a never-before-seen clip of Garland singing 'Mr Monotony') and live performances by Beatrice Arthur, Michael Feinstein, Joel Grey, Walter Matthau, Debbie Reynolds and others. Jack Lemmon, who hosted the event, played 'Let Me Sing and I'm Happy' and 'Always' on the piano. The tribute closed with Mel Torme performing – what else? – 'There's No Business Like Show Business'.

On 6 February, the Academy joined forces with the Hollywood Section of the Society of Motion Picture and Television Engineers to present a retrospective tribute to the lesser-known but very important Academy Awards, those dedicated to Scientific or Technical Achievement. Karl Malden opened the

evening's activities by bowing to an oversize statue of Oscar – Malden has considerable personality and has made a great Academy president. Unfortunately that was the highspot of the evening, which sank into a tedious assemblage of tired old film clips, introduced with tired old remarks.

The Oscar season got under way in Hollywood with the British Academy of Film and Television Arts hosting a part of its awards ceremony in Hollywood – at the Bel Age Hotel – on Sunday 17 March. On hand were Whoopi Goldberg, Shirley MacLaine, Anthony Hopkins, Jane Seymour and others. On 22 March, the American Cinematheque's annual Moving Picture Ball honoured Martin Scorsese, who was fêted by Jodie Foster, Robert De Niro, Robert Wise and Robin Williams. The following day, Kevin Costner was guest speaker at the Independent Spirit Awards, where at least two other Oscar nominees – Annette Bening and Andy Garcia – were present.

The Academy Awards were much as was expected, with many of the winners obvious in advance. The evening was devoted to the 100th anniversary of the motion picture (a somewhat dubious claim), but little was made of this supposed landmark in film history. Around town on Oscar night, there were the usual parties, with the major one hosted by agent Swifty Lazar at Spago's restaurant. That same night, the American Foundation for the Performing Arts honoured Stanley Kramer, and the American Spirit Foundation hosted Ginger Rogers and James Stewart on the 50th anniversary of their Academy Awards – for *Kitty Foyle* and *Philadelphia Story* respectively.

Almost eclipsing the Academy Awards in the amount of publicity it received was the opening of the Academy's new Center for Motion Picture Study. The Academy of Motion Picture Arts and Sciences has taken over the City of Beverly Hills Water Treatment Plant No. 1, a Spanish-Romanesque building dating from 1927 and located

in La Cienega Park. The structure has been completely refurbished and now houses the Academy's film archives and its Margaret Herrick Library. Michael Douglas, Meryl Streep and Steven Spielberg were named to chair an Endowment Campaign Committee, dedicated to raising $15 million. To date, more than half that amount has been received, with major donations coming from Bob Hope and the Cecil B. DeMille Foundation. The library's reading room has been named in honour of DeMille, and patrons of the centre now enter through the Bob Hope Lobby. Academy president Karl Malden is well known as the spokesman for American Express travellers' cheques, and American Express donated funds for a conference room named in Malden's honour. (Unlike the English, Americans are very fond of naming memorials to the living.)

The Center for Motion Picture Study opened on 23 January 1991, with a well-organised dinner reception and continuous tours of the facility. The Academy's new executive director, Bruce Davis, was so carried away by the event that he compared the work of creating the centre to that of the craftsmen working on a fourteenth-century European cathedral!

The Academy's Margaret Herrick Library remains one of the greatest film resources in the world. It houses more than 18,000 books, five million still photographs, 5000 scripts, clippings files on 82,000 films and 73,000 film personalities, and the papers of celebrities as varied as Cary Grant, Mary Pickford, George Cukor, Martin Ritt, John Huston, George Stevens and two British directors, Alfred Hitchcock and Bryan Forbes. Unlike, say, the British Film Institute, it receives no public funding, and unlike its British counterpart, it is open to anyone – at no charge. Its founding, its growth and its new home are a lasting tribute to the concern of the Academy and its members to preserve Hollywood history in the community where it all happened.

Movie Quotations of the Year

'I hate you more! If hate were people, I'd be China!'
Daniel Stern having a row with his wife (Karla Tamburelli) in *City Slickers*

'Actually, I don't remember being born. It must have happened during one of my blackouts.'
Val Kilmer as Jim Morrison, at a press reception, in Oliver Stone's *The Doors*

'You could park a car in the shadow of Darryl's ass.'
Geena Davis describing her husband's physique in *Thelma & Louise*

'Sandy, your breasts feel weird.' 'That's because they're real.'
LA sophisticate Steve Martin in bed with the *au naturel* Sarah Jessica Parker, in *LA Story*

'Most of our passengers arrive alive.'
Airline advertisement in *Crazy People*

'God created all men, but Sam Colt made them equal.'
Alan Rickman extolling the virtues of America's famous gunsmith in *Quigley Down Under*

'Never hate your enemies. It affects your judgement.'
Michael Corleone (Al Pacino) in *The Godfather Part III*

'I used to have a speech impediment. I couldn't say "no".'
Reformed bad girl Annabella Sciorra in *The Hard Way*

'You're not important. You're dinner. This time next week they won't remember what they ate.'
Newshound Bruce Willis to media celebrity Tom Hanks in *The Bonfire of the Vanities*

'Consider that a divorce!'
Arnold Schwarzenegger shooting wife Sharon Stone in the head in *Total Recall*

'I know how you feel: you don't know if you want to hit me or kiss me. I get a lot of that.'
Madonna in *Dick Tracy*

Doctor: 'We're gonna have to pump your stomach.' Patient: 'Do I have to be there?'
Richard Dreyfuss and Meryl Streep in *Postcards from the Edge*

'When *I* grow up and get married, I'm gonna live alone.'
A ten-year-old Macaulay Culkin in *Home Alone*

Journalist to English film star at press conference: 'What do you think of British cinema?' Film star: 'Oh, that would be a very good idea.'
Extra and Peter O'Toole in *Wings of Fame*.

'Nice party – a lot of familiar face-lifts.'
Leslie Nielsen walking into a smart do in *The Naked Gun 2½ – The Smell of Fear*

'God – I *love* being a turtle!'
Michelangelo in *Teenage Mutant Ninja Turtles*

The year's most famous line:
'Ditto.'
The ghost of Patrick Swayze in *Ghost*

'I once heard a wise man say there are no perfect men, only perfect intentions.'
A wise Morgan Freeman in *Robin Hood: Prince of Thieves*

The year's second most famous line:
'Pleased to meet you.'
Anthony Hopkins – as Dr Hannibal Lecter – transforming a common courtesy into a chilling threat, in *The Silence of the Lambs*

'Women need a reason to have sex, men need a place.'
Billy Crystal in *City Slickers*

'There are only two things to do around here. You got a TV? No? Well, you're now down to one.'
Virginia Madsen on the entertainment her town has to offer, in Dennis Hopper's *The Hot Spot*

'Some people are born not to do things – and I am one of them.'
Rupert Graves in E. M. Forster's *Where Angels Fear to Tread*.

The year's strangest line:
'This whole world is wild at heart and weird on top. I wish I was somewhere over the rainbow.'
Laura Dern in *Wild at Heart*

125

TV Feature Films of the Year

In this section you will find listed all the made-for-television movies shown for the first time in the UK during the year. Films shown during the year which have been previously televised in the UK are not listed, but can be found in the edition of *Film Review* for the year when they were first shown. The date given in brackets after each title is the year the movie was made or originally shown (often in the US).

Adam (1983). True-life story about the struggle of worried parents to get a government bill passed which would allow them access to the FBI's national crime computer – a move which led to the locating of many missing youngsters. Emmy nomination performances by Daniel J. Travanti and JoBeth Williams. Dir: Michael Tuchner. Screenplay: Allan Leicht. Channel 4, 25 September 1990.

Aimée (1991). The problem: a millionaire former rock show promoter vanishes for two years and then returns to murder his mother. Why should he do it? The answer seems an awful long time coming, but the waiting is reasonably well filled by the performances of Donald Sumpter and Juliet Stevenson. Also with Simon Chandler, Christine Rose. Dir: Pedr James. Screenplay: Guy Hibbert. BBC2, 7 April 1991.

Anastasia: The Mystery of Anna (1986). Lavish, literate, star-studded and well-produced telefilm based on the fascinating puzzle of Anna Anderson's claim to be the only member of the Russian royal family to escape death at the hands of the Soviets. With Amy Irving in the title role, Rex Harrison, Olivia de Havilland, Omar Sharif, Claire Bloom, Edward Fox etc. Dir: Martin Chomsky. Screenplay: James Goldman; based on the book by Peter Kurth. BBC2, 24 July 1990 (Part 1) and 25 July 1990 (Part 2).

Annihilator (1986). The now all-too-familiar SF story about aliens from outer space taking over earthly bodies as a way of infiltrating our planet. With Mark Lindsay Chapman, Susan Blakely. Dir: Michael Chapman. Screenplay: Roderick and Bruce Taylor. ITV, 7 July 1990.

Ask Max (1986). Typical Disney family comedy, about a precocious 12-year-old who invents a 'sky bike'. With Jeff B. Cohen, Kareem Abdul-Jabbar, Ray Walston. Dir: Vincent McEveety. Screenplay: Andy Guerdat, Steve Kreinberg and Gil Grant. ITV, 30 December 1990.

Assassin (1986). Averagely silly minor science-fiction film about a mechanical man programmed to kill major scientists etc. Robert Conrad investigates. Also with Karen Austin, Richard Young. Dir and Screenplay: Sandor Stern. ITV, 4 March 1991.

The Atlanta Child Murders (1985). Absorbing courtroom drama with brilliant performances and a consistent documentary style. An undercurrent of racial prejudice makes itself felt when a man is finally accused of a series of child murders. A deservedly much-praised TV movie. With Jason Robards, Martin Sheen, James Earl Jones, Rip Torn and Morgan Freeman etc. Dir: John Erman. Screenplay: W. Mann. BBC2, 18 August 1990 (Part 1) and 25 August 1990 (Part 2).

The Autobiography of Miss Jane Pittman (1973). The story of a 110-year-old black woman, born into slavery, who survived the American Civil War to take part in the Civil Rights agitation. Cicely Tyson, in the central role, won a well-deserved Emmy award. As a cinema release outside America it achieved considerable success, one critic calling it 'one of the best TV movies ever made'. With Michael Murphy, Richard Dysart. Dir: John Korty. Screenplay: Tracy Keenan Wynn. Channel 4, 20 November 1990.

Baby M. Superior tear-jerking 'women's picture' about the problems of surrogate motherhood. Mother agrees to part with her child, then goes back on the contract and refuses to let the baby go: a tricky real-life case for the law courts. With JoBeth Williams, John Shea. Dir and Screenplay: James Steven Sadwith. BBC1, 7 August 1990.

Barnaby and Me (1977). Listed by the BBC as a telefilm, but by ITV as a cinema production (though it's never been released as such in the UK), this is an easy-to-forget Australian production starring Sid Caesar – playing an American con-man seeking buried treasure 'down under'. Also with Juliet Mills. Dir: Norman Panama. BBC1, 20 April 1991.

Bay Cove (1987). (US: *Bay Coven.*) Pretty daft, highly unlikely tale of modern witchcraft. With Tim Matheson, Pamela Sue Martin. Dir: Carl Schenkel. ITV, 13 May 1991.

Beauty and Denise (1988). Familiar story about a tough policewoman (Dinah Manoff) assigned to protect a lovely model who has witnessed a political assassination and thus become the assassin's next target. Also with David Carradine, Julia Duffy. Dir: Neal Israel. No writing credit. Channel 4, 2 October 1990.

Beverly Hills 90210 (1990). Poor (comparatively!) folk in rich people's territory. Dad's transfer from Minneapolis to his firm's Beverly Hills office isn't easy for the family. Feature intro to a new series. With Jason Priestley, Shannon Doherty. Dir: Tim Hunter. No writing credit. ITV, 5 January 1991.

Blind Justice (1986). Tim Matheson as a young photographer wrongly arrested for rape and murder: as the case against him proceeds, he becomes increasingly terrified by the horrible trap around him. Also with Mimi Kuzak. Dir: Rod Holcomb. ITV, 25 March 1991.

B. L. Stryker: The Dancer's Touch (1989). Pilot feature for a Burt Reynolds series. Pallid and far too casually presented story of a retired cop called back into action to catch the criminal murdering upper-class young girls. Also with Rita Moreno, David Hunt. Dir: Bill Fraker. ITV, 27 April 1991.

B. L. Stryker – the series. No. 1 **Carolann**. Likeable rogue Reynolds is hired to protect a queen from the assassins who have already bumped off her royal spouse. Also with Deborah Raffin and Ossie Davis. ITV, 4 May 1991. No. 2 **Blind Chess**. A good deed turns to disaster: Stryker's private eye licence is revoked after an unjustly imprisoned man whom he's helped organises a jailbreak. With Ossie Davis and Michael O. Smith. ITV, 11 May 1991. No. 3 **Auntie Sue**. Some fiercely independent old-age pensioners get tangled up with a gang of jewel smugglers: Stryker unravels the mess. Superb performances from a cast of veterans, including Douglas Fairbanks Jr, Maureen Stapleton, Harry Carey Jr and Rita Moreno. ITV, 18 May 1991. No. 4 **Blues for Buder**. Burt Reynolds self-directs this story of Stryker's efforts to save an obnoxious teenager and his fortune from a crooked evangelist. Also with Ossie Davis and Rita Moreno. ITV, 25 May 1991.

Blue de Ville (1986). Quite entertaining 'road' film with Jennifer Runyon throwing in her job (and throwing over

her boyfriend) in order to help her friend (Kimberley Pistone) search for her long-lost dad. Dir: Jim Johnston. Screenplay: Brad Buckner and Eugenie Ross-Leming. ITV, 1 January 1991.

Bonanza: The Next Generation (1988). Routine pilot for a new *Bonanza* series, with the youngsters taking over the defence of the Ponderosa. With John Ireland, Robert Fuller. Dir: Bill Claxton. BBC1, 30 June 1991.

Bread (1986). This Israeli story of a loyal and hard-working baker who suddenly loses his job after twenty years' service didn't find great favour with the authorities – unsurprisingly, as it levels plenty of criticism at the Israeli establishment. With Rami Dannon. Dir: Ram Loevy. Screenplay: Meir Doran, Gilad Evron and Loevy. Channel 4, 20 October 1990.

Burnout (1988). Out-of-the-rut US drama about a female cop who takes to drugs and booze when her life turns sour, but is switched back to the straight and narrow by a nice old professor and two orphaned youngsters. Good acting by Lindsay Wagner and good direction by Michael Switzer make it well worth watching. BBC1, 12 June 1991.

Buster's World (1984). Six episodes of a Danish TV series stitched into feature length. A quite charming youngster's movie about a boy (Mads Bugge Andersen, an 8-year-old with great appeal) whose dreams come true when his stage magician grandad leaves him his box of tricks. Dir: No credit. Channel 4, 6 May 1991.

Callie and Son (1981). Callie's a Texas waitress who determinedly rises to power and financial success in order to track down and renew the ties with her illegitimate son. She's played more than competently by Lindsay Wagner, heading a cast that includes Michelle Pfeiffer, Dabney Coleman and Jameson Parker as the son. Dir: Waris Hussein. Screenplay: Thomas Thompson. BBC1, 15 February 1991.

Can Ellen Be Saved? (1974). Ellen's worried parents call in a private eye (Leslie Nielsen) to prise her away from the bizarre religious sect that has taken

her in. Also with Cathy Cannon. Dir: Harvey Hart. Screenplay: Emmett Roberts. ITV, 7 July 1990.

Can You Hear Me Thinking? (1990). In another BBC-made telefilm, a happily married sitcom couple have to play out their light comedy series while watching their son gradually going crazy. Good performances by real-life husband and wife Michael Williams and Judi Dench as the unhappy parents. Dir: Christopher Morahan. Screenplay: Monty Haltrecht and Beverley Marcus. BBC1, 30 September 1990.

Caroline? (1990). Is she (as she claims) or isn't she the daughter of the couple who were convinced she had died in a plane crash thirteen years ago? Proficiently produced telefilm with an ever tightening screw of suspense. With Stephanie Zimbalist, Patricia Neal, Dorothy McGuire, George Grizzard. Dir: Joseph Sargent. Screenplay: Michael Guzman. Channel 4, 25 July 1990.

A Christmas Carol (1985). Aussie animated version of the classic Dickens tale of a miser frightened into the seasonal spirit. Dir: Warwick Gilbert. ITV, 25 December 1990.

The Clean Machine (1988). Australian telefilm about ex-cop Steve Bisley, called back into action as the leader of an anti-corruption squad, decimated as it sets out to clean up organised crime. Dir: Ken Cameron. No writing credit. BBC1, 5 December 1990.

Cocaine: One Man's Poison (1983). At 50, Eddie Gant (Dennis Weaver) is passed over for promotion. With the real-estate business in recession, he turns to drugs – and then finds he can't give them up. Good performances by Weaver and James Spader (as his son). Dir: Paul Wendkos. BBC2, 15 April 1991.

Colette (1985). Two-part French TV film about the authoress of *Gigi*, *Chéri* etc. With Macha Merie, Clementine Amoureux. Dir: Gerard Poitou Weber. Part 2, BBC2, 6 July 1990. (Part 1 was broadcast in June 1989.)

Columbo: Dead Weight (1973). A much-bemedalled war hero (Eddie

Albert) is accused of murder, and Columbo takes up the case. With Peter Falk. Dir: No credit. BBC1, 25 May 1991.

Columbo: Etude in Black (1972). Columbo's at it again – irritating his murder suspects so much that they play into his hands. With Peter Falk, John Cassavetes, Myrna Loy, Anjanette Comer, Blythe Danner and James Olson. Dir: Nick Colosanto. Screenplay: Steven Bochco. ITV, 12 October 1990.

Columbo: How to Dial Murder (1978). Creepy little cop Columbo (Peter Falk) solves a murder apparently committed by two pet Dobermans. Also with Nicol Williamson and Tricia O'Neill. Dir: James Frawley. BBC1, 18 May 1991.

Columbo: Lady in Waiting (1971). When Richard Anderson refuses to let his sister marry the firm's attorney, she rebels and the fatal result has to be sorted out by Columbo. Also with Peter Falk, Susan Clark and Leslie Nielsen. Dir: No credit. BBC1, 1 June 1991.

Columbo: Lovely But Lethal (1973). Beastly work in the beauty trade: enter the scruffy cleaner-up. With Peter Falk. Dir: No credit. BBC1, 22 June 1991.

Columbo: The Most Crucial Game (1972). The intrepid little cop solves the murder of a wealthy football fan. With Peter Falk. Dir: No credit. BBC1, 8 June 1991.

Columbo: Murder by the Book (1972). Another routine investigation – with a notable director. With Peter Falk. Dir: Steven Spielberg. BBC1, 15 June 1991.

Columbo: Ransom for a Dead Man (1971). The world's worst-dressed 'tec winkles out the truth from a beautiful and bored lady lawyer after her nice old hubbie gets the chop. The perfect crime – almost. With Peter Falk, Lee Grant and John Fink. Dir: Richard Irving. Screenplay: Dean Hargrove. ITV, 28 September 1990.

Confessions of a Married Man (1982). A routine eternal triangle, made very watchable by the fine performance of

Jennifer Warren. With Robert Conrad as the cad. Dir: Steven Gathers. ITV, 24 March 1991.

The Connection (1973). Charles Durning as the scruffy ex-reporter whose knowledge of the New York underworld leads to his becoming the go-between for jewel thieves and crooked insurance companies. And the *French Connection* producer – Philip D'Antoni – tops the movie with a car chase which is second only to the one in his earlier success. All edge-of-the-seat stuff. Also with Dana Wynter. Dir: Tom Gries. Screenplay: Albert Ruben. ITV, 6 February 1991.

Conspiracy of Terror (1975). A man-and-woman 'tec team uncover devil worship in the suburbs while keeping a promise to find a boy's lost dog, in this pilot feature for a series that never was. The feature certainly set a higher standard than some of the series that *did* make it. With Michael Constantine and Barbara Rhoades. Dir: John Llewellyn Moxey. Screenplay: Howard Rodman; from the book by David Delman. ITV, 26 August 1990.

Convicted: A Mother's Story (1987). Double value: both a melodramatic tearjerker and a women-in-prison drama, about a mother who puts boyfriend before children, shouldering his guilt and going to jail for him. Better have a spare handkerchief for this one. With Ann Jillian, Kiel Martin. Dir: Richard Heffron. Screenplay: Ellen Kesand. Channel 4, 31 January 1991.

Cop Killer (1988). Cop's partner and best pal killed: can't get on with replacement: recipe for crisis. Another entertaining story from the files of ex-cop Joseph Wambaugh. With Ken Olin, Joseph Bottoms, Glynnis O'Connor. Dir: Larry Shaw. Screenplay: Wambaugh. BBC1, 27 October 1990.

The Count of Monte Cristo (1975). Routine re-make of the classic Dumas adventure tale, with Richard Chamberlain a very poor substitute for Robert Donat, who played the hero in the previous big-screen version. Also with Tony Curtis, Trevor Howard. Dir: David Greene. No script credit. BBC1, 9 September 1990.

Courage (1986). Sophia Loren splendid as the mother so sickened and angry at her son's obsession with drugs that she volunteers to become an agent for the US Drugs Enforcement Agency. Supposedly based on a true story. Also with Hector Elizondo, Billy Dee Williams. Dir: Jeremy Paul Kagan. Screenplay: Jack E. Neuman. BBC1, 22 February 1991.

Crossfire (1975). Reasonably entertaining if routine hokum about an undercover cop whose colleagues wrongly suspect him of drug trafficking and steadfastly ignore him. With James Farentino, John Saxon and Pamela Franklin etc. Dir: William Hale. Screenplay: Philip Saltzman. ITV, 15 July 1990.

Crossing the Mob (1988). On New York's waterfront the local Mafia boss, Frank Stallone (Sylvester's less famous brother), gives Jason Bateman a job . . . and then expects a return favour. Tough stuff. Also with Maura Tierney. Dir: Steven Stem. BBC1, 19 January 1991.

Daddy (1987). Weepie about teenage pregnancy, marriage and parenthood problems: a lesson to the young to play it safe. With Dermot Mulroney, Patricia Arquette. Dir and screenplay: John Herzfeld. Channel 4, 1 August 1990.

Dark City (1990). Political thriller set in South Africa (but filmed in Zimbabwe) about seven innocent men accused of murdering a local councillor. A BBC film, directed by debuting British director Chris Curling. Screenplay: David Lan. BBC1, 11 December 1990.

The Darker Side of Terror (1979). Well-produced and entertaining (if daft) science-fiction tale about a professor who clones himself. After early success he develops a 'metabolic imbalance' and the shade of Mr Hyde takes over . . . ! With Robert Forster, Adrienne Barbeau, Ray Milland. Dir: Gus Trikonis. Screenplay: John Herman Shaner and Al Ramrus. ITV, 21 December 1990.

Day of Terror, Night of Fear (1977). Cool cop Chad Everett trying to 'talk out' the two villains holding five innocent people as hostages. Intended as the first of a series that never took off. Also with Warren Oates, Sandy Dennis. ITV, 11 October 1990.

Deadly Deception (1987). Average psychological thriller about a man's desperate and determined search for his son after his wife's death, apparently from suicide. With Matt Salinger, Lisa Eilbacher. Dir: John L. Moxey. ITV, 9 March 1991.

Dear Detective (1979). Much-vaunted series that only lasted for four weeks, although based on a very successful French series about a lady detective – Brenda Vaccaro, very good in the role first created on French TV by Annie Girardot – who brings in the killer almost in her spare time. Also with Arlen Dean Snyder, Ron Silver. Dir: Dean Hargrove. Screenplay: Roland Kibbee and Hargrove. ITV, 25 August 1990.

Deceptions (1985). Well-worn tale about identical twin sisters – one a bored high-flyer, the other an even more bored and depressed New York housewife – who decide to swap roles for a week, hardly expecting the murder that follows. With Stefanie Powers, Gina Lollobrigida, Brenda Vaccaro, Joan Sims etc. Dir: Robert Cherault. Screenplay and Co-Dir: Melville Shavelson. BBC1, 14 August 1990.

Desperado (1987). Alex McArthur dons Clint Eastwood's mantle as the stern, fast-drawing, deadly-shooting loner looking for the one man who can clear his name of murder. On the way he takes time off to fight for the right in a mining town tyrannised by the local mine-owner. Good old action in the good old Western way – simple and satisfying. Also with David Warner, Robert Vaughn, Yaphet Kotto. Dir: Virgil Vogel. Screenplay: Elmore Leonard. ITV, 29 September 1990.

Desperado: Avalanche at Devil's Ridge (1988). Still searching for the man who can clear his name, desperate Duell McCall (Alex McArthur) takes over from a murdered lawman and tangles with nasty piece of work Silas Slater – played at full throttle, with no holds barred, by Rod Steiger. Third and best so far of this series, and grand

stuff! Also with Alice Adair and Lise Cutter. Dir: Richard Compton. Screenplay: Larry Cohen. ITV, 13 October 1990.

Desperado: Badlands Justice (1989). Duell McCall (Alex McArthur) rides into more trouble, but still hasn't, by the end of the film, caught up with his quarry – so everything points to another 'Desperado' series to come. Also with Patricia Charbonneau, John Rhys-Davies. Dir: E. W. Swackhamer. Screenplay: Andrew Mirisch and Leslie Bohem. ITV, 27 October 1990.

Desperado: The Outlaw Wars (1989). Fourth in the Western series with Alex McArthur. In this episode the Desperado becomes embroiled with some of Quantrell's evil Raiders . . . and finds a son! Dir: E. W. Swackhamer. Screenplay: William Wusner: from a story by Andrew Mirisch. ITV, 20 October 1990.

Desperado: The Return of Desperado (1988). Taking his cue from Clint Eastwood in the 'Man with No Name' movies, Alex McArthur sits tall and taciturn in the saddle in this second movie as he determinedly continues his search for the man who can clear his name. It's good to see an all-shootin' Western once more: even if it took three writers to create the familiar storyline! Dir: E. W. Swackhamer. Screenplay: John Makiewicz, Daniel Pyne and Charles Grant Craig. ITV, 6 October 1990.

Disaster at Silo 7 (1988). Somewhat less than thrilling, though ploddingly effective, thriller about an atomic near-disaster in Texas. A true story. With Dennis Weaver, Perry King, Michael O'Keefe, Patricia Charbonneau. Dir: Larry Elikan. ITV, 29 April 1991.

Do Not Disturb (1991). Yet another new BBC telefilm, this one, though on the gloomy side, is an acceptable modern ghost story, helped by good performances and a memorable setting in the Norfolk dunes and marshes. With Frances Barber, Peter Capaldi. Dir: Nicholas Renton. Screenplay: Timberlake Wertenbaker. BBC2, 17 March 1991.

Do Not Fold, Spindle or Mutilate (1971). Amusing thriller about four American senior citizens addicted to jokes – until they create one that rebounds very unpleasantly on them. A delightful showcase for four past stars of the 'golden age': Helen Hayes, Myrna Loy, Mildred Natwick and Sylvia Sidney. Also with Vince Edwards, Griffith Jones and Patrick Troughton. Dir: Ted Post. Screenplay: John D. F. Black. Channel 4, 30 August 1990.

Dogtanian – the Movie (1989). A canine cartoon feature based on the Dumas classic *The Three Musketeers*: an offshoot from the children's TV series. Dir: Luis Ballester. Screenplay: Claudio Biern Boyd. ITV, 4 January 1991.

Doing Life (1986). Based on the true story of a killer who spent his time in jail studying law, passed his exams, and became a defender of his fellow prisoners, especially when they rose up against the authorities. Fascinating; well above the usual jail melodrama. With Tony Danza, John de Vries. Dir: Gene Reynolds. Screenplay: Steve Bello; adapted from his book. BBC2, 29 October 1990.

Double Switch (1986). Another version of the often used 'Prince and Pauper' yarn about switched identities, only this time the 'Prince' is a rock star. Modestly entertaining with the boys of the Disney special effects department scoring over all else. With George Newbern, Elisabeth Shue. Dir: David Greenwalt. Screenplay: John McNamara. ITV, 5 August 1990 (Part 1) and 12 August 1990 (Part 2).

Dr Scorpion (1978). Pretty mediocre sub-James Bond stuff with a former CIA agent smashing the plans of the evil mastermind. With Nick Mancuso, Christine Lahti. Dir: Richard Lang. Screenplay: S. J. Cannell. ITV, 22 July 1990.

Draw! (1984). As long as a few of the veteran stetson stars keep going, the Western will never fade away. Here Kirk Douglas and James Coburn shoot it out in Alberta, but nobody takes things too seriously. Not tops, but still a lot of fun. Dir: Steven Hilliard Stern. ITV, 16 March 1991.

Dreaming (1991). Shades of *Billy Liar!*. Ewen Bremner stars in this new BBC telefilm about an Ayrshire youngster on the dole who dreams of the better lives he might have had. Pleasant comedy with some music. Also with Mary McCusker. Screenplay: William McIlvanney. Dir: Mike Alexander. BBC2, 24 March 1991.

Everybody's Baby: The Rescue of Jessica McClure (1989). Ding, dong, dell; Baby's down the well! As the worried parents fret, frantic attempts are made to get the child out, as the tension mounts. A true story, made in a very effective documentary style. Will they or won't they rescue her in time? With Beau Bridges, Roxanna Zal, Patty Duke. Dir: Mel Damski. Screenplay: David Eyre Jr. Channel 4, 11 September 1990.

The Exo-Man (1977). Daft thriller about a paralysed professor hitting back at the mob who attacked him. With David Ackroyd. Dir: Richard Irving. ITV, 14 April 1991.

The Execution (1985). Far-fetched and missable drama about five ex-inmates of a Nazi death camp who come across the camp's doctor, now a successful Los Angeles restaurateur, and decide to bring him to their own brand of justice. With Loretta Swit, Jessica Walter, Valerie Harper, Sandy Dennis. Dir: Paul Wendkos. No writing credit. ITV, 11 March 1991.

F. Scott Fitzgerald and 'The Last of the Belles' (1974). Biopic about the writer which quite ingeniously introduces one of his own semi-autobiographical short stories. With Richard Chamberlain, Blythe Danner, Susan Sarandon. Dir: George Schaefer. Screenplay: James Costigan. Channel 4, 27 November 1990.

The Fantasy Man (1984). Tame Aussie sex comedy which misses out on many potential laughs. Harry Hopkins is the happily married man who suddenly gets a mid-life amorous itch. Glamorous trio of itch-inducers are Jeanie Drynan, Kerry Mack and Kate Fitzpatrick. Dir: John Meagher. ITV, 1 May 1991.

Fatal Confession (1987). Father Dowling (a modern day Father Brown) is a parish priest who, with his nun assistant (an odd couple), has a taste for and an ability to solve crimes; in this case the suicide that isn't and the Mob that is. With Tom Bosley, Tracy Nelson. Dir: Christopher Hibler. Screenplay: Donald E. Westlake; based on stories by Ralph McInerny. ITV, 28 December 1990.

The Fifth Victim (1983). Full marks to this suspenseful thriller with Karen Valentine as Doe (the film's initial title), the amnesiac victim of an attack, and William Devane as the cop sorting out the suspects and the motive. Very watchable. Also with Eva Marie Saint, David Huffman. Dir: Ivan Nagy. Screenplay: Cynthia Mandelberg and Walter H. Davis. ITV, 18 August 1990.

Fourteen Going On Thirty (1988). Below-standard Disney film about a teenager determined to stop the teacher he's got a crush on from marrying her admittedly ill-judged swain. With Steve Eckholdt, Daphne Ashbrook, Loretta Swit. Dir: Paul Schneider. ITV, 28 April 1991 (Part 1) and 5 May 1991 (Part 2).

Frankenstein's Baby (1990). Completely tasteless and infantile so-called comedy about a man so obsessed with becoming a parent that with the devil's help he achieves pregnancy! Dir: Robert Bierman. Screenplay: Emma Tennent. BBC1, 9 September 1990.

Gambit (1986). Powerful and fascinating – and frightening – German two-part telefilm about atomic power and the authorities' inability to control it. Shades of Chernobyl. With Despina Pajanou, Rolf Zacher, Heinz Bennent. Dir: Peter Bringmann. No writing credit. BBC2, Part 1 on 15 February, Part 2 on 22 February 1991.

The Gift (1979). A far from jolly tar comes home from the sea on Christmas leave to find that he has been ditched by his girlfriend. The background is that of the grim tenements of Brooklyn and the lower-class life he would like to break away from, wistfully dreaming of painting in Paris. With Gary Frank, Julie Harris, Glenn Ford. Dir: Don

Taylor. Screenplay: Robert Malloy. Channel 4, 18 December 1990.

Gladiator School (1988). The 'school' is San Quentin jail, where tough, uncompromising cop Robert Conrad is sent for supposedly murdering a prostitute, and finds it a dangerous place to be. Dir: James Darren. Screenplay: Joseph (ex-cop) Wambaugh. BBC1, 20 October 1990.

Glitz (1988). Competent adaptation of Elmore Leonard's tough, exciting book about a rough-edged Miami cop (Jimmy Smits) who's drawn into the seedy world of gamblers, gangsters and their cohorts. Also with Markie Post, John Diehl. Dir: Sandor Stern. BBC1, 26 April 1991.

Glory! Glory! (1989). TV evangelism in America – a perfect subject for one of Britain's wittiest and most ironical of directors, Lindsay Anderson. To be savoured and treasured. With Ellen Greene, Richard Thomas, James Whitmore. Screenplay: Stan Daniels. BBC2, 4 August 1990.

Goodnight My Love (1972). Stylish thriller set in the 1940s and reminiscent in many ways of *The Maltese Falcon*. Blonde beauty Barbara Bain hires Richard Boone, the tough private eye with a dwarf sidekick (Michael Dunn). And the magnificent villain of the piece is played by Victor Buono. Dir and Screenplay: Peter Hyams. Channel 4, 16 August 1990.

Hallelujah Anyhow (1991). BBC telefilm about the rekindling of an old love affair. The former boyfriend of a woman preacher arrives from America and she has to face up to some difficult decisions. Nice performances from Dona Kroll, Keith Davis. Dir: Matthew Jacobs. Screenplay: Jacobs and Jean Breeze. BBC2, 27 January 1991.

Happy Feet (1990). Excellent BBC film about a dance school teacher (Phyllis Logan) coping with her various pupils. Their parents are more difficult, all seeing their own offspring as budding Pavlovas as they take part in the 1960 Classical Dance Festival at Scarborough. A comedy which even includes a mysterious ghost. Also with Marjie

Lawrence, Stephen Hancock. Dir and Screenplay: Mike Bradwell. BBC1, 1 January 1991.

Hardball: Till Death Do Us Part (1989). Feature-length intro to a tough new American cop series, the main interest of which is that it is directed by British actor David Hemmings. Routine stuff about the cops assigned to protect a star witness whose gangster hubbie is determined to stop her reaching the witness box. With John Ashton, Richard Tyson, Kay Lenz. Dir: David Hemmings. Screenplay: Frank Lupo. ITV, 5 January 1991.

Haunts of the Very Rich (1972). A variation on the *Outward Bound* story, with a small group of puzzled and frightened people marooned, by invitation, on a desert island where scary things happen. . . . Well done until the end, which leaves you feeling let down . . . as so often with this kind of thriller. With Lloyd Bridges, Cloris Leachman. Dir: Paul Wendkos. Screenplay: William Wood. Channel 4, 3 December 1990.

Heading Home (1991). The first of the BBC's 1991 films gets an early airing: Joely Richardson plays the innocent at home, the naive young girl from the provinces who finds poets and crooks and other oddball characters in London soon after World War II. Redolent of the atmosphere of those rationed years. Also with Gary Oldman, Stephen Dillane. Dir and Screenplay: David Hare. BBC2, 13 January 1991.

Heartsounds (1984). Marvellous performances by James Garner as the doctor who suffers heart attacks and Mary Tyler Moore as his brave wife make this a memorable experience. It won Garner the best actor award at the International TV Movie Festival and both of them gained Emmy nominations. Also with Sam Wanamaker, Wendy Crewson. Dir: Glenn Jordan. Based on Martha Lear's account in her best-selling book. BBC1, 2 September 1990.

Hero in the Family (1986). Disney family fun in a space fantasy about a boy who realises his astronaut dad has lost his marbles . . . and a chimp has them! With Christopher Collet, Cliff de

Young. Dir: No credit. Screenplay: No credit. ITV, 26 May 1991 (Part 1), 2 June 1991 (Part 2).

Home for Christmas (1990). Sad little piece about a once expert thief (Mickey Rooney) finding age has made inroads into his art. Shed a Christmas tear. Also with Chantalese Kent, Simon Richards. Dir and (with Peter Ferri) Screenplay: Peter McCubbin, ITV, 22 December 1990.

Hostage (1987). Real-life mum and daughter Carol Burnett and Carrie Hamilton give nice performances in this otherwise undistinguished telefilm. A young woman, accused of murder, escapes from jail and takes a wealthy widow as hostage . . . and then, of course, a relationship begins to flower between the duo. Dir: Peter Levin. Screenplay: Stephen H. Foreman. ITV, 4 February 1991.

I, Desire (1982). Telepic shudderer expert John Llewellyn Moxey directs this tale of modern vampirism, with a law student getting suspicious when a cadaver is found to have been drained of blood! With David Naughton, Dorian Harewood and Brad Dourif heading a large cast. Dir: J. L. Moxey. Screenplay: Robert Foster. ITV, 11 August 1990.

I Know My First Name Is Steven (1989). Based on a true story, but as good as any fiction: seven years after he is abducted, a California lad turns up at a police station to tell the grim story of those missing years. A fascinating and powerful film, likely to leave a deep impression. With Corin Nemec (the boy), Cindy Pickett and John Ashton. The real Steven appears, briefly, playing a cop.) Dir: Larry Elikann. BBC1 24 July 1990 (Part 1) and 25 July 1990 (Part 2).

I-Man (1986). Typical, entertaining fantasy from the Disney studios about a taxi driver (Scott Bakula) whose accidental inhaling of a magic gas makes him virtually indestructible. Fun for the family. Dir: Corey Allen. Screenplay: No credit. ITV, 14 April 1991.

I Married Wyatt Earp (1983). Marie Osmond (yes, she of the singing

Osmonds) as real-life character Josie Marcus, a Jewish singer/actress who married the famous marshal, and slept with his rival sheriff. Schmaltzy but fascinating. Also with Bruce Boxleitner, John Bennett Perry. Dir: Michael O'Herlihy. ITV, 9 June 1991.

Incident in San Francisco (1970). Another pilot feature for yet another series that never took off. Once again it's easy to see why it didn't. A journalist tries to prove the man charged is not guilty of a brawl killing. With Chris Connelly, Richard Kiley. Dir: Don Medford. ITV, 16 March 1991.

Intrigue (1988). Pretty poor writing can't quite kill off this reasonably convincing thriller, thanks to good work in most other departments including excellent acting performances from Scott Glenn, Robert Loggia and Martin Shaw. Dir: David Drury. Screenplay: Jeff Melvoin and Robert Collins. ITV, 14 January 1991.

Johnny Belinda (1982). TV loves Belinda! . . . Well, they made three previous small-screen versions of the 1948 large-screen weepie (which gave Jane Wyman one of her greatest triumphs), in 1955, 1958 and 1967. Rosanna Arquette in this new version (updated and *sans* the famous climactic court scene) plays the deaf-mute girl to splendid effect. She makes this fourth *Belinda* about the best of the lot. Also with Dennis Quaid. Dir: Anthony Page. Screenplay: Sue Milburn; based on the original 1940 Elmer Harris stage play. BBC2, 3 September 1990.

Judge Horton and the Scotsboro Boys (1976). Reconstruction of a big US court case of 1931, when nine blacks in Alabama were accused of the rape of two white women. With Arthur Hill, Vera Miles, Lewis Stadlen. Dir: Fielder Cook. BBC2, 13 June 1991.

Kids Like These (1987). Prepare to shed tears while watching this story of a gallant mother (Tyne Daly, getting the last ounce and the last tear-drop out of the role) with a Down's Syndrome child. Seriously and sensitively handled by Ms Daly's real-life hubbie, director George Stanford Brown. Also with Richard Crenna, Martin Balsam etc. Screenplay: Allan Sloane and Emile

Pearl Kingsley; based on the story by the latter. Channel 4, 21 August 1990.

The Lady from Yesterday (1985). Formerly categorised as a 'women's picture', the story of a man suddenly confronted by his former Vietnam mistress with the son he never knew existed. With Wayne Rogers, Bonnie Bedelia. Dir: Robert Day. Screenplay: Tim Maschler and Ken Pettus. ITV, 1 July 1990.

Laguna Heat (1987). Yet another pilot feature for a private eye series (based on T. Jefferson Parker's best-seller) that failed to make the grade. Harry Hamlin trying to sort out and solve a 20-year-old murder. Good acting and atmosphere can't make up for an indifferent story. Also with Jason Robards, Rip Torn, Anne Francis. Dir: Simon Langton. BBC1, 19 March 1991.

The Last Crop (1990). Aussie film which had a successful showing at the London Film Festival. Quirky story (by Elizabeth Jolley) about a Sydney char (Kerry Walker) who decides to distribute her clients' wealth to more deserving characters. Dir: Sue Clayton. Channel 4, 20 April 1991.

The Last Ride of the Dalton Gang (1979). Once more the Dalton brothers do their bad-guy thing, which they did in real life and then several times on the cinema screen. This time they do it in an ambitious TV Western feature. With Jack Palance, Randy Quaid, Larry Wilcox, Dale Robertson, Royal Dano. Dir: Dan Curtis. Screenplay: Earl W. Wallace. ITV, 8 August 1990.

The Laughter of God (1991). British telefilm about a husband and wife who hate each other enough to wish each other dead . . . Foul-mouthed, but impressive performances from Amanda Donohoe (showing her all), Peter Firth and Sylvia Syms. Dir and Screenplay: Tony Bicât. BBC2, 3 March 1991.

Laura Lansing Slept Here (1988). A specially written vehicle for 81-year-old Katharine Hepburn. She plays a novelist who bets her agent she *can* live with an ordinary family – at least for a week – in spite of her feisty ways. And there are plenty of reminders of Katie at her unique best. Also with Karen Austin,

Joel Higgins etc. Dir: George Schaefer. Screenplay: James Prideaux. BBC1, 24 August 1990.

The Leftovers (1986). Familiar Disney 'family' feature about the fight to keep the greedy hands of the developers off singing star John Denver's orphanage for unwanted kids. Also with Cindy Williams. ITV, 12 May 1991 (Part 1) and 19 May 1991 (Part 2).

Les Misérables (1978). Costly and reasonable TV re-make of the numerous cinema movies based on the classic story. Starry cast includes Richard Jordan, Anthony Perkins, John Gielgud, Celia Johnson, Flora Robson, and plenty more. An unjustly convicted woodcutter is relentlessly hounded by a really nasty policeman. Dir: Glenn Jordan. Screenplay: John Gay. BBC1, 5 April 1991.

Letting Go (1985). Modestly entertaining (in spite of poor script) hearts-and-flowers stuff about the romance of widower John Ritter and ditched-by-her-lover Sharon Gless, neither of whom seem to be able to forget their former partners. Dir: Jack Bender. ITV, 10 March 1991.

Little Spies (1986). Disney film about dognapping which looks like a transcription of an animated feature – but apparently isn't! Mickey Rooney (as one might expect) does a hefty bit of scene-stealing as Jimmie the Hermit, while the dogs themselves upstage the youngsters who've sworn to catch the pooch stealers. Grand family fun. Dir: Greg Beeman. Screenplay: Stephen Greenfield and Stephen Bonds. ITV, 19 August 1990 (Part 1) and 26 August 1990 (Part 2).

The Long Hot Summer (1985). A re-make (sort of) of the 1958 cinema film based on the William Faulkner stories of sex and sin in hot and sticky small-town Louisiana. To enhance a good script, there's a marvellous cast including Cybill Shepherd, Jason Robards, Ava Gardner, Don Johnson etc. Dir: Stuart Cooper. Screenplay: Rita Mae Brown and Dennis Turner. BBC1, 18 December 1990 (Part 1) and 20 December 1990 (Part 2).

Loose Cannon: Flashback (1989). Pilot feature for a new mad-cop series which will soon be reaching your TV set. Shandoe Stevens as the tough New York cop who charges through bombs, bullets and car crashes with equal aplomb and always gives the crooks what they deserve. Good fast-and-furious action-fun. Also with Bruce Young, Shelagh McLeod. Dir: No credit. ITV, 1 June 1991.

Lorca, Death of a Poet (1987). Spanish telefilm about the distinguished poet who was assassinated just after the outbreak of the Spanish Civil War. With Nickolas Grace. Dir: J. A. Bardem. Screenplay: Ian Gibson, Mario Camus and Bardem. Channel 4, 4 August 1990.

Lorna Doone (1990). The producers really splashed out on this re-make of the classic tale of passion on Dartmoor by R. D. Blackmore . . . even though they made it in Scotland! With Clive Owen, Polly Walker (as Lorna), Sean Bean. Dir: Andrew Grieve. Screenplay: Matthew Jacobs. ITV, 26 December 1990.

Love Is Never Silent (1985). Tear-jerking story about a dutiful daughter who finds it difficult to cut the strings that keep her tied to her deaf parents. (Many of the players were really deaf.) Winner of an Emmy Award as well as several nominations and critical favour. With Mare Winningham, Phyllis Frelich, Ed Waterstreet. Dir: Joseph Sargent. BBC2, 18 March 1991.

The Mafia Priest Mystery (1989). G. K. Chesterton's Father Brown walks again! Probing priest Tom Bosley uncovers more than he bargained for when he sets out to prove a fellow cleric innocent of the murder with which he is charged. Pleasant watching. Also with Tracy Nelson, Mary Wickes. No writing or directing credits given. ITV, 23 March 1991.

Mama's Going to Buy You a Mocking Bird (1988). Sincere if minor Canadian weepie about a happy family suddenly thrown into tragedy when it is discovered dad has terminal cancer. With Geoff Bowes, Linda Griffiths, Louis Tripp. Dir: Sandy Wilson. Screenplay: Anna Sandor; based on the novel by

Jean Little. Channel 4, 24 January 1991.

Manhunter (1974). Made as a pilot for a TV series (and not to be confused with the recent cinema film release with the same title), this is an exciting thriller about bank robbers of the 1930s who become killers, and the one man who is determined they shall pay for their crime. With Ken Howard, Gary Lockwood and Stefanie Powers. Dir: Walter Grauman. Screenplay: Sam H. Rolfe. ITV, 2 September 1990.

Mayflower Madam (1987). Candice Bergen as real-life character Sydney Biddle Barrows, who ran an up-market New York introduction bureau, and obviously enjoyed herself greatly in the role. And Miss Barrows herself takes a cameo role, playing one of her own friends! A socialite descendant of the original *Mayflower* pilgrims, Madam shocked New York with her call girls. Also with Chris Sarandon. Dir: Lou Antonio. No writing credit. BBC1, 28 August 1990.

The Memory of Eva Ryker (1980). Painfully overlong, over-directed and patchy TV movie about a search for the truth. The background is the sinking of the *Queen Anne* with the loss of nearly a thousand lives in the first year of World War II. With Natalie Wood, Robert Foxworth, Roddy McDowall. Dir: Walter Grauman. Screenplay: Laurence Heath; based on the D. A. Stanwood novel. ITV, 5 January 1991.

Mercy or Murder (1987). A brilliant performance by veteran movie star Robert Young, as the tragic husband accused of (mercy) killing his terminally ill wife, makes this a memorable telefilm. Based on a factual case. Also with Frances Reid, Eddie Albert. Dir and Screenplay: Steven Gethers. Channel 4, 16 October 1990.

Mickey Spillane's Mike Hammer: Murder Takes All (1989). Stacy Keach as gumshoe Mike Hammer picking his way through the corpses in Las Vegas to find the killer and clear his own name. Also with Linda Carter. Dir: John Nicolella. ITV, 26 June 1991.

Midnight Breaks (1990). Pretty rough going about rock'n'roll, reggae and the drug pushers always waiting off-stage. Robbie Coltrane as a dope baron. Routine. Dir and Screenplay: Laurens C. Postma. Channel 4, 18 October 1990.

Monster Manor (1988). A direct descendant of the crude 'Police Academy' series: a couple of jokey cops take over a manor house, with predictable farcical results. With Brian McNamara, Clayton Rohner etc. Dir: Ron Lipstadt. Screenplay: Joseph Wambaugh. BBC1, 3 November 1990.

A Month of Sundays (1991). Good performances by Vincent Gardenia and particularly Hume Cronyn (still going strong at 80) make this tear-flecked telecomedy about a couple of nursing home pals very watchable. And note the assured performance by Hume's daughter Tandy. Dir: Alan Kroeker. Screenplay: Bob Larbey. ITV, 31 March 1991.

Morphine and Dolly Mixtures (1991). An adaptation by Karl Francis (who also directs) of Carol Ann Courtney's autobiographical novel about her traumatic childhood in Cardiff with her drug-addicted and often very violent father. A strong addition to the new series of BBC films. Powerful performances by Patrick Bergin and Joanna Griffiths. BBC2, 10 March 1991.

✓**Moving Target** (1988). When young Jason Bateman returns home he finds family and furniture vanished. And when he tries to find out what has happened he is soon immersed in a dangerous mystery that threatens his own life. Sounds better than it is, with too many weaknesses to keep it – in spite of the pace – engrossing. With Tom Skerritt, Jack Wagner. Dir: Chris Thomson. No writing credit. BBC2, 15 February 1991.

Murder in the City of Angels (1988). Intended as the feature introduction to a series that never materialised, this is the story of tough LA cop George Peppard's 1940s fight against the Mob's plans to take over the city. (The alternative title was *Man Against the Mob*.) Fairly gripping crime drama. Also with Kathryn Harrold. Dir: Steven H. Stern. BBC1, 5 March 1991.

Murder Me, Murder You (1983). Private eye Mike Hammer's search for the daughter he didn't know he had leads him down a tortuous path of vice and international politics. With Stacy Keach, Tanya Roberts, Don Stroud. Dir: Gary Nelson. Screenplay: Bill Stratton. ITV, 25 December 1990.

Murder in Music City (1979). (A.k.a. *The Country Music Murders*.) Murder-and-music mystery which is unlikely to keep you hooked. A songwriter turns detective when he finds a body in his bath. With Sonny Bono and lots of country-and-western warblers. Dir: Leo Penn. Screenplay: Jimmy Sangster and Ernie Frankel. ITV, 21 July 1990.

My Boyfriend's Back (1989). What happens when a trio of female pop singers get back together again after twenty years and try their luck? A pity it's such a poor script . . . and why didn't they get the bubbling Beverley Sisters to make the whole affair more plausible and enjoyable? With Sandy Duncan, Jill Eikenberry, Judith Light. Dir: Paul Schneider. Screenplay: Lindsay Harrison. ITV, 11 December 1990.

My First Love (1988). Lonely widow Beatrice Arthur tries to rekindle the romance she once had with a now highly successful doctor, but finds his young mistress doesn't like the idea at all. A film that falters at times but is generally quite charming. Also with Richard Kiley, Joan Van Ark. Dir: Gilbert Cates. Screenplay: Ed Kaplan. Channel 4, 6 November 1990.

Naked Lie (1987). Life has been sweet for lady lawyer Victoria Principal and her superior court judge lover . . . until she takes the case of a murdered prostitute and uncovers a lot of nasty maggots in unexpected places. Also with James Farentino. Dir: Richard Colla. ITV, 26 March 1991.

New Columbo: Columbo Goes to the Guillotine (1989). With Peter Falk, Anthony Andrews and Karen Austin. Dir: No credit. ITV, 2 March 1991.

New Columbo: Grand Deception (1989). With Peter Falk, Robert Foxworth and Janet Eilber. Dir: Sam Wanamaker. ITV, 9 March 1991.

New Columbo: Murder, Smoke and Shadows (1989). Peter Falk as shabby and ill-mannered as ever, driving the killer to confess. With Fisher Stevens, Steven Hill and Molly Hagan. Dir: Richard A. Simmons. ITV, 23 February 1991.

The Night Nurse (1977). When night nurse Kate Fitzpatrick takes on the routine job of minding an ageing diva (Davina Whitehouse) she doesn't know that she's walking into a murder mystery. Dir: Igor Auzins. Screenplay: Tony McLean. ITV, 28 July 1990.

The Night They Took Miss Beautiful (1977). The terrorists actually hi-jack not one but *five* beauty queens, along with the other cargo of deadly germs. Dull and badly done. With Chuck Connors, Victoria Principal. Dir: Robert Michael Lewis. BBC1, 7 June 1991.

Night Walk (1989). Familiar story: Lesley-Anne Down takes a night walk on the beach, witnesses a murder and, when the cops scoff at her story, moves to the top of the killers' hit list. Surprisingly easy-going performances in spite of Jerrold Freedman's splendidly tight direction. Also with Robert Urich. ITV, 8 June 1991.

No Room to Run (1978). Routine Aussie TV thriller about a visiting PR man who becomes enmeshed in a net of down-under crookery. Richard Benjamin, Paula Prentiss and Barry Sullivan went from the USA to Australia to make this minor TV movie, but one has to ask – was it worth it? Dir: Robert Michael Lewis. No writing credit. BBC1, 6 December 1990.

Nocturne (1990). Going back to her childhood home for her mother's funeral, Marguerite (Lisa Eichhorn) becomes beset by memories – and two young runaway girls. Also with Caroline Paterson, Karen Jones. Dir: Joy Chamberlain. Screenplay: Tash Fairbanks. Channel 4, 29 November 1990.

Olive (1987). An acting husband-and-wife team go to live in Australia, and when wife Olive (Kerry McGuire) discovers she has cancer, their life together changes. Also with Nick Tate. Dir: Stephen Wallace. Screenplay: Anthony Wheeler. Channel 4, 4 December 1990.

Once Upon a Texas Train (1988). A real, nostalgic treat for Western fans, with a cast that includes Willie Nelson (the old villain leading a gang of other old villains), Richard Widmark (as the old Texas Ranger grimly determined to thwart Willie's robbery plan), Chuck Connors, Jack Elam, Kevin McCarthy, Dub Taylor, Royal Dano, Stuart Whitman, Harry Carey Jr, Angie Dickinson etc. Terrific fun. Dir and Screenplay: Burt Kennedy. BBC1, 27 July 1990.

One Cooks, the Other Doesn't (1984). Comedy about an estate agent whose inability to sell property puts him in a tight financial corner, and leads to his former wife moving in with his present one, with all the expected comic results. With Joseph Bologna, Suzanne Pleshette, Rosanna Arquette. Dir: Richard Michaels. Screenplay: Larry Grusin. ITV, 24 November 1990.

102 Boulevard Haussmann (1991). BBC telefilm starring Alan Bates as French writer Marcel Proust, who develops a passion for the playing of a string quartet and, more particularly, its young viola player. Delicate writing by Alan Bennett, a sensitive performance by Bates, plenty of classical music, virtually no movement, and gloomy photography. Not an easy film to sit through. Also with Paul Rhys, Janet McTeer. Dir: Udayas Prasad. BBC2, 17 February 1991.

One Last Chance (1990). Yet another new BBC-made TV movie and not a bad one at that: a blackish comedy about goings-on in the London Greek-Cypriot community. Heavy on the London background, with a nice script and very reasonable performances. Decorative ex-*Star Trek* (and real Greek-Cypriot) Marina Sirtis adds to the glamour. Also with George Jackos, Mark Jefferis. Dir: Gabriel Beaumont. No writing credit. BBC1, 6 October 1990.

Original Sin (1988). Generally excellent, well out of the normal rut Mafia melodrama – until the end, when it falls completely apart. With Charlton Heston, Ann Jillian. Dir: Ron Satlof. Screenplay: Philip F. Messina. ITV, 12 November 1990.

The Other Lover (1985). Apparently it took no fewer than five (unnamed) writers to produce this very ordinary love story set in the world of novelists and publishers. But the cast (Lindsay Wagner, Jack Scalia etc.) and director Robert Ellis Miller do their best to hold one's attention. BBC2, 11 February 1991.

Perilous Voyage (1976). Routine 1968 (made then but understandably kept on the shelf until eight years later) adventure telefilm about a ship's passengers held hostage by South American revolutionaries. It might as well have stayed on the shelf. With William Shatner, Michael Parks. Dir: William Graham. ITV, 20 April 1991.

Perry Mason: The Case of the All-Star Assassin (1989). Not the best of Perry (nor the most: he's not on screen for long). Here he helps a lesser mortal to prove the innocence of a hockey player accused of murder. With Raymond Burr, Barbara Hale, William Moses, Alexandra Paul. Dir: Christian I. Nyby II. BBC1, 11 May 1991.

Perry Mason: The Case of the Avenging Ace (1979). Another of the new crop of Mason telefeature court victories: this time he's facing a very difficult time proving that his pilot pal did not do the murder of which he has been convicted. With Raymond Burr, Barbara Hale, William Katt, Larry Wilcox. Dir: Christian I. Nyby II. BBC1, 20 April 1991.

Perry Mason: The Case of the Lady in the Lake (1987). The first in a new series of Mason telemovies; this time he defends the husband of a happily married woman on a murder charge. It's not really that difficult to solve the case, but for Mason fans it's great stuff! With Raymond Burr, Barbara Hale, David Hasselhoff. Dir: Ron Satlof. BBC1, 13 April 1991.

Perry Mason: The Case of the Lethal Lesson (1989). Perry defends one of his law class pupils accused of murdering a fellow student. With Raymond Burr, Barbara Hale, Brian Keith. Dir: Christian I. Nyby II. BBC1, 27 April 1991.

Peter Lundy and the Medicine Hat Stallion (1977). Based on the Marguerite Henry novel, this pleasant family Western is about a likely lad (Leif Garrett) who volunteers to ride Pony Express in Nebraskan territory, and finds plenty of adventures along the way. A delightful movie for the young and young in heart. Also with Milo O'Shea. Dir: Michael O'Herlihy. BBC1, 12 August 1990.

The Phantom of the Opera (1990). They just can't let the poor fellow alone, can they? (I've seen at least six previous versions of the story, starting with the Lon Chaney silent version made in 1925.) Tony Richardson chose Charles Dance for his lavish telefilm version of the classic story, which I think might now be left in peace on the shelves for a while. Teri Polo dances her way into your heart and Burt Lancaster makes everything seem worthwhile with his superb performance. Also with Ian Richardson, Adam Storke and Andrea Ferreol. Dir: Tony Richardson. BBC1, 19 August 1990 (Part 1) and 26 August 1990 (Part 2).

The Pickwick Papers (1985). Aussie feature-length cartoon version of the classic Dickens novel. Dir: Warwick Gilbert. Screenplay: Steven Fosbery. ITV, 27 December 1990.

The Police (1990). Disturbing new BBC telefilm about a group of school-boys who form their own police force to stop bullying, but enjoy it so much they start work on a teacher who has earned their displeasure. With Guy Faulkner as the lad who starts it all. Dir: Ian Knox. Screenplay: Arthur Ellis. BBC1, 16 September 1990.

Popeye Doyle (1986). The real-life cop played by Gene Hackman in both *The French Connection* movies is revived (though now played by Ed O'Neill) for this fast-moving thriller. The murder of a rich man's mistress leads tortuously to a plot to start a war in the Middle East and a rapidly approaching dead-line if the conflict is to be prevented. Also with Matthew Laurence, Audrey Landers. Dir: Peter Levin. Screenplay: Richard Dilello. ITV, 30 December 1990.

Pray for the Wildcats (1974). Remember *Deliverance*? Well, here is the TV version of the story; four men take a motorcycle trip into the wild and, not satisfied with fighting nature, end up fighting among themselves. Familiar stuff, but watchable. With Andy Griffith (as a real bad 'un here), William Shatner, Janet Margolin, Angie Dickinson. Dir: Robert Michael Lewis. Screenplay: Jack Turley. ITV, 7 October 1990.

Pressure Point (1977). It's put-upon, worried-and-worn cop David Janssen (did he ever smile? If he did it was a miracle of miscasting). Actually this is a couple of stitched together episodes of the old 'Police Story' series, following the police and personal problems of a cop who takes everything very seriously. Also with Diana Muldaur, Macdonald Carey, Scott Brady etc. Dir: Jerry London. Screenplay: Mark Rodgers. ITV, 20 September 1990.

Promises to Keep (1985). A family affair (Robert Mitchum, son Chris and grandson Bentley – his sorry debut! – in the three main male roles) which gradually is revealed as a let-down, thanks to a mediocre story and undistinguished handling. Also with Claire Bloom, Tess Harper. Dir: Noel Blanck. No writing credit. BBC2, 24 September 1990.

Quincy: The Thigh Bone's Connected to the Knee Bone (1976). From the four-part mystery murder series, part of the 'Mystery Movies' films of the period. Quincy (Jack Klugman) sets his pathology class the problem of solving the murder of the owner of the thigh bone being used to illustrate a visiting professor's lecture. And the students come up with all the answers to the twenty-year-old killing! Clever lot. Also with Lynnette Mettey, Gaey Walberg. Dir: Alex March. Screenplay: Tony Lawrence and Lou Shaw. ITV, 14 December 1990.

The Rainbow Warrior Conspiracy (1988). Brilliant Jack Thompson (remember his outstanding performance in the Australian film *Breaker Morant*?) in a New Zealand film based on the sensational true story about the French agents who scuttled Greenpeace's ship *Rainbow Warrior* while it was floating peacefully at anchor in a New Zealand harbour in 1985. First-class stuff. Also with Brad Davis. Dir: Chris Thompson. No writing credit. BBC2, 7 August 1990 (Part 1) and 8 August 1990 (Part 2).

Rape and Marriage: The Rideout Case (1980). Semi-documentary centred on the Oregon housewife who claimed her husband had raped her, and took her case to court. Sensational at the time, and still fascinating to watch, as the case breaks new legal ground. Linda Hamilton plays the wife and Mickey Rourke, happily cast, the drunken bully of a husband. Also with Rip Torn. Dir: Peter Levin. Screenplay: Hesper Anderson. ITV, 16 December 1990.

Return to Earth (1976). And not a particularly happy return for astronaut Buzz Aldrin when he comes back from the moon in 1969 to find everything, including his marriage, going wrong. A serious, real-life story, with plenty of breathtaking footage of the expedition and a masterly performance by Cliff Robertson as the unfortunate astronaut. Also with Shirley Knight and Ralph Bellamy. Based on the book by George Malko and Wayne Waga, *Buzz Aldrin*. Dir: Jud Taylor. Channel 4, 23 August 1990.

The Return of Mickey Spillane's Mike Hammer (1986). Pilot feature for the series of private eye adventures that followed, with Stacy Keach back in the role that fits him like a battle-worn boxing glove. A trail of kidnap and extortion leads from New York to Hollywood . . . Also with Don Stroud, Lauren Hutton, Vince Edwards, Mickey Rooney. Dir: Ray Danton. Screenplay: James Miller, Larry Brody and Janis Hendler. ITV, 23 July 1990.

Rock 'n' Roll Mom (1988). Good-humoured, easy-going Disney product about a suburban housewife who finds surprising fame as a singer – and nobody is more surprised than her teenage brood. With Dyan Cannon, Michael Brandon, Heather Locklear. Dir: Michael Schultz. ITV, 9 and 16 June 1991.

The Room Upstairs (1987). Routine comedy about the lodgers in Stockard Channing's boarding house, and how cellist Sam Waterston undermines her intention never to become personally involved with any of them. Dir: Stuart Margolin. Screenplay: Steve Lawson. BBC2, 8 October 1990.

135

The Runaways (1975). Simple and quite endearing film for youngsters (and adults) about a boy and his leopard, the runaways of the title. A very enjoyable 1½ hours, with charming performances by Dorothy McGuire and John Randolph. From the Victor Canning novel. Dir: Harry Harris. Channel 4, 31 March 1991.

Save the Dog! (1988). Cindy Williams trying to save her film star dog (and her financial future) when he's stricken down with junk-food fever! Typical, pleasant Disney 'family' watching. Also with Tony Randall. Dir: Paul Aaron. ITV, 23 June 1991 (Part 1) and 1 July 1991 (Part 2).

Scandal in a Small Town (1988). Raquel Welch at 50 still looks great and knows how to put herself across; here playing a waitress in a seedy bar who courageously fights the racism expressed by her daughter's schoolmistress, and doesn't count the cost of the battle. Also with Christa Denton (the daughter), Ronny Cox. Dir: Anthony Page. No writing credit. BBC1, 22 January 1991.

Scream of the Wolf (1974). Routine little thriller about a novelist who becomes the investigator of a series of murders, apparently the work of a wolf-man. With Peter Graves, Clint Walker, Jo Ann Pflug. Dir: Dan Curtis. Screenplay: Richard Matheson. ITV, 22 December 1990.

Secret Weapon (1990). Spying in the secret world of Israel's atom bomb programme – based on the stories that grabbed newspaper headlines in 1986. With Griffin Dunne, Karen Allen. Dir: Ian Sharp. Screenplay: Nick Evans. ITV, 23 December 1990.

Sessions (1983). The psychological problems of a high-class prostitute are made consistently interesting by the intelligent and illuminating performance of Veronica Hamel – a woman 'on the edge of a nervous breakdown'. Also with Jeffrey DeMunn, Jill Eikenberry. Dir: Richard Pearce. Screenplay: Barbara Turner. Channel 4, 18 September 1990.

The Shiralee (1987). One of the rare occasions when the TV re-make is a great improvement on the cinema original. A splendid adaptation of the D'Arcy Niland classic Australian novel about a tough Aussie sheep shearer who keeps on the move and whose 'shiralee' (burden) is the small daughter who travels the road with him. Superbly credible performances by Bryan Brown and Rebecca Smart and the rest of the cast. And you can almost smell the outback backgrounds. Also with Noni Hazelhurst. Dir: George Ogilvie. BBC1, 10 and 11 January 1991.

Silent Witness (1985). Though made in 1985, a very topical story. Dilemma: should the sister-in-law of one of three rapists give him away to the police? With Valerie Bertinelli, John Savage. Dir: No credit: ITV, 29 May 1991.

Skulduggery (1991). More screen time for idle, layabout London East End youth, from actor-turned-director/writer Philip Davis. It may be 'realistic', but it bored me to switch-off. With Steve Sweeney, David Trewlis and some other promising youngsters. And lots of foul language. BBC1, 20 June 1991.

A Small Killing (1981). Infuriatingly daft film about a cop-and-professor team who go undercover to find a killer, and fall in love along the way. Just – *only* just – worth a look for the stars, Jean Simmons, Sylvia Sidney and Edward Asner. Dir: Steven Hilliard Stern. ITV, 19 June 1991.

Small Sacrifices (1989). Pretty horrific tale – apparently a true one – about an Oregon mother who in 1983 allegedly attempted to kill her three offspring in the hope that this would persuade her married lover to swap his wife for her! Two of the children survived, but one death was quite enough to ensure the unbalanced lady got a life sentence. A testing role for ex-Charlie's Angel Farrah Fawcett, who pulls it off quite commendably. (A neat touch: FF's real-life lover Ryan O'Neal plays her fictional lover.) Also with John Shea. Dir: David Greene. Screenplay based on the bestseller by Ann Rule. BBC1, 31 July 1990 (Part 1) and 1 August 1990 (Part 2).

Snake Treaty (1989). (A.k.a. *Red Earth, White Earth*.) A Canadian Western about the Redskins which can't make up its mind if it wants to be an actioner or a sentimental weepie, and falls with a thud between the two. With Genevieve Bujold, Timothy Daly, Richard Farnsworth. Dir: David Greene. Screenplay: Michael Deguzman; from a story by William Weaver. Channel 4, 23 October 1990.

A Special Kind of Love (1978). About a mentally retarded youngster who finds a joy in life through sport. Charles Durning gives a moving and sympathetic portrait of the lad's widowed dad, trying to keep the family together. Also with Irene Tedrow, Debra Winger. Dir: Lee Philips. Screenplay: John S. Young. ITV, 12 February 1991.

Sticky Wickets (1990). And pretty sticky going, too. A new BBC telefilm production which might affront German and Welsh viewers as it takes the mickey out of both. A local Welsh cricket team's annual dinner at the Dragon Inn, with a World War II theme, is complicated by the arrival of a coachload of Germans. All good fun . . . maybe? With James Bolam, Alun Armstrong, George Sewell etc. Dir: Dewi Humphreys. Screenplay: Fletcher Watkins. BBC1, 14 October 1990.

A Stranger Waits (1983). Suzanne Pleshette as the unsuspecting widow who starts an affair with her estate manager – Justin Deas – without knowing the dastardly fellow is planning to murder her. Dir: Robert Lewis. ITV, 29 June 1991.

Strike Force (1975). A young Richard Gere is one of the cops assigned to investigate the murder of two mobsters by the Mob. Also with Cliff Gorman, Marilyn Chris. Dir: Barry Shear. Screenplay: R. O. Hirson. ITV, 23 December 1990.

Survival of the Fittest (1990). New BBC black comedy about an entirely selfish old lady of 80 (Jean Anderson in delightful top form) who stirs up the villagers. Nice work, too, from supporting players Timothy West, Elizabeth Spriggs and Nerys Hughes. Dir: Martyn Friend. Screenplay: Julian Mitchell. BBC1, 21 October 1990.

Sweet Nothing (1990). Highly unlikely story of parents who up and off to Canada without letting their shocked schoolboy son know anything of their plans, leaving him to join London's 'cardboard city' down-and-outs. (At times it seems almost like an excuse for the writer to get some of his anger about social conditions off his chest.) Some may find it compulsive viewing; more, I suspect, won't. With Lee Ross, Charlotte Coleman, Janet McTeer. Dir: Tony Smith. Screenplay: Vincent O'Connell. BBC1, 23 September 1990.

Sworn to Silence (1986). Superior telefilm with an intriguing social problem at its heart: should a defence lawyer reveal confidential information about his client or not? That's the worrying situation facing Peter Coyote. Dabney Coleman walked off with an Emmy award for his performance as the inebriated pal. Dir: Peter Levin. Screenplay: No credit. BBC1, 12 January 1991.

Take My Daughters, Please (1988). A routine re-make (why?) of the TV movie *All My Darling Daughters*, about a determined mother scheming to get her four daughters off her hands. Nice performance by Rue McClanahan as Ma. Also with Stefanie Kramer. Dir: Larry Elikann. Screenplay: Lindsay Harrison. Channel 4, 10 January 1991.

Tarzan in Manhattan (1989). What will they do to the everlasting Ape Man next? Here he leaves his comfy African jungle to fight the vivisectionists in the far less civilised jungle of New York. This one is good carefree fun, with the monkey man played by the eighteenth actor to essay the role, Joe Lara. A sympathetic taxi driver (Kim Crosby) is his 'Jane' for the occasion. With Tony Curtis. Dir: Michael Schultz. No screenwriting credit. BBC1, 3 August 1990.

The Tenth Month (1979). Nicely acted, often touching story (which, alas, goes on far too long) about a middle-aged, self-sufficient woman who suddenly finds herself pregnant and facing all sorts of unexpected problems. Though based on a novel it was apparently scripted especially for the star, Carol Burnett. Also with Keith Michell, Dina Merrill, Cristina Raines. Dir. and Screenplay: Joan Tewkesbury;

based on the novel by Laura Z. Hobson. Channel 4, 13 November 1990.

Terror on Highway 91 (1988). Remember Ricky Schroder, the little blond lad who won a million moviegoers' hearts? Well, he's grown into quite an actor, shown here as a lawman with ethics, untainted by the corruption all around him. Very watchable. Dir: Jerry Jameson. Screenplay: Stuart Schoffman. ITV, 18 February 1991.

That Secret Sunday (1986). Originally titled *Betrayal of Trust*. The police cover up the murder of two girls at a wild party, but a grubby journalist gets on the trail in the hope of making his name. Routine TV feature. With James Farentino, Parker Stevenson, Daphne Ashbrook. Dir: Richard Colla. ITV, 15 June 1991.

There Must Be a Pony (1986). This extremely interesting film, based on a James Kirkwood novel, sees Elizabeth Taylor as a former top-flight screen star who comes out of a mental home determined to climb back to her old pinnacle by way of TV 'soaps'. Also with Robert Wagner and James Coco etc. Dir: Joseph Sargent. BBC1, 12 August 1990.

They Never Slept (1991). Women spies at work in this send-up of MI5 in World War II. Emily Morgan plays the driver who suddenly finds herself in the midst of the confusion of the French Resistance, but finally emerges with honour. Also with Edward Fox and James Fleet as her superiors, hugely enjoying themselves. Dir: Udayan Prasad. Screenplay: Simon Gray. BBC2, 20 January 1991.

Tidy Endings (1988). Television adaptation of Harvey Fierstein's play about the confrontation of the wife and male lover of a man who has just died of AIDS. With Harvey Fierstein, Stockard Channing. Dir: Gavin Millar. Channel 4, 24 November 1990.

Tilt (1979). A cinema general release in June 1980, and reviewed in *Film Review 1979–80*. ITV, 6 April 1991.

Timestalkers (1987). Weird but quite entertaining fantasy about a nutty old

scientist who turns the clock back enough for him to participate in and change the story of the Old West by bringing back to the present a character from the future! Are you with me so far? With William Devane, Lauren Hutton, Klaus Kinski and, his final film, Forrest Tucker. Dir: Michael Schultz. (Originally scheduled to be transmitted on 25 June 1990.) BBC1, 13 July 1990.

Tubby the Tuba (1977). Delightful animated version of the classic for children, about the tuba who gets bored with just going 'oompa, oompa' all the time. With the voices of Hermione Gingold, Pearl Bailey and Dick Van Dyke. Dir: Alexander Schure. BBC1, 1 June 1991.

Uncommon Valour (1983). No relation to the Gene Hackman film released in 1984 with the same title. This one was made as a try-out feature for a possible series about firefighters but never really lit up. (Understandably.) However, if you like watching fires . . . With Mitchell Ryan, Barbara Parkins. Dir: Ron Amateau. ITV, 25 March 1991.

A Very Brady Christmas (1988). Feature-length episode from the US TV series which ran in the 1970s, 'The Brady Bunch'. Mom and Dad's Christmas family reunion plans falter and fail because their progeny all have reasons not to turn up. With Robert Reed, Florence Henderson. Dir: Peter Baldwin. Screenplay: S. and L. J. Schwartz. ITV, 24 December 1990.

Where the Spirit Lives (1989). A Canadian telefilm about a shameful chapter in the white man's treatment of the North American Indians, when youngsters were forcibly taken from their parents to schools where they were beaten into accepting the white man's God. The story of a courageous Indian girl rebel (Michelle St John). Lovely photography of glorious backgrounds must have helped the film to win its several Film Festival awards. Don't miss this one. Dir: Bruce Pittman. BBC1, 6 May 1991.

Whisperkill (1987). Laughably incredible murder mystery in which the killer gives advance warning of his intentions by making phone calls to the victims, all of whom are connected with a local newspaper. With Loni Anderson, Joe Penny, June Lockhart. Dir: Christian I. Nyby II. Screenplay: J. R. Bensink. ITV, 26 February 1991.

The Widowmaker (1990). Seemingly based on the Hungerford tragedy, the story of a man, apparently normal, who one day goes out with a gun and shoots down fourteen innocent people in the street for no apparent reason. With David Morrissey, Annabelle Apsion. Dir: John Madden. Screenplay: Jeremy Brock. ITV, 29 December 1990.

Wild Jack (1988). Disney family comedy about Alaskan wilderness guide W. J. suddenly faced with running a vast publishing company in the Big City. Sit back and enjoy it! With John Schneider, Carol Huston, Mel Ferrer. Dir: Harry Harris. Screenplay: William Blinn. ITV 15 July 1990 (Part 1), 22 July 1990 (Part 2) and 29 July 1990 (Part 3).

Winnie (1988). The moving story of a slightly mentally retarded woman who has spent most of her life (wrongly, one feels) in institutions, but who now sees her love for another inmate as the possible key to freedom. A marvellous performance by Meredith Baxter Birney in a memorable TV movie. Also with David Morse. Dir: John Korty. Screenplay: Joyce Eliason; based on the book (itself based on a true story) by Jamie Pastor Bolnick. Channel 4, 17 January 1991.

Women in Tropical Places (1989). Newcastle, England, in fact, where Miss Jones is left stranded – arriving from abroad to rejoin her lover, he's not there to meet her as promised, nor is he anywhere to be found. So there she is, trying to keep afloat in a sea of Geordies! With Alison Doody, Scarlet O'Hara, Hufty Reah. Dir and (with Candy Guard) Screenplay: Penny Woolcock. Channel 4, 8 November 1990.

The Wrestler (1986). Award-winning Finnish telefilm about the romance between an ex-wrestler and a not-so-young woman, both of whom are in an institution. Those awards were well earned. With Esko Hukkanen, Esko Pesonen. Dir and Screenplay: Matti Lias. Channel 4, 27 October 1990.

Video Releases

FILMS BETWEEN JULY 1990 AND JUNE 1991

ANTHONY HAYWARD

Britain's video industry weathered the recession to experience only a small fall in trading during 1990–1, although dealers made clear their disappointment at the quality of releases during the year.

There were few major blockbusters to thrill the video-viewing public. *Total Recall, Pretty Woman, Die Hard 2* and *Back to the Future, Part III* were the most popular tapes in a rental market that lost one in twenty customers. A one per cent fall in income was cushioned by an increase in nightly rental charges.

Total Recall was an instant No. 1, accounting for 13 per cent of all cassette rentals in its first week. The Arnold Schwarzenegger hit took £9 million at the British box office – probably the most successful 18-certificate film ever released – and was welcomed by video dealers.

Pretty Woman – released simultaneously in the rental and 'sell-through' markets – was also No. 1 in the 1990–1 sales chart, with shops taking 800,000 tapes during the film's first six weeks. It quickly became the third-biggest-selling video ever, behind *Lady and the Tramp* and *Dirty Harry*.

Walt Disney's *Lady and the Tramp*, the other major 'sell-through' success of the year, sold 1.7 million copies, surpassing the sales achievements of *Sleeping Beauty* and *Pinocchio* during the previous two years. Disney and McDonald's launched a joint promotion, giving the burger chain's customers money-off vouchers to buy *Lady and the Tramp*, and buyers of the video free children's meals.

Another first was the marketing campaign by film distributors Twentieth Century-Fox and video company CBS/Fox for *Die Hard* in the 'sell-through' market, with the tape carrying a trailer for the theatrical release of *Die Hard 2*. The sequel came out on cassette in early 1991, reflecting the shorter gap between cinema and video release that was becoming a trend for feature films.

There was also less time between rental and 'sell-through' video release, four months in the case of *Indiana Jones and the Last Crusade* which then retailed at £12.99, more than most other tapes on sale. This trend for higher-price blockbusters available in a shorter time had begun the previous year, although some distributors preferred to wait and keep the standard price of £9.99, as Buena Vista did with *Good Morning Vietnam*, released fifteen months after its first appearance in the rental market.

The British Government's decision to increase the VAT rate to 17.5 per cent resulted in most 'sell-through' tapes breaking through the £10 barrier. However, Warner launched a mid-price range of films such as *Arthur* and *Dirty Harry* – which had exhausted their potential in the standard-price market – retailing at £7.99.

Another sign of the closer links between cinema and video came with CBS/Fox's change of name to FoxVideo as part of a new agreement between the two giants, which had been partners in the home video business since 1982. As well as being responsible for past and future video releases, the new company was to take up theatrical distribution of Twentieth Century-Fox films. The film industry, which had once viewed video with suspicion, was coming to accept that it could no longer live without it.

Above the Law: The Blond Fury (VPD) October 1990
Across the Tracks (Big Pictures) March 1991
The Adventures of Ford Fairlane (FoxVideo) June 1991
Aftershock (Medusa) August 1990
After the Shock (CIC) April 1991
Air Raid Wardens (MGM/UA) November 1990
The Alien Factor (Box Office) November 1990
All Dogs Go to Heaven (Warner) October 1990
Allnighter (CIC) July 1990
Almost a Virgin (Big Pictures) May 1991
Amazon Women on the Moon (CIC) July 1990
American Angels (CIC) February 1991

American Kickboxer (Warner West Coast) June 1991
American Ninja 4: Annihilation (MGM/Pathé) April 1991
The Andromeda Strain (CIC) September 1990
Angel Town (VPD) March 1991
Another 48 Hours (CIC) March 1991
Any Man's Death (Braveworld) May 1991
Any Time, Any Play (Braveworld) June 1991
A.W.O.L. (Guild) November 1990
Baby It's You (CIC) July 1990
Back to Back (MGM/UA) August 1990
Back to the Future, Part II (CIC) July 1990
Back to the Future, Part III (CIC) January 1991
Backstreet Dreams (First Independent) June 1991
Bad Dreams (CBS/Fox) August 1990

Bad Influence (EV) March 1991
Bad Jim (Castle) September 1990
Beach Balls (Cineplex) August 1990
Best of the Best (EV) September 1990
Betsy's Wedding (Touchstone/Buena Vista) April 1991
Beverly Hills Brats (Virgin Vision) February 1991
Beverly Hills Vamp (New World) July 1990
Beyond the Stars (Braveworld) April 1991
The Big Hurt (RCA/Columbia) September 1990
The Big Man (Palace) November 1990
Big Store (MGM/UA) November 1990
The Big Sweat (Colourbox) October 1990
Bill and Ted's Excellent Adventure (Castle) July 1990
Bird on a Wire (CIC) June 1991

Black Rain (CIC) September 1990

Black Rainbow (Palace) August 1990

Blaze (Touchstone) January 1991

Blind Vengeance (CIC) June 1991

Blind Witness (Excalibur) March 1991

Blood Moon (Capital) June 1991

Blood River (FoxVideo) June 1991

Bloodfight 2: The Death Cage (VPD) February 1991

Bloodhounds of Broadway (20:20 Vision) December 1990

Blue Heat (Virgin Vision) June 1991

Blue Steel (First Independent) March 1991

Blue Vengeance (RCA/Columbia) February 1991

Bonds of Love (Futuristic) October 1990

Bonnie Scotland (MGM/UA) November 1990

The Boost (20:20 Vision) March 1991

Born on the Fourth of July (CIC) November 1990

Born Killer (MGM/UA/Pathe) February 1991

Boxer Blow (VPD) July 1990

Breaking In (Capital) May 1991

Brenda Starr (RCA/Columbia) June 1991

Broken Dream (ITC) May 1991

The Bronx War (Big Pictures) May 1991

Bullseye! (RCA/Columbia) May 1991

Buried Alive (CIC) November 1990

Buried Alive (1989) (EV) August 1990

By Dawn's Early Light (Warner) November 1990

Cadillac Man (20:20 Vision) April 1991

Call Me Anna (Guild) June 1991

Captain America (20:20 Vision) April 1991

Cartel (New World) October 1990

Cast the First Stone (Odyssey) June 1991

Casualties of War (RCA/Columbia) August 1990

Catchfire (First Independent) June 1991

Celia (Box Office) August 1990

Chains of Gold (Medusa) January 1991

Chameleons (Ingram) June 1991

Chances Are (20:20 Vision) July 1990

Changes (NBC) June 1991

Cheetah (Walt Disney) July 1990

Chicago Joe and the Showgirl (Palace) July 1990

Child in the Night (Odyssey) February 1991

Cold Comfort (Prism) August 1990

Cold Feet (Virgin) October 1990

Cold Sassy Tree (Turner) August 1990

Come See the Paradise (FoxVideo) May 1991

Commander (VPD) April 1991

Communion (First Independent) February 1991

Cool Blue (EV) June 1991

Cop Target (VPD) January 1991

Cops (Guild) July 1990

Courage Mountain (EV) December 1990

Crash and Burn (EV) July 1990

Crazy Moon (RCA/Columbia) July 1990

Creator (EV) April 1991

Crimes and Misdemeanors (Virgin Vision) April 1991

Criminal Law (RCA/Columbia) May 1991

Crusoe (Virgin) September 1990

Cry Baby (CIC) January 1991

A Cry for Help (Odyssey) July 1990

Curiosity Kills (CIC) January 1991

Dakota (RCA/Columbia) August 1990

Daddy's Dyin', Who's Got the Will? (Palace) April 1991

Damned River (RCA/Columbia) February 1991

Dark Angel (EV) November 1990

Dark Side of the Moon (Medusa) June 1991

Darkman (CIC) April 1991

Daughter of the Streets (CBS/Fox) January 1991

David (ITC) April 1991

A Day at the Races (MGM/UA) November 1990

Days of Thunder (CIC) February 1991

Dead Men Don't Die (New World) November 1990

Dead Reckoning (CIC) February 1991

Dead Trouble 2 (New World) October 1990

Dead Trouble 3 (New World) January 1991

Deadly Dreams (Cineplex) July 1990

Death Force (New World) August 1990

Death of the Incredible Hulk (New World) August 1990

The Death Merchants (Warner East Coast) June 1991

Death Warrant (MGM/Pathé/Warner East Coast) April 1991

Deathstone (Bano) November 1990

Deceit (Castle) October 1990

The Delinquents (Warner) July 1990

Delta Force 2 (MGM/Pathé/Warner East Coast) May 1991

Desire and Hell at Sunset Motel (First Independent) April 1991

Destiny to Order (Colourbox) July 1990

Devil's Treasure (Warner) February 1991

Diamond Skulls (MCEG Virgin Vision) June 1991

Dick Tracy (Touchstone/Buena Vista) February 1991

Die Hard 2 (CBS/Fox) February 1991

Dinner at Eight (Turner) August 1990

Dirty Games (Braveworld) November 1990

Do You Know the Muffin Man? (Odyssey) November 1990

The Donor (FoxVideo) April 1991

Downtown (CBS/Fox) August 1990

Driving Miss Daisy (Warner) August 1990

Drugstore Cowboy (Virgin) August 1990

A Dry White Season (MGM/UA) August 1990

Duel of the Dragons (VPD) June 1991

Dying Time (Big Pictures) December 1990

E.A.R.T.H. Force (CIC) March 1991

Earth Girls Are Easy (Braveworld/MGM/UA) August 1990

Eat a Bowl of Tea (RCA/Columbia) December 1990

Eddie & The Crusaders 2: Eddie Lives (Medusa) July 1990

El Diablo (Warner East Coast) March 1991

Emmanuelle 6 (VPD) August 1990

Enemies, A Love Story (20:20 Vision) November 1990

Enemy Unseen (Medusa) December 1990

Ernest Goes to Jail (Touchstone) May 1991

Ernest Saves Christmas (Touchstone) November 1990

The Eternity (Braveworld) April 1991

Everybody's All American (Warner) August 1990

Exile (Buena Vista) September 1990

The Exorcist III (CBS/Fox) March 1991

The Eyes of the Amaryllis (First Independent) March 1991

Eyewitness to Murder (RCA/Columbia) November 1990

The Fabulous Baker Boys (MGM/UA) November 1990

Face of Fear (Warner East Coast) April 1991

Family Reunion (Big Pictures) November 1990

Far North (Vestron) August 1990

Far Out Man (First View) November 1990

Fearstalk (New World) January 1991

Felix the Cat (RCA/Columbia) June 1991

Fellow Traveller (BFI Connoisseur Video) November 1990

The Field (Granada/High Fliers) June 1991

Fight to Win (Braveworld) February 1991

Fighting Justice (20:20 Vision) August 1990

Fine Things (NBC) May 1991

Fist of Vengeance (VPD) June 1991

The Flash (Warner East Coast) March 1991

Flatliners (RCA/Columbia) June 1991

Flesh Gordon 2 (EV) June 1991

For Better or Worse (EV) August 1990

Forbidden Nights (Warner) February 1991

The Forgotten One (Warner East Coast) June 1991

The Fourth War (Guild) October 1990

Framed (Warner West Coast) June 1991

Frankenhooker (Medusa) October 1990

Fresh Horses (20:20 Vision) January 1991

The Freshman (20:20 Vision) April 1991

Funny About Love (CIC) April 1991

Future Zone (20:20 Vision) June 1991

Ganglands (Braveworld) June 1991

Garwood: Prisoner of War (Box Office) March 1991

The Gate 2 (MGM/UA/Pathé) Feb 1991

Getting Lucky (Colourbox) October 1990

Ghost (CIC) May 1991

Ghost Dad (CIC) June 1991

Ghosts Can't Do It (EV) November 1990

Ghoulies: Ghoulies Go to College (Vestron) December 1990

A Girl to Kill For (EV) October 1990

Gleaming the Cube (MGM/UA) July 1990

Go West (MGM/UA) November 1990

The Gods Must Be Crazy (CBS/Fox) January 1991

Goldy 2 (Vestron) July 1990

GoodFellas (Warner West Coast) May 1991

Goodnight Sweet Wife (CBS/Fox) February 1991

Grave Misdemeanours (Medusa) February 1991

Grave Secrets (SGE) March 1991

Great Balls of Fire! (Virgin) July 1990

The Great Outdoors (CIC) July 1990

Gremlins II: The New Batch (Warner West Coast) March 1991

The Grifters (Palace) May 1991

The Guardian (CIC) February 1991

Guns (RCA/Columbia) April 1991

Gunsmoke: The Last Apache (CBS/Fox) November 1990

The Guys (CIC) March 1991

Halloween 5: The Revenge of Michael Myers (Capital) March 1991

The Handmaid's Tale (Virgin) March 1991

Hard to Kill (Warner) October 1990

Hardware (Palace) February 1991

Harlem Nights (CIC) November 1990

Havana (CIC) May 1991

Have a Nice Night (20:20 Vision) June 1991

Hawkeye (VPD) April 1991

Heart Condition (RCA/Columbia) April 1991

Heart of a Champion (CBS/Fox) July 1990

Heart of Dixie (Virgin) February 1991

Hell Hath No Fury (Guild) June 1991

Henry V (20:20 Vision) July 1990

Henry and June (CIC) April 1991

Hi Honey, I'm Dead (FoxVideo) June 1991

Hidden Agenda (FoxVideo) June 1991

High Desert Kill (CIC) July 1990

Hired to Kill (CIC) June 1991

Hiroshima (Prism) August 1990

Hitler's Daughter (CIC) May 1991

Hometown Boy Makes Good (Warner) June 1991

Hoodwinked (Futuristic) October 1990

House Party (RCA/Columbia) February 1991

The House of Usher (Castle) August 1990

Howling VI: The Freaks (Palace) April 1991

The Hunt for Red October (Palace) October 1990

The Hunted (RCA/Columbia) March 1991

I Bought a Vampire Motorcycle (Braveworld) March 1991

I Love You to Death (RCA/Columbia) March 1991

The Image (Warner) September 1990

Immediate Family (20:20 Vision) November 1990

In the Best Interests of the Child (CIC) March 1991

In Country (Warner) July 1990

In Gold We Trust (First View) May 1991

In the Line of Duty (VPD) December 1990

An Innocent Man (Touchstone) June 1991

Istanbul (Odyssey) December 1990

Jezebel's Kiss (SGE) June 1991

Johnny Handsome (Guild) September 1990

Jour de Fête (BFI Connoisseur Video) November 1990

Judgement in Berlin (Warner East Coast) May 1991

Kaleidoscope (NBC) May 1991

Keaton's Cop (Pathé) November 1990

Kickboxer Champion (VPD) February 1991

Kid (EV) April 1991

The Kid Who Loved Christmas (CIC) December 1990

The Killer (Palace) October 1990

Killer Instinct (ITC) April 1990

A Killing in a Small Town (Odyssey) May 1991

King of the Kickboxers (EV) February 1991

King of the Wind (Vestron) December 1990

Kings of the Road (BFI Connoisseur Video) November 1990

LA Connection (VPD) August 1990

LA Crimewave (Prism) September 1990

La Belle et la Bête (BFI Connoisseur Video) November 1990

Ladder of Swords (Odyssey) August 1990

Lady and the Tramp (Walt Disney/Buena Vista) October 1990

Lambada – Set the Night on Fire (Pathé) February 1991

Last Call (SGE) May 1991

Last Stand at Lang Mei (RCA/Columbia) May 1991

The Last to Go (ITC) June 1991

Lean on Me (Warner) February 1991

Leap of Faith (Braveworld) January 1991

Leathernecks (VPD) July 1990

Legion of Iron (EV) December 1990

Let It Ride (CIC) April 1991

Lethal Charm (ITC) June 1991

Leviathan (CBS/Fox) October 1990

Life Is Sweet (Palace) June 1991

Lionheart (Warner West Coast) April 1991

Lisa (Warner East Coast) April 1991

The Little Kidnappers (CBS/Fox) March 1991

Little Monsters (Vestron) August 1990

Lock Up (Guild) July 1990

Lockdown (RCA/Columbia) May 1991

Longtime Companion (Palace) March 1991

Look Who's Talking (20:20 Vision) October 1990

Lord of the Flies (Palace) October 1990

The Lost Capone (New World) March 1991

Love Hurts (First Independent) April 1991

Love at Stake (20:20 Vision) August 1990

Loverboy (RCA/Columbia) December 1990

Mack the Knife (20:20 Vision) March 1991

Mad House (20:20 Vision) June 1991

Magic Crystal (VPD) February 1991

Making a Case For Murder (Prism) October 1990

A Man Called Sarge (Pathé) February 1991

The Man Inside (Virgin) March 1991

Manhunt: Search for the Night Stalker (Braveworld) August 1990

Maniac Cop 2 (Medusa) May 1991

Mariah (New World) January 1991

Marked for Murder (New World) August 1990

Martial Law (EV) April 1991

The Masque of the Red Death (Castle) August 1990

May Wine (Touchstone) June 1991

Me and Him (20:20 Vision) April 1991

Memphis Belle (Warner East Coast) May 1991

Men Don't Leave (Warner East Coast) March 1991

Metropolitan (Palace) April 1991

Midnight Run (CIC) July 1990

The Miracle (Palace) June 1991

Miracle Landing (CBS/Fox) October 1990

Miracles: The Canton Godfather (VPD) November 1990

Mirage (New World) December 1990

Mirror Mirror (SGE) February 1991

Misfits of Science (CIC) September 1990

Miss Firecracker (MGM/UA) December 1990

Mission Impossible: Golden Serpent (CIC) August 1990

Mo' Better Blues (CIC) March 1991

Modern Love (Medusa) March 1991

Money, Power, Murder (CBS/Fox) August 1990

Monkey Shines (Virgin) September 1990

Monster High (RCA/Columbia) August 1990

Montana (Warner West Coast) April 1991

A Month of Sundays (Futuristic) July 1990

Moon 44 (Medusa) November 1990

Mortal Passions (Virgin Vision) May 1991

Mountains of the Moon (Guild) February 1991

Mr Frost (FoxVideo) April 1991

Mr and Mrs Bridge (Palace) May 1991

Murder in Mississippi (Warner West Coast) March 1991

Music Box (Guild) March 1991

My Blue Heaven (Warner West Coast) June 1991

Mystery Train (Palace) July 1990

Narrow Margin (Guild) May 1991

Nasty Boys 2: Kill or Be Killed (CIC) February 1991

National Lampoon's Christmas Vacation (Warner) November 1990

Never Cry Devil (Medusa) August 1990

Night of the Cyclone (EV) February 1991

Night of the Fox (ITC) March 1991

Night of the Warrior (First Independent) April 1991

Night Rider (CIC) August 1990

The Night Stalker (Vestron) September 1990

A Nightmare on Elm Street Part 5 (CBS/Fox) November 1990

Nightwish (Medusa) July 1990

Nikita (Palace) March 1991

No Place Like Home (Odyssey) April 1991

Not Quite Human 2 (Walt Disney) July 1990

Nothing But Trouble (MGM/UA) November 1990

Nuns on the Run (CBS/Fox) November 1990

Obsessione (BFI Connoisseur Video) November 1990

Old Gringo (RCA/Columbia) July 1990

On the Block (Capital) June 1991

One Man Force (RCA/Columbia) March 1991

Open Fire (Braveworld) April 1991

Out Cold (20:20 Vision) March 1991

Out on Bail (EV) November 1990

The Overthrow (VPD) May 1991

The Package (Virgin) February 1991

Paint It Black (Vestron) July 1990

Pair of Aces (Warner) September 1990

Paper Mask (Enterprise) February 1991

Parenthood (CIC) August 1990

Payback (First View) February 1991

Peacemaker (Medusa) October 1990

Perfect Witness (Warner) August 1990

Phantom Soldiers (VPD) June 1991

The Plot to Kill Hitler (Warner) February 1991

Prancer (Medusa) November 1990

Presumed Innocent (Warner West Coast) April 1991

Pretty Woman (Touchstone) December 1990

The Price of Passion (Touchstone) August 1990

Project S (EV) June 1991

Prom Night 3 – The Last Kiss (CBS/Fox) October 1990

A Promise to Keep (Warner West Coast) May 1991

Psychocop (RCA/Columbia) November 1990

Puppet Master 2 (EV) February 1991

The Quare Fellow (BFI Connoisseur Video) November 1990

Rabid Grannies (Virgin) August 1990

Re-Animator 2 (Medusa) September 1990

Red Blooded American Girl (20:20 Vision) April 1991

The Reflecting Skin (Virgin Vision) May 1991

Relentless (Warner) September 1990

Renegades (20:20 Vision) September 1990

Repo Man (CIC) September 1990

Repossessed (Guild) April 1991

The Rescuers (Buena Vista) March 1991

Return of the Family Man (Braveworld/MGM/UA) November 1990

The Return of Sam McCloud (CIC) August 1990

Revealing Evidence (CIC) April 1991

Revenge (20:20 Vision) November 1990

Revenge of the Radioactive Reporter (CIC) July 1990

The Rift (RCA/Columbia) May 1991

Rising Storm (RCA/Columbia) November 1990

Riverbend (Prism) November 1990

Road House (Warner) August 1990

Robocop 2 (Virgin) April 1991

Rockula (Pathé) August 1990

Roger & Me (Warner East Coast) April 1991

Romero (Warner) August 1990

Rooftops (CBS/Fox) August 1990

The Rookie (Warner East Coast) June 1991

The Room of Words (Braveworld) April 1991

Salute of the Jugger (Virgin) December 1990

Sarah, Plain and Tall (Palace) May 1991

Schizo (Medusa) April 1991

The Sealed Train (Futuristic) September 1990

Second Sight (Warner) July 1990

The Secret of the Ice Cave (Pathé) July 1990

See You in the Morning (Guild) July 1990

Settle the Score (ITC) February 1991

Seven Minutes (Warner West Coast) May 1991

Shadow of the Cobra (Futuristic) September 1990

Shadows Run Black (Vestron) November 1990

Shadowzone (EV) July 1990

She-Devil (Virgin) November 1990

She Said No (Odyssey) March 1991

She'll Take Romance (New World/High Fliers) June 1991

The Sheltering Sky (FoxVideo) June 1991

She's Having a Baby (CIC) July 1990

She's Out of Control (20:20 Vision) February 1991

Shirley Valentine (CIC) August 1990

A Shock to the System (Medusa) April 1991

Shocker (Guild) August 1990

A Show of Force (CIC) February 1991

Side Out (RCA/Columbia) June 1991

Signs of Life (Virgin Vision) May 1991

Sinbad of the Seven Seas (Pathé) July 1990

Single Women, Married Men (CBS/Fox) August 1990

Ski Patrol (EV) October 1990

Snake Eater's Revenge (20:20 Vision) February 1991

Snow Kill (CIC) March 1991

Society (Medusa) August 1990

Some Kind of Wonderful (CIC) July 1990

A Son's Promise (Capital) June 1991

Sorry, Wrong Number (CIC) July 1990

Space Chase (SGE) March 1991

Spaced Invaders (Medusa) March 1991

Sparks – The Price of Passion (Excalibur) April 1991

Spies, Lies & Alibis (Vestron) October 1990

Spyder (RCA/Columbia) July 1990

Spymaker: The Secret Life of Ian Fleming (First Independent) May 1991

Stanley and Iris (MGM/UA) March 1991

Steel Magnolias (RCA/Columbia) November 1990

Stella (Touchstone/Buena Vista) March 1991

Stepfather 2 (Virgin Vision) March 1991

Stockade (EV) May 1991

Stranded (20:20 Vision) July 1990

The Stranger Within (New World) February 1991

Strapless (Virgin) January 1991

Street Hunter (Capital) April 1991

Streets (MGM/UA) July 1990

Student Affairs (First Independent) February 1991

Summer Dreams: Story of the Beach Boys (PolyGram) August 1990

Sun Dragon (VPD) March 1991

Sundown – The Vampire in Retreat (Vestron) September 1990

Sunset Beat (20:20 Vision) February 1991

Sweet Murder (New World) September 1990

The Sword of the Bushido (Futuristic) August 1990

Talk Radio (CBS/Fox) August 1990

Talking Back (RCA/Columbia) December 1990

Tango and Cash (Warner) September 1990

Teenage Mutant Ninja Turtles (Virgin Vision) May 1990

Terror at the Opera (Virgin Vision) March 1991

Terror Eyes (VPD) January 1991

Texasville (Guild) June 1991

That Magic Moment (New World) November 1990

Thundering Mantis (VPD) February 1991

Tie Me Up! Tie Me Down! (Enterprise) December 1990

The Tiger Strikes Again (VPD) July 1990

Tiger's Cage (VPD) June 1991

To Be the Best (Odyssey) May 1991

To Make a Killing (RCA/Columbia) June 1991

Too Much Sun (First Independent) June 1991

Too Young To Die? (Odyssey) September 1990

Total Recall (Guild) January 1991

Transformations (CBS/Fox) September 1990

Travelling Man (Warner) November 1990

Tremors (CIC) November 1990

Trenchcoats in Paradise (MGM/UA) July 1991

Trial by Vengeance (Oasis) September 1990

Triumph of the Spirit (Guild) January 1991

Troma's War (Virgin) July 1990

True Betrayal (ITC) April 1991

Try This One for Size (20:20 Vision) June 1991

Tunnels (Vestron) July 1990

Twisted Justice (Big Pictures) June 1991

Two Evil Eyes (Medusa) December 1990

Two Moon Junction (CBS/Fox) July 1990

UFO Cafe (ITC) May 1991

UHF (Virgin) October 1990

Uncle Buck (CIC) December 1990

Under the Boardwalk (20:20 Vision) May 1991

Unspeakable Acts (Braveworld) December 1990

Upworld (Vestron) November 1990

Videodrome (CIC) September 1990

Vietnam Texas (EV) October 1990

Vietnam War Story: The Last Days (Warner) November 1990

The Visitors (New World) July 1990

Vital Signs (CBS/Fox) January 1991

Voodoo Dawn (20:20 Vision) November 1990

The Voyage of the Rock Aliens (Prism) July 1990

Waiting for the Light (EV) May 1991

Want to Stay Alive? (20:20 Vision) June 1991

The War of the Roses (CBS/Fox) September 1990

Warm Summer Rain (EV) September 1990

Watchers 2 (RCA/Columbia) November 1990

W. B. Blue and the Bean (EV) September 1990

Web of Deceit (CIC) June 1991

Wedding Day Blues (Excalibur) March 1991

Welcome Home (Warner) August 1990

We're No Angels (CIC) December 1990

When He's Not a Stranger (Prism) October 1990

Where the Heart Is (Guild) April 1991

Why Me? (EV) March 1991

Wild at Heart (Palace) January 1991

Wild Orchid (EV) January 1991

Wings of the Apache (Medusa) February 1991

Winter People (Vestron) October 1990

Wishful Thinking (Medusa) April 1991

Witch Story (Medusa) January 1991

The Witches (Warner) November 1990

Without Her Consent (Warner) August 1990

The Wizard (Guild) November 1990

Worth Winning (CBS/Fox) July 1990

Young Guns II: Blaze of Glory (FoxVideo) April 1991

The Ten Most Promising Faces of 1991

JAMES CAMERON-WILSON

Annette Bening has become a victim of the leading lady syndrome. But if you're gonna play second fiddle to your leading men, you couldn't find a more impressive line-up than the guys Annette has been hanging out with.

The five-foot-seven actress from Kansas made her film debut as Dan Ackroyd's sexually frustrated wife in the properly ignored *The Great Outdoors*, and lately has been hogging the screen with Robert De Niro (in *Guilty by Suspicion*), Harrison Ford (in *Regarding Henry*) and Warren Beatty (in *Bugsy Siegel*). Not bad company for a newcomer.

Bening's breakthrough role was as the scheming, lecherous Myra Langtry in Stephen Frears's dark, acclaimed *The Grifters*. John Cusack was the tall, dark leading man, but Annette was the girl who stalked off with the National Society of Film Critics award and an Oscar nomination. Then she was the envy of the likes of Cher, Sean Young and Julia Roberts – for winning the coveted role of Catwoman in *Batman 2*. Later, of course, she had to relinquish the role in order to carry Warren Beatty's child.

Born in 1959 in Topeka, Kansas, and raised in San Diego, Annette says, 'I just always wanted to be an actress – I can't say exactly why.' Certainly, she wasn't born into it. Her father was an insurance salesman, her mother a housewife. 'We were just a regular family,' she says. 'I'm afraid there's nothing in my background that is either twisted or amazing.' One brother grew up to be an electrician, another entered law and her sister became a gynaecologist.

'A boyfriend's mother tried to talk me out of becoming an actress,' she recalls. ' "You're just going to be disap-pointed, so don't do this to yourself," she told me. I realised then that there was nothing I could say that would make her understand. If someone doesn't have a passion – whether it's playing the guitar or manipulating the stock market – you can't explain it to them, because it's got nothing to do with practicality. It's something no one else in the world can judge.'

Bening's first play was a Spanish production of *The Three Little Pigs*, and in junior high school she landed the role of Maria von Trapp in *The Sound of Music*. While enrolled at college she was hired as a dancer in a local show and then landed a walk-on in a Shakespearean production. After graduation, Bening was one of 32 out of 600 candidates to join the renowned American Conservatory Theater in San Francisco, where she met her former husband Steve White.

Mr and Mrs White moved to New York in 1986 and within a few months Annette had secured a role in the Broadway-bound *Coastal Disturbances*,

Annette Bening in Guilty by Suspicion

143

for which she earned herself a Tony nomination and won the Clarence Derwent Award. A sprinkling of TV followed (including a spot as a bad girl in *Miami Vice*), and then came *The Great Outdoors*.

The film, she says, was 'the best lesson in Hollywood I could've had. It left me a lot wiser about the whole machinery of moviemaking, and how what happens depends on why people are doing what they're doing.' In spite of the presence of Aykroyd and John Candy, the film was a resounding dud.

Now for the good news. Back in New York, Bening auditioned for both Milos Forman and Stephen Frears for their respective versions of Choderlos de Laclos's *Les Liaisons Dangereuses*. She had already won the role of the Marquise de Merteuil in Forman's *Valmont* when Frears invited her back to play a courtesan in his *Dangerous Liaisons*.

Unfortunately, *Valmont* was not the success everybody has expected, although Annette Bening made a suitable impression in the role which Glenn Close made famous in Frears's film.

'With Annette you have a star and a character actress in one person,' Forman enthused. 'She knows real acting is not in technique but in what you feel and how you behave. She is not at all interested in looking for safe havens or preconceived ideas.'

She had a good role as Carol Burnett's iron-willed daughter in the

Lara Flynn Boyle with Charlie Sheen in The Rookie

superior TV movie *Hostage*, and then landed a prime scene with Meryl Streep in *Postcards from the Edge*. In the latter she was the bitchy actress who bedded Dennis Quaid and turned Streep green, all but stealing the scene for herself.

Frears returned with the offer of Myra Langtry in *The Grifters* and Bening was on her way. In *Guilty by Suspicion* she secured second billing (after De Niro), playing the sympathetic ex-wife who stands by De Niro during the horrific McCarthy witch-hunts of the early 1950s.

'With *Guilty by Suspicion* I found the issues so compelling,' she explains, 'and I really liked the woman. She was a solid person, very grounded – the voice of reason – who had a sense of sanity in the middle of this crazy Hollywood time. I was very moved by the story. And that is basically what draws me to something on a real gut level.'

In *Regarding Henry*, directed by the great Mike Nichols, she and Harrison Ford play a couple whose marriage is threatened by crisis.

'When I read the story, I was so taken by its theme, that through a catastrophe we are often forced to turn inward and change ourselves, and that *that* is the moment at which self-growth happens. Also, the fact that Mike Nichols was directing and that Harrison Ford was in it were two very compelling reasons to do *Henry* in the first place.'

In *Bugsy Siegel*, Annette is directed by another great, Barry Levinson, and

gets to play Mob hostess Virginia 'Flamingo' Hill. Besides Warren Beatty, the film stars Ben Kingsley, Harvey Keitel, Joe Mantegna and Elliott Gould.

'Virginia was a real-life "moll",' the actress reveals, 'a girl from the South who went to Chicago and got a job in a restaurant and met a gangster. He was the first boyfriend who took care of her, and he became one of several men in the Mob whom she went with.'

Prompted to discuss her relationship with Beatty, Annette's hackles rise. 'Oh, give me a break,' she snaps. 'Look at his work. Talk to me about that. It's really that simple. There's nothing else to say.' Except: 'I guess what I feel is somewhat protective of Warren.'

After *Seigel* the actress was announced to star in *The Playboys*, opposite Aidan Quinn, to be paid $1 million up-front, plus 5 per cent of the gross. However, when Bening turned her back on the project the Samuel Goldwyn Company sought $1 million in damages from her. The actress denies ever signing to do the film and told the company she would not abide by their terms.

Since then, she's had the unenviable task of turning down Catwoman, the most coveted woman's film role of the year, to take the most coveted role of all – motherhood.

Lara Flynn Boyle. *Somebody* from *Twin Peaks* had to make these pages this year. Sherilyn Fenn was a possibility, but did you see *Two Moon Junction*? And then there was Laura Palmer herself, alias Sheryl Lee, but she was killed off too soon. So my choice from the cult hit series for inclusion in this year's Top Ten is Lara Flynn Boyle. In *Peaks* she played Laura's best friend, Donna Hayward, and Clint Eastwood has described her as 'being in the Katharine Hepburn mould'.

The actress co-starred with Eastwood in the truly awful *The Rookie* – as Charlie Sheen's law-student girlfriend – and she seemed to be the only member of the cast playing a real person. And seldom do Charlie Sheen's screen girlfriends show a propensity for *that*.

'I don't mind playing the "girlfriend",' she says, modestly: 'I figure I'll go from girlfriend parts to wife parts to mother parts to grandmother parts. That's how it works, isn't it? Maybe

once in a while I'll get a role like Jessica Lange's in *Frances.*'

So we have Lara Flynn Boyle, only child of a middle-class Irish family, born in Davenport, Iowa, 21 years ago – brought up in Rogers Park, a suburb of Chicago, by her mother.

'We lived in this decrepit two-storey building my mum got out of the divorce,' the actress recalls. 'I remember how she would put out bait for the rats, and how I would have to shovel up the dead rats.'

Lara took acting lessons to ease her shyness and found the bug had bit. In 1987 she secured a small part in the gargantuan mini-series *Amerika* (as Robert Urich's daughter), an experience which involved nine months of shooting in Nebraska and Toronto.

After that she played another Donna (Gardner) in the less-than-perfect *Poltergeist III*. However, as a scream queen she gave Jamie Lee Curtis a run for her money, and had a decent slice of the action. Also, the movie was conveniently filmed in her home town (Chicago), after which she moved to LA. There, she found the competition tough.

'When I audition for things they say, "If Winona Ryder doesn't get it, you will",' laments Lara. 'I used to think I would never work, but Hollywood makes so many movies Winona can't possibly do all of them.'

There was the female lead in *How I Got Into College* – as the dream queen of Corey Parker's senior college boy – but the film went nowhere, while her part in *Dead Poets Society* was negligible (the film went everywhere).

Then *Twin Peaks* happened.

'People ask me if it was weird to work on *Twin Peaks*,' says the actress who didn't know who David Lynch was until the series started. 'To be honest, I was upset about how *normal* my character was. But David Lynch's characters are normal people pushed to their extremes.'

Besides the fame that the must-see series brought her, it also brought Lara romance – in the shape of 33-year-old co-star Kyle MacLachlan (FBI agent Dale Cooper to you).

'It's so great,' she oozes. 'We're very happy. We're both goofy and it's hard to find someone you can be silly with. I used to laugh at people who said, "He's my lover and he's my best friend." It sounded so cornball, but

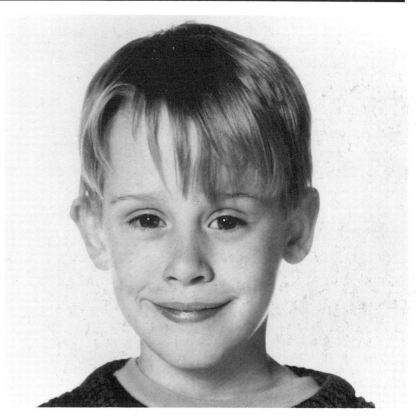

Macaulay Culkin

that's really what Kyle is. We even run in the rain together.'

Lara Flynn Boyle also won considerable attention for the TV movie *The Preppie Murder* – as Jennifer Levin, the girl who became a media sensation when she was killed in Central Park in 1987.

Back then she joked, 'Maybe this is my big victim year – but I'd like to start doing things where I put the pressure on another person.'

Well, the future seems to hold a myriad possibilities. Lara plays a Californian in Paris in the French comedy *May Wine*, in which she competes with her mother (Joanna Cassidy) for the attentions of Guy Marchand. The film is a trifle, and Lara won all the good reviews for herself.

In the Lynch-esque *The Dark Backward* she played Judd Nelson's waitress girlfriend who's turned off by the little human hand growing out of his back. The film received respectful notices and once again Lara Flynn Boyle won her share (Rob Lowe's contribution was dismissed). Next, she stars opposite Dennis Hopper in *Eyes of the Storm* and is the female lead in the starry Brat Pack gangster epic *Mobsters*, and also appears with MacLachlan in *Where the Day Takes You.*

With the good reviews she repeatedly gets, and with the company she keeps (Hopper, Lynch & Co.), Lara Flynn Boyle should end up very hot indeed.

Macaulay Culkin. At the end of Adrian Lyne's powerful psychological thriller *Jacob's Ladder*, Tim Robbins is led up an ominous stairway by an unbilled child actor. That child later became such a hot property that he was used to promote *Jacob's Ladder* when it was released on video. The new poster illustrated the said scene – although the kid is only seen in silhouette and the episode comes at the very end of the film. In some ads Tim Robbins – the film's star – isn't even mentioned, but the kid – Macaulay Culkin – is. *That* is misleading advertising for you.

Culkin is of course the unbelievably cute ten-year-old star of the runaway mega-hit *Home Alone*, a superbly crafted Christmas film that mixed up sentimentality, comedy and cartoon violence. Six months after it had opened in the States, *Home Alone* had sucked up over $270 million dollars at the box office and was still showing at over a thousand cinemas. And this was a *Christmas* movie. The second round

Harley Jane Kozak with John Goodman in Arachnophobia

of advertising suggested audiences should see the film again – and they did.

Culkin, admittedly, holds the film together. Besides being the most beautiful kid to grace the movies for some time, he has a winning rapport with the camera, has an uncanny knack for comedy timing and boasts a personality as big as his stature is small.

Culkin, one of seven children, was born on 26 August 1980 in Manhattan and studied a year of pre-ballet at the age of four. He was delivered into showbusiness. His father, Christopher (Kit) Culkin, is the former New York stage actor, and his aunt is Bonnie Bedelia, female lead of the box-office hits *Die Hard, Presumed Innocent,* and *Die Hard 2.* His oldest brother, Shane, is an actor who (Macaulay proudly relates) once threw up on stage; while younger brother Kieran also appeared in *Home Alone* and has a role in the new Steve Martin–Diane Keaton comedy *Father of the Bride.*

Macaulay himself cut his milk teeth on commercials promoting the wonders of Apple Mac Computers, Dr Pepper, Gillette and Kraft Foods, and made his

film debut as Burt Lancaster's favourite grandchild in *Rocket Gibraltar.* A year later he played the adorable son of Jeff Bridges and Farrah Fawcett in the unfairly dismissed *See You in the Morning,* and then battled John Candy as *Uncle Buck.*

It was the last-named that won him the role in *Home Alone.* 'I knew he'd be perfect,' says the film's director, Chris Columbus. 'I looked at three hundred other kids, and none of them came close. Mac's a kid that adults like and are happy to spend two hours with.'

So it would seem. Macaulay was paid $1 million to co-star with Dan Aykroyd and Jamie Lee Curtis in *My Girl,* the story of a little girl growing up in her father's funeral parlour. 'I play this kid who lives next door,' Mac informs us. 'We bike ride and do stuff like that.' He also gets his first screen kiss, with ten-year-old newcomer Anna Chlumsky.

After that anything could happen. Imagine Films offered Culkin $1.5 million to play a precocious ten-year-old boy in *Cop and a Half,* opposite Kurt Russell's unorthodox cop – but the child star bowed out when an agreement failed to materialise.

Warner Brothers meanwhile courted Culkin with $1.5 million to star in

Richie Rich, but dropped the idea when the boy's agent asked for no less than $4 million and 10 per cent of the gross. For the sequel to *Home Alone (Home Alone, Again)* a salary of $5 million is being negotiated. But sources indicate that Twentieth Century-Fox are unwilling to pay such an outlandish sum. We'll see.

However, Macaulay Culkin *will* appear in *Only the Lonely,* the Chris Columbus–John Hughes comedy starring John Candy and James Belushi.

Harley Jane Kozak. It is something short of miraculous that Harley Jane Kozak made an impression in the all-star *Parenthood.* Perhaps it was the fact that she *was* an unknown face – in such weighty company as Steve Martin, Rick Moranis, Jason Robards, Keanu Reeves et al – that made us sit up and take notice. Yes, she is pretty, but she also comes across as something entirely real – even in the silliest of movies.

She made her first impression as Billy Crystal's ex-wife Helen in *When Harry Met Sally . . . ,* in a small but key scene in which she catches Crystal and Meg Ryan goofing off and singing together (out of tune) in a department store.

Immediately after that she was snapped up to play Rick Moranis's wife and the mother of a prodigious three-year-old daughter in *Parenthood.* Few actresses starting out can boast two hit movies in a row. It certainly gave Harley Jane the exposure she needed.

By her next film, produced by none other than Steven Spielberg, she had snared the female lead and second billing as the formula wife of Jeff Daniels. However, this was no normal suburban couple thrown into the deep end of Spielberg's imagination. Daniels was the wimp, Kozak the soothing centre of gravity in a town besieged with killer spiders. *Arachnophobia* was a widely publicised flop in America, but it did much better overseas, sweeping up the number one spot in the UK and knocking *Home Alone* rudely off its perch.

Born in Pennsylvania, Harley Jane was raised in North Dakota and Nebraska and joined the Nebraska Repertory Theater as a tap dancer while still in high school. Two years later she was a paid-up member, and after appearing in over thirty plays left for New York – aged nineteen. There, she was accepted at NYU's School of the Arts, where she studied for three years before making her film debut in the low-budget *The House on Sorority Row* (forget it). She had a regular part in the soap opera *Texas*, and spent two years on TV's *The Guiding Light*. In 1985 Harley Jane moved to California to cement her soap experience as Mary in the popular *Santa Barbara*, and after her character was crushed to death (by a giant neon letter, no less), she took bits and pieces in various small-screen offerings.

She had a small part as a receptionist in *Clean and Sober*, with Michael Keaton, and claimed a decent role in the TV film *So Proudly We Hail*, about a neo-Nazi movement headed by David Soul. She had an even bigger contribution to make in the lame-brained volleyball saga *Side Out*, with C. Thomas Howell, and then starred opposite Ken Wahl in the dramatic *The Taking of Beverly Hills*.

Next, Harley Jane has the leading role in Donald Petrie's *The Favor*, supported by Elizabeth McGovern, Bill Pullman and old pal Ken Wahl, and this summer (of '91) she joined Scott Bakula, Robert Loggia, Hector Elizondo and Jason Bateman in Paramount's *Necessary Roughness*, and Jamie Sheridan and Lauren Bacall in Disney's *All I Want For Christmas*.

If *The Favor* is even remotely successful, Harley Jane Kozak should be on the way to a very successful career in the movies.

Ray Liotta has a habit of making startling debuts. He's always popping up as the most promising man of the moment. This year, following on the heels of *GoodFellas*, the most critically acclaimed movie of 1990, Liotta is no longer in a position to make another debut. He has made it.

Combining an unpredictable danger with a rakish, sweeping charm, Ray Liotta knocked our socks off as the gangster-wannabe Henry Hill in *Good-Fellas*. Exhaling fire and enthusiasm, he wore his macho charisma like a banner and became the proverbial overnight star in a twinkle. His hard-edged good looks, his unforeseen explosions of energy and off-centre sex appeal cemented his name in neon.

Guardedly shy, the Italian-American charmer reveals little of his background. To find out more, you have to ask around.

Steven Bauer, who starred opposite

Ray Liotta in Something Wild

Pacino in *Scarface*, studied drama with Liotta at the University of Miami. 'Ray was an enigma, a loner – like James Dean,' Bauer reveals. 'No one could get close to him. He was incredibly cool. He was my idol. I wanted to wear my jeans like he did, I wanted to walk like him.'

Liotta wandered down to Florida and settled into the university drama class because a friend was doing it and because the weather was nice. It was better than tending cemetery grounds back in New Jersey, or working in his father's car shop.

Moving to New York to find work as an actor, Liotta landed a K-tel record commercial his third day out. After that he found his way on to the TV soap *Another World*, playing Mr 'Nice Guy' Joey Perinni for three years. In 1981 he speared one of the three leading roles in the TV movie *Crazy Times* (1981) – alongside Michael Paré and David Caruso – a nostalgic look at three teenage guys living it up in 1955. Talia Balsam and Amy Madigan also starred. Not a bad living for a guy more interested in basketball than the films of Martin Scorsese. 'It was never one

of my things, checking out movies,' he reveals.

Born on 13 December 1955, in Union, New Jersey, Liotta admits that 'becoming an actor wasn't a big, burning passion for me. I just did the whole jock thing in high school. When it came time to go to college, my parents said, "Go wherever you want for a year." Acting was sort of just something to do, but I liked it. Once you're committed to doing it – I mean, what's the sense unless you hope that you can work in movies some day?'

So Liotta wandered down to Los Angeles to see what movies he could pick up. He hung out with fellow out-of-work actors Andy Garcia and Kevin Costner and 'played a lot of paddle tennis,' according to Costner, 'and wondered why everyone was working except us.'

When the script for Jonathan Demme's *Something Wild* surfaced, Liotta fought for the part of Ray Sinclair, Melanie Griffith's tempestuous husband – but found the role earmarked as 'a star vehicle'. Next, Liotta contacted Melanie Griffith, ex-wife of Steve Bauer. As a favour she put Demme and Liotta together and Liotta won the part.

'I like to play people who feel deeply about something,' he explained, 'and that's pretty much what Ray Sinclair was about. And I was angry, waiting around for five years to be in a movie. I was *primed*. I worked my ass off.'

The film became a critical success and built up a cult following. Melanie Griffith at last became a star of some reckoning and Liotta's performance as the psychotic, edgy Sinclair launched him into the Filofaxes of casting agents everywhere. He was also nominated for a Golden Globe and won the Boston Critics' award for best supporting actor.

Although Ray Liotta could now *see* the scripts that circulated through Hollywood, he wasn't going to take any old role that required a psycho.

Two years elapsed, during which time Liotta was 'offered a couple of bad guys, a lot of comedies', adding: 'Life is short, but there's still a lot of time. I'd rather do the right things.' He took the role of promising medic Eugene Luciano in *Nicky and Gino*, co-starring Jamie Lee Curtis as his girlfriend and Tom Hulce as the backward Nicky. 'Those of us who know Ray's work also know his sensitivity,' volunteered the film's producer, Mike Farrell. 'But those who saw him only in *Something Wild* are in for a surprise.'

The film was well acted and well intentioned, but on the soggy side, and quickly slid out of sight. There was a movie announced with Linda Fiorentino, *The War at Home*, and then came the role of Shoeless Joe Jackson in Kevin Costner's whimsical baseball hit *Field of Dreams*.

But Liotta was yet to fulfil the promise he'd displayed in *Something Wild*. Three years earlier, Robert De Niro and Martin Scorsese were in Tahiti discussing their new movie *GoodFellas*. De Niro was to play James Conway, but who could sustain the innocence and hot-headed bravura of Henry Hill? De Niro remembered *Something Wild* and suggested Liotta to Scorsese.

'But it was a matter of meeting him to know that the other aspects – the vulnerability, the sympathy people would need for Hill – would also work,' Scorsese relayed. It worked. And how. Liotta acted De Niro off the screen.

Next, Ray Liotta stars in *Article 99* as the chief of surgery in a Veterans Administration hospital. Along with Kiefer Sutherland, Forest Whitaker, Amy Madigan and Lea Thompson, he fights bureaucracy to save lives, and the film promises to stir up some controversy. After that Liotta teams up with Jonathan Kaplan (*The Accused*) for the psychological thriller *Unlawful Entry*.

Michael Madsen oozes macho charisma like a leaking gasoline tank. He looks entirely comfortable on screen, not so much a man reading lines as a truck driver who has accidentally wandered on to the set. He squints like Clint Eastwood, hauls his masculinity around like Nick Nolte and has the dangerous edge of a man who's never heard of nerve endings. He's the sort of guy film directors love.

The magic of Madsen is that he doesn't try to be recognised. He just *is*. And you notice him. In the awful *Blood Red*, Eric Roberts strutted around like a cockerel, but Madsen fitted into the background like the genuine article. Maybe he wasn't an actor at all, but an Italian farmer from the region.

In *The Doors* you didn't know who he was, but he looked like one of the guys. He belonged there: perhaps he was a *real* Door who was hanging

Michael Madsen in Kill Me Again

around the film set. He smelt authentic enough.

Michael Madsen was born in Chicago on the South Side, the son of a fire-fighter weighed down with medals for bravery. Madsen began his acting career at the Steppenwolf Theater, at the time under the direction of John Malkovich. After appearing in productions of *A Streetcar Named Desire* and *Of Mice and Men*, the actor set off for Los Angeles to build a film career and made his debut in John Badham's *WarGames*, in 1983. He followed this with small roles in *Racing with the Moon*, *The Natural* (as baseball player 'Bump'), *Blood Red*, *Perfect Strangers*, *The Killing Time*, *Iguana* and *Shadows in the Storm*.

He also clocked up such TV credits as *St Elsewhere*, *Miami Vice*, *Cagney and Lacey* and the mini-series *War and Remembrance*, but didn't achieve the instant stardom of his sister, Virginia, who had followed him out to LA.

His break came in the stylish *film noir* thriller *Kill Me Again*, in which he played the psychotic boyfriend of Joanne Whalley-Kilmer. The film was not a success, but generated enough favourable reviews to get Madsen noticed. He had a good role in *One Point of View*, produced, directed by and starring Dyan Cannon, and then secured the part of Tom Baker in Oliver Stone's *The Doors*, a privilege if not a career milestone.

Another big break was the role of Susan Sarandon's hot-headed boyfriend, Jimmy, in Ridley Scott's superb *Thelma & Louise*. Again, Madsen played the macho heel, hurling furniture around and squinting his way into Sarandon's heart. The film belonged to Sarandon and Geena Davis, but Madsen held every scene he was in.

In John Dirlam's *To Kill For*, Michael Madsen has landed his first starring role. After that he stars in *Double Cross*. Our fingers are crossed.

Penelope Ann Miller. Suddenly Penelope Ann Miller was everywhere. Last Christmas she was starring opposite Robert De Niro in *Awakenings* and Arnold Schwarzenegger in *Kindergarten Cop*. Last year she played Marlon Brando's daughter in *The Freshman* and then she replaced Michelle Pfeiffer in *Other People's Money*. Next, she top-bills in

Peter Yates's big budget *The Year of the Comet*, from a screenplay by William Goldman.

Of course, there's no such thing as overnight stardom, and Penelope Ann Miller, now 27, has paid her dues.

Born in Los Angeles, she grew up in a showbusiness environment, the daughter of actor-filmmaker Mark Miller. At eighteen, she moved to New York to study drama and after only one year was cast as Daisy, the soft-spoken convent girl, in Neil Simon's Broadway premiere of *Biloxi Blues*. Co-star Matthew Broderick recalls that Penelope 'was a breath of fresh air. The play was all men and she came in during the second act and changed the whole show.'

Before she recreated her role in the successful film version, Penelope made her film debut as Brenda, the short-sighted friend of Elisabeth Shue in Chris Columbus's *Adventures in Baby Sitting* (known as *A Night on the Town* in the UK). A somewhat zany, plain girl, Brenda flees her wicked step-mother to land up at a Chicago bus station, where she rings Shue to rescue her. While the latter is experiencing a hair-raising night on the town, poor Brenda is becoming more and more intimidated by the human refuse around her, waiting hysterically for her deliverance. It was a plum role and Penelope made the most of it, revealing a comedy talent that even now has yet to be fully tapped.

In the under-valued *Miles from Home*, she played a local girl who tags along with outlaw Kevin Anderson, and then re-created Daisy in the film version of *Biloxi Blues*, her first female lead on celluloid. She was Pee-Wee Herman's wholesome fiancée in the disastrous *Big Top Pee-Wee*, and then went on to surprise her critics by playing a tough, independent woman who beds Don Johnson in John Frankenheimer's stylish *Dead-Bang* (terrible title, though).

She got good reviews as Anthony Edwards's wife in the mediocre cop thriller *Downtown*, but was pretty much wasted, and was then re-teamed with Matthew Broderick in *The Freshman*. As the daughter of Mafia don Marlon Brando she exhibited a toughness and sexiness unseen before, particularly in the scenes in which she seduces film student Broderick into the Mob.

Penelope Ann Miller with Arnold Schwarzenegger in Kindergarten Cop

The film's director, Andrew Bergman, was impressed. 'She has amazing concentration and amazing technique. You can tell Penelope to make her character five per cent more girlish and she'll be five per cent more girlish. She can shade her characters that precisely.'

In between movies she made appearances on TV in *St Elsewhere*, *Family Ties* and *Miami Vice* and romanced Woody Harrelson (Woody in *Cheers*). However, all this exposure seemed to have little effect on her private life.

'I like being anonymous,' she says. 'As long as directors and producers know who I am, that's fine.'

Her recognition factor went up when she won a Tony nomination for her performance (as Emily Webb) in a Broadway production of *Our Town*, later filmed for PBS. And then came the big roles.

In *Awakenings* she played the girl who breathes some life into the post-catatonic days of Robert De Niro, and then she co-starred as the teacher who hooks up with Schwarzenegger in *Kin-*

dergarten Cop. Neither film supplied her with the kind of muscle she had shown earlier, but they were both highly visible at the box office.

Before either opened, she was signed up to play the lawyer at loggerheads with Danny DeVito's unctuous liquidator in *Other People's Money*. The advance word is that she's sensational, and that the scenes between her and DeVito are particularly mesmerising. This, obviously, is the film that will make her or break her. Chances are she'll make the grade.

Ed O'Neill is an American TV phenomenon now working the movies. I include him here for the record. Not because he might succeed where Peter Falk, Farrah Fawcett and, bless her, Tanya Roberts failed (to seduce the great cinemagoing public), but because we'll be hearing a lot more of him. At least, for the time being.

A native of Youngstown, Ohio, O'Neill dabbled with acting at school, but directed his energies towards football, winning himself scholarships to Ohio University and Youngstown

Ed O'Neill, starring in Dutch, *with Ethan Randall and JoBeth Williams*

State, and playing the gridiron for them both. For a while he even played for the Pittsburgh Steelers, but was dropped from the team shortly afterwards. In Florida, of all places, he worked as a bellhop for six months, before returning to Ohio to teach. But O'Neill had never entirely lost the acting bug and enrolled in drama classes, winning the part of Randall P. McMurphy in a local production of *One Flew Over the Cuckoo's Nest*.

Inspired by his leading role at the Playhouse, O'Neill packed a single suitcase and headed for New York. Following work as a waiter, he won a part in an off-off-Broadway production of *Requiem for a Heavyweight*, and then walked off with the lead in *Knockout* on Broadway – after the star had been fired.

Bits in films (*Cruising*, *The Dogs of War*) followed, and more plays, until

the actor was signed up by NBC to appear in the TV movie *The Day the Women Got Even* (1980) and to star in their *Farrell for the People* (1982). The latter received OK reviews and O'Neill found himself all over the small screen. He popped up in the very first season of *Miami Vice* (as FBI undercover agent Artie Rollins) and won the title role in *Popeye Doyle* (1986), the TV movie and subsequent series based on *The French Connection*. Other TV bits have included a regular spot on the daytime soap *Another World* and cameos on *Spenser: For Hire* and *Hunter*, before landing the role of the workaholic, frustrated and long-suffering shoe salesman Al Bundy in the hit sitcom *Married . . . with Children*.

Described as 'a cult hero to every victimised male in America' and pegged 'the most loveable slob since Archie Bunker', Al Bundy made Ed O'Neill a household name in every American home with a TV.

Since the success of the show O'Neill has been picked up by the movies, playing Lt Brannigan in the canine *K–9* and

joining the all-star cast of *Disorganized Crime*. There was a TV movie, *Gladiator School* ('90), and then another cop (and former disco star), Lt Amos, in the disastrous, high-profile *The Adventures of Ford Fairlane*.

In Carl Reiner's *Sibling Rivalry* he played the fumbling, loveable cop Wilbur Meany, more interested in Jamie Gertz than in solving crime. In the acclaimed TV film *The Whereabouts of Jenny*, O'Neill won excellent reviews as a divorcee denied visiting rights to his daughter when she and her mother are swallowed up by a government witness relocation programme. Following this, the actor landed his first major starring role in a major motion picture. In *Dutch*, the second film from Peter Faiman (the director of *'Crocodile' Dundee*), O'Neill takes the title role and is supported by JoBeth Williams. More notably, the movie is produced and written by John Hughes, the force behind such success stories as *Home Alone* and the *National Lampoon's Vacation* films.

Described as a cross between *Planes, Trains and Automobiles* and *Uncle Buck*, the comedy sees O'Neill as a self-made man who has to transport his new girlfriend's snotty son home from boarding school. 'All sorts of horrible things happen,' the star illuminates. 'The kid is a precocious young boy. Very upperclass. But he's never experienced America as it really is out there at the truck stop.'

Saskia Reeves's range as a performer on screen has yet to be determined. However, there is no denying that she is the most in-demand new actress working in the piffling few films being made in Britain.

Born in London, Saskia left the Guildhall drama school in 1982 and performed puppet shows with the Covent Garden Community Theatre to earn her Equity card. From there she joined the respected Cheek by Jowl Company for eighteen months, performing plays on tour and at London's Donmar Warehouse. At the Mermaid Theatre she played Greta in Steven Berkhoff's *Metamorphosis*, which was later filmed by the BBC, and also appeared at the Young Vic, Hampstead Theatre and the Royal Court. On television she has been seen in *The Last of the Summer Wine*, *Lytton's Diary* and *A*

Woman of Substance before being cast in the title role of Thaddeus O'Sullivan's haunting, award-winning film *December Bride*.

As Sarah, the 'heathen' servant girl who sleeps with her employers (the Echlin brothers), Saskia displayed a simple, understated sexuality tinged with iron. The film was not of the stature to produce stars, but obviously all the right people were watching.

Saskia was next cast in the central role of Natalie, a bored and restless wife, in the steamy, London-set erotic drama *Close My Eyes*. This time she was asked to play a woman who changes dramatically over the course of five years, and here Saskia was less effective. As Natalie she lacked the latent spirit that she exhibited so well in her first film. Nevertheless, it was an important, demanding role and a provocative one at that.

'Incest isn't something we find easy to talk about,' the actress explains. 'But once you start looking, you realise that the theme of love between a brother and sister has always fascinated people. It's there in the legends of Isis and Osiris and in present-day novels like *The Hotel New Hampshire*.'

Stephen Poliakoff's dialogue is not the easiest to get your tongue round, and at the screening at which I saw the film, the audience was in hysterics. Before Natalie is about to seduce her brother (Clive Owen) she asks, 'Are you clean everywhere?' Under the circumstances, it would take a Meryl Streep to carry that line off. Only Alan Rickman – as Saskia's cuckolded husband – seemed at ease with the stilted script.

Anyhow, Saskia Reeves survived this tricky second film to land the lead in *The Bridge*, directed by debuting filmmaker Sidney McCartney. Receiving top billing for the first time, the actress was supported by an impressive cast, including Joss Ackland, Anthony Higgins, Geraldine James and Rosemary Harris.

She played the bored and restless wife again, this time striking up an affair with a young artist. Set in 1887, the film was variously described as being 'in the Laura Ashley school of genteel British cinema' (*Variety*) and as 'cornily enjoyable' (*Film Review*). Saskia herself was not blessed with the best reviews of her career.

Today the actress says, 'I've been

Saskia Reeves in Close My Eyes

lucky to be able to combine so much film and television work with work for the theatre as well, but I don't have a particular preference.

'I know it's what everybody says, but all I want to do is work with people who are good at their job in order to make me better at my job – whether that's on film or in theatre.'

Well, this year she's certainly been visible on the large screen.

Alan Rickman. Whether nasty or nice, Alan Rickman is veritably hypnotic. Whether alchemising the cryptic dialogue of Stephen Poliakoff into speakable dialogue, or just snarling at Tom Selleck's cowboy hat, Rickman slinks to centre stage and steals the show.

Filmically it all happened with *Die Hard*, the wildly entertaining blockbuster that gave Rickman the spotlight as the gentlemanly, snarling, ice-cold villain Hans Gruber.

'All sorts of people asked me why I wanted to be in a film like *Die Hard*,' Rickman says. 'I thought it could turn out to be a fabulous film – something like the best ride at the best funfair.'

It was, and in Hollywood Rickman became an overnight . . . villain. He repeated his role as the smarmy, sarcastic malefactor in two more BIG movies, opposite Tom Selleck in *Quigley Down Under* and Kevin Costner in *Robin Hood: Prince of Thieves* (as the Sheriff of Nottingham). However, it was a trio of leading roles in *Truly, Madly, Deeply* and *Close My Eyes* which established Rickman as a serious acting force on the large screen.

Truly, Madly, Deeply, made by the BBC, is the unusual and often very funny story of a ghost (Rickman) and his bereaved girlfriend (Juliet Stevenson). A sharply scripted, English variation of Paramount's *Ghost*, the film succeeds as a unique entertainment – against the odds. *Truly, Madly, Deeply*

Saskia Reeves and Alan Rickman

was written and directed specially for Stevenson by the playwright Anthony Minghella, and the actress excels in her first top-billing central role on the large screen. Rickman, meanwhile, exhibits a nifty deadpan humour and some superbly subtle playing as the virtuoso cellist back from the dead.

In *Closet Land*, another low-budget, small-scale production, Rickman won ecstatic reviews as a brilliant interrogator, a man weaving an intellectual nightmare around his victim Madeline Stowe (complete with confusing accents). The entire film takes place in one room, but due to the power of Rickman's multi-layered performance the film bolts you to your seat.

Close My Eyes was a less successful exercise, but once again Rickman strolled off with the acting honours. The potentially torrid story of an incestuous liaison, the film saw Rickman as a jilted husband and betrayed brother-in-law, a successful financial advisor and apparent bore. However, as Rickman was the only interesting character in sight, his performance upended the film. And for this we must be thankful, for without him *Close My Eyes* would have been a lot duller.

Trained as a graphic designer at the

Chelsea School of Art, Rickman managed a design group for three years until being struck by the acting bug. 'It was time,' he said, and so at the age of 26 he enrolled at RADA – paying for his course by doing a bit of graphic design here and there.

Following drama school he performed the classics at such London establishments as the Royal Court, the Hampstead Theatre and the Bush, before signing on with the august Royal Shakespeare Company.

For the BBC he created the inimitable Obadiah Slope in the highly acclaimed *The Barchester Chronicles*, and in 1985 he originated the role of the Vicomte de Valmont in Christopher Hampton's *Les Liaisons Dangereuses*, performing the part more than 500 times in London and on Broadway.

For the Broadway production, Rickman received a 1987 Tony nomination as Best Actor, but it was John Malkovich who landed the part in Stephen Frears's film version.

'I don't know what the word is to describe how I feel,' he said after Malkovich snared the role. 'Not disappointed exactly. In fact, I'm really not sure a word has been coined for the sensation. I don't want to spend my time thinking about it.'

Alan Rickman's other work includes such celebrated TV productions as *Smi-*

ley's People, *Romeo and Juliet*, *Girls on Top* and *Benefactors*, and playing Kevin Kline's computer graphics friend in the ill-received film *The January Man*.

But on film, Rickman is still best remembered as Hans Gruber, the brilliant, calculating terrorist in *Die Hard*. 'He was wonderful because he made us all stop and think about "Why?" ', explained Rickman's co-star Bonnie Bedelia. 'It's very easy to make this kind of film by numbers, but Alan kept the truth in the film. The man is a wonderful actor.'

In *Robin Hood: Prince of Thieves*, a Spielbergesque roller-coaster ride that had little to do with the English legend, Rickman appeared to be the only member of the cast enjoying himself. Kevin Costner, Morgan Freeman and Christian Slater looked ill-at-ease and unconvincing, while Rickman twisted the film round his arm and made it *his* – albeit comic – vehicle. Whether sliding a sword through the gut of Guy of Gisborne or threatening Robin with a spoon, Rickman was delightfully despicable. He also had the best angle on the script. In one scene, furious that the poor had sided with the noble outlaw, Rickman's sheriff screams in vengeful frustration, 'That's it! Call off Christmas!' As usual, the devil had all the best lines, but Alan Rickman made sure he had the devil of a part.

Film World Diary

JAMES CAMERON-WILSON

July

Jodie Foster starts production on her directorial debut, *Little Man Tate*, in Cincinnati. Dianne Wiest and Harry Connick Jr co-star ★ Denzel Washington signs a two-year development and production deal with Tri-Star Pictures, for whom he made *Glory* ★ Howard Duff, 76, dies of a heart attack in Santa Barbara, California. Most recently he made appearances in TV's *Knot's Landing* and *The Golden Girls*, and co-starred in *Too Much Sun*, his last film (in which he dies at the very beginning) ★ Mel Gibson is injured during a fight scene for *Hamlet*. Filming is delayed for a week ★ Margaret Lockwood dies, aged 73, after spending her last years as a recluse – devoting her time to gardening and doing crosswords ★ *Total Recall* clocks up $104 million in 45 days in the US ★ Dennis Quaid and his company, Summers/Quaid Prods, enter into a three-year development pact with Tri-Star ★ The first wife of Laurence Olivier, actress Jill Esmond, 82, dies in Wimbledon ★ Sting and his girlfriend Trudie Styler have their third child, Eliot Pauline Sumner – a girl ★ Rosanna Arquette reveals that she posed nude for *Playboy* magazine . . . and is terrified that her boyfriend, rock star Peter Gabriel, will disapprove ★ Brigitte Nielsen becomes engaged to British film producer Sebastian Copeland at a secret ceremony in Malta ★ Zsa Zsa Gabor leaves prison after three days inside – for slapping a traffic policeman. An American magazine offers her $60,000 for the diary she kept as a convict ★

August

Accused murderer Christian Brando, son of Marlon, is released on $2 million bail after his father put up his Hollywood mansion as security ★ Woody Allen extends his exclusive contract with Orion Pictures, committing his next three films to them as writer, director and producer ★ Charlton Heston resigns from American Equity in protest over the union's decision to ban Jonathan Pryce from playing the leading 'Asian' role in the Broadway musical *Miss Saigon* ★ *Dick Tracy* passes the $100 million mark at the US box office ★ *Die Hard 2* likewise clocks up $100 million ★ The Brooklyn Bridge in New York is closed to the public so that Bruce Willis can film scenes from *Hudson Hawk* ★ William Hurt replaces Warren Beatty in the title role of Touchstone's *The Doctor* ★ Michael Moore, creator of the documentary *Roger & Me*, donates half his net profits ($1 million) from that film to a fund that will help support displaced residents of Flint, Michigan, the town immortalised by his film ★ Jodie Foster signs a two-year contract with Orion Pictures to star in, direct and produce features. Her first film will be with Woody Allen ★ Steven Spielberg announces his film of *Peter Pan*, to be called *Hook*. Dustin Hoffman will take the title role as the Cap'n and Robin Williams will co-star as Pan. Julia Roberts is mooted as Tinkerbell. The stars will repeat their roles in the sequel, to be called, er . . . *Peter Pan* ★

September

Irene Dunne, 88, dies of heart failure in her Los Angeles home ★ Lou Diamond Phillips is given a clean bill of health by the Navajo nation to play a Navajo cop in Robert Redford's *The Dark Wind*. An earlier press report, which said that they were upset over the casting, is denied. Lou Diamond points out that he is part American Indian anyway ★ British actress Athene Seyler dies aged 101. Her last film was the 1963 *Nurse on Wheels*, with Juliet Mills ★ *GoodFellas* and *Miller's Crossing* receive rave reviews in New York. The gangster movie has returned ★ Danny DeVito is announced as the star of Norman Jewison's film version of Jerry Sterner's off-Broadway play *Other People's Money*. Gregory Peck and Penelope Ann Miller will also appear ★ Spike Lee refuses to comment when a white florist is vandalised after he rented the shop for a scene in *Jungle Fever*. The police classified the incident as racially

Jodie Foster: big deals, new directions

Kim Basinger: showing her style, but dropping Helena

motivated ⋆ The Motion Picture Association of America introduces the new NC17 rating in America. This is so that 'serious' adult films like *Tie Me Up! Tie Me Down!* and *The Cook, Thief, His Wife & Her Lover* can receive proper distribution – without the stigma of an X-rating. X-rated pictures were invariably associated with pornography and refused proper distribution and advertising. Philip Kaufman's *Henry and June* is the very first feature to be honoured with the new certificate ⋆ *Memphis Belle* does sensational business in Britain ⋆ *Texasville* is given the kiss of death by Gotham critics ⋆

October

It is reported that Carolco Pictures will pay Ronald Bass (*Rain Man*) a guaranteed $2 million to write a script based on T. M. Wright's supernatural thriller *Manhattan Ghost Story*. The commission is a record for an unseen screenplay ⋆ *Henry and June*, in spite of its new respectable NC17 rating, is banned in a suburb of Boston, Massachusetts – by 'city fathers' ⋆ The *Birmingham* (Alabama) *News* refuses to advertise *Henry and June* in spite of the film's new rating ⋆ Michael Cimino's *Desperate Hours* is a box-office catastrophe in the US ⋆ The Golden State Theater in Riverside, California, the site of the first screening of *The Birth of a Nation*, will be razed to the ground following a fire that gutted it ⋆ Sidney Poitier signs an exclusive three-year contract with Columbia Pictures. He will produce all the films himself and take turns at directing, writing and starring ⋆ The French actress-director Delphine Seyrig, 58, dies of lung disease. She will be best remembered for her roles in *Last Year at Marienbad*, *The Discreet Charm of the Bourgeoisie* and *The Day of the Jackal* ⋆ *Reversal of Fortune* opens to rave reviews in New York ⋆ Bob Guccione is ordered by a State Supreme Court Justice to pay Marjorie Lee Thoreson $4.06 million for treating her as a sex slave and making her perform pornographic scenes in the film *Caligula*. Guccione is the head of the Penthouse empire and Thoreson a former Penthouse 'Pet of the Year' ⋆ Western star Joel McCrea dies, aged 84 ⋆ Dennis Hopper, who directed Don Johnson in *The Hot Spot*, publicly denounces his star on the Arsenio Hall Show. Hopper accuses Johnson of being a 'sleazebag' for refusing to promote the film, adding, 'I realise Johnson's just insecure, because before this film he just couldn't act.' ⋆ 21st Century announces production of *The Cherry Orchard*. Lindsay Anderson will direct and Maggie Smith, Bob Hoskins and Alan Bates will star ⋆ It is out: Madonna uses protein collagen injections to increase the fullness of her lips. The public exposure of her secret has the star pouting ⋆ David Lynch and Isabella Rossellini split up after five years of love and harmony ⋆ Paul Hogan is offered £10 million to make a second sequel to '*Crocodile*' *Dundee* ⋆ Canadian drag queen Craig Russell, 42, dies of AIDS. He starred in the 1977 *Outrageous!* and its 1987 sequel *Too Outrageous!* ⋆ Steve Martin visits the American troops in Saudi Arabia ⋆ British actress Freda Jackson, 82, dies. Her last film was the 1981 *Clash of the Titans*, with Laurence Olivier ⋆ Italian film star Ugo Tognazzi (*La Cage Aux Folles*, *Il Petomane*), 68, dies of a cerebral haemorrhage in Rome ⋆ Bruce Willis denies rumours of a split with Demi Moore. It is reported that Ms Moore had Dutch actress Marushka Detmers removed from Bruce's current film *Hudson Hawk* in a jealous fit. Marushka was replaced by the married Andie MacDowell ⋆ Whitney Houston goes public about her love affair with Eddie Murphy. 'We are friends and we are lovers,' she announces ⋆

November

Kim Basinger is paid $1 million to show off her legs for a 30-second TV commercial made by an Italian stocking company ⋆ Marlon Brando's son, Christian, is charged with a second shooting when drop-out Ricardo Alvarez claims that the actor's son nearly shot him dead while under the influence of drugs ⋆ British Satellite Broadcasting, the TV company that invested in at least twelve British movies (including *Hidden Agenda*, *Memphis Belle* and *Scandal*), is consumed by Sky Television in a surprise takeover ⋆ Giancarlo Parretti merges his Pathé Communications with MGM/United Artists – at a cost of $1.3 billion. But where did he get the money? And is MGM/UA worth it? ★ Peter Bogdanovich, still suffering from the critical stings inflicted on his *Texasville*, is removed from Tri-Star's *Another You*, starring Richard Pryor and Gene Wilder. Apparently, the production was ten days over schedule ★ Sean Young ties the marital knot with a little-known Spanish thespian ★ Screenwriter Carol Sobieski (*Annie*, *Winter People* etc), 51, dies of a blood disease ★ Twentieth Century-Fox signs up Patrick Dempsey and his production company in a new development deal. Dempsey will both star in and produce films for the studio ★ The London gentlemen of the press wield their collective hacksaws on Michael Winner's *Bullseye!* ★ *Ghost* dominates the British box office ★ *Hudson Hawk* goes five weeks over schedule and *at least* $15 million over budget. And there are still another four weeks of filming to be completed . . . ★ A fire rages through Universal Studios, destroying the set of John Landis's *Oscar*, starring Sylvester Stallone. Other famous sets burned to the ground include those used for *The Sting*, *Back to the Future* and *Dick Tracy* ★ Michael J. Fox signs a multi-year contract with Universal Studios ★ The New York critics are ecstatic over *Dances with Wolves* ★ Super-producers Don Simpson and Jerry Bruckheimer (*Top Gun*, *Beverly Hills Cop*) leave Paramount after nine months. Their sole film with the studio, *Days of Thunder*, is not the success that they had hoped ★ Representatives of Alexander and Ilya Salkind file a $40-million suit charging English director Ridley Scott with misappropriating the idea for their planned 1992 production of a Christopher Columbus biography. However, the name of Scott's movie – plain *Christopher Columbus* – does not clash with the five titles registered by the Salkinds ★ Comic actress Eve Arden, aged somewhere between 78 and 88, dies of heart failure ★ *Adios* is given an NC17 rating ★ The New York press take *Cyrano de Bergerac* to their hearts ★ *Home Alone* breaks box-office records in the States, and blocks *Rocky V* from making it to No. 1. *Rocky* is dead. Long live Rocky Balboa! ★ The New York critics approve of James Ivory's *Mr and Mrs Bridge* ★ The London press love *Metropolitan* ★ Robert De Niro, Nick Nolte, Jessica Lange, Gregory Peck, Robert Mitchum and Martin Balsam are con-

firmed as the stars of Martin Scorsese's *Cape Fear*. Wow ★ English director Don Chaffey (*One Million Years BC*, *Pete's Dragon*), 72, dies of heart disease at his New Zealand home ★ Paramount informally suggests to the Los Angeles Film Critics' Association that they postpone their annual awards so that Francis Ford Coppola can complete *The Godfather Part III* in time to qualify ★ *Ghost* grosses $300 million worldwide ★

December

Burt Lancaster is seriously ill ★ Bob Cummings, 80, dies of kidney failure and pneumonia in California. His last film was the 1967 crime melo *Five Golden Dragons* ★ The Brat Pack turns to crime: *Mobsters* starts filming in LA with Christian Slater, Patrick Dempsey and Richard Grieco top-cast. F. Murray Abraham and Anthony Quinn co-star ★ Whoopi Goldberg signs an exclusive 'acting' contract with Paramount Pictures. She kicks off with the TV-spoof *Soapdish* ★ *Ghost* clocks up $201 million in the US and Canada alone – in 23 weeks ★ Carolco signs English director Tony Scott to a first-look agreement under which he will produce and direct movies through his own company Asylum Productions. He is currently preparing *The Last Boy Scout* for Warner Bros and Bruce Willis ★ Joan Bennett, 80, dies of a heart attack ★ Martin Ritt, 76, also dies of a heart attack ★ English director Alan Parker and Tri-Star Pictures dissolve their 'exclusive three-year, first-look agreement'. Parker will no longer direct the film version of *Les Misérables* for the company ★ Jeff Goldblum and Geena Davis separate after three years of marriage. The tall couple starred together in *Transylvania 6–5000*, *The Fly* and *Earth Girls Are Easy* ★ On Christmas Eve Tom Cruise and Nicole Kidman marry in secret in Aspen, Colorado ★ Madonna, 32, and Tony Ward, 27, lose their baby. Although rumours suggest the singer-actress had the child aborted, Madonna declares the loss a miscarriage ★ Anne Revere, 87, dies of pneumonia. She will be best remembered for her Oscar-winning role as Mrs Brown in *National Velvet* (1944) ★ *GoodFellas* sweeps the New York and Los Angeles Film Critics' awards. Martin Scorsese wins the plaudit for best director twice over ★ *Home Alone*

knocks up $103 million in five weeks ★ *The Godfather Part III* opens to violence in New York. At a first-night showing at Long Island two gangs of teenagers open fire. Two teens and two adults are wounded in the melee and Tremain Hall, 15, dies from a shot in the head ★ In its opening week, *The Godfather Part III* makes less than half of *Home Alone*'s take the same week. And *Home Alone* has already been on release for six weeks ★

January

In the UK, Ian McKellen, 55, is knighted in the New Year Honours list. Marius Goring walks home with a CBE ★ *Home Alone* makes $152 million in seven weeks in the US ★ *Alien III* starts production at Pinewood Studios. Sigourney Weaver, Charles Dance, Charles Dutton and Paul McGann topbill ★ An internal 28-page memo from Disney Studio chairman Jeffrey Katzenberg to his staff is leaked to the press. Urging staff and filmmakers to cut down on their costs, Katzenberg comes across as patriarchal and officious. A parody memo follows a week later, and is likewise leaked. Katzenberg becomes the laughing stock of Hollywood ★ *Dances with Wolves*, a.k.a. *Kevin's Gate*, sweeps the Golden Globes. Gerard Depardieu wins a trophy as best actor for *Green Card* ★ Mel Gibson is signed up by Warner Bros to a four-picture deal worth $60 million. The package includes *Lethal Weapon III* and the romantic fantasy *The Rest of Daniel* ★ Tom Cruise moves his production company, Odin Prods, from Paramount to Universal. For the latter he will film *Far and Away*, co-starring Mrs Cruise ★ *Home Alone* makes $205 million in the United States and Canada – in eleven weeks ★

February

Character actor Dean Jagger, 87, dies in Los Angeles. He will be best remembered for his Oscar-winning performance in the 1949 *Twelve O'Clock High* ★ Ruth Morley, 65, costume designer extraordinaire, dies of breast cancer in New York. Her credits include *Taxi Driver*, *Annie Hall* and *Ghost* ★ Meg Ryan and Dennis Quaid finally tie the knot – on St Valentine's Day ★ *The Silence of the Lambs* opens to ecstatic reviews in New York ★ *Dances with*

Wolves runs off with *twelve* Oscar nominations ★ Sean Penn has his heart-shaped tattoo of Madonna removed to convince pregnant fiancée Robin Wright of his love ★ The New York critics condemn Paul Mazursky's *Scenes from a Mall* ★ *Dances with Wolves* passes the $100-million mark at the US box office ★ *Hook* starts production in Hollywood. Spielberg directs Dustin Hoffman, Robin Williams, Julia Roberts, Bob Hoskins, Maggie Smith and Phil Collins ★ Ryan O'Neal says he will finally marry Farrah Fawcett *if* their TV sitcom *Good Sports* is a hit ★ Marlon Brando's son, Christian, is sentenced to ten years in prison for voluntary manslaughter. Marlon refers to his son as a 'basket case' ★ Pathé Films sues John Travolta for $200,000 for failing to return his salary after a film in which he was due to star folded ★ Representatives of Macaulay Culkin ask $5 million for the ten-year-old actor to star in the *Home Alone* sequel ★ Oliver Stone's new film, *JFK*, is announced. Kevin Costner will star as New Orleans district attorney James Garrison, investigating the assassination of John F. Kennedy. Gary Oldman is signed to play Lee Harvey Oswald, and the supporting cast includes Sissy Spacek, Tommy Lee Jones, Donald Sutherland, Jack Lemmon, Walter Matthau, Glenn Ford, John Candy, Kevin Bacon, Sally Kirkland and Joe Pesci.

March

Reputedly, Sean Penn leaves Robin Wright to return to the arms of ex-wife Madonna ★ Gerard Depardieu confesses to an American journal that he once raped a girl. The furore that ensues looks guaranteed to lose him an Oscar later in the month ★ French singer, songwriter, filmmaker and actor Serge Gainsbourg, 62, dies in Paris. He is, perhaps, best remembered for his long-standing relationship with British actress Jane Birkin and for their illicit hit record, *Je T'Aime, Moi Non Plus*, which he later directed as a film ★ It is official: the tabloids reveal that Ryan O'Neal and Farrah Fawcett have split ★ Steven Spielberg marries actress Kate Capshaw (*Indiana Jones and the Temple of Doom*) ★ Mickey Rourke announces plans for his next film, a controversial account of the H-block terrorists. Rourke promises to glorify the IRA and is himself planning to star as Francis

Hughes. He has pencilled in such co-stars as Gabriel Byrne, Matt Dillon, Richard Harris and, as Bobby Sands, Sean Penn ★ Steven Spielberg starts production in London of *An American Tail: Fievel Goes West*, utilising the voices of James Stewart, John Cleese and ex-wife Amy Irving ★ Aldo Ray, 64, dies of complications from throat cancer and pneumonia. Best remembered for *Pat and Mike* and the 1955 *We're No Angels*, his last film was *Shock 'Em Dead*, with former porn princess Traci Lords ★ Ralph Bates, 50, dies of cancer in London. His last film was *King of the Wind*, but recently he was best known for the TV sitcom *Dear John* ★ *Home Alone* clocks up a phenomenal $250 million Stateside ★ John Hughes asks $14 million to write, direct and produce his next film, Hollywood studio chiefs are appalled ★ Outsider Kathy Bates wins the Oscar as Best Actress for *Misery*, beating out the heady competition of Meryl Streep, Joanne Woodward, Anjelica Huston and Julia Roberts. For Britain, Jeremy Irons walks off with the statuette for Best Actor for *Reversal of Fortune*. Kevin cleans up the rest ★

April

The Silence of the Lambs clocks up over $100 million at the US and Canadian box office ★ Martin Scorsese signs an exclusive six-year contract with Universal Pictures. He is currently completing *Cape Fear*, with Robert De Niro, Nick Nolte, Jessica Lange, Gregory Peck and Robert Mitchum for the company ★ Hollywood's highest-paid screenwriter, Joe Eszterhas, makes up with director Paul Verhoeven after a row over the treatment of the former's screenplay, *Basic Instinct*. Eszterhas will now collaborate on the erotic thriller he created, which is starring Michael Douglas and Sharon Stone. Besides, Eszterhas was paid $3 million for his script ★ *Dances with Wolves* passes the $150-million mark ★ *Home Alone* overtakes *Jaws* to become the fourth biggest grosser in American cinema history. The top three places are now held by: 1) *E.T.*; 2) *Star Wars*; and 3) *Return of the Jedi* ★ *Star Trek VI – The Undiscovered Country* goes into production under Nicholas Meyer's direction. Christopher Plummer guest stars ★ Sir David Lean, 83, dies – shortly after suspension of his last film,

Nostromo, which was to have starred Marlon Brando ★ John Hughes signs a seven-picture multi-deal with Twentieth Century-Fox ★ Robert Evans announces a big-budget movie of Leslie Charteris's *The Saint*, to be produced by Paramount Pictures with Renny Harlin directing ★ The Samuel Goldwyn Co. is suing actress Annette Bening for $1 million for ducking out of their movie *The Playboys*. She is later replaced by Robin Wright ★ The remake of the Spencer Tracy–Elizabeth Taylor *Father of the Bride* goes into production with Steve Martin and Diane Keaton starring ★ Director Don Siegel, 78, dies after a long illness. He will be best remembered for the 1956 *Invasion of the Body Snatchers* and *Dirty Harry*.

May

Wilfrid Hyde-White, 87, dies of congestive heart failure in California ★ Jon Peters parts ways with his long-time colleague Peter Guber and exits his post as co-chairman of Columbia Pictures ★ Sydney Samuelson is named head of the newly-funded British Screen Commission ★ Cinema attendances in America are disastrous, with only the rap gangster pic *New Jack City* making a profit. Casualties include Sylvester Stallone's *Oscar* and Michael Keaton's *One Good Cop* ★ Arthur Hiller's film biography of baseball legend Babe Ruth goes into production in Chicago. John Goodman stars as *Babe* and is supported by Kelly McGillis and Trini Alvarado ★ The film version of *Evita*, to have starred Madonna, is abandoned by Disney's Hollywood Pictures because of spiralling costs. Katzenberg's memo lives on ★ *Truth or Dare*, the documentary on Madonna's world tour – 'Ambition' – is given rave reviews by New York's gentlemen of the press ★ Meanwhile the London critics give the thumbs up to Rob Reiner's *Misery* ★ Madonna corners the publicity at the 44th Cannes Film Festival. Even Arnold Schwarzenegger cannot drum up the same kind of media frenzy ★ Kevin Costner is in negotiations to relocate his Tig Productions from Orion Pictures to Warner Bros ★ *Noises Off*, the film version of Michael Frayn's hit play, goes into production under Peter Bogdanovich's direction. The cast includes Carol Burnett, Michael Caine, Denholm Elliott, Julie Hagerty, Christopher Reeve and John Ritter ★ English actor Ronald Lacey, 55, dies in London of cancer. He will be best remembered for his role as the villainous Toht in *Raiders of the Lost Ark* ⋆ Crispin Glover seeks compensation for the use of his 'likeness' in the *Back To the Future* sequels. He was turned down for the two films because Universal refused to pay his $1 million fee ⋆ Joel and Ethan Coen's *Barton Fink* wins the Palme d'Or at Cannes. John Turturro, the film's star, wins the best actor accolade and the Coens are jointly awarded best director. No British film was represented ⋆ Timothy Dalton is officially announced as the star of the next James Bond film. But first he will play *Christopher Columbus* in the Salkinds' epic about the Italian explorer ⋆ The New York critics rave over Ridley Scott's offbeat road movie *Thelma & Louise*. They condemn *Hudson Hawk* ⋆ The $65-million *Hudson Hawk* is dubbed *Hudson the Duck* (in memory of the box-office turkey *Howard the Duck*) when the Bruce Willis adventure dies at American cinemas. Following the disastrous returns of *The Bonfire of the Vanities*, Mr Willis is in dire need of a hit. Meanwhile, his new epic, *The Last Boy Scout*, is going wildly over budget ⋆ Australian-born actress Coral Browne, 77, dies in Los Angeles of breast cancer. She is survived by her husband Vincent Price ⋆ *Backdraft* grosses $15,723,480 in its first weekend in the States, the biggest summer opening ever for a non-sequel.

June

Julia Roberts calls off her star-studded wedding to Kiefer Sutherland – to have taken place on the Twentieth Century-Fox backlot. She leaves her fiancé to be with her mother ⋆ Dame Peggy Ashcroft, 83, dies of a stroke in London ⋆ It's official: Julia Roberts is now the highest-paid actress in the world, commanding more than $7 million a movie. Move over, Ms Streep and Ms Streisand ⋆ Ms Roberts leaves the US for Ireland, accompanied by Jason Patric – Keifer's co-star in *The Lost Boys*. The tabloids have a field day. One eye witness reveals that Julia and Jason 'all but made love on the plane' ⋆ *The Silence of the Lambs* breaks all-time house records in 22 British Odeons. Grossing £4,260,472 in its first week in the UK, *Lambs* breaks another all-time record. Grossing £290,939 at the Odeon Leices-

Julia Roberts (with Campbell Scott in Dying Young*): taking Tinkerbell, dropping Kiefer*

ter Square, the thriller lassoes the world record for the most money taken at a single cinema in a week ⋆ Kim Basinger pulls out of the psychological thriller *Boxing Helena*, to have co-starred Ed Harris. The director, 23-year-old Jennifer Lynch (daughter of David), has already suffered a six-month setback when Madonna pulled out of the same role last December. A legal battle ensues ⋆ Lord Bernard Miles, 83, dies ⋆ Jean Arthur, 90, dies of heart failure in Carmel, California. Her last film was *Shane*, in 1953 ⋆ In the US, *Robin Hood: Prince of Thieves* clocks up a staggering $39,190,653 in its *first week*! – besting the previous summer's blockbusters *Total Recall* and *Die Hard 2*. Is Kevin the most wanted man in the world? ⋆ Nicole Kidman reveals she is

pregnant. Her husband, Tom Cruise, is over the moon ⋆ Paramount Pictures, who have refused to pay writer Art Buchwald his slice of the profits from their film *Coming to America*, admit that the Eddie Murphy comedy has made 'tens of millions of dollars' in so-called 'actual profits'. However, they point out that it has yet to show a *net* profit, and only then would Buchwald be entitled to his share. For the record, *Coming to America* has actually *grossed* around $128 million – in the US alone ⋆ It is announced that Brigitte Nielsen has ditched her third husband, pop video producer Sebastian Copeland ⋆ In just two weeks, *Prince of Thieves* has racked up $66,244,014 in the US ⋆ As Julia Roberts holidays with Jason Patric in Ireland, Michelle Pfeiffer is brought in to replace her as Tinkerbell in Steven Spielberg's *Hook*. However, Julia returns in the nick of time, and Michelle bows out ⋆

In Memoriam

Once described as a perfect English rose, delicate-looking, slender but Yorkshire-tough **Elizabeth Allan** died, aged 80, on 27 July 1990. She made her professional debut with a tiny role in the Hammersmith Lyric production of *The Taming of the Shrew* at the age of eighteen; in 1927 she appeared at the Old Vic, prior to her winning a major role in A. A. Milne's play *Michael and Mary* at the St James's in 1930. She made her screen debut the following year in Agatha Christie's whodunnit, *Alibi*, a performance which brought Hollywood interest and a number of easily forgettable films there. But her

Elizabeth Allan

American film career came to an end in 1937 when MGM (who had her under contract) replaced her in one of the leading roles in their production of *The Citadel*, and she sued them over it. No Hollywood company would employ her thereafter, and she came back to Britain, where she was offered more stage

roles than she could cope with, remaining one of our busiest theatrical stars throughout the forties and fifties, fitting in the occasional supporting role in a number of films during that time. She gained new popularity as one of the panel of the TV show *What's My Line?*. With the death of her agent-husband in 1977, ending a marriage that had lasted for 45 years, she finally retired. Her films include *The Lodger* (1932), *David Copperfield* and *A Tale of Two Cities* (1935), *Camille* and *Michael Strogoff* (1937), *He Snoops to Conquer* (1944), *The Heart of the Matter* (1953), *Front Page Story* (1954) and, her final film, *The Haunted Strangler* in 1958 (sometimes known as *The Grip of the Strangler*).

Eve Arden died on 12 November 1990 at an unconfirmed age – various sources listed her as being 78, 82 and 88 and she herself never divulged which was correct. I well remember her scene-stealing and sometimes entire film-stealing performances as the heroine's wise-cracking friend in a string of vintage (and non-vintage) films of my youth. Apparently she didn't like the tough, caustic-tongued characters she so often played, but early on she became typecast, playing these parts to hilarious perfection. Born Eunice Quedens, she made her first two screen appearances with that name, in *Song of Love* (1929) and *Dancing Lady* (1932), and in the latter year adopted her stage name. She made her stage debut at the age of sixteen and in 1934 appeared on Broadway in the 1934 production of *Ziegfeld Follies*. Her subsequent crowded career on radio, stage, film and television included many stage musicals, more than fifty movies and a great deal of radio and television work. Early

on, she averaged three feature films a year and in 1941 she appeared in no fewer than eight releases. But during her long and very successful career she achieved only one Oscar nomination, as supporting actress in *Mildred Pierce* in 1945. For my part, I remember many of her films solely for the sake of her performance in them: she was that kind of performer. I shall miss her acerbic, wisecracking wit and perfect timing, qualities which are in all too short supply in today's films. Eve Arden's films include: *Oh Doctor* and *Stage Door* (her debut as Eve Arden in 1937), *A Child Is Born* and *No, No, Nanette*

Eve Arden

(1940), *Ziegfeld Girl* (1941), *Whistling in the Dark* and *Bedtime Story* (1942), *Cover Girl* (1944), *Mildred Pierce* (1945), *The Kid from Brooklyn* and *Night and Day* (1946), *One Touch of Venus* (1948), *Tea for Two* (1950), *Our Miss Brooks* (1956), *Anatomy of a Murder* (1959), *The Dark at the Top of* the Stairs (1960), *The Strongest Man in the World* (1975) and, more recently, *Grease* and *Grease 2*, *Pandemonium* and *Under the Rainbow*.

Essentially a lady of the theatre – and the First Lady at that – (Dame) **Peggy** (Edith Margaret Emily) **Ashcroft**, who died on 14 June 1991, at the age of 83, was generally acknowledged to have been the greatest British actress of at least the decade. Probably at her best in Shakespearean roles, she was certainly very versatile, and she did latterly become equally respected in the cinema – though the imbalance of the two mediums in her career can be judged by the fact that *The Daily Telegraph* devoted 90 column inches of their obituary to Dame Peggy's stage work and only 4 inches to her films, important as they were.

Born in Croydon, where the Ashcroft Theatre is a lasting memorial to her, Dame Peggy made her stage debut in 1926 at the Birmingham Repertory Theatre, making her Broadway debut just ten years later. She made her screen debut in *The Wandering Jew* in 1933, which was to be followed by *The 39 Steps* (1935), *Rhodes of Africa* (1936), *Quiet Wedding* (1940), *The Nun's Story* (1959), *Secret Ceremony* (1968), *Three Into Two Won't Go* (1969), *Sunday, Bloody Sunday* (1971), *Hullabalou Over Georgie and Bonnie's Pictures* (1978), *A Passage to India* (1985), *Madame Soulatzka* (1989), *She's Been Away* (1989) and the remarkably memorable TV film *Caught on a Train* (1980).

Ina Balin (real name Ina Rosenberg), the Brooklyn-born model who became a stage, screen and television actress, died on 20 June 1990 at the age of 52. She earned lasting fame for her efforts, along with her friend Betty Tisdale, to evacuate more than two hundred South Vietnamese youngsters to America, subsequently dramatised in a television feature entitled *The Children of An Lac*, which she wrote and co-produced and in which she played herself. Making her Broadway stage debut in *Compulsion* in 1957, her first film (*The Black Orchid*) was premiered the same year. Voted 1961's Star of Tomorrow, she never in fact achieved stardom, and her screen career ended with *The Don Is Dead* in 1973. Among a total of around ten movies were *The Comancheros* in

Peggy Ashcroft

1961, *The Patsy* in 1964, *The Greatest Story Ever Told* (1965), and *Charro!* in 1969. Apart from her stage and film work she appeared in a considerable number of television features and series.

Joy Batchelor, who died, aged 77, on 14 May 1991, was responsible with her partner and husband John Halas – they were the celebrated Halas and Batchelor – for putting Britain well and truly on the animation map with the feature cartoon *Animal Farm* in 1954. The pair had made their first coloured animated short (*Handling Ships*) for the Admiralty in 1945, and went on to make some 2000 other shorts of all kinds, mostly advertisements for companies like Lux and Kelloggs. The firm also produced a number of films for the Ministry of Information and similar government departments, and they did considerable work for both the BBC and American TV. During constant production work by the Halas and Batchelor studios they managed to develop new techniques, several of which made a significant contribution to animated film.

The news of the death of **Ralph Bates** on 27 March 1991 at the age of 50, from cancer, will have special interest for the many fans of the old Hammer 'horrors', for his screen career was largely spent at the Bray Studios, where he made such Hammer films as *Dr Jekyll and Sister Hyde*, *Taste the Blood of Dracula*, *Persecution* and *The Devil Within Her*, to name only a few.

I always admired Constance Bennett as an actress but it was her sister **Joan Bennett** (who died, aged 80, on 7 December 1990) who stole my young heart, and I shall never forget her in the two Fritz Lang movies, *The Woman in the Window* (1944) and *Scarlet Street* (1946). I have fond memories too of her performances in her third Lang film, *The Secret Beyond the Door* (1948), and in Renoir's *Woman on the Beach* (1947) and Max Ophuls's *The Reckless Moment* (1949), in which she co-starred with James Mason. The youngest of three sisters (the eldest, Barbara, also appeared in films but to nothing like the extent of her sisters), Joan came of a theatrical family, making her stage debut in 1928 with her father in the Broadway production of *Jarnegan*. She had made her initial appearance in front of the movie cameras the previous year, in a short film of *Alice in Wonderland*. In 1928 she also had a minor role in *Power*, her only non-starring role for many years to come, as she became an overnight star after being cast opposite Ronald Colman in *Bulldog Drummond* in 1929. Married at sixteen, a mother at seventeen and a divorcee at eighteen, Joan Bennett married for the third time in 1940: her husband this time was producer Walter Wanger, with whom in 1951 she shared the newspaper headlines when he shot and wounded her agent in a fit of jealous rage. Wanger was subsequently imprisoned for attempted murder. The case and its

Joan Bennett

publicity did her career considerable harm, and she did not work again until 1954, when she took a role in *Highway Dragnet*. She was never again offered a starring role. In all, Joan Bennett appeared in more than seventy films, in her early career appearing in as many as seven a year. (One film of hers has never yet been seen in the cinema or on TV, the 1974 production *Inn of the Damned*.) Miss Bennett's work in later years, apart from a few stage productions, was almost entirely confined to TV, including a horror soap, *Dark Shadows* (which ran continuously from 1966 to 1971), and a number of telefilm features. Her final cinema film, the Italian production, *Suspiria*, appeared in 1977. A natural blonde, Miss Bennett became a brunette in 1938 and remained one for the rest of her career. Her final appearance in front of the cameras was in 1986, when she took part in the TV documentary, *The Spencer Tracy Legend*. In addition to those

Edwina Booth

mentioned above, her films include: *Little Women* (1933), *The Texans* (1938), *The Man in the Iron Mask* (1939), *The House Across the Bay* (1940), *Wild Geese Calling* (1941), *Confirm or Deny* (1941), *Margin for Error* (1943), *Nob Hill* (1945), *The Macomber Affair* (1947), *Father of the Bride* (1950), *Navy Wife* (1956) and *Desire in the Dust* (1960).

Now almost totally forgotten, 'White Goddess' **Edwina Booth** (some sources give her real name as Edwina Woodruff, others say it was Constance Booth Woodruff) died, aged 82, in May 1991. Her sensational story was constantly in the headlines and probably took up more space in the newspapers than that of any major Hollywood star. Originally a stage actress, Miss Booth played minor roles in several silent films before being chosen by W. S. Van Dyke to play the star role of 'The White Goddess' in his film *Trader Horn* in 1928. It appeared to be a golden step to stardom but it was to prove a disaster which ended her short career. On location in the jungle, working almost naked, Miss Booth contracted one disease after another, including malaria and dysentery, and was being continually struck down by bad bouts of sunstroke. After the unit moved to the Belgian Congo, she fell out of a tree and all but cracked her skull. Life was made even more harrowing by the producers deciding to switch from silent to

sound film midway through the production. The final result was that Miss Booth had a nervous breakdown followed by a complete collapse, after which she spent six years in bed in a darkened room. She fought back and won both a divorce case against her first husband, Anthony Schuck, and a suit against MGM for a million dollars – the latter case was apparently settled out of court. In recent years Miss Booth had worked in, a Los Angeles Mormon Temple – a far cry from the horrors of *Trader Horn*.

Pierre Braunberger, who died at the age of 85 in Paris on 16 November 1990, produced films in his native France for well over sixty years, starting with silents in 1924 and ending with *Knights of the Round Table* in 1989. He had a considerable influence on the French cinema, taking the avant-garde and the New Wave in his stride, and producing films with such leading directors as Renoir (including his first feature, *Catherine*), Buñuel (including the controversial *Un Chien Andalou*), Cavalcanti, Resnais, Truffaut and Godard. His films owed much of their success to his precise judgement of the balance between the artistic and the popular.

Born in Melbourne, Australia, **Coral Browne**, who died, aged 78, in June 1991, gets no mention in *Who's Who in British Films*, and didn't get mentioned either in *Variety*'s very comprehensive Obituary column. Although she was primarily a stage actress, this treatment seems unfair, in that she did appear in some thirteen British and American movies, including *The Amateur Gentleman* (her screen debut in 1936), *Auntie Mame* (1958), *The Roman Spring of Mrs Stone* (1961), *The Night of the Generals* (1967), *The Killing of Sister George* (1968), *The Ruling Class* (1962), *Theatre of Blood* (1973), *The Drowning Pool* (1975), and, notably, *Dreamchild* (1985). Miss Browne was married to Vincent Price.

Although primarily a stage actress, who made her debut in rep. and then established herself with Joan Littlewood's Theatre Workshop at Stratford, East London, **Avis Bunnage**, who died on 4 October 1990 at the age of 67, did also appear in a number of British films.

These include *Sparrers Don't Sing*, *Tom Jones*, *The L-Shaped Room*, *The Whisperers*, *The Loneliness of the Long Distance Runner* and, most recently, *The Krays*. Her career as a wholly dependable character actress spanned some forty years.

A trained artist who entered films through the art department of the old Gainsborough Studios, **Don Chaffey** was British-born (in Hastings), but died in New Zealand after long residence there, aged 72, on 13 November 1990. Moving from Gainsborough to Gaumont-British, Chaffey directed his first film there – a documentary on dogfish! But he was soon directing features, the first of which, a children's film, *The Mysterious Poacher* (1950), brought him an award at the Venice Film Festival of that year. He subsequently directed a number of other films for children, both shorts and features, the latter including Disney's *The Three Lives of Thomasina* in 1963. Some of his other thirty-odd features (ranging from thrillers and dramas to comedy) include: *Time Is My Enemy* (1954), *The Girl in the Picture* (1957), *The Man Upstairs* (1958), *Dentist in the Chair* (1960), *Greyfriars Bobby* (1961), *The Prince and the Pauper* (1962), *Jason and the Argonauts* (1963), *One Million Years BC* (1966), *The Terror of Sheba* (1974), *Pete's Dragon* (1977), and *The Magic of Lassie* (1978). He also directed hundreds of television episodes of series such as 'Charley's Angels', 'Vegas', 'Fantasy Island', 'T. J. Hooker' and 'Mission Impossible'.

Although he made comparatively few movies and is not mentioned in most film reference books, **Alan Clarke**, who died at the age of 54 on 24 July 1990, deserves a niche for his grim and gritty large- and small-screen output, reflecting his Liverpudlian background: films like *Rita, Sue and Bob Too* and *Billy the Kid and the Green Baize Tree*. His *Scum* (originally intended for a small-screen debut), about life in Borstal, was too grim for the BBC, who shelved it. His telefeature *Made in Britain* (skinheads and glue-sniffing) brought him the Prix Italia drama prize.

Robert (Bob) Cummings, the ever-youthful, resourceful (and, as I recall

Coral Browne

him, cheeky) American actor who died, aged 80, on 2 December 1990, won his first stage and screen roles by subterfuge. He obtained his first role on the stage by adopting the name of Blade Stanhope Conway and passing himself off as a true-blue Britisher: similarly, he got his first film role by presenting himself to the studios, complete with authentic Texas drawl, as Brice Hutchens of the Lone Star State. He later used his real name, and had considerable success as a debonair young light comedy actor in some notable films during the 30s, 40s and 50s (although he successfully switched to dramatic roles in several films including *King's Row* and Hitchcock's *Dial M for Murder*). As well as a great deal of work in television and the theatre, Cummings made some sixty-odd films, including *The Virginian Judge* (1935), *Hollywood Boulevard* and *The Accusing Finger* (1936), *Wells Fargo* (1937), *The Texan* (1938), *Three Smart Girls Grow Up* (1939), *The Devil and Miss Jones* (1941), Hitchcock's *The Saboteur*

161

Robert Cummings

(1942), *Princess O'Rourke* (1943), *Let's Live a Little* (which he also co-produced, in 1948), *The Carpetbaggers* (1964), *Stagecoach* (1966) and *Five Golden Dragons* (1967), which appears to have been his final screen appearance. His considerable work on TV included sit-coms and his own show, which ran initially from 1955 to 1959, and then, as 'The New Bob Cummings Show', from 1961 to 1962. On stage, his performance in *Twelve Angry Men* in 1954 brought him an Emmy award. In his retirement he wrote a book, *How to Stay Young and Vital*: his five wives and seven children perhaps qualified him as an authority on the subject.

If he had never made another film, **Jacques Demy** – who died in Paris on 27 October 1990, aged 59 – would have

established his rightful place in the Cinema Hall of Fame with his *Les Parapluies de Cherbourg*, a revolutionary departure from the conventional, in which every word of dialogue was sung. With a delightful musical score by Michel Legrand, artistic and imaginative dancing and a youthful freshness, the film well deserved the Golden Palm award it won at the Cannes Film Festival in 1964. Three years later Demy attempted to repeat the formula with *Les Demoiselles de Rochefort* which, delightful as it was, lacked the impact of novelty. After art and film studies in Nantes and Paris, Demy became an assistant director of animated movies and documentaries before making a number of shorts. He made his debut as a feature director with *Lola* in 1960, which he dedicated to Max Ophuls and which had much of that director's style. In 1968 Demy, with his film director wife, Agnes Varda, went to America, where he made the critically acclaimed

but financially not very successful *The Model Shop*. Back in France in 1971 Demy made *Peau d'Ane* (starring Catherine Deneuve) and then the following year came to England to direct David Puttnam's *The Pied Piper*. In 1982 his *Une Chambre en Ville* had a somewhat bumpy production because of casting troubles, but was warmly praised by the critics. Unfortunately, however, the public stayed away. After *Parking* in 1985 Demy returned to animation and co-directed with some success the amusing and inventive feature *La Table Tournante*. His last film was another attempt to marry the American musical with French style and refinement, but although *Trois Places pour le 26* starred Yves Montand it failed to please the public and must be considered a failure. Demy made only a dozen movies and he did very little television work, but although he never again achieved the success of *Les Parapluies*, that film alone made him one of the most innovative directors in the history of the cinema.

Specialist 'tough-guy' actor **Howard Duff** died, aged 76, on 8 July 1990, after a day devoted to raising money for the Santa Barbara victims of the Californian fires of the previous month. After studying drama as a young man, Duff began his professional acting career in the Seattle Repertory Theatre, but turned to radio in 1935 when he was offered the chance of creating the famous Dashiell Hammett private eye Sam Spade on the airwaves. It was not until after the war and his military service that Duff entered the film studios, appearing in the classic *film noir* duo, *Brute Force* and *The Naked City*, both directed by Jules Dassin. After appearing in *Calamity Jane and Sam Bass* and *Johnny Stool Pigeon*, Duff was teamed with Ida Lupino in *Women in Hiding* in 1949, the first of several films in which they were successfully co-starred – including *Private Hell 36* (1954), *Women's Prison* (1955) and Fritz Lang's *While the City Sleeps* (1956). So successful did this partnership become that they decided both to marry and to set up their own production company. During 1957 and 1958 they carried their joint success into television, playing husband and wife in the series 'Mr Adam and Eve', and later guest starring together in the 'Batman' series. Their

Howard Duff

able movies, ranging from tear-jerking 'women's' pictures to the craziest of comedies and fine musicals. Her performances were always professional and polished to the extreme, her timing meticulous and her approach to her varied roles intelligent. Altogether Miss Dunne, who died on 4 September 1990 at the age of 88, gave me some of my most memorable hours in the cinema. Of Irish descent, and a graduate of the Chicago Musical College, opera was her original aim, but when she failed an audition with the New York Metropolitan Opera in 1920 she turned to musical comedy, achieving stardom in her first engagement, a tour of *Irene*. She made her Broadway debut in *The Clinging Vine*, and in 1929 was the star of Ziegfeld's touring company in *Showboat*. Signed up by RKO, she made the indifferent *Leathernecking*, but the following year starred in no fewer than four films, one of which was *Cimarron*, the only Western ever to take the Best Film Oscar. During the next twenty years she appeared in a large number of often outstanding movies, proving her versa-

Irene Dunne

marriage and professional association ended with divorce in the early 1970s. Duff continued to concentrate on TV, and after *Panic in the City* in 1968 he didn't enter a film studio until 1977. It was Robert Altman who lured him back to the large screen with a role in *The Late Show* and then persuaded him to appear in *A Wedding* (1978). Duff also had a featured role in Robert Benton's *Kramer vs Kramer* (1979). Several less memorable movies followed including the yet-to-be-seen *Too Much Sun*, which Duff completed in 1990. Florid of feature and powerfully built, Duff's character range was wider than the tough roles in which he tended to be typecast.

It has long seemed that **Irene Dunne**, one of the greatest of Hollywood's 'golden era' stars, was one of the least honoured and the most forgotten of them. Her films are seldom if ever shown on TV, yet she gave a series of glowing performances in many memor-

Jill Esmond

tility again and again. Some of the best of them were: *Back Street* (1932), *The Silver Cord* (1933), *Roberta* and *Magnificent Obsession* (1935), *High, Wide and Handsome* (1937), *My Favourite Wife* (1940), *A Guy Named Joe* (1943), *The White Cliffs of Dover* (1944), *Anna and the King of Siam* (1948), *Life with Father* (1947), *The Mudlark* (in which she played Queen Victoria, 1950) and *It Grows on Trees* (1952). After this she made no more films, although she did make a few appearances on television. Not every performance of hers was a great one, but all were good enough to be recalled with real pleasure. Though she never won an Oscar (though she richly deserved one), she did gain five Academy nominations with her roles in *Cimarron* (1931), *Theodora Goes Wild* (1936), *The Awful Truth* (1937), *Love Affair* (1939) and *I Remember Mama* (1948).

Jill Esmond (real name Jill Esmond-Moore) who died at her Wimbledon home, aged 82, on 28 July 1990, was a RADA graduate who first appeared professionally on the stage at the age of fourteen in a production of *Peter Pan*. She made her screen debut in the 1930 movie *Chinese Bungalow*, to be followed in 1931 by roles in *The Skin Game* and *The Eternal Feminine*. She had previously met Laurence Olivier while acting with him in John Drinkwater's *Bird in Hand* and they married in 1930,

subsequently crossing the Atlantic to appear together in the Broadway production of *Private Lives*, co-starring with Noel Coward and Gertrude Lawrence. Miss Esmond's first Hollywood film was *Once a Lady*, which was followed by *This Above All, The Pied Piper, Random Harvest, Journey for Margaret* (all 1942), *The White Cliffs of Dover, Casanova Brown* and *My Pal Wolf* (all 1944), and *The Bandit of Sherwood Forest* (1946). She returned to Britain in 1946 to make *Bedelia*, staying to make *Escape* in 1948, and then returning to America to star in *Night People* in 1954 and, her final film, *A Man Called Peter* in 1955, completing a total of some 22 films. Having borne Olivier a son (Tarquin), she was divorced from him in 1940, and she never re-married.

British-born **Gloria Holden**, who died aged 82 on 22 March 1991, had spent so long in Hollywood that she was often thought to be American. Ex-model and stage actress, she starred in her second film (the first was *Wife v. Secretary*), *Dracula's Daughter* (1936), and with it established herself. From then until the late 1950s she was in pretty constant demand, appearing in *The Life of Emile Zola* (1937), *Test Pilot* (1938), *Dodge City* (1939), *The Corsican Brothers* (1941), *Miss Annie Rooney* (1942), *The*

Gloria Holden

Hucksters (1947), *Killer McCoy* (1948), *The Eddy Duchin Story* (1956), *This Happy Feeling* (1958) and many others. She made a total of more than twenty features, in addition to considerable radio and television work.

Raymond Huntley, who died in June 1990 at the age of 86, was still acting almost up to the time of his death; one of his more recent performances was in the popular TV series 'Upstairs, Downstairs'. Huntley began his career in the 1920s in repertory, making it to the West End stage in the title role in *Dracula*, with which he subsequently – 1928–30 – toured America. His film debut came in 1935 with the Sandy Powell film *Can You Hear Me Mother?*, which he followed in 1936 with the more prestigious duo, *Rembrandt* and *Whom the Gods Love*. Among the more than sixty films that followed, there were a number of classic British productions including *Knight Without Armour* (1937), *The Ghost Train* (1941), *The Way Ahead* (1944) and *The Dam Busters* (1955). His range was formidable, for as well as the more weighty films, he appeared in such comedies as *The Ghost of St Michael's* (1941), *Doctor at Sea* (1955), *The Pure Hell of St Trinian's* (1961) and *Rotten to the Core* (1965).

Wilfrid Hyde-White (who died, aged 87, on 6 May 1991 at the Palm Springs house he had occupied since 1960) played often highly contrasting roles in a career that spanned more than 45 years and more than 150 films. I shall always picture him, however, in a Savile Row tweed suit, topped by a jauntily worn trilby hat and with a pair of binoculars slung over his shoulder, with that mischievous, slightly mocking smile on his face, leaning over the rails, or making his way to the bookie's . . . picture him, in fact, as the perfect public-school educated, impeccable English gent having a day at the races.

Born in lovely Bourton-on-the-Water, educated at Marlborough School, Hyde-White started out with the plan of being a stage magician, but switched to acting when he won a scholarship to RADA. He made his West End stage debut in *Beggars on Horseback* in 1925, having appeared in his first film, *Ton of Money*, three years

and (without a credit) co-directed *It Grows on Trees*. Others of his more than sixty films include *The Robe* (1953), *White Christmas* (1954), *Bad Day at Black Rock* (1955), the British thriller *X, The Unknown* (1957), *The Nun's Story* (1959) and *Elmer Gantry* (1960). Jagger made no films between *Jumbo* in 1962 and *First to Fight* in 1967, but followed the latter by *Tiger by the Tail* and *The Kremlin Letter* in 1970 and *Vanishing Point* in 1971. But the films that followed were easily forgettable and his better work was in the vast number of appearances he made on TV, in both features and series, winning an Emmy award in 1989 for his performance in *This Is the Life*. Jagger's performances on large or small screen were never less than good, and were often outstanding, but nothing else he did ever equalled that inspired performance he gave in *Twelve O'Clock High*.

You won't find the name of **Harry Lauter** – who died at the age of 75 on 30 October 1990 – in many film reference books, but he was a familiar face in Westerns and even more familiar on the small screen in such popular series

Wilfrid Hyde-White

previously. Thereafter, it was just one film after another; to pick out a favourite few, *Rembrandt* (1936), *The Demi-Paradise* (1943), *The Winslow Boy* (1948), *The Third Man* (1949), *The Browning Version* (1950), *The Adventures of Quentin Durward* (1955), *Tarzan and the Lost Safari* (1957), *Libel* (1959), *Crooks Anonymous* (1962), *My Fair Lady* (1964; a made-to-measure role in which he had a career-best success, as the debonair Colonel Pickering), *Run a Crooked Mile* (1969), *The Cat and the Canary* (1978), and *Fanny Hill* (1983). In addition to all these films, Hyde-White appeared in a number of telefilms and periodically returned to the theatre to appear in the classics as well as in modern plays. Of his two sons and one daughter, one of the sons is also an actor.

It is strange how some moments, brief scenes or performances among the thousands I have seen have become indelibly and vividly etched in my memory. One such performance is **Dean Jagger**'s playing of Major Stovell

in *Twelve O'Clock High*, a performance which deservedly brought him an Oscar. That was more than forty years ago, but I recall Jagger's performance in that film as clearly as if it had been yesterday. Dean (Jeffries) Jagger, who died on 5 February 1991 at the age of 87, was already a seasoned stage and vaudeville performer when he made his screen debut in Fox's silent film *Woman from Hell* in 1929. He didn't make another movie until five years later (*You Belong to Me*) but in the following two years he made six B features and got his first leading role, in *Revolt of the Zombies*, in 1936. For the next four years he concentrated on his stage performances but in 1940 returned to face the cameras to play his first major role in a major film, *Brigham Young – Frontiersman*, which established him and brought him thereafter a constant stream of character and supporting work in a range of movies. Following a big success in *When Strangers Marry* in 1944 (alt. title *Betrayed*) he came to England in 1945 for the Anna Neagle film *I Live in Grosvenor Square*, returning home to earn his Oscar in *Twelve O'Clock High*. In 1952 he co-starred

Dean Jagger

Harry Lauter

as 'Gunsmoke', 'Wagon Train', 'Rawhide', 'Wyatt Earp' and 'Bonanza'. He twice achieved his own TV series: 'Waterfront' in 1954, and 'Tales of the Texas Rangers' from 1955 to 1959.

Philip Leacock, who died in his birthtown of London, while on a holiday from his long-time California home, on 14 July 1990 at the age of 73, entered the movie business as a disciple of the master of the documentary John Grierson. And it wasn't until the early fifties, after making a series of non-fiction films like *Island People* and *The Story of Wool* in 1940, and *Life in Her Hands* and *Festival of London* in 1951, that he turned to fictional features, concentrating initially on children's and young people's features. But when he began to make features for adult moviegoers he had immediate success with films like *Escapade* (1955), *The Spanish Gardener* – with Dirk Bogarde – in 1956 and *High Tide at Noon* in 1957. At which point the Hollywood siren called, and there he made *The Rabbit Trap* in 1959, and *Let No Man Write My Epitaph* and *Take a Giant Step* in 1960. He then came back to England to make *The War Lover* (1962) and *Tamashine* (1963). In 1970 he went to Australia to make *Adam's Woman*. Leacock continued to make films both in Britain and in Hollywood where he won kudos for his TV action and Western series, including the classic 'Gunsmoke'. (He was also the executive

producer of *The Wild, Wild West* feature.) In recent years he confined himself to small-screen work, but in 1988 he decided to retire from the film business altogether in order to concentrate his energies wholly on environmental issues. Philip's elder brother, Richard Leacock, has been working in Hollywood since he first went there at the age of seventeen.

David Lean, writer, director, editor and producer, who died on 16 April 1991 at the age of 83, was one of Britain's most versatile and talented men of the cinema, and was internationally respected and admired for his films. The son of Quakers, who considered the cinema a sin, Lean started as a tea boy at the old Gainsborough Studios in 1927, working his way up from clapper-boy to newsreel editor, from where he graduated to co-directing, with Noel Coward, the memorable *In Which We Serve* in 1942.

A perfectionist who took great care with the preliminary work, and was not to be hurried once he took his chosen subject on to the studio floor, he in fact made only sixteen films in five decades. He was extremely versatile, being equally at home with intimate romantic drama, like his *Brief Encounter* (1945), sweeping spectacle, like his *Doctor Zhivago* (1965), *Lawrence of Arabia* (1962) and *The Bridge on the River Kwai* (1957), and classic texts, as in his screen Dickens in *Great Expectations* (1946) and *Oliver Twist* (1948). His influence on Hollywood may be judged by the fact that although he never worked there, in 1990 the American Film Institute bent their own strict rules by awarding Lean their Life Achievement Award, topping the fact that his films won 24 Oscars, with two of them going to him personally.

Lean's final film was his distinguished and sensitive adaptation of E. M. Forster's *A Passage to India*, released in 1985, though he also supervised the recent revival of his *Lawrence of Arabia*. At the time of his final illness Lean was preparing a lavish screen version of Joseph Conrad's novel *Nostromo*, which was slated to start actual production on 4 March in the South of France with Dennis Quaid and Isabella Rossellini as the stars; but on news of Lean's death the whole project was shelved. David Lean's other films were *This Happy Breed* (1944), *Blithe Spirit*

Alison Legatt

(1945), *Passionate Friends* (1949), *Madeleine* (1950), *The Sound Barrier* (1952), *Hobson's Choice* (1954), *Summer Madness* (1955) and *Ryan's Daughter* (1970). His outstanding skills as an editor are to be seen in *Pygmalion*, *The 49th Parallel* (1941) and *One of Our Aircraft Is Missing* (1942).

A great artist of the cinema medium, David Lean leaves a gap in British cinema not likely to be filled for many years to come.

Although ignored by Katz in his *International Film Encyclopedia*, British actress **Alison Legatt**, who died at the age of 86 on 15 July 1990 in her native London, deserves a place in any list of British film actresses for her performances in a number of movies. Notable are *This Happy Breed* (she was a favourite Noel Coward player who, as well as being cast in his original stage production of *Cavalcade*, toured with him and Gertrude Lawrence in *Tonight at 8.30*), the musical re-make of *Goodbye Mr Chips*, *Far From the Madding Crowd*, *Waterloo Road*, *A Funny Thing Happened on the Way to the Forum* and *The Card*. A star of many West End stage productions, Miss Legatt starred in the Broadway production of *Epitaph for George Dillon* in 1959. She was also a favourite star of TV dramas.

Margaret Lockwood (real name, Margaret Day), who died in London on 15 July 1990 at the age of 73, was one of the few British stars of the 1940s who didn't decide that their careers would be best furthered by settling in Hollywood. After her considerable success in Alfred Hitchcock's *The Lady Vanishes* in 1938 she was lured across the Atlantic, but after two indifferent movies (*Susannah of the Mounties* with Shirley Temple, and *Rulers of the Sea* with Douglas Fairbanks Jr), she decided that Hollywood didn't suit her and she returned to Britain, never again to make a film elsewhere. Born in India (like Merle Oberon and Vivien Leigh), Miss Lockwood came to Britain and became a RADA pupil. Her professional career began in 1928 when, while still in her early teens, she was engaged to play a fairy in a London production of *A Midsummer Night's Dream*. After further stage work she made her initial entry into a film studio in 1934 with a role in *Lorna Doone*. A number of parts followed, including roles in *Midshipman Easy* the following year, *The Beloved Vagabond* in 1936, *Dr Syn* in 1937 and *Bank Holiday* in 1938, the year that she achieved a major success in Hitchcock's *The Lady Vanishes*. After that she was seldom out of a film studio, for following her Hollywood sojourn she came back to Britain to star in *The Stars Look Down*, followed by *Night Train to Munich* the same year (1940), *Quiet Wedding* in

Margaret Lockwood

Keye Luke

1941 and *Alibi* (1942), the first of the four films in which she co-starred with James Mason. The others were *The Man in Grey* in 1943, *A Place of One's Own* and – her most boisterous success – *The Wicked Lady* (both in 1945). Among the other films that followed *Alibi* were *Dear Octopus* (1943), *Love Story* (1944), *Hungry Hill* (1946), *Cardboard Cavalier* (as Nell Gwynn) (1949), *Highly Dangerous* (1950), *Trent's Last Case* (1952), *Laughing Anne* (1953), *Trouble in the Glen* (1954) and *Cast a Dark Shadow* (1955), after which she announced her retirement from films and future concentration on her stage work. But 21 years later she was briefly back in the studios again, when Bryan Forbes persuaded her to play a major

role in his 'Cinderella' musical, *The Slipper and the Rose*, thus completing a total of 44 films. Margaret Lockwood's autobiography, *My Life and Films*, was published in 1948, and there is an excellent recent biography available, *Once a Wicked Lady*, by Hilton Tims.

Keye Luke, the Chinese, Canton-born actor who made almost one hundred Hollywood films after his screen debut opposite Greta Garbo in *The Painted Veil* in 1934, died on 12 January 1991, aged 86. In the 1930s he appeared in nine films in the Charlie Chan series, returning to the role in 1948–9 in *The Feathered Serpent* and *Sky Dragon*. Many famous directors chose him for feature roles in their films, including Alfred Hitchcock (*Mr and Mrs Smith*),

W. S. Van Dyke (*Journey for Margaret*), Michael Curtiz (*Young Man with a Horn*), John Huston (*Across the Pacific*), Wesley Ruggles (*Somewhere I'll Find You*) and many others. He also appeared in a number of films in the 'Andy Hardy' and 'Dr Kildare' series. His versatility was proved in the musicals *No, No, Nanette* and *The Gang's All Here*: and, incidentally, in the Broadway stage production of *The Flower Drum Song*. Luke also appeared in a large number of TV productions, including telefeatures and series. He was also featured in a number of film serials. His final screen appearance was in Woody Allen's *Alice*, released in 1991.

James MacDonald, ex-engineering student, ex-percussionist and the voice of Mickey Mouse for 30 years (1946–1976), died on 1 February 1991 at the age of 84. Apart from Mickey's voice he provided Pluto's bark and the voices of the dwarfs in *Cinderella*, the dormouse in *Alice in Wonderland* and

Dorothy Mackaill

the dragonfly Evintrude in *The Rescuers*, as well as many other voices and sound effects for the Disney cartoons. Though officially retired, at the time of his death he was still creating sound effects for the Disney studios and was scheduled to work next for the Walt Disney World in Japan.

Few modern moviegoers will know the name of Hull-born silent-screen star **Dorothy Mackaill** who died, at the age of 87, on 12 August 1990. But she was an important screen actress of her day, appearing in some fifty silent and sound films before retiring to her house in Hawaii in 1938, thereafter making just one or two brief appearances, particularly as a guest star in a few episodes of the TV series 'Hawaii Five-O'. A child student at her father's dancing school, she made her professional debut on stage when she was only sixteen in the London Hippodrome show *Joybells*. In 1920 she made her screen debut in *The Face at the Window*. After a period as a showgirl at the Café de Paris, she decided to try her luck in America, and was there quickly given

a role by Florence Ziegfeld in two of his musical shows, *Midnight Follies* and *Sally*. She was seen in the latter by Hollywood director Marshall Neiland, who was impressed enough to offer her a part in his production of *The Lotus Eater* (1921) and an even more important role in his next film, *Bits of Life*, the same year. By 1925 she had become the star of films like *The Bridge of Sighs*, *Shore Leave* and *Joanna*, and the following year she headed the cast of *Dancer of Paris*. Star of the silent version of Gershwin's *Lady Be Good*, Dorothy Mackaill made an easy transition to sound films in *Two Weeks Off* in 1929, although her own favourite performance was in the silent *The Barker* in 1928, in which she played opposite Douglas Fairbanks Jr. Her subsequent talkies tally included *The Reckless Hour* and *Safe in Hell* in 1931 (a hectic year for her with four movies completed), *Love Affair* in 1932, *Curtain at Eight* the following year, *Cheaters* in 1934 and, back in Britain, what was virtually her final screen appearance in *Bulldog Drummond at Bay* in 1937.

Earlier in his career especially, **Joel McCrea** made many other kinds of movies, but it is as a Western star that he is best known, remembered and loved. Reputedly as charming off-screen as on, McCrea, who died on 20 October 1990 at the age of 84, came of Western stock; one grandfather drove a stagecoach and fought Apache Indians, while the other took part in the 1894 California Gold Rush. McCrea's first job was holding horses for Tom Mix and William S. Hart (later becoming a stuntman and bit player in silents), and he once said that he was a lot more comfortable playing roles that involved a horse, a stetson and cowboy boots. Away from the screen he became a wealthy rancher and farmer and at one time owned 3000 acres at Thousand Oaks, with another 20,000 acres in Nevada. McCrea took the sound film in his stride, becoming a featured player in 1929 and a star the following year. He alternated between drama, sophisticated comedy and tough adventure films in the 1930s and early 1940s. During this period, he starred in some outstanding movies such as Alfred Hitchcock's *Foreign Correspondent*, George Stevens's *The More the Merrier*, Preston Sturges's *Sullivan's Travels* and

William Wellman's *Reaching for the Sun*. His co-stars included Greta Garbo (with whom he danced in *The Single Standard*), Constance Bennett, Dolores del Rio, Irene Dunne, Miriam Hopkins, Barbara Stanwyck and Ginger Rogers. Around 1946 he took the decision to concentrate almost exclusively on Westerns, though he did break this rule in 1953 when he came to Britain to star in Eric Ambler's thriller *Shoot First*. After *Gunfight at Dodge City* in 1959 he did not make another film until Sam Peckinpah persuaded him to star in *Ride the High Country*, a classic of its kind, in 1962. McCrea did not make another film until his last (in 1970), *Cry Blood-Apache*, which he produced and which featured one of his three sons, Jody – who made a few films before turning rancher. However, McCrea did subsequently make a trio of documentaries: *The Great American Cowboy* in 1974, *George Stevens: A Film-maker's Journey* in 1984 and *Preston Sturges: The Rise and Fall of an American Dreamer* in 1990. Apart from the films already mentioned, McCrea's tally of nearly one hundred films included: *The Silver Cord* (1935), *Barbary Coast* (1935), *Wells Fargo* (1937), *Union Pacific* (1939), *The Palm Beach Story* (1932), *Buffalo Bill* (1944), *The Virginian* (1946), *Ramrod* (1947), *Colorado Territory* (1949), *Black Horse Canyon* (1954), *Wichita* (1955) and *Fort Massacre* (1948). In 1959 McCrea produced and starred in a TV Western series called *Wichita Town*. He met the lovely Frances Dee while they were co-starring in *The Silver Cord* in 1933, and they remained happily married until he died. They had three sons, Jody and David (both ranchers in New Mexico) and Peter. Hollywood always overlooked McCrea when the awards were handed out, but he was elected to the Cowboy Hall of Fame and awarded the Hall's Award. An actor of great range and talent, and a delightful character, McCrea deserved more from Hollywood.

It is surprising to find that **Mary Martin**, who died, aged 76, on 4 November 1990, made only eleven films. Most of these were at the beginning of her career, between 1938 and 1946 under the Paramount contract she received in 1938 as a result of her great success in the Broadway production of *Leave It To Me*, in which she sang the

Joel McCrea

show-stopping number 'My Heart Belongs to Daddy' (later to serve Eartha Kitt so well). When films were made of some of her other great stage successes, such as *South Pacific* and *The Sound of Music*, the leading roles for various reasons were always given to others. Mary Martin's complete tally of movies, together with a bit-part she played in *Rage of Paris* in 1938, is as follows: *The Great Victor Herbert* (1939), *Rhythm on the River* and *Love Thy Neighbour* (1940), *Birth of the Blues*, *New York Town* and *Kiss the Boys Goodbye* (1941), *Star Spangled Rhythm* (1942), *True to Life* and *Happy Go Lucky* (1943), *Night and Day* (1946), and *Main Street to Broadway* (1953). Larry 'Dallas' Hagman is Mary Martin's son by her first marriage.

Large, craggy and bulldog-featured **Mike Mazurki** (real name Mikhail Mazurwski), who died on 9 December 1990 at the age of 82 after a long fight against illness, was a college footballer and professional wrestler before he made *The Shanghai Gesture* in 1941, the first of his more than one hundred films. He was fated to be typecast and most of his roles were as a tough guy or

gangster, although there was occasional relief in films like Jack Benny's *The Horn Blows at Midnight*, Jerry Lewis's *The Errand Boy*, *It's a Mad, Mad, Mad, Mad World*, *Kismet* and *Some Like It Hot*. It was generally agreed that his most memorable performance was as Moose Malloy in the classic Dmytryk adaptation of Raymond Chandler's *Murder, My Sweet*; but his most surprising success was a leading role in the family film *Challenge To Be Free*, made in 1976.

The achievements of (Sir) **Bernard** (James) **Miles**, who died aged 83 on 14 June 1991, were many and considerable, though possibly the most noteworthy was the creation and running of his famous Thames-side Mermaid Theatre at Puddle Dock (where he also played leading roles). For me, though, his name will always conjure up a ruddy-faced yokel with a straw in his mouth coming on stage – at the Palladium, I seem to recall – to lean against a large wagon wheel and deliver a marvellously amusing and witty monologue in Buckinghamshire dialect. But that was long before he developed into a brilliant actor and outstanding theatrical impresario.

Born in Uxbridge, the son of a suc-

Bernard Miles

cessful market gardener and a Scots cook mother, Miles attended the local High School before going on to Pembroke College, Oxford. Leaving university, he became a teacher, for just a year, before his theatrical ambition took over and he took the job of stage carpenter at the Theatre Royal, Windsor, where he made his acting debut when one of the cast failed to turn up and he stepped into the part.

Miles made his screen debut in 1933 in *Channel Crossing* and went on to appear in some 26 movies including one which he also produced and co-directed (*Tawny Pippit* in 1944) and another which he both directed and produced as well as co-scripted (*Chance of a Lifetime* in 1950). His film acting credits also included *Pastor Hall* (1940), *In Which We Serve* (1942), *Great Expectations* (1946), *Nicholas Nickleby* (1947), *The Magic Box* (1951), *Moby Dick* (1956), *The Smallest Show on Earth* and *Saint Joan* (1957), *Tom Thumb* (1958) and, apparently his last movie, *Run Wild, Run Free* (1969). Sir Bernard had been confined to a wheelchair for some years and was reportedly living on a state pension when he died, having lost all the money he invested in his beloved Mermaid.

Though best and most fondly remembered for his radio series, such as 'Much Binding in the Marsh', **Richard B. Murdoch** ('Stinker Murdoch' of the airways), who died on 9 October 1990, was a versatile performer who made a success in all the entertainment media. A professional entertainer for 60 of his 83 years, he appeared on television, in the theatre and in the music hall and, although his name is unfairly omitted from *Who's Who in British Films*, he did in fact also appear in many British films, including *Band Waggon*, *The Ghost Train*, *Three Men and a Girl*, *Charlie's Big Hearted Aunt* and many others. His professional career began as a chorus 'boy' in the 1927 musical *The Blue Train* and more or less ended with a regular appearance in the popular TV series 'Rumpole of the Bailey'. Another of his recent TV roles was in the mini-series 'Winston Churchill, the Wilderness Years'. But it will nevertheless probably be in 'Much Binding' that he will be remembered for longest.

Dying just two months after his 100th birthday on 16 August 1990, **Myron (Grim) Natwick** was one of the greatest of film animators, two of his triumphs being as the creator of Betty Boop and the animator of Snow White in Disney's first feature cartoon. Having stud-

ied art in Chicago, New York and Vienna, Natwick started his professional career as a magazine and sheet music-cover illustrator, switching to film animation in 1921. Then, after a period of studying painting in Europe, he returned to New York and landed a job with the Fleischer brothers, Max and Dave, with whom he stayed until 1929, when he began to work on his Betty Boop character, which he introduced in a 1930 short named *Dizzy Dishes*. Miss Boop was an immediate success with moviegoers and continued to delight them for eight years, though most of the films were not directly Natwick's work, for he had joined Ub Iwerks, Disney's former partner, in 1931 and became the studio's supervisor. In 1935 he joined Disney and after working on a number of shorts helped to make *Snow White*. After Disney's first feature was launched, Natwick returned to the Fleischers to work on *Gulliver's Travels* and their *Popeye* cartoons. After working on training and other films for the Forces during the war, he joined UPA in 1949, working on the famous *Mister Magoo* and other series before more or less retiring, only to be persuaded to return to the drawing board by Britain's Richard Williams, who brought him to London as lecturer, consultant and animator on Williams's *Raggedy Ann and Raggedy Andy* and *The Thief and the Cobbler* (as yet unreleased). But failing eyesight and advancing old age in recent years meant a gradual withdrawal from work, and Natwick eventually slipped into definite retirement.

Though his output was minor – under ten features (five of the earlier ones he dismissed as 'garbage') – **Sergei Paradjanov**'s impact was major, most especially on his fellow Armenians. He was 66 when he died of cancer on 21 July 1990. The features which made a big impact in the West were *Shadows of Forgotten Ancestors*, *The Colour of Pomegranates*, *Legend of Suram Fortress* and *Ashik Kerib*. Neither his life nor his career ever ran smoothly, and in 1973 he was imprisoned by the Soviets on various charges including that of being openly homosexual. His films, though hailed by some as masterpieces, have only a minority appeal; static, colourful, poetical and sometimes avant-garde, I must admit I always had reservations about them.

A favourite juvenile lead of the 1920s and 1930s, **Eddie Quillan** died in Hollywood on 19 July 1990 at the age of 83. His Scots parents were vaudeville performers and while still a child he was included in their act, along with another four of their ten children. He entered films via a series of Mack Sennett short comedies, but his first feature was *Show Folk* in 1928, followed by four films the following year, including Cecil B. de Mille's *The Godless Girl*. But it was seven years later that Eddie Quillan achieved his first real impression, in Frank Lloyd's *Mutiny on the Bounty*. Other major successes were achieved in *The Young Mr Lincoln* (1939) and *The Grapes of Wrath* (1940). In total he appeared in some 39 films, including a couple of serials. A few of the more familiar titles are *The Flame of New Orleans* (1941), *Kid Glove Killer* (1942), *This Is the Life* (1944), *Brigadoon* (1954), *Move Over Darling* (1963) and *Angel in My Pocket* (1969). Quillan, with his prominent eyes, was a master of the double-take.

Anyone who ever heard **Aldo Ray**'s (real name Aldo DaRe) gravel-grating voice on the screen is unlikely to have forgotten him. Ray died from throat cancer on 27 March 1991 at the age of 64. Joining the US Navy on his graduation day in 1944, he served as a frogman at Okinawa and elsewhere in the Pacific. Demobbed in 1946, he returned to university, where he was a stalwart of the football team, and it was as a cynical, hard-faced college player that he obtained his first screen role in *Saturday's Hero* in 1950. Two years later he appeared in the critically acclaimed George Cukor film *The Marrying Kind*, co-starring with Judy Holliday, and he followed this as a tough boxer in another Cukor success *Pat and Mike*, with Tracy and Hepburn. Then came a succession of films with a military background, but his career took a decided dip in the sixties and seventies when the break up of his third marriage resulted in a drink problem. But he went on working, even if some of the movies he appeared in were rather dubious affairs. His final screen appearance was in 1990, in *Shock 'Em Dead*,

sharing the lead with a former porno film star, Traci Lords. Never an outstanding performer, Aldo Ray could nevertheless be very watchable in the right part, and his unique voice was painful to listen to, but certainly memorable. His films include *Miss Sadie Thompson* (1953), *We're No Angels* (1955), *The Naked and the Dead* (1958), *The Green Berets* (1968), *The Centrefold Girls* (1974) and a couple of British productions, *The Day They Robbed the Bank of England* in 1960 and *Johnny Nobody* the following year.

Actor-turned-director **Martin Ritt** – who died on 8 December 1990 at the age of 76 – made a number of very good films, but few were successful at the box-office, possibly because he often focused on social and racial themes. Nevertheless it was the racial overtones of his first film, *Edge of the City* (retitled *A Man is Ten Feet Tall* in the UK), a raw and realistic waterfront drama, that

Aldo Ray

brought him considerable critical acclaim. Others of his more successful films which pleased critics and public alike were *The Long Hot Summer* (1958), *Hud* (1963), and *The Spy Who Came in from the Cold* (1965); *Hombre* (1967) was less successful and his career ended with the starry (Jane Fonda and Robert De Niro) 1990 flop *Stanley and Iris*. For six years in the 1950s Ritt was blacklisted by the infamous McCarthy witch-hunting Un-American Activities Committee, but spent the period fruitfully as a teacher at the Actors Studio where his pupils included Paul Newman, Joanne Woodward, Lee Remick and Rod Steiger. Among his later films were *Nuts* (starring Barbra Streisand), *Cross Creek* (with Mary Steenburgen) and *Murphy's Romance*. He also made a great number of TV shows (*Variety* gives 250 live shows, of which he acted in 150 and directed 100). Ritt was known for getting the best out of his actors and actresses, and was rewarded by seeing Sally Field (in *Norma Rae*) and Patricia Neal and Melvyn Douglas (in *Hud*) pick up Oscars: the latter film also brought Ritt a Best Director nomination.

Although she was never in any way involved in actual film production, **Irene Mayer Selznick** – who died, aged 83, on 10 October 1990 – deserves mention here if only for the fact that she was the daughter of Louis B. Mayer and became the wife of David O. Selznick. During an argument with Elia Kazan, the director of her Broadway production of *A Streetcar Named Desire*, she is reported to have said, 'I've survived Louis B. Mayer and I've survived David O. Selznick, so it's no use. You'd better lay off.' After *Streetcar* she went on to produce a string of big Broadway stage successes such as *The Chalk Garden* and *Bell, Book and Candle*.

Athene Seyler, who only a few months previously had made her final public appearance at the National Theatre on the occasion of a 101st birthday tribute, died on 12 September 1990. During a long career which began when she appeared in a children's theatrical company at the age of seven, she appeared in more than a hundred stage plays and more than fifty films. A graduate of RADA – where in 1950 she was elected the President – her initial performances were with such famous players of the past as Sir Gerald Du Maurier and Ellen Terry, and she was directed by such great Victorians as Herbert Beer-

Athene Seyler

bohm Tree. Her film career began in 1923 with a role in *This Freedom*, but really took off in 1931 with *The Perfect Lady*; thereafter she made at least one film a year and sometimes more – in 1935 and 1937 she made five films, and in many other years appeared in at least three. Principal films include *The Mill on the Floss* (1937), *The Citadel* (1938), *The Saint in London* (1939), *Tilly of Bloomsbury* (1940), *Quiet Wedding* (1941), *Dear Octopus* (1943), *Nicholas Nickleby* (1947), *Queen of Spades* (1949), *The Pickwick Papers* (1952), *Doctor at Large* (1957), *A Tale of Two Cities* and *Inn of the Sixth Happiness* (1958), *Make Mine Mink* (1960), *The Devil Never Sleeps* (1962) and, her last screen appearance, *Nurse on Wheels* (1963). She excelled in comedy roles; her crinkled, unforgettable face and distinctive voice made her especially suitable for them. It really was a case of once seen, and heard, never forgotten: and she was, surely unintentionally, a great scene stealer. In 1959 Athene Seyler became a Commander of the British Empire. Her book on *The Craft of Comedy* was republished on her 101st birthday.

For most moviegoers the name of **Delphine Seyrig** will be associated with the heroine in that controversial Alain Resnais movie puzzler *Last Year in Marienbad* (1961), and they will be unaware of her other extensive stage and screen work. Ms Seyrig, who died in Paris on 15 October 1990 aged 58, was born in Beirut and studied theatre at several Paris drama schools. After her first significant roles, in *Ondine* and *The Seagull*, she went to the USA in 1956 to study at the Actors Studio and appeared in New York productions of plays by Pirandello and Giraudoux. There followed crowded years of film, theatre and television (including a role in the BBC production of Henry James's *The Ambassadors*); to record them in full would take up pages. Her most notable films included Resnais's *Muriel* (which won her the best actress award at the Venice Film Festival of 1963), Losey's British film *Accident*, Buñuel's *The Discreet Charm of the Bourgeoisie*, *The Day of the Jackal* and others in Germany, Italy and Switzerland. In 1968 she starred in Truffaut's lovely *Stolen Kisses* and then made *The Milky Way* for Buñuel. Always

Delphine Seyrig

interested in avant-garde productions on both stage and screen (in 1968 she served on various committees appointed to modernise drama teaching methods), she starred in several Marguerite Duras plays and films including the experimental *India Song*, and in the 1970s made a number of experimental videos. She continued to work and was due to open in a new play in Paris in September 1990, but had to cancel when lung disease made it impossible for her to carry on. In 1967 the French Académie de Cinéma honoured her with a Star of Crystal award. Though always known for her enigmatic performance in *Marienbad*, the lovely Ms Seyrig deserves to be remembered for a great deal more than that.

With approximately 175 feature films (as well as 35 TV productions and a further 200 small-screen episodes) to his credit, **George Sherman**, who died at the age of 82 on 15 March 1991, was one of the most prolific Hollywood directors. For Republic Pictures he made a vast collection of Westerns – generally on something between a six-day and eight-day schedule, at minimum cost – often starring John Wayne or Gene Autry. He began his career in 1932 at the old Mack Sennett studios and started directing in 1937, the following year starting the series *The Three Mesquiteers*. His last film (and the last of almost a score with Wayne) was *Big Jake* in 1971.

Prolific director and occasional producer, **Don Siegel**, who died after a long illness, aged 78, on 20 April 1991, got to the top the hard way. Though born in Chicago (his father was a mandolin virtuoso) Siegel completed his education in England (at Jesus College, Cambridge) and then attended RADA with the intention of becoming an actor. But he met with no success and returned to America to begin his film career at Warner Studios in 1933. He started in the Warner film library and worked through several departments before getting his chance to direct three shorts, one of which (*Star of the Night*) brought him an Oscar in 1945.

After the shorts, his first feature chance came with *The Verdict* in 1946, after which the offers came steadily. His films include *The Big Steal* (1949), *Riot in Cell Block 11* (1954 – his first real critical success), *Duel at Silver Creek* and *Invasion of the Body Snatchers* (1956), *Baby Face Nelson* (1957), *Flaming Star* (the Elvis Presley Western in 1960), *Coogan's Bluff* and *Madigan* (1968), *Death of a Gunfighter* (1969), *Two Mules for Sister Sara* (1970), *Dirty Harry* (1971), *The Shootist* (John Wayne's final film, in which he played a dying gunfighter, 1976), *Escape from Alcatraz* (1979), the much troubled *Rough Cut* (during which he was fired and later re-hired) and *Jinxed* (during which he suffered the heart attack that led to others finishing the film).

Siegel also did a great deal of TV work, including a number of feature-length telefilms. As a result of his long training, he was a brilliant technician whose on-the-floor improvisations and alterations did not endear him to scriptwriters, especially as many of these amendments and innovations were highly successful!

Although **Ugo Tognazzi** – who died on 27 October 1990 in Rome at the age of 68 – made almost 150 films during his career, only a handful reached this country, where he was best known for the hilarious homosexual comedy *La Cage aux Folles* and the two sequels that followed. An accountant by training, Tognazzi entered films by way of amateur theatricals. His screen debut was in 1950 in Mario Matoli's *The Cadets of Guascogna*, which does not appear ever to have been shown in Britain. During the next ten years he never stopped working, appearing on stage, television, radio and film, making more than thirty movies in three years. Although primarily a star of comedy, Tognazzi was equally good in straight drama. In the early 1960s he concentrated on films, working for all the top Italian directors and co-starring with Italian and French stars like Fernandel, Catherine Spaak, Marina Vlady, Annie Girardot, Marcello Mastroianni, Michel Piccoli and Philippe Noiret. In 1973 he was one of the stars in the classic but controversial *La Grande Bouffe*, and some may recall his performance in Roger Vadim's *Barbarella* in 1968 with Jane Fonda. In the 1960s he began to direct some of his own films, including *Il Fischio al Naso* (1967) and *Sissignore* (1968) although to the best of my memory none was ever seen in Britain. His performance in Bertolucci's *The Tragedy of a Ridiculous Man* brought him the Best Actor award at the Cannes Film Festival, and he also deserved some recognition for his brilliant performance in the 1974

Max Wall

release *All My Friends*. Another of his films which reached this country starred Tognazzi as the French music-hall star 'Le Petomane', whose forte was the passing of musical wind! More recently, with the decline of the Italian film industry, Tognazzi made a triumphant return to the stage in the Comédie Française production of Pirandello's evergreen classic *Six Characters in Search of an Author*.

Primarily a star of the music-hall, **Max Wall**, who died at the age of 82 on 22 May 1990, in recent years showed his versatility by appearing, with great success, in Samuel Beckett's play *Waiting for Godot*. But the Wall we always affectionately remember is the Wall who created Professor Wallofski, the eccentric pianist and comic dancer who could make merely walking into a major comic experience. During his 65 years in show business of all kinds, Maxwell George Lorimer (to give him his real name) appeared on Broadway in the 1932 'Earl Carroll Vanities', in London's West End in a production of John Osborne's *The Entertainer* and on television. He also appeared in some ten films, including *Chitty Chitty Bang Bang*, *The Nine Ages of Nakedness*, *Jabberwocky*, the recent re-make of *The Hound of the Baskervilles*, *Little Dorrit*, *We Think the World of You* and *Strike It Rich*. He had many ups and downs during his career: after a period of obscurity, his popularity revived in the 1970s after his appearance in a one-man show *Aspects of Max Wall*. More recently he had not been getting any work and was living frugally in a small council flat. It was a sad ending for one of Britain's most inspired clowns and laughter-makers.

Stop Press: **Jean Arthur**, the reclusive star of the three Frank Capra classics, *Mr Deeds Goes to Town* (1936), *Mr Deeds Goes to Washington* (1939) and *You Can't Take It With You* (1938), died aged 90 on 19 June 1991, as did the 69-year-old **Joan Caulfield**, who, after her debut in *Duffy's Tavern* (1945), went on to make a score of films including *Dear Ruth* (1947), *Dear Wife* (1950), *The Rains of Ranchipur* (1955), *Buckskin* (1968) and *Pony Express Rider* (1976). (Extended biographies will appear in next year's *Film Review*.)

Bookshelf

A selection of the year's books on cinema

IVAN BUTLER

Alfred Hitchcock and the Making of ***Psycho***, Stephen Rebello; Marion Boyars, £14.95.

This engrossing book traces the history of Hitchcock's most famous film from its inception, as a book by Robert Bloch, to its triumphant release and aftermath. Every aspect of the work entailed in its production – finance, script, casting, design, photography, promotion, censorship evasion (with Hitchcock at his most cunning), promotion, critical reception and public acclaim – is covered in detail, based on intense research. Comments and anecdotes from stars, technicians, writers and others connected with the film are incorporated in the story, and not the least interesting part of the account involves the sidelights thrown on Hitchcock's working methods and on his character. Problems involved in achieving tricky effects (such as those in the notorious shower sequence and the killing of the detective) are described together with the secrets of their solution. This knowledge in no way detracts from their shock value – the impact of *Psycho* seems indestructible!

Appendices include career details of the cast, writers, technicians and others who worked on the film, including Bernard Herrmann who provided the wonderfully atmospheric score. Altogether, an essential addition to Hitchcockiana.

American Animated Films: The Silent Era, 1897–1929, Denis Gifford; McFarland, dist. Shelwing, £22.50.

This monumental example of painstaking documentation lists all available titles of animated films made in America during the silent years. It opens with three cartoons by J. Stuart Blackton (known later for many live-action films such as *The Clean Heart* and the British spectacle *The Glorious Adventure*) and closes with two Mickey Mouse episodes, *Plane Crazy* and *The Gallopin' Gaucho*, which were originally silent but released only after the advent of sound. Names of studios, animators and production companies are included, together with other relevant

details, and a 44-page index makes research easy. Just a glance down the long lists of titles provides entertainment. This is perhaps a book for the specialist, but for anyone interested in the history of animation it is an indispensable possession.

American Film Music, William Darby & Jack Du Bois; McFarland, dist. Shelwing, £41.25.

This year has seen a notable recognition of the part played by the composer in the creation of a film. In this large (600-page), handsome volume, lengthy essays are given on some fifteen major composers of American scores, and many others are more briefly discussed in separate sections on each decade from 1940. Other chapters deal with studio arrangements and foreign composers. An opening section covers the music specially written for 'silent' films, the first of these in all probability being a score by no less a composer than Camille Saint-Saëns in 1908 for *The Assassination of the Duc de Guise*. Full filmographies of the main entries are given. Particularly convenient is the large number of simply presented themes that can be picked out on the piano with one finger. Appendices include Academy Awards and a bibliography. A number of good stills and portraits complete a valuable reference book. (See also *The Composer in Hollywood*.)

Bad Girls of the Silver Screen, Lottie Da & Jan Alexander; Pandora, £15.95.

At first glance the main attraction of this large-format book may be the lavish, excellent and rare stills, but the accompanying text is of equal interest – a detailed, often amusing (though occasionally rather clumsily written) history of the white slaves, prostitutes, madams and gold-diggers who have passed across the cinema screens. Various scandals and sensations – not always of unchallenged authenticity – are also touched upon. It is a lightly feminist account that can be set beside other books dealing with

the influence of, and work by, women in films, with numerous touches of pleasantly acerbic wit – e.g. 'The heavyweight leading ladies – Crawford, Bette Davis, Vivien Leigh, Ingrid Bergman, Barbara Stanwyck – managed to avoid becoming stereotyped, and played themselves playing whatever role the occasion demanded.'

One small point: the captions might usefully have contained more names of the supporting players appearing in the stills.

Behind the Mask of Innocence, Kevin Brownlow; Jonathan Cape, £35.

Kevin Brownlow, author of one of the great tributes to the silent cinema, *The Parade's Gone By*, here explores the darker side of life as depicted on the screen during that momentous period. 'Sex', 'Crime', 'Drugs', 'Poverty' and 'Political Corruption' are among the chapter headings of his book, and each discusses the way in which real life was reflected in the movies of the time. Each section consists in essence of a general survey followed by analyses of relevant 'social' films. Included are many fascinating details of the individual films, such as the original (and surely strange) choice of George Fawcett to play Lillian Gish's young Chinese devotee in *Broken Blossoms*, before Richard Barthelmess was finally cast in the part. Among lighter moments, Jesse Lasky's comment on the comparative failure of the film version of the long-running play *Abie's Irish Rose* is worth perserving: 'I cannot understand why it didn't do phenomenal business,' he wrote, 'since the picture was every bit as bad as the play.'

At 579 pages, this book is beautifully produced, with outstandingly good stills and an excellent index, and is a serious and valuable study of a rarely treated aspect of the silent cinema.

British Cinema – The Lights that Failed, James Park; Batsford, £14.95.

The author has achieved a miracle of compression by surveying the British cinema scene from the earliest days to the Goldcrest fiasco in a book of under 200 pages, including many full-page photographs. The Goldcrest affair, with all its complications, is succinctly reported in only a dozen of those pages. The theme is the sad story of the way in which British filmmakers have achieved through the years a series of popular periods of success crowned with magnificent movies, only to sink back again. 'Too few filmmakers', the author says, 'have recognised that the argument for a British cinema could only begin when they showed a readiness to listen to people's dreams and nightmares, and play them back to audiences in exciting narratives that would enable those watching to know themselves a little better, and to feel a widening sense of possibility in the way they shaped their lives.' A ten-page appendix of exceptional interest contains a detailed analysis of *Dance with a Stranger* (1985), the film based on the Ruth Ellis case of 1955.

Classic Universal Filmscripts, Philip Riley; MagicImage Film Books, dist. Gazelle Book Services (Lancaster), £15.95, paperback.

Each volume of this interesting and important series, now available in this country, consists of a full facsimile shooting script of a silent or early sound period Universal film, mainly in the horror/fantasy category, together with a fascinating collection of stills, portraits, production photographs, newspaper articles and publicity material. These very rare scripts include *Dracula, Frankenstein, The Bride of Frankenstein, The Mummy* – and, for contrast, *Abbott and Costello Meet Frankenstein*. Careful and painstaking research has been aimed at producing as close an approximation as possible to the original film as presented on the screen. Perhaps the plum of the collection to date is the long-lost Lon Chaney 'vampire' film, *London After Midnight* (price in this case £27.95 hardback), which is not an actual facsimile but a reconstruction with stills and full titles; but all the volumes are part of a valuable series for both historian and early horror enthusiast.

The Composer in Hollywood, Christopher Palmer; Marion Boyars, £19.95.

It has been said that the test of good film music is that it should be unnoticeable – which is like saying the best jam is that which can't be tasted! Composers (in common with photographers and editors) have rarely been given their full share of appreciation for their part in the effectiveness of a film, yet one only has to imagine watching in complete silence the shower sequence in *Psycho* or the gradual approach of the fatal hour in *High Noon* to realise the value of the music of Bernard Herrmann and Dimitri Tiomkin respectively. The more welcome, therefore, is this excellent book, which studies in detail the work of

eleven leading composers of the great days of the Hollywood studios. Each article is accompanied by a photograph of the composer, together with a page from his score to a particular film. The author, who has written a number of books on musical subjects as well as arranging film scores, analyses a large number of famous examples in clear and non-technical language. He concludes his survey with a nostalgic and somewhat wistful glance back at the great days of film music: his book, together with the blessings of video, will do something at least to keep them alive.

The Continental Actress, Kerry Segrave & Linda Martin; McFarland, dist. Shelwing, £26.25.

A well-illustrated and -indexed handbook on the background and careers of European stars of the postwar era, together with filmographies and photographs. Forty-one actresses are represented, arranged chronologically under country of origin, and varying from the famous, such as Jeanne Moreau, Sophia Loren, Catherine Deneuve and Britt Ekland, to the lesser-known – Hanna Schygulla, Laura Antonelli and Fanny Ardant. This is a companion volume to the same authors' *The Post-Feminist Hollywood Actress*; useful and well researched, but unfortunately with the same irritating habit of jumping from forename to surname – see *Film Review 1990–1*.

A Darling of the Twenties, Madge Bellamy; Vestal Press, dist. Gazelle Book Services (Lancaster), £19.95.

Though few of her films are remembered today (*The Iron Horse*, perhaps, or *Mother Knows Best*) and even fewer appear on television (Bela Lugosi's *White Zombie*), Madge Bellamy was one of the brightest and most sparkling of the silent stars of the cinema – and also had a certain career in the theatre. Her autobiography is extraordinary in its frankness, invaluable as a picture of its period, and moving in the courage with which she faced the decline of her later years. Traumatic events such as her loss of the leading part in *Seventh Heaven* (indirectly because of her refusal to dirty her fingernails sufficiently to please director Frank Borzage in an earlier film), her bankruptcy after the 1939 Wall Street Crash, her sensational arrest after firing three revolver shots at a former lover, her extraordinary period of working as a shipyard welder – all these, in addition to a full account of her film career and her private life, are recounted with honesty, warmth and humour. Kevin Brownlow provides a long and sympathetic introduction: 'We look back on the silent era as a period of astonishing achievement,' he writes, 'but the Hollywood system had its victims. This is the dramatic and touching

history of one of them.' Madge Bellamy died of a long-standing heart complaint on 24 January 1990.

The book is attractively produced and contains a good filmography and many rare stills and portraits. One slip (which might have been spotted by an alert editor): Charles Frohman met his death in the sinking of the *Lusitania*, not the *Titanic*.

Deadly Illusions – Who Killed Jean Harlow's Husband?, Samuel Marx & Joyce Vanderveen; Century, £14.99.

The major (and even the minor) Hollywood scandals of the past have an apparently undying interest. The alleged suicide of Paul Bern shortly after his marriage to 'blonde bombshell' Jean Harlow in 1932 was one of the most notorious of these scandals, and one that gave rise to some of the most unsavoury 'revelations' of all time among the muckrakers. A close friend of Bern, Samuel Marx – ably assisted by his collaborator – has unravelled an extremely tangled skein of half-truth and whole-falsehood, and come up with a solution that seems totally convincing. The reader is drawn with an iron grip into the authors' engrossing and convincing investigations; and the astonishing conclusion provides a satisfying climax that any crime writer might envy.

Dick Tracy: America's Most Famous Detective, ed. Bill Crouch Jr; Plexus, £9.95.

Originally published to tie in with the Warren Beatty film, this brightly produced paperback consists mainly of a large number of extracts from Tracy strip cartoon features, but there is also an interesting brief account of his adventures on film, mainly during the thirties and forties. There are some good stills, and the cartoons themselves are reproduced with commendable crispness. Fun for the fans, and useful for the film buff.

Dustin Hoffman, Ronald Bergan; Virgin, £14.99.

'Frank' is nowadays an almost unavoidable cliché word when describing a show-business biography, generally indicating a plentiful injection of venom. Ronald Bergan does not attempt to gloss over the less attractive aspects of his subject – his 'Methodical' fussing over small details (often described as 'perfectionism') which can drive his directors and fellow artistes to distraction, his egotism, his occasional ruthlessness and lack of consideration for others, such as his treatment of an ageing and ailing Laurence Olivier during a scene in the making of *Marathon Man* (though in this case, the author points out, it seems that Hoffman was not aware of the true position). On balance, however, this is a warm and sympathetic study of a man of much humour, charm and generosity who, through determination and hard work, triumphed over considerable initial difficulties to achieve a position high among the stars.

The book contains many fascinating details of the eternal wheeling and dealing during the pre-production period of filmmaking, and fills in relevant facts of the careers of people with whom Hoffman worked. It is notably well written (except for a use of the horrible non-word 'unfraught') and is entertainingly witty throughout.

Elizabeth, Alexander Walker; Weidenfeld & Nicolson, £16.00.

Among the mass of material available on Elizabeth Taylor, this long and detailed book stands out as a major biography. As he does in his other 'Lives', Alexander Walker approaches his famous subject with a delicate balance of frankness and sympathy, concentrating largely on her personal life but with adequate treatment of the films themselves. The reference section is excellent: with source notes, detailed index, full chronology, and two fascinating pages on the star's 'marriage web'. Three generous sections of illustrations round off a book that should remain the standard work on Elizabeth Taylor for a long time to come.

Fade Out, Peter Bart; Simon & Schuster, £15.95.

Increasing interest has been shown lately in the commercial side of movie-making, in particular the high dramas that have erupted during the last decade or so, as evidenced by books such as *Indecent Exposure, Final Cut* and, from Britain, the vast volume on the history of Goldcrest Films, *My Indecision is Final* (also reviewed here). *Fade Out* deals with the 'calamitous final days of MGM' and is a year-by-year account (1983–8) of the regime of Frank Lablans and the activities of the somewhat mysterious 'Kirk' Kerkorian. Vividly and lucidly told, it is a sad but engrossing story of the disintegration of not just one but two famous American companies: MGM and United Artists, the latter founded in 1919 by such famous names as Douglas Fairbanks, Mary Pickford, Charles Chaplin and D. W. Griffith.

The Films of the Eighties, Douglas Brode; Virgin, £9.99.

The 'eighties saw the production of a number of notable films – for example, *The Elephant Man, Excalibur, Chariots of Fire, The Killing Fields, Amadeus, Hope and Glory*. Over one hundred of these – some very good, others not quite so good – are covered in this volume from the excellent 'The Films of . . .' series. The book opens

with a general introduction which is followed by an essay and cast-and-credits list for each film. The essays throughout are excellent, from both the informative and the critical point of view. As always in this series the illustrations are lavish and superbly reproduced. One criticism: the cast lists are in many cases disappointingly meagre.

At the end of the book is a complete list to date of this long-running Citadel series. These are now being made available in the UK in glossy paperback by Virgin Publishing, with additional titles published every month. The general standard is extremely high and a complete (or even near-complete) collection would form a valuable and attractive reference survey of the cinema (principally in the US) from its earliest days. Many of the 125 Citadel books have been covered in former editions of *Film Review*, and others will be reviewed as they appear.

The Films of Susan Hayward, Eduardo Moreno; Virgin, £9.99.

The name of Susan Hayward may not figure at the very top of the superstar hierarchy, but to countless filmgoers from the forties to the sixties she was one of those actresses whose performances *could not* be missed. Her eventful, determined climb to success, as well as her supremely courageous, indeed furious, two-year battle against the illness that finally killed her, are described here in one of the fullest and best of the Citadel reprints. Notable among the usual features is an unusually large Portrait Gallery extending over eighteen pages and followed by a unique section of photographs from her time as an advertising model. The lively, frank and affectionate text includes a list of 32 'cinematic mishaps' that she underwent, including execution in a gas chamber, harassment by a hyena and (a bitter irony) death from a brain tumour. Among the hundreds of illustrations are a couple of rare ones taken during her test for *Gone with the Wind*.

George Robey, James Harding; Hodder & Stoughton, £17.95.

Although the major share of this wholly delightful biography is, not unexpectedly, given over to Robey's work in music hall and theatre, due attention is paid to his work in the cinema – despite the fact that, as he himself said, it was not a medium he ever really enjoyed. Even so, he made a considerable number of films, especially if the shorts are included, from 1900 right up to the 1950s, when he appeared, at the age of 83, as Sam Weller in *The Pickwick Papers*. The silent features are apparently gone beyond recall, but *Chu Chin Chow* (1934) was shown quite recently on television and his cameo role as the dying Falstaff will last as long as Laurence Olivier's memorable *Henry V* (1944). Among the most unusual and

interesting of his film roles was that of Sancho Panza in *Don Quixote* with the famous opera singer Chaliapin in the title part: sadly, despite having the renowned G. W. Pabst as director, the film was a financial failure, mainly due to overrunning schedules.

James Harding has previously written an entrancing book on Jacques Tati (see *Film Review 1985–6*). This new biography is in every way its equal – in careful and detailed research, and above all for its enthusiasm, frankness and affection for its subject. Amongst numerous fascinating side issues is the story of the origin of the villainous Dr Fu Manchu and his creator Sax Rohmer – of interest to all horror-film addicts.

George Robey died in 1954, very soon after being knighted. The quiet, gentle last days of the great comedian are most movingly told.

***Gone with the Wind* on Film**, Cynthia Marylee Molt; McFarland, dist. Shelwing, £35.15.

For once the subtitle 'A Complete Reference' is undoubtedly justified. In a book of over 500 pages the authoress (who edited and wrote a periodical on *GWTW* for nearly ten years) has assembled an awe-inspiring mass of material on every aspect of the production. The first section describes in detail all the characters in the book and their translation into film; the second is a cast and crew list that (while not claiming to be absolutely conclusive) gives the names of many of the smallest parts and extras, together with 'Contenders' – those who tried but failed to obtain a share in the epic production. This is followed by full filmographies of all major and minor members of the cast and crew. Over 100 pages are given to detailed descriptions of costumes (together with an introductory account of the general fashions of the period), and other sections cover the sets, music and 'collectables'. A colossal annotated bibliography fills 150 pages, divided into 3835 separate items.

In dealing with this gargantuan amount of material the writer maintains an easy, lucid style; and the print size (except for the section on sets) is mercifully kind to the eyes. For every devotee this book is – it need hardly be said – a must.

Good Movie Guide, David Parkinson; Bloomsbury, £17.99.

The principle behind this very originally arranged guide is that, rather than looking upon each film as an individual entity, the viewer should be led from one 'good' one to another, and from there to others, covering in the journey a wide field of different approaches and discovering on the way forgotten pleasures in old favourites. In order to get the best out of this ingenious and quite complicated plan it is desirable to read carefully the explanatory notes before embarking on a series of interesting and at times surprising journeys. Headings throughout the book are arranged in alphabetical order and consist of names (stars, directors), film titles and rating symbols, and such widely varying subjects as – on one page only – Impersonation, Incest, Injustice and Insanity, or – on another – Pop Stars, Popes and Pot-pourri. There are complete lists of the main Oscar and BAFTA awards, with a brief description of each. In all, over 5000 films are represented. There is an excellent (and essential) index of film titles. A second index, of people and themes, is also useful to some extent but – perhaps inevitably – many headings are followed merely by lengthy columns of bare page numbers; anyone looking up films about Nazis, for instance, would have to hunt through about 120 pages to find a particular point of interest. This small point apart, it is a thoroughly entertaining and instructive survey, in the making of which the author must indeed, as he states, have seen in his 28 years 'more films than are good for him'.

The Great Combat Pictures, James Robert Parish; Scarecrow, dist. Shelwing, £35.65.

On his own this time, Mr Parish has compiled a 'Great Pictures' reference book on twentieth-century warfare, following the same lines as others in the series. The principal conflicts covered are World Wars I and II, Korea and Vietnam. A list of exclusions is given in the introduction, and among them are training service dramas. It is presumably for this reason that Carol Reed's *The Way Ahead* (retitled *Immortal Battalion* in the US) does not appear. This is regrettable: though a large part of the film deals with army training, combat is certainly featured in the later sequences, and the film – one of the finest war films – is an essential companion to *In Which We Serve* (Navy) and *One of Our Aircraft is Missing* (Air Force). Among other British films, *The Wooden Horse* and even *Dangrous Moonlight* (*Suicide Squadron* in the US) are present, but surprisingly not *The Way to the Stars*. Perhaps, however, these important movies will find their way into the inevitable *The Great Combat Pictures II*! A useful filmography conveniently sorts the titles into their respective wars, and a list of TV films is included. The usual painstaking research over such details as cast lists is well in evidence.

The Great Cop Pictures, James Robert Parish; Scarecrow, dist. Shelwing, £46.90.

Another 'Great Pictures' guide from the arch-compiler. As the title suggests, this volume concentrates on American cinema and TV. Production is well up to standard; many of the cast lists appear even fuller than usual, and the commentaries longer. Entries range from 1923 to 1989, becoming more numerous as the years pass. The 680-page volume includes a list of TV and radio series, a large bibliography on various aspects of the American police, a film chronology and some (but not many) good stills.

The Great Detective Pictures, James Robert Parish & Michael R. Pitts; Scarecrow, dist. Shelwing, £44.65.

The indefatigable Messrs. Parish and Pitts have produced this new addition to their valuable 'Great Pictures' series, and no doubt it will be followed by a supplementary volume in due course. It is well up to the standard of its forerunners, both in comprehensiveness and attractiveness, and covers more than 350 feature films as well as shorts, serials and TV movies. Notable are the very full cast lists and the lively commentaries. Agatha Christie TV titles are listed under her name.

As the authors make clear the word 'Great' refers to the specific genre and *not* to all the titles included: inevitably the Rathbone/Bruce updated travesties (with Holmes presumably over ninety years of age) have to be included. Silent films are included. The authors note that the first Holmes film, *Sherlock Holmes Baffled*, appeared around 1900, and give brief details of another, *Adventures of Sherlock Holmes* (1905, director J. Stuart Blackton) in which the entire action took place in only eight minutes!

The Great Movie Stars 3 – The Independent Years, David Shipman; Macdonald, £19.95.

David Shipman here brings his two former volumes of *The Great Movie Stars* up to date with an equally valuable collection of articles on over ninety actors and actresses of the present day. Apart from a complete filmography in each case (including important television productions), biographical details, photographs and critical judgements are provided. The latter are sometimes trenchant and refreshingly outspoken – see, for instance, the piece on Meryl Streep. He is always entertaining, and enlivens his pages with happily apt phrases such as his description of actor Nick Nolte turning up to be photographed and staring defiantly at the camera 'looking like an unmade bed'. A useful list is given of the names in the two former volumes: one is left wondering a little how many of the faces in the present collection (particularly among the men) will stand the test of time and remain as instantly recognisable as the earlier great stars.

The Hollywood Musical, Clive Hirschhorn; Pyramid, £19.99.

Reappearing under the Pyramid imprint, this is an updated and revised edition of the book from the Octopus studio history series (see *Film Review 1982–3*) and might be described as a splendid offshoot. A number of film titles have been added, bringing the contents up to date to 1990. Each film is provided with a still, a lively commentary, and lists of songs and leading players. A lengthy introduction points out the difficulty of defining the term 'musical', but the author is generous in his selection of films (they total, after all, nearly 4000) and also includes marginal films in three appendices. No fewer than five huge indexes complete this handsome volume, the reappearance of which with its new additions is very welcome.

Hooked, Pauline Kael; Marion Boyars, £14.95 (paperback).

Another mammoth volume of reviews from the indomitable American film critic covering some two hundred productions from 1985 to 1988, in 500 pages. Trenchant and lively as ever, they provide a splendidly varied collection of commentaries and information, so much so that – as I have mentioned before – it is a pleasure on occasion even to disagree with her. It may seem invidious to pick out one item among so many, but her review of *The Dead*, for instance, is both moving in itself and a worthy tribute to John Huston's hauntingly beautiful last film. Among the film articles is one on a book – *Final Cut* – telling the story of the making of the United Artists debacle, *Heaven's Gate*. Pauline Kael describes *Final Cut* as 'the only good that has ever come from the movie'; but the film does have its devotees who find much to admire in this sprawling though admittedly flawed masterpiece.

Hooked is excellently indexed. It is good to see from the publisher's catalogue that paperback editions of several of the critic's earlier books are to be reissued at £5.95 each.

How I Made a Hundred Movies in Hollywood and Never Lost a Dime, Roger Corman with Jim Jerome; Muller, £16.99.

Until a few years ago not very much was known about Roger Corman outside Hollywood; it was even difficult to obtain a photograph of him for a book. Now, however, he is well known as a maverick, and has been called, as he says, everything from 'King of the B's' to the 'Pope of Pop Cinema'. There is, however, more to his achievements than this, as he clearly reveals in this lively and enjoyable autobiography. He writes about his working methods and the wide variety of his interests, and gives details in particular about the series of Edgar Allan Poe films for which he is probably still best known. Inserted into his story are numerous entertaining anecdotes and comments from people with whom he was associated, such as Peter Fonda, Bruce Dern, Francis Coppola, Shelley Winters and Martin Scorsese. There are some interesting (but not very well reproduced) illustrations. A filmography and index would have been welcome.

The International Dictionary of Films and Filmmakers, Vol. 1, ed. Nicholas Thomas; St James Press, £60.00.

This enormous reference book, 1100 pages long and covering over 650 films from the US, the UK and most European countries, first appeared about five years ago under a slightly different title, but has been so much enlarged and embellished as to make it virtually a new work. As before, it contains full cast and credit lists for each film, a lengthy critical article and (particularly valuable because of its rarity), a very detailed list of relevant publications, both books and periodicals. All the articles have been updated, 150 more entries have been added, and the page and print sizes have been enlarged to make for easier reading. A major new attraction is the inclusion of 380 excellent stills. The emphasis is, naturally, on the more distinguished or historically important productions, but the contents are by no means limited to accepted 'masterpieces'; Lugosi's *Dracula* fits in quite comfortably with *Citizen Kane*. Whereas the earlier edition, for all its worthiness, was somewhat congested and appealed mainly to the serious student, this new one is for all lovers of the cinema, and essential for libraries. The four remaining volumes will appear in due course.

Two other reprints are announced for St James Press: *Dark City: Film Noir*; and *Cinema Sequels and Remakes, 1903–87* (see *Film Review 1989–90*).

John Wayne – Actor, Artist, Hero, Richard D. McGhee; McFarland, dist. Shelwing, £26.25.

This long book is one of the best to have appeared on one of the arch-superstars of the movies. It is not a straight chronological biography, but an examination of Wayne's career and film persona in the three main aspects indicated in the subtitle. Chapter headings such as Tragic, Comic, Ironic and Romantic Heroes, 'It's Going to Be All Right' and 'Your Country Needs You' indicate the general approach, and each subject is considered in depth. Numerous non-Wayne films are referred to in comparison or contrast. It is a scholarly, absorbing study, concluding with a full filmography.

Kenneth Williams, Michael Freedland; Weidenfeld & Nicolson, £15.00.

The 'Carry On' films were arguably the most popular comedies of their genre (in Britain, that is – America would have none of them) and Kenneth Williams was generally regarded as their brightest star. In this biography Michael Freedland has endeavoured, in his own words, to bring down the walls that surrounded Williams. Whether he has altogether succeeded may be open to question, but in all probability he guides us as close to the truth as we are likely to get. He writes sympathetically and fully, for instance, of Williams's sexual problems – perhaps more fully than is pleasant at times, but since so much of his conversation turned on this or on his 'anal complaints', his 'bum' and other (one would have thought) personal matters, such areas must have been difficult to avoid. Williams's more disagreeable characteristics – his petty meannesses, his frequent ingratitude towards friends and colleagues, his immature desire to shock, his rudeness to people who inadvertently displeased him, his childish misbehaviour to attract attention – are also recounted, and inevitably they become repetitious because they occurred so often. Against this, set out with equal frankness and fullness, are his professionalism, his capacity for commanding friendship, his wit and bookish intelligence, above all his brilliance in all forms of popular entertainment. The mystery of his death – accident or suicide? – is apparently not yet fully solved. Perhaps the kindest and truest words come from Sheila Hancock, who knew him well: 'I think the real Kenneth Williams was a lonely, sad, desolate individual.'

The Legend of Garbo, Peter Haining; W. H. Allen, £14.95.

For this finely produced, lavishly illustrated coffee-table book, Peter Haining has assembled over thirty articles and memoirs, including a long essay from Garbo herself. His list of contributors is indeed an impressive one, opening with a brief selection of tributes from stars no longer living, such as John Gilbert, Clark Gable, Ramon Novarro, and John and Lionel Barrymore. In the main section are such famous names as Victor Seastrom, Pola Negri, Val Lewton, Cecil Beaton, Laurence Olivier, Rouben Mamoulian, Tallulah Bankhead, Clarence Brown and George Cukor. In many cases the author adds a brief, interesting introduction. The comments, opinions and stories, personal and professional, are many and varied; and if the famous (and at times – dare one say – somewhat tedious) mystique/enigma/legend remains inviolate, this is only to be expected in a book that is described by the author himself as 'not . . . a sensational or prying work – more a memorial to a great actress'.

The illustrations are superbly reproduced, but the still said to be from *The Temptress* resembles neither the stars nor the situation as they appeared in that film – it was taken perhaps from a scrapped version? Two uncaptioned photographs, however, facing pp. 100 and 278, do show Garbo in *The Temptress* as she actually was.

Lethal Innocence – The Cinema of Alexander Mackendrick, Philip Kemp; Methuen, £17.99.

When Alexander Mackendrick retired from directing (around 1968) and went to teach film in Los Angeles, he had made only nine feature films. These included, however, three of Ealing's finest successes, *The Man in the White Suit*, *Mandy*, and *The Ladykillers*, and, from America, *The Sweet Smell of Success* and a brave if not wholly successful attempt to capture the unique quality of Richard Hughes's haunting novel, *A High Wind in Jamaica*. In this splendid book Philip Kemp sensitively and perceptively covers Mackendrick's career in detail, with each film examined in long essays that are fine examples of critical analysis. Fascinating practical details (such as the origin of the man in the white suit's 'bubble bubble, high drip, low drip' patent machinery) blend with examination of the social implications and underlying themes of the films as a whole.

In the chapter on *The Ladykillers* the author refers to the 'circular nightmare' that encloses the British film *Dead of Night*, but, in company with other writers on this famous collection of the macabre, he has evidently missed the crucial brief shot towards the very end that reveals that *this* time round what is about to happen is no simple nightmare, but a terrifying reality.

A filmography of exemplary fullness and three good sections of illustrations complete an important and engrossing study of one of the cinema's most memorable directors.

The Man Between, Nicholas Wapshott; Chatto & Windus, £18.00.

A major book on Carol Reed has been a long time coming, but this biography is well worth the wait. Reed himself does not appear for over forty pages, as Nicholas Wapshott paints a vivid picture of the character and career of the flamboyant Victorian/Edwardian theatrical manager Sir Herbert Tree, Reed's father by his mistress Mary Reed, a most attractively drawn character in the book. It is an essential introduction, as Tree's influence on his son lasted, if inconspicuously, through his life. Reed's own character is a far more complex one, as becomes clear from the author's painstaking research into the contradictions, for instance, between his sympathetic direction of actors and children and his occasional ruthlessness; between his claim to be mainly a technician, and the artistry found in much of his work. The detailed descriptions of the making of his three masterpieces, *Odd Man Out*, *The Third Man* and *The Fallen Idol*, make engrossing reading, and his later fall from critical esteem (despite the huge success of *Oliver!*) form a moving close to the story.

There are some interesting illustrations and an excellently full index.

The MGM Story, John Douglas Eames & Ronald Bergan; Pyramid, £19.95.

In *Film Review 1976–7* this was enthusiastically described as a 'stupendous cornucopia of nostalgia' in which every one of MGM's 1705 films was listed, with each being given a cast and credit list, a still, and a brief and frequently witty commentary. The book is now reissued in a revised and updated form (bringing the total number of films, up to 1988, to 1774) and looks more handsome than ever. The illustrations appear to have lost little, if any, of their previous clarity, and the binding is sounder and more attractive. It is perhaps a pity that two errors pointed out in the original have not been corrected: first, *Kind Lady* was based on Hugh Walpole's short story 'The Silver Mask' and not 'The Silver Casket'; second, the still from Garbo's *The Temptress* shows a scene (and an actor, H. B. Warner) that never appeared in the final print. However, the book is packed with facts, interest, entertainment and fond memories; the advice given in the earlier review can be repeated: reinforce the bookshelf if necessary, but do find room on it for this unique – if weighty – record of a great period.

The Modern Horror Film, John McCarty; Virgin (Citadel series), £9.99.

This glossy paperback starts with *The Curse of Frankenstein* (1957) and ends with Ken Russell's *Lair of the White Worm* (1988), covering in all fifty classics of the genre. Hammer Films is generously treated, as are Ken Russell, with four films, and Roman Polanski, with five films and his *Macbeth* (1971), which McCarty undoubtedly views for its horror content rather than its poetical. As he says, with such a wide field the selection must be personal (for example, De Palma's 1973 *Sisters* is included, but not his much more horrifying *Carrie*), and there are a number of entries, such as Russell's *The Devils* (1971), which he admits are not horror films in the traditional sense. The text is crisp and incisive and includes many points of historical interest on the film under examination. The illustrations are profuse and generally excellent: there are, however, two egregious errors – in the *Repulsion* still it is not Carol's friend Colin forcing himself into her flat, but the fantasised rapist creeping through the bedroom door; and in the *Dance of the Vampires* picture Alfred (played

by Polanski himself) is certainly not admiring the vampire and his victim – in fact he does not appear in the still at all.

The Motion Picture Guide, 1990 Annual; Cinebooks, dist. Bowker-Saur, £95.

This magnificent record of the films of 1989 is the fifth volume published as a follow-up to the massive twelve-volume encyclopedia reviewed in *Film Review 1987–8*. It covers 557 films from over forty countries, and while resembling the earlier volumes in general, it has the considerable advantage of larger print. It also includes many stills, together with several full-page illustrations to introduce the various sections. A few films, mainly foreign-language productions, are treated briefly, but the majority of the reviews are very detailed and quite frequently extend beyond short essays beyond the particular movie being discussed. A 'v' indicates video availability, the number of which must make many mouths water in the UK.

A major feature is the massive illustrated obituary, with nearly sixty pages of entries including players, directors, composers, writers, cinematographers and others, no matter how minor their contributions may have been, and in many cases giving long lists of their films. Five indexes (of country, star rating, genre, family viewing recommendation, and an enormous one of names) round off a volume which no self-respecting library should be without even if, sadly, the price may put it beyond the reach of many private buyers.

Motion Picture Players' Credits, Jeffrey Oliviero; McFarland, dist. Shelwing, £108.75.

This gargantuan tome of just over 1000 pages covers 'Worldwide Performers of 1967 through 1980, with Filmographies of Their Entire Careers, 1905–1983'. About 15,000 artistes are included, and the term 'worldwide' is scarcely an exaggeration. Births, deaths and brief personal descriptions are supplied together with, in many cases, present addresses. Important American (and a few British) television credits are listed. To have such a mass of information crammed into a single volume is obviously a boon beyond belief – even though the price is similarly incredible – and within its stated limits it is surely the most complete reference book as yet available.

A word of advice: it is helpful to have a good magnifying-glass handy when using the book. The print is microscopic – though this is a small inconvenience compared to the overall convenience of having so comprehensive a reference source readily accessible.

The Movie List Book, Richard B. Armstrong & Mary Willems Armstrong; McFarland, dist. Shelwing, £22.50.

An original reference guide to film themes,

settings and series, with 376 entries arranged alphabetically from 'Abominable Snowman' to 'Zombies'. At first glance the headings may seem to suggest a somewhat jumbled collection ('Acronyms in Title', 'Henry Aldrich', 'Baseball', 'Dracula', 'Having Babies Series', 'Nuns', 'Elvis Presley', 'Plants', 'Ellery Queen', 'Twins', 'Vietnam') but soon their very variety becomes intriguing, and they do indeed fill a void which may hamper researchers anxious to trace contrasts or similarities between different subjects or classes of films. Complete lists of series, such as 'East Side Kids', 'Hopalong Cassidy', 'Carry On . . .', etc., are useful as checklists, and a quick guide to 'Long Running Times', 'Television Series', 'Reunion Movies' or 'Strippers' may help specialist researchers or quiz masters.

The Musical Worlds of Lerner and Loewe, Gene Lees; Robson Books, £16.95.

Well written, well produced and well researched, this 'double biography' (of Alan Jay Lerner and Frederick Loewe) is of equal interest to the filmgoer and the musical theatre enthusiast. Pride of place, not unexpectedly, goes to *My Fair Lady* and *Camelot*, but there is much also on the creation and fortunes of other productions such as *Brigadoon*, *Paint Your Wagon*, *Gigi* and *Coco*. There are frank (on occasion devastatingly frank) accounts of working with the famous artists encountered by Lerner and Loewe, and also on the sometimes turbulent relationship between the two partners themselves. One fault is the paucity of quick reference material; a book that is claimed (not without justification) to be 'definitive' should surely include at least a joint chronology. Otherwise this is a useful and entertaining account.

My Indecision Is Final, Jake Eberts & Terry Ilott; Faber & Faber, £17.50.

This 650-page book deals in painstaking detail with the rise and fall of Goldcrest Films – the great hope of the British cinema between 1977 and 1987. Though its reign lasted only about a decade it was involved with the production of such varied and notable films as *Chariots of Fire*, *Gandhi*, *The Killing Fields*, *Hope and Glory*, and *The Dresser*; and with TV features such as *The Far Pavilions* and the 'Robin of Sherwood' series. It collected nineteen Oscars and numerous other awards.

What might at first seem a mass of intractable material – involved accounts of board meetings, financial deals, executive rivalry, transactions with leading directors and stars – is made clear and easy to follow by a highly original method of presentation. The story is approached from two angles: firstly from the personal and inevitably partial viewpoint of Jake Eberts, Goldcrest's founder and moving spirit; and secondly from that of journalist Terry Ilott, editor throughout the period of the trade paper *Screen International*, who provides an objective running commentary throughout, together with interviews from many of the people involved, such as David Puttnam, Sir Richard Attenborough and Sandy Lieberson. A useful cast list of key personalities and companies helps to keep the reader on the right track throughout a journey of interest – and often dramatic excitement – for student, historian and ordinary film enthusiast.

Nancy Reagan, Kitty Kelley; Bantam Press, £16.99.

The film career of Nancy Davis (a.k.a. Reagan) may not have achieved the heights of stardom, and forms only a minor part of this widely publicised biography, but Kitty Kelley's account, well written and fairly balanced, is probably as full as any that is likely to appear. Nancy Davis did in fact appear in eleven feature films, two of which achieved one critical 'star'. Mervyn LeRoy, William A. Wellman and Curtis Bernhardt (all omitted from the index) were among her directors. Glenn Ford, Barbara Stanwyck, Ava Gardner, Cyd Charisse, Ray Milland and Lew Ayres were among those appearing in her cast lists, together with Ethel Barrymore, Fredric March, Gary Cooper – and Gene Kelly, in an episodic film entitled *It's a Big Country*, which was described as 'showing the glory of being an American citizen'. Her only film with Ronald Reagan (*Hellcats in the Navy*) received notices varying from 'satisfactory' to 'flimsy jingoistic potboiler'. Remarks from those who worked with her ranged from 'delightful to work with' and 'beautiful to direct' to 'wooden' and 'she just wasn't star material'.

In a book published in 1974, entitled *Star Quality – Great Actors and Actresses of Hollywood*, her photograph appears with others in the section headed 'Star Gallery'. This seems generous treatment, and certainly nothing in Kitty Kelley's thorough account would justify it.

1939 – The Year in Movies, Tom Flannery; McFarland, dist. Shelwing, £30.

The 'last year of peace' was a high spot in the history of the cinema, with films such as – to name but a handful – *Dark Victory, Destry Rides Again, Of Mice and Men, The Wizard of Oz, Stage Coach, Mr Smith Goes to Washington, Goodbye Mr Chips, The Stars Look Down* and, of course, *Gone with the Wind*. It was an excellent idea to gather some of them, major and minor, into a single volume and provide each with cast-and-credit lists, synopsis and notes. Unfortunately, in too many cases the cast lists are very skimpy. Anyone sufficiently interested

in the period to obtain the book would surely want to be told not only who was in the cast, but also the parts they played, particularly in the case of the smaller-scale films on which details are not so readily available elsewhere. Academy Awards are provided in an appendix.

No Guts, No Glory, Whitney Stine; Virgin, £12.99.

It must be fairly difficult nowadays to find a fresh angle from which to write a book on Bette Davis. Whitney Stine however achieves this in his record of a long series of personal conversations (rather than interviews) with the star whom he had admired from childhood, and on whom he had already written a biography, *Mother Goddam*. All the famous feuds reappear – with Miriam Hopkins, Joan Crawford and others – together with comments, favourable or cuttingly unfavourable, on dozens of well-known people, from George Arliss to Maggie Smith. Davis was really fond, the author states, of only four of her co-stars – Olivia de Havilland, Mary Astor, Anne Baxter and Gena Rowlands. The men appear to have come off slightly better. It is an enjoyable few-holds-barred account of her eventful, often stormy life. The title is taken from a motto embroidered on one of her cushions.

Bette Davis died from cancer on 6 October 1989; Whitney Stine, by then her friend, died of a heart attack five days later.

Norma Shearer, Gavin Lambert; Hodder & Stoughton, £17.95.

The lure of old-time Hollywood seems inexhaustible, and this splendid biography will surely arouse interest even in those whose knowledge of the late silent/early sound period can at best be only second-hand. Norma Shearer was determinedly a survivor, overcoming physical shortcomings to become one of the most popular, glamorous and accomplished stars of the time. She married the young Irving Thalberg – 'wonder-boy' head of production first of Universal, then of MGM – incurring the envy of Joan Crawford and others, and after his death formed relationships with film notables as dissimilar as Mickey Rooney and George Raft.

Gavin Lambert tells her story with a mixture of sympathy and cool appraisal. Of equal interest are the many and varied details he gives of the world in which she lived. A large number of the stories he relates may be familiar, but he gathers them together in a colourful tragi-comic pageant, correcting numerous publicity-engendered myths, and revealing carefully closeted skeletons. The book is handsomely produced and printed, well indexed and lavishly illustrated.

Order in the Universe – The Films of John Carpenter, Robert C. Cumbow; Scarecrow, dist. Shelwing, £22.15.

John Carpenter is probably best known for the apparently endless *Halloween* series (No. 5, the last mentioned here, receives fairly drastic treatment from the author), but he also directed such well-known horror-sci-fi movies as *Someone's Watching Me!, The Fog, Christine* and the early, low-budget but engaging and witty outer-space comedy-thriller *Dark Star*. His untypical bio-pic *Elvis* achieved high ratings in America. The films are examined in depth with interesting references to other directors. A full filmography, some notes from a talk with the director, and a reasonable number of stills round off this nicely produced book, no. 23 in the Filmmakers series edited by Anthony Slide.

Out of Focus – David Puttnam in Hollywood, Charles Kipps; Century, £14.99.

The story of David Puttnam's tempestuous months in Hollywood during the late eighties is excitingly told by Charles Kipps, features editor of *Variety*, with personal knowledge of the events he relates. Puttnam's professional relationships and confrontations with Columbia Pictures and its owner the Coca-Cola Company were turbulent, to put it mildly, and caught up in the turbulence were such famous Hollywood names as Dustin Hoffman and Warren Beatty. The book's subtitle, *Power, Pride and Prejudice*, is an apt comment. Studio politics and business are often involved, but the author whisks the reader through them with great zest and reasonable clarity despite the large cast of characters, from the arrival of the idealistic, acclaimed British producer of *Chariots of Fire* and *The Killing Fields* to the grim warning in the final sentence of the book: '*Never* hire a studio chief who needs a visa to work in California.'

The Passionate Life of Bette Davis, Lawrence J. Quirk; Robson Books, £15.95.

There are enough 'revelations' here to justify the slightly sensational title, but this biography (the fullest to date) is much more than a mere succession of scandals. It is a full, uncompromising, well-balanced and eminently readable account of the life and career of one of the most famous and glittering of all film stars. The films themselves are dealt with in detail and Bette Davis's performances in them analysed and criticised fairly and frankly. On the personal side her kindnesses and cruelties, generosity and pettiness, unprofessional tantrums and professional skills are described fairly and frankly by an author who has known and written about her for over forty years. Her famous feuds – with Joan Crawford, Warner Brothers, Errol Flynn, Robert Montgomery and (above all) Miriam Hopkins – are here, as are the tensions and strains that so often plagued the sets on which she was performing. In the final analysis it is those performances (fortunately preserved and now readily available on video) on which her reputation rests and will remain secure for long to come.

(Among the many illustrations in the book is a shot on the set of *Old Acquaintance* of Miss Davis and Miss Hopkins cuddling each other affectionately; the author warns us not to be fooled by this apparent friendliness – but he need not have worried; a close examination of the photograph amusingly reveals the truth in their expressions!)

Past Tense – The Cocteau Diaries, Volume II, Jean Cocteau; Methuen, £18.50.

This attractively presented book deals with the year 1953 – an important one for anyone interested in the cinema, as it covers the author's Presidency of the Cannes Film Festival. Not unexpectedly, Cocteau has some trenchant remarks to make on the general conduct of the occasion, the manners of some of the visitors, the resentment, rivalry and – as he underlines in talking with Orson Welles – the sheer hatred that is aroused.

Among the films shown that year were Walt Disney's *Peter Pan* ('Delighted by its grace and surprising technical achievements'), Alfred Hitchcock's *I Confess* ('. . . at least told by a *storyteller*, a great director'), Graham Greene's *The Heart of the Matter* ('. . . a grim bore, which is surprising from Graham Greene after films like *Brighton* [sic] and *The Fallen Idol*'), Clouzot's *The Wages of Fear*, and Jacques Tati's *Monsieur Hulot's Holiday*, about which he is surprisingly dismissive. An amusing comment is that on Edward G. Robinson, one of the judges at the Festival, who 'the other day was trying so hard to understand the French subtitles that he didn't realise the film was in English' – unfortunately the title of the film in question is not revealed.

The Cannes Festival fills only a minor part of this very enjoyable book, but the rest of the Diary (which contains much about Picasso, Jean Marais, François Mauriac, Salvador Dali and others) is full of human interest, written with the lively, sharp and at times acerbic wit to be expected from this charismatic, multi-talented 'poet, playwright, novelist, film maker and artist'.

Included are several of Cocteau's sketches and a useful list of works.

Remembering Peter Sellers, Graham Stark; Robson Books, £14.95.

Peter Sellers has on occasion been given rather a rough ride in print since his death. This affectionate collection of memories by a fellow actor and friend of many years does much to redress the balance. It may be regarded as a lightweight book (as the absence of an index despite blank pages being available seems to indicate) but it is full of charm, humour and interest. It may indeed present the most revealing portrait of Sellers that has yet appeared, and is also full of new, often hilarious stories of the hazards of filmmaking, as well as containing one almost incredible childhood coincidence. The author, known as an accomplished photographer as well as an actor in some ninety films, has included a generous number of rare illustrations.

There are a few comparatively inoffensive misspellings, such as Richard Burton's appearance in the film *Beckett* and the naming (in an illustration) of the famous Parisian transvestite club as the 'Carousel', but the grammatical howler in the caption to the lower photograph facing page 29 should have been spotted by an attentive editor.

Renoir on Renoir, Jean Renoir, trans. Carol Volk; Cambridge University Press, £10.95.

Jean Renoir was one of the more articulate exponents of his own work, and this large collection of 'Interviews, Essays and Remarks' presents a fascinating and instructive account of his views and theories as writer and director, in addition to many practical details of the making of individual films. The interviews, which form the greater part of the book, come from the leading French magazine *Cahiers du cinéma* and from television. Among the interviewers are Jacques Rivette and François Truffaut. Of equal interest is the third main section, consisting of short talks by Renoir on twenty of his productions, intended to be used as introductions to a retrospective screening of the films on television – an event that apparently never came to pass.

The book is fully illustrated with stills, frame enlargements and other photographs, and also includes a full filmography.

Richard Harris – A Sporting Life, Michael Feeney Callan; Sidgwick & Jackson, £14.99.

This first full-length life of Richard Harris is a good, workmanlike biography which preserves a nice balance between the actor and the roisterer. What is arguably his greatest performance, as the rugby player in *This Sporting Life*, came fairly early in his career, but his range throughout has been adventurously wide: from Cain in *The Bible* to a whaler in *Hawaii* (concerning which he remarked of his co-star Julie Andrews that rarely if ever had he experienced such hatred for a person); from *Cromwell* to *A Man Called Horse*; from *Maigret* in a TV film to King Arthur in the film version of *Camelot* – a role he created on stage. His co-star in *This Sporting Life* was Rachel Roberts, then the wife of Rex Harrison, who later married Harris's ex-wife Elizabeth (née Rees-Williams). Harris spoke in 1966 of his regard for John Huston, and said of his part as Cain in Huston's *The Bible* (taking up six of the film's 175 minutes), 'I think it's the best thing I've ever done. I really do.'

Michael Callan well catches the flamboyance of his subject's colourful character in this book, which concludes with a good filmography and list of stage appearances.

Robert Ryan, Franklin Jarlett; McFarland, dist. Shelwing, £22.50.

It is extraordinary that comparatively little has been written about this fine and sensitive actor, who was able to play hero or villain with equal ease and conviction. He could be described as king of the *film noir* (with fourteen films in the genre to his credit), but could also give very different and unforgettable performances such as Claggart in *Billy Budd* and, towards the end of his life, Larry Slade in Eugene O'Neill's *The Iceman Cometh*. Among his stage appearances were Antony in *Antony and Cleopatra* with Katharine Hepburn, and Coriolanus in a production by John Houseman. In addition he visited England to give an electrifying portrayal of Tyrone in O'Neill's *Long Day's Journey Into Night* at the Nottingham Playhouse – the first time, he said, the British had ever seen the part played by an American-Irishman. He followed this with *Othello*, which, however, was not deemed so successful. Finally, he is in all probability the only film star who founded a school: together with his wife Jessica he opened the Oakwood elementary school in North Hollywood (on liberal or, in his words, 'watered-down progressive' principles) in 1951, and it still flourishes today. All this and more is fully recounted in this well-written and well-illustrated biography, which also includes a splendid 90-page annotated and critical filmography.

The Rock and Roll Movie Encyclopedia of the 1950s, Mark Thomas McGee; McFarland, dist. Shelwing, £19.50.

A welcome reference book for the enthusiast, providing each film with an article covering its history, musical content, critical reception, cast and credits. Elvis Presley, not unexpectedly, figures prominently, as does Bill Haley (and his Comets). There are two original and useful appendices – a Song–Film List placing each song in its film, and a Performer–Song List doing the same with the original singers and musicians. Plenty of illustrations, comprising both stills and publicity reproductions.

Ronald Colman, R. Dixon Smith; McFarland, dist. Shelwing, £26.25.

A very likeable biography of a very likeable actor – aptly described in the book's subtitle as 'Gentleman of the Cinema'. The author follows Colman's career in straightforward fashion, film by film from the earliest days; the full cast and credit lists are integrated into the text in their rightful place instead of being lumped together at the end, thus saving the reader from having to jump from place to place in order to check some particular point – a welcome innovation. Each film is given a full synopsis, together with production and other details. Well illustrated, with a foreword by Colman's friend and fellow actor, Brian Aherne.

Russ Meyer – The Life and Films, David K. Frasier; McFarland, £30.

However little one might feel inclined to spend an afternoon in the company of Russ Meyer's sub-softporn movies there is no denying that they form part of the widely varied world of the cinema – if only because of the millions of dollars earned by such anti-masterpieces as *The Immoral Mr Teas*; *Cherry, Harry and Raquel*; *Faster, Pussycat! Kill! Kill!* and *Vixen* (followed by *Supervixens* and – ultimately – *Beneath the Valley of the Ultravixens*). The bulk of the book is arranged as a series of 1148 brief entries dealing with actresses, reviews, censorship, production notes, videos etc. These are followed by extensive filmographies. There are numerous illustrations – few of these are of a quality to attract the average filmgoer to a Russ Meyer screening.

Schrader on Schrader, and Other Writings, ed. Kevin Jackson; Faber & Faber, £12.99.
Scorsese on Scorsese, ed. David Thompson & Ian Christie; Faber & Faber, £5.99.
Taxi Driver, Paul Schrader; Faber & Faber, £5.99.
***The Comfort of Strangers** and Other Screenplays*, Harold Pinter; Faber & Faber, £7.99.

These books have been issued as an interlinked quartet, with Paul Schrader as the main thread. He wrote the scripts of *Taxi Driver*, *Raging Bull* and *The Last Temptation of Christ*, all directed by Martin Scorsese; Harold Pinter wrote the script of *The Comfort of Strangers*, directed by Paul Schrader.

Schrader on Schrader, and Other Writings consists of four lengthy interviews conducted by Kevin Jackson on his life, work and opinions, together with a collection of his critical writings between 1969 and 1971. Of particular interest among the latter are his *Notes on Film Noir*, his brief (and condemnatory) review of Peter Fonda's *Easy Rider* and his essay on Rossellini's atypical and strangely haunting *The Rise of Louis XIV*.

For *Scorsese on Scorsese* the editors have skilfully blended interviews, articles and a series of three *Guardian* Lectures given at the National Film Theatre in 1987 into a smoothly running account of his life and work, full of details of the making of his films, his views, ambitions, setbacks and

successes, all told with an engaging frankness and modesty. It also contains a thirty-page chapter on the controversial *The Last Temptation of Christ*. An introduction is provided by Michael Powell, whose influence on the younger director was considerable, and whose films and advice are referred to on several occasions.

Taxi Driver is the script (with stills) of one of the most innovative and discussed films of its year. The screenplay is preceded by an interview between Schrader and Scorsese recorded in 1982.

Harold Pinter's *The Comfort of Strangers* is followed in the same volume by his *Reunion, Turtle Diary* and the as yet unmade *Victory*.

Both *Taxi Driver* and *The Comfort of Strangers* are set out in the clear and easy-to-read form of other Faber Screenplays. The four books taken together present a valuable addition to the library of modern cinema; it is difficult to believe that *Taxi Driver* was in fact made fourteen years ago, in 1976.

Screen World, 1990, John Willis; Muller, £16.99.

This long-running reference book makes its welcome 41st appearance with even more information than usual crammed into its glossy pages. No synopses are here, no comment, no criticism, no opinions (except perhaps obliquely in the handful of photographs of Outstanding New Actors). Apart from a section of brief biographical notes, a list of past and current Academy Awards, an obituary and a huge index, all its 270-odd pages are devoted to covering hundreds of films of the period with photographs (1000 in all) and the fullest cast lists obtainable. An essential data bank of the American cinema year.

Second Feature, John Cocchi; Virgin, £12.99.

Anyone turning the first pages of this glossy paperback on the history of the B-picture will be invited to a feast of nostalgia by a parade of large photographs of the main titles of small studios familiar to all slightly older filmgoers – Monogram, Invincible, Republic, Mascot and others – and further tempted by a glimpse of the vast collection of rare stills and portraits. The book, however, is of equal value as a reference work, containing as it does informative paragraphs on several hundred films, arranged chronologically under such headings as Comedies and Dramas, Westerns, Musicals etc, and extending from 1929 to the late 1970s. Some of the titles included as second features are surprisingly prestigious, and the number of famous names appearing in them is impressive. One could have wished for fuller actual cast lists rather than the somewhat abbreviated catalogue of names – but that might

have necessitated saving space on the illustrations, and nobody, surely, would agree to such an exchange.

This is an original 'Citadel' book, and one of the best.

Silent Portraits, Anthony Slide; Vestal Press, dist. Gazelle Book Services (Lancaster), £19.95.

This superb and beautifully produced book of photographs of the stars (and many supporting players) from the silent cinema is not only a feast of nostalgia for those who can remember those great days, but also a treat for anyone sharing the growing interest in a vital part of the past history of the cinema. Tony Slide, expert on film history, one-time editor of the fondly-remembered periodical *The Silent Picture* and longtime contributor to this annual, has collected an astonishing variety of over 500 portraits. Thumbing through the 276 pages (not 208 as the back-cover blurb ungenerously says) in search of even a lesser-known player, one is continually delighted at how complete his coverage is. Each photograph is accompanied by a brief biography and a list of important films. These, together with a silent picture bibliography, make the book an invaluable reference source.

In the author's notes we are disarmingly made aware – without any doubt – of his personal preferences (on Mae Marsh: 'Without question, the greatest dramatic actress of the silent era . . .') and also, occasionally, of those regarded with slightly less affection.

Speaking of Silents, William M. Drew; Vestal Press, dist. Gazelle Book Services (Lancaster), £19.95.

In this handsome, large-format book William Drew presents ten lengthy autobiographical essays on ten 'First Ladies of the Screen' derived from personal interviews. The stars concerned are Madge Bellamy (see also *A Darling of the Twenties*, reviewed here), Eleanor Boardman, Leatrice Joy, Laura La Plante, May McAvoy, Patsy Ruth Miller, Colleen Moore, Esther Ralston, Blanche Sweet and Lois Wilson. He has very skilfully drawn out the varying personalities of his subjects, and the result is a highly enjoyable collection of frank, forthright and frequently amusing memoirs from ladies who are certainly no longer in the first flush of youth, but whose recollections are as bright and sharp as ever. The book is crammed with fascinating stills and portraits – among them a remarkable one of May McAvoy driving a Roman chariot, in a scene cut from the release print of *Ben-Hur* owing to the film's length. (She was injured while filming this scene, fortunately not seriously.)

As Charles Buddy Rogers (who married Mary Pickford in 1936) remarks: 'Those who haven't had the good fortune to be around during the silent era of the movies may wish they had been born in better times after reading these fascinating and revealing interviews with the ladies of the silent screen.'

Stages, Norman Lloyd; Scarecrow, dist. Shelwing, £24.40.

Though working largely as an actor and director in the theatre or on TV, Norman Lloyd also appeared in a number of films, including Hitchcock's *Saboteur* and *Spellbound*, and Chaplin's *Limelight*. (In the first he had the famous fall from the Statue of Liberty.) He also became associated with many well-known Hollywood figures, and the book contains special sections on Chaplin, Renoir and Lewis Milestone as well as much on Hitchcock. This is an interesting volume in the Directors Guild Oral History series: the 'questions', unobtrusively asked by Francine Parker, are less numerous than in other books in the series, which makes for easier reading. Mr Lloyd's replies are frank, detailed and generous. One interesting small item is that Chaplin considered producing a film from Horace McCoy's novel *They Shoot Horses, Don't They?*. It is tantalising to imagine what the result would have been.

Stars of the Screen, Don MacPherson, Julie Welch, Louise Brody; Conran Octopus, £12.99.

Though the names and faces of the stars represented here may be familiar, many of the photographs and stills are not – and even those that are have been so beautifully reproduced as to give fresh pleasure. As indicated by the chapter headings, the period covered extends from the Silent Era (rather shabbily treated, with only nine entries), through the Studio Years, the War Years, the Fifties, Sixties and Modern Times, finishing up with Kelly McGillis and Harrison Ford. The photographs are accompanied by an intelligent and informative text, providing a brief biography in each case. Altogether this forms a worthy addition to the Conran Octopus series of glossy portrait albums.

Terry-Thomas . . . Tells Tales, Terry-Thomas with Terry Daum; Robson Books, £14.95.

In a moving epilogue, Terry Daum describes how in 1983 Terry-Thomas called on him to help in writing the story of his life: 'some years have elapsed since he dictated it to me,' he says, 'but I have not updated it. These were Terry's tales, as he told them . . .' The result is a worthy memorial to one of the most charming and best-loved 'cads' in movie history. It sparkles with good stories of his famous film career, and in its later pages glows with the courage he

showed in facing the Parkinson's Disease that so cruelly struck him down. His own favourite of his films was the American *How to Murder Your Wife*, but to many his early British films of the 1950s will be equally memorable.

A list of titles is provided, but unfortunately no index.

Those Fabulous Serial Heroines, Buck Rainey; Scarecrow, dist. Shelwing, £44.65.

It is only rarely that Scarecrow film books appear in a large-page format, but its use is certainly justified here – a big and beautiful volume which is surely the definitive reference work on the great serial queens (and princesses) of the silent and early sound periods. Each entry is given a full-page portrait and one or more stills, a biographical/critical essay and a full filmography of *all* the films in which the actress appeared, serial or otherwise, including early one-reelers, set out in crisp, clear type. The main part of the book is divided into two sections: the first contains all the most famous names, such as Pearl White, Helen Holmes and Allene Ray. This runs to 22 entries, and is followed by 24 heroines who made minor or very few serials, and a list of hundreds of other actresses who appeared (even briefly) in one or two serials only. Bibliographies on all the leading stars and a huge index round off this comprehensive and enjoyable compilation. There are numerous titbits for film buffs, e.g. two silent serial heroines appear in Laurel and Hardy's *Way Out West*; Pearl White played in over one hundred shorts (mostly one-reelers) before making *The Perils of Pauline* in 1914; the first *Superman* lady was Noel Neill, in 1948.

Universal Horrors, Michael Brunas, John Brunas & Tom Weaver; McFarland, £33.75.

Plenty of material has for a long time been available on the horror film, but it was a good idea to collect together the output of the leading producers of the genre's heyday, from 1931 to 1946. The book, some 600 pages long, covers around eighty 'classics' arranged in chronological order, from the seminal Lugosi *Dracula* to *The Brute Man* (Rondo Hatton) in 1946 when the series was in sad decline. Each is given a lengthy descriptive and critical essay, with numerous interesting side issues, and a full filmography. Many lesser-known titles can be found among the Draculas, Frankensteins, Invisible Men, Werewolves, Mummies, Mad Doctors and other familiar faces. It is surprising, however, to find the Sherlock Holmes/Basil Rathbone series included. 'Horrible' they certainly are, with their ludicrous travesties of Holmes fighting the Nazis etc. (he would have been around ninety at

the time), but they hardly qualify as 'horror films' in the accepted sense.

The White Brothers, David N. Bruskin; Scarecrow, dist. Shelwing, £37.15.

Look in the majority of film reference books, and it is unlikely you will find much, if any, information in the 'directors' section on Jack, Jules and Sam White; yet between them they produced, directed or otherwise worked on dozens of one- and two-reelers for various companies, including MGM and Columbia. Well-known players who appeared in their films include the Three Scrooges, Buster Keaton, Harry Langdon, Charley Chase, Leon Errol, Franklyn Pangborn, Ruth Etting, Betty Grable and the George Sidney–Charlie Murray duo. Sam White also worked on various musical sequences, television programmes, and 175 commercials.

In this handsome 400-page volume David Bruskin interviews the three brothers in depth, and their articulate and lively replies make a delightfully entertaining book which sheds light on hitherto unrecorded corners of the film industry. Included are a section of rare photographs, three filmographies and a good index.

William Friedkin, Thomas D. Clagett; McFarland, dist. Shelwing, £26.25.

With films as varied as *The Exorcist*, *The Night They Raided Minsky's*, *The French Connection* and Harold Pinter's *The Birthday Party* (the latter in an unfortunately cut version) to his credit, the work of William Friedkin certainly calls for a full-length study. This has been admirably undertaken here. The lengthy essays are thorough, perceptive and full of interesting details about Friedkin's working methods. There is a commendably full filmography and a list of interviews conducted by the author. The subtitle of his book is 'Films of Aberration, Obsession and Reality' – an apt summary of the basic subjects of the films.

The Wizard of Oz, Noel Langley, Florence Ryerson & Edgar Allan Woolf; Faber & Faber, £6.99.

'No final screenplay of *The Wizard of Oz* survives – if indeed there was one,' writes Michael Patrick Hearn in a long and detailed introduction. This, however, is the actual shooting script together with scenes that were cut from the final release (such as the Scarecrow's Dance) and many other revisions and notes. It includes full cast and credit lists as they were shown in the film. The result is an essential companion to the various glamorously coloured books already available on this classic movie.

There is a generous selection of illustrations, but unfortunately these are very poorly and smudgily reproduced.

Awards and Festivals

There are now over 150 film festivals and award ceremonies around the world every year, many of which have only a minority interest. Fascinating as the Banff Festival of Mountain Films, the Festival des Migrations et Immigrations and the La Rochelle Sailing Film Festival may be to a small number of enthusiasts, there seems little reason to include them here, so we have as usual concentrated on the major established events. China, Japan, Egypt, Cuba and Taiwan, to name only a few, have their own film and TV festivals in addition to those held in Africa, Europe, Russia and the USA, and fuller details about most of them are periodically published in *Variety*.

This year the British Critics' Circle Awards have a special importance to us: included among them is a special award to F. Maurice Speed for long service to the film industry, and in particular for having produced this annual for nearly 50 years. (The first *Film Review* was published in 1944–5.) This gesture of appreciation and support from fellow critics is deeply appreciated.

Nationality is stated only where films do not originate from the country in which the awards are given.

The American Academy of Motion Picture Arts and Sciences Awards (Oscars) and Nominations for 1990, March 1991

Best Film: *Dances with Wolves*. Nominations: *Awakenings*; *Ghost*; *The Godfather Part III*; *GoodFellas*.

Best Director: Kevin Costner, for *Dances with Wolves*. Nominations: Francis Ford Coppola, for *The Godfather Part III*; Martin Scorsese, for *GoodFellas*; Stephen Frears, for *The Grifters*; Barbet Schroeder, for *Reversal of Fortune*.

Best Actor: Jeremy Irons, for *Reversal of Fortune*. Nominations: Kevin Costner, for *Dances with Wolves*; Robert De Niro, for *Awakenings*; Gerard Depardieu, for *Cyrano de Bergerac* (France); Richard Harris, for *The Field* (UK).

Best Actress: Kathy Bates, for *Misery*. Nominations: Anjelica Huston, for *The Grifters*; Julia Roberts, for *Pretty Woman*; Meryl Streep, for *Postcards from the Edge*; Joanne Woodward, for *Mr and Mrs Bridge*.

Best Supporting Actor: Joe Pesci, for *GoodFellas*. Nominations: Bruce Davison, for *Longtime Companion*; Andy Garcia, for *The Godfather Part III*; Graham Greene, for *Dances with Wolves*; Al Pacino, for *Dick Tracy*.

Kevin Costner, riding off with the Oscars for Dances with Wolves

Best Supporting Actress: Whoopi Goldberg, for *Ghost*. Nominations: Annette Bening, for *The Grifters*; Lorraine Bracco, for *GoodFellas*; Diane Ladd, for *Wild at Heart*; Mary McDonnell, for *Dances with Wolves*.

Best Original Screenplay: Brian Joel Rubin, for *Ghost*. Nominations: Woody Allen, for *Alice*; Barry Levinson, for *Avalon*; Peter Weir, for *Green Card*; Whit Stillman, for *Metropolitan*.

Best Screenplay Adaptation: Michael Blake, for *Dances with Wolves*. Nominations: Steven Zaillian, for *Awakenings*; Nicholas Pileggi, for *GoodFellas*; Donald E. Westlake, for *The Grifters*; Nicholas Kazan, for *Reversal of Fortune*.

Best Cinematography: Dean Semler, for *Dances with Wolves*. Nominations: Allen Daviau, for *Avalon*; Vittorio Storaro, for *Dick Tracy*; Gordon Willis, for *The Godfather Part III*; Philippe Rousselot, for *Henry and June*.

Best Editing: Neil Travis, for *Dances with Wolves*. Nominations: Walter Murch, for *Ghost*; Barry Malkin, Lisa Fruchtman and Walter Murch, for *The Godfather Part III*; Thelma Schoonmaker, for *GoodFellas*; Dennis Virkler and John Wright, for *The Hunt for Red October*.

Best Original Score: John Barry, for *Dances with Wolves*. Nominations: Randy Newman, for *Avalon*; Maurice Jarre, for *Ghost*; David Grusin, for *Havana*; John Williams, for *Home Alone*.

Best Original Song: 'Sooner or Later (I Always Get My Man)' from *Dick Tracy*, music and lyric by Stephen Sondheim. Nominations: 'Blaze of Glory' from *Young Guns II*, music and lyric by Jon Bon Jovi; 'I'm Checkin' Out' from *Postcards from the Edge*, music and lyric by Shel Silverstein; 'Promise Me You'll Remember' from *The Godfather Part III*, music by Carmine Coppola, lyric by John Bettis; 'Somewhere in My Memory' from *Home Alone*, music by John Williams, lyric by Leslie Bricusse.

Best Art Direction: Richard Sylbert (art direction) and Rick Simpson (set decoration), for *Dick Tracy*. Nominations: Ezio Frigerio (art) and Jacques Rouxel (set), for *Cyrano de Bergerac* (France); Jeffrey Beecroft (art) and Lisa Dean (set), for *Dances with Wolves*; Dean Tavoularis (art) and Gary Fettis (set), for *The Godfather Part III*; Dante Ferretti (art) and Francesca Lo Schiavo (set), for *Hamlet*.

Best Costume Design: Franca Squarciapino, for *Cyrano de Bergerac* (France). Nominations: Gloria Gresham, for *Avalon*; Elsa Zamparelli, for *Dances with Wolves*; Milena Canonero, for *Dick Tracy*; Maurizio Millenotti, for *Hamlet*.

Best Sound: Russell Williams II, Jeffrey Perkins, Bill W. Benton and Greg Watkins, for *Dances with Wolves*. Nominations: Charles Wilborn, Donald O. Mitchell, Rick Kline and Kevin O'Connell, for *Days of Thunder*; Thomas Causey, Chris Jenkins, David E. Campbell and D. M. Hempbill, for *Dick Tracy*; Richard Bryce Goodman, Richard Overton, Kevin F. Cleary and Don Bassman, for *The Hunt for Red October*; Nelson Stoll, Michael J. Kohut, Carlos deLarios and Aaron Rochin, for *Total Recall*.

Best Sound Effects Editing: Cecelia Hall and George Watters II, for *The Hunt for Red October*. Nominations: Charles L. Campbell and Richard Franklin, for *Flatliners*; Stephen H. Flick, for *Total Recall*.

Best Make-Up: John Caglione Jr and Doug Drexler, for *Dick Tracy*. Nominations: Michele Burke and Jean-Pierre Eyche, for *Cyrano de Bergerac* (France); Ve Neill and Stan Winston, for *Edward Scissorhands*.

Best Foreign Language Film: *Journey of Hope* (Switzerland). Nominations: *Cyrano de Bergerac* (France); *Ju Dou* (China); *The Nasty Girl – Das Schreckliche Madchen* (Germany); *Open Doors – Portas Apertas* (Italy).

The Australian Film Institute Awards, October 1990

Best Film: *Flirting*, by John Duignan.
Best Actor: Max von Sydow, for *Father*.
Best Actress: Katheryn McClements, for *Weekend with Kate*.
Best Director: Ray Argall, for *Return Home*.

The 21st Belgrade International Festival Awards, February 1991

Grand Prize for Best Film: *The Nasty Girl – Das Schreckliche Madchen*, by Michael Verhoeven (Germany).
Best Actress: Krystina Janda, in *Interrogation* (Poland).
Best Actor: Peter Malceiner, in *On Death Row* (Hungary).
Special Prize: Robert Dornhiem, for *Requiem for Dominic* (Austria).
Special Mention: Zoran Masirevic, for *The Border* (Yugoslavia).
Life Achievement Award: Andrzej Wajda.

The 41st Berlin International Film Festival, February 1991

Golden Bear for Best Film: *House of Smiles*, by Marco Ferreri (Italy).
Silver Bear for Special Jury Prize shared by: *The Judgement*, by Marco Bellocchio (Italy); and *Satan*, by Victor Aristov (USSR).
Best Director shared by: Ricky Tognazzi, for *Ultra* (Italy); and Jonathan Demme, for *The Silence of the Lambs* (USA).
Best Actress: Victoria Abril, in *Lovers* (Spain).
Best Actor: Maynard Eziashi, in *Mister Johnson* (UK).

Silver Bear for Best Achievement: Kevin Costner, for *Dances with Wolves* (USA).
FIBRESCI Prize for Best Film: *The Little Gangster*, by Jacques Doillon (France).

The 1990 British Academy of Film and Television Arts Awards, March 1991

Best Film: *GoodFellas*, by Martin Scorsese (USA). *GoodFellas* also won the awards for Best Director (Martin Scorsese), Best Editing (Thelma Schoonmaker), Best Costume Design (Richard Bruno) and Best Screenplay Adaptation (Scorsese and Nicholas Pileggi).
Best Actor: Philippe Noiret, in *Cinema Paradiso* (Italy).
Best Actress: Jessica Tandy, in *Driving Miss Daisy* (USA).
Best Supporting Actor: 11-year-old Salvatore Cascio, in *Cinema Paradiso* (Italy).
Best Supporting Actress: Whoopi Goldberg, in *Ghost* (USA).
Best Original Screenplay: Giuseppe Tornatore, for *Cinema Paradiso* (Italy).
Best Score: Ennio and Andrea Morricone, for *Cinema Paradiso* (Italy).
The Academy's Fellowship, the top honour, went to Louis Malle.
The Michael Balcon Award went to UK producer Jeremy Thomas.
Special Award: Deborah Kerr.
(Only one British film was nominated: it received no award.)

The 12th (British) Critics' Circle Film Section Awards, March 1991

Best Film: *Crimes and Misdemeanors*, by Woody Allen (USA). Woody Allen also won the Best Direction and Best Screenplay awards.
Best Actor: Philippe Noiret, in *Cinema Paradiso* (Italy).
Best Actress: Pauline Collins, for *Shirley Valentine*.
Best Foreign Language Film: *Cinema Paradiso*, written and directed by Giuseppe Tornatore (Italy).
Special Awards for Services to the Cinema: Penelope Houston, Simon Relph and F. Maurice Speed.

The British Film Institute Awards, 21 October 1990

Best Film: *Henry V*, by Kenneth Branagh. *Henry V* also won the award for Technical Achievement.
Archival Achievement Award: David Sim, for the documentary *The Making of a Legend: Gone with the Wind*.
Film Music Award: Michael Kamen, for *The Krays*.

John Grierson Award for Best Documentary: Kevin Sum, for *Four Hours in My Lai*.

Maria Kuttner Award for Best Animated Film: Nick Park, for *Creature Comforts*.

Career in the Industry Award: Monty Berman, for 40 years in the theatrical costumier business.

BFI Fellowships: Derek Jarman, Jeanne Moreau, Fred Zinnemann and Krzystof Kieslowski.

The 44th Cannes Film Festival Awards, May 1991

Palme d'Or for Best Film: *Barton Fink*, by Joel and Ethan Coen (USA).

Special Prize: *La Belle Noiseuse*, by Jacques Rivette (France).

Best Direction: Joel and Ethan Coen, for *Barton Fink* (USA).

Best Actor: John Turturro, in *Barton Fink* (USA).

Best Actress: Irene Jacob, in *The Double Life of Weronika* (France/Poland).

Best Supporting Performance: Samuel L. Jackson, in *Jungle Fever* (USA).

Jury Prize shared by: *Europa*, by Lars von Trier (Denmark/Germany); and *Hors de la Vie*, by Maroun Bagdadi (France).

Palme d'Or for Best Short: *With Hands in the Air*, by Mikto Panov (Poland).

Golden Camera for Best First Feature: *Toto the Hero*, by Jaco van Dormael (Belgium).

International Film Critics' Prize for Best Film: *The Double Life of Weronika* (France/Poland).

The 3rd European Film Festival Awards, Glasgow, December 1990

Best Film: *Open Doors*, by Gianni Amelio (Italy).

Best Actor: Kenneth Branagh, in *Henry V*.

Best Actress: Carmen Maura, in *Ay, Carmela!* (Spain).

Best Documentary: *Skersiela*, by Ivars Seletski (USSR).

Music Prize: not awarded, as the jury (including Ingmar Bergman, Deborah Kerr, Jeanne Moreau and Margarethe von Trotta) could not decide between *Cyrano de Bergerac* (France), *December Bride* (Ireland) and *New Wave* (France).

The 16th French Academy (César) Awards, March 1991

Best Film: *Cyrano de Bergerac*, by Jean-Paul Rapeneau. *Cyrano* won nine other Césars, including Best Actor (Gerard Depardieu), Best Director (Jean-Paul Rapeneau), Best Supporting Actor (Jacques Weber), Best Cinematography (Pierre Lhomme), Best Editing (Noelle Boisson) and Best Score (Jean-Claude Petit).

Best Actress: Anne Parillaud, in *Nikita*.

Best Script: Christian Vincent and Jean-Pierre Ronssin, for *La Discrète*, which also won Césars for Best First Film by a Director (Christian Vincent) and Most Promising Actress (Judith Henry).

Best Supporting Actress: Dominique Blanc, in *May Fools*, by Louis Malle.

Lifetime Achievement Award: Sophia Loren.

The 48th Hollywood Foreign Press Association (Golden Globe) Awards, 19 January 1991

Best Film – Drama: *Dances with Wolves*.

Best Film – Comedy or Musical: *Green Card*.

Best Actor – Drama: Jeremy Irons, in *Reversal of Fortune*.

Best Actress – Drama: Kathy Bates, in *Misery*.

Best Actor – Comedy or Musical: Gerard Depardieu, in *Green Card*.

Best Actress – Comedy or Musical: Julia Roberts, in *Pretty Woman*.

Best Supporting Actor: Bruce Davison, in *Longtime Companion*.

Best Supporting Actress: Whoopi Goldberg, in *Ghost*.

Best Director: Kevin Costner, for *Dances with Wolves*.

Best Screenplay: Michael Blake, for *Dances with Wolves*.

Best Original Score: Ryuichi Sakamoto and Richard Horowitz, for *The Sheltering Sky*.

Best Foreign Language Film: *Cyrano de Bergerac* (France).

The Locarno Festival Awards, August 1990

Golden Leopard for Best Film: *Slouchainij Vals*, by Svetlana Proskourina (USSR).

Silver Leopard shared by: *Metropolitan*, by Walt Stillman (USA); and *The Reflecting Skin*, by Philip Ridley (UK).

Bronze Leopards: *Reise der Hoffnung*, by Xavier Koller (Switzerland); Miklos Gurban (photography) and Emer McCourt (performance), *Hush-a-Bye-Baby* (N. Ireland).

The Los Angeles Film Critics' Association Awards, December 1990

Best Film: *GoodFellas*.

Best Actor: Jeremy Irons, in *Reversal of Fortune*.

Best Actress: Anjelica Huston, in *The Witches* and *The Grifters*.

Best Supporting Actor: Joe Pesci, in *GoodFellas*.

Best Supporting Actress: Lorraine Bracco, in *GoodFellas*.

Best Director: Martin Scorsese, for *GoodFellas*.

Best Foreign Film: *Life And Nothing But – La Vie et Rien d'Autre* (France).

The 14th Montreal World Film Festival Awards, September 1990

The Grand Prize of the Americas for Best Film: *Fallen from the Sky*, by Francisco Lombardi (Peru).

Second Prize shared by: *Funeral Ceremony*, by Zdenek Sirovy (Czechoslovakia); and *Landscape with a Woman*, by Ivica Matic (Yugoslavia).

Best Director: Teng Wenji, for *Ballad of the Yellow River* (China).

Best Screenplay: Giles Walker, for *Princes in Exile*.

Best Actor shared by: Andres Pajares, in *Ay, Carmela!* (Spain); and Marcel Leboeuf in *Blizzard*.

Best Actress: Natalia Goundareva, in *Dog's Feast* (USSR).

Best First Film shared by: *Time of the Servants*, by Irina Pavlaskova (Czechoslovakia); and *Lost Spring*, by Alain Mazars (Fránce).

Grand Prize for Best Short Film: *Feelings of Mountains and Water*, by Te Wei (China).

The National Board of Review, December 1990

Best Film: *Dances with Wolves*.

Best Actor: Robert De Niro/Robin Williams, in *Awakenings*.

Best Actress: Mia Farrow, in *Alice*.

Best Supporting Actor: Joe Pesci, in *GoodFellas*.

Best Supporting Actress: Winona Ryder, in *Mermaids*.

Best Director: Kevin Costner, for *Dances with Wolves*.

Best Foreign Film: *Cyrano de Bergerac*.

The 56th New York Film Critics' Circle Awards, December 1990

Best Film: *GoodFellas*.

Best Actor: Robert De Niro, in *GoodFellas* and *Awakenings*.

Best Actress: Joanne Woodward, in *Mr and Mrs Bridge*.

Best Supporting Actor: Bruce Davison, in *Longtime Companion*.

Best Supporting Actress: Jennifer Jason Leigh, in *Last Exit to Brooklyn* and *Miami Blues*.

Best Director: Martin Scorsese, for *GoodFellas*.

Best Foreign Film: *The Nasty Girl – Das Schreckliche Madchen*, by Michael Verhoeven (Germany).

The 38th San Sebastian Film Festival Awards, September 1990

Best Film: *Letters from Alou – Las Cartas de Alou*, by Montxo Armendariz (Spain).

Best Actor: Mulie Jarju, in *Letters from Alou* (Spain).

Best Actress: Margherita Buy, in *The Week of the Sphinx – La Settimana delle Singe* (Italy).

Best Director: Joel Coen, for *Miller's Crossing* (USA).

Special Jury Prize: *Red Daybreak – Rojo Amanecer*, by Jorge Fons (Mexico).

Note: According to *Variety*, the seven-strong jury were reluctant to select a best film in view of the low standard of this year's entries.

The 23rd Sitges Film Festival Awards, October 1990

Best Film: *Henry: Portrait of a Serial Killer*, by John McNaughton (USA).

Best Director shared by: John McNaughton, for *Henry: Portrait of a Serial Killer*; and Sam Raimi for *Darkness* (USA).

Best Actress: Lindsay Duncan, in *The Reflecting Skin* (UK).

Best Actor: Jeff Goldblum, in *Mister Frost* (UK/France).

Best Screenplay: Jean-Claude Carrière and Peter Fleischmann, for *Hard to Be a God* (Germany/USSR).

Best Photography: Dick Pope, for *Hard to Be a God*.

Best Short: *For God's Sake*, by Enric Folch (Spain).

The 36th Taormina Film Festival, July 1990

Best Film: *Small Time*, by Norman Loftis (USA).

Best Actor: M. K. Harris, in *Horseplayer* (USA).

Best Actress: Krista Erickson, in *Mortal Passions* (USA).

Best Director: Christian Faber, in *Bail Jumper* (USA).

Note: All the competitive awards were this year devoted to 'Young American Cinema'.

The 15th Toronto Festival of Festivals Awards, September 1990

Best Film (winner of the John Labatt Class Award): *Cyrano de Bergerac*, by Jean Paul Rappeneau (France).

Toronto City Award for Best Canadian Film: *H*, by Darrell Wasyk.

Four Seasons International Critics Award: *An Angel at My Table*, by Jane Campion (New Zealand).

National Film Board Award for Best Short: *Shaggie*, by Janis Cole.

The 25th US National Society of Film Critics Awards, January 1991

Best Film: *GoodFellas*.

Best Actor: Jeremy Irons, in *Reversal of Fortune*.

Best Actress: Anjelica Huston, in *The Grifters* and *The Witches*.

Best Supporting Actor: Bruce Davison, in *Longtime Companion*.

Best Supporting Actress: Annette Bening, in *The Grifters*.

Best Director: Martin Scorsese, for *GoodFellas*.

Best Screenplay: Charles Burnett, for *To Sleep With Anger*.

Best Cinematography: Peter Suschitzky, for *Where the Heart Is*.

Best Foreign Film: *Ariel*, by Aki Kaurismaki (Finland).

Best Documentary: *Berkeley in the Sixties*, by Mark Kitchell.

Special Citation: Jean-Luc Godard.

The Valladolid Film Festival Awards, October 1990

Golden Sheaf for Best Film: *Ju Dou*, by Zhang Yimou (China/Japan).

Silver Sheaf for Runner-Up: *An Angel at My Table*, by Jane Campion (New Zealand).

Best First Film: *Freeze, Die, Come to Life – Zamri, Umri, Voskres Ni*, by Vitaly Kanevski (USSR).

Best Actress: Kerry Fox, in *An Angel at My Table*.

Best Actor: Dirk Bogarde, in *Daddy Nostalgia* (France).

Best Photography: Tonino Nardi, for *Open Doors – Portas Apertas* (Italy).

Special Prize shared by: *Curfew Nights – Karartma Geceleri*, by Yusef Kurcenli (Turkey); and *The Moon in the Mirror – La Luna en el Espejo*, by Silvio Caiozzi (Chile).

Golden Sheaf for Best Short: *A Day Will Come – Va Veni O Zi*, by Copel Moscu (Romania).

The 47th Venice International Film Festival Awards, September 1990

Golden Lion for Best Film: *Rosencrantz and Guildenstern Are Dead*, by Tom Stoppard (UK).

Special Jury Prize: *An Angel at My Table*, by Jane Campion (New Zealand).

Best Director: Martin Scorsese, for *GoodFellas* (USA).

Best Script: Helle Rysling and Peter Boensen, for *Sirup* (Denmark).

Best Actress: Gloria Munchmeyer, in *The Moon in the Mirror – La Luna en el Espejo* (Chile).

Best Actor: Oleg Borisov, in *The Sole Witness – Edinstvenijat Svidetel* (Bulgaria). (This film also won the Best Musical Score award for Valeri Mjilovanski).

Italian Senate Medal: *Raspad*, by Mikhail Belikov (USSR).

Career Awards: Miklos Jancso and Marcello Mastroianni.

The 10th Vevey International Festival of Comedy Films, August 1990

Golden Cane for Best Film: *Nuns on the Run*, by Jonathan Lynn (UK).

Best Performances: Mathias Gnaedinger, in *Leo Sunnyboy* (Switzerland); and Patrika Darbo, in *Daddy's Dyin', Who's Got the Will?* (USA).

Index

Page numbers in *italic* refer to illustrations

Video releases are listed separately between pages 139 and 142